Fleeing Homophobia

Each year, thousands of lesbian, gay, bisexual, transgender and intersex (LGBTI) asylum seekers apply for asylum in EU Member States. This book considers the position of LGBTI asylum seekers in European asylum law. Developing an encompassing approach to the topic, the book identifies and analyzes the main legal issues arising in relation to LGBTI people seeking asylum, including: the underestimation of the large scale violence against trans people in countries of origin by some European states; the requirement to seek State protection against violence even when they originate from countries where sexual orientation or gender identity is criminalized, or where the authorities are homophobic; the particular hurdles faced during credibility assessment on account of persisting stereotypes; and queer families and refugee law.

The book gives a state of the art overview of law in Europe, both at the level of European legislation and at the level of Member State practice. While being largely focused on Europe, the book also takes into account asylum decisions from Australia, New Zealand, Canada and the United States, and is of relevance internationally, offering analyses of issues which are not specific to particular legal systems.

Thomas Spijkerboer is Professor of Migration Law at VU University Amsterdam. He has published on gender and sexuality (*Gender and Refugee Status*, Ashgate 2000; *Women and Immigration Law*, with Sarah van Walsum, Routledge 2007). He also publishes on the role of courts in migration law, and on border deaths.

Fleeing Homophobia

Sexual orientation, gender identity and asylum

Edited by
Thomas Spijkerboer

Routledge
Taylor & Francis Group
LONDON AND NEW YORK

First published 2013
by Routledge
2 Park Square, Milton Park, Abingdon, Oxon OX14 4RN

Simultaneously published in the USA and Canada
by Routledge
711 Third Avenue, New York, NY 10017

Routledge is an imprint of the Taylor & Francis Group, an informa business

British Library Cataloguing in Publication Data
A catalogue record for this book is available from the British Library

Library of Congress Cataloguing in Publication Data
Fleeing homophobia : sexual orientation, gender identity and asylum / edited by Thomas Spijkerboer.
pages cm
Includes bibliographical references.
1. Sexual minorities—Legal status, laws, etc.—Europe. 2. Asylum, Right of—Europe. 3. Refugees—Legal status, laws, etc.—Europe. I. Spijkerboer, T. (Thomas), 1963-, editor of compilation.
KJC5144.G39F58 2013
342.408'3—dc23

2012043605

ISBN 978-0-415-62817-4 (hbk)
ISBN 978-0-203-51572-3 (ebk)

Typeset in Garamond
by Keystroke, Station Road, Codsall, Wolverhampton

MIX
Paper from responsible sources
FSC
www.fsc.org
FSC® C013056

Printed and bound in Great Britain by
TJ International Ltd, Padstow, Cornwall

Contents

Acknowledgements

This collection of chapters has come out of the *Fleeing Homophobia* conference, which was held at VU University Amsterdam on 5–6 September 2011. I am grateful to the participants of this conference, who created the environment where the ideas presented in this volume could be developed.

The *Fleeing Homophobia* project was funded by the European Refugee Fund, the Dutch Ministry of Justice, and the organizations which carried out the project: COC Nederland, VU University Amsterdam, the Hungarian Helsinki Committee, Avvocatura per i dritti LGBT/Rete Lenford and the European Council on Refugees and Exiles. The *Fleeing Homophobia* project has benefited from the expertise of the advisory panel members: S. Chelvan (Barrister of the Inner Temple, No5 Chambers, London), Joël Le Déroff (ILGA-Europe), Maria Hennessy (European Council on Refugees and Exiles), Borbála Ivány (Hungarian Helsinki Committee), Simone Rossi (Avvocatura per i dritti LGBT/Rete Lenford) and Gisela Thäter (UNHCR).

Louis Middelkoop has been instrumental in editing this volume. Reschin Hassan has compiled the case law index.

Thomas Spijkerboer
Amsterdam, October 2012

Notes on contributors

Dr Thomas Spijkerboer is Professor of Migration Law at VU University Amsterdam since 2000. Before that, he was a lawyer specialising in asylum cases (1986–92) and Lecturer in Migration Law at Nijmegen University (1993–2000). His publications include *Gender and Refugee Status* (Ashgate, 2000) and *Women and Immigration Law. New variations of classical feminist themes* (editor with Sarah van Walsum, Routledge 2007). He is a member of the editorial board of the *European Journal of Migration and Law*, and has published widely in international and Dutch journals and edited volumes.

Hemme Battjes is Professor of European Asylum Law at VU University Amsterdam.

Laurie Berg is Lecturer at the Faculty of Law of the University of Technology Sydney.

Giulia Cragnolini holds a Master of Arts in Human Rights and Conflict Management from the *Scuola Superiore Sant'Anna*, Pisa, Italy. Currently, she works as a consultant for UNHCR in Italy.

Sabine Jansen is Legal Researcher, and Policy Officer LGBTI and asylum at COC Netherlands.

Nicole LaViolette is Associate Professor, Faculty of Law, University of Ottawa. She has close to 20 years' experience in international human rights and refugee law. She has focused a significant part of her scholarly research on sexual minorities and the refugee determination system, and has published extensively on this issue. She has also conducted professional development training on sexual orientation and gender identity for the Immigration and Refugee Board of Canada. She is a recipient of the *Lambda Foundation Award for Excellence in Gay and Lesbian Studies* for her work on the Canadian *Gender Guidelines* and their impact on sexual orientation and gender identity refugee claims. She is also involved in a Canadian initiative that supported the resettlement of a lesbian refugee couple from abroad.

Louis Middelkoop is a lawyer and criminologist, presently legal intern, Trial Chambers, UN International Criminal Tribunal for Rwanda. He previously worked as a legal aid volunteer with the Dutch Refugee Council, as research assistant for the Migration Law Research Programme of VU University Amsterdam, and as editor in chief of *Amsterdam Law Forum*.

Jenni Millbank is Professor at the Faculty of Law of the University of Technology, Sydney.

Petra Sußner is PhD Fellow at the Faculty of Social Sciences at University of Vienna.

Janna Weßels is Quentin Bryce Doctoral Scholar at the Faculty of Law of the University of Technology, Sydney. She holds a Master of Science in Forced Migration from the Refugee Studies Centre at the University of Oxford, and is Co-founder and Vice-Chair of the *Oxford Monitor of Forced Migratio* n.

Table of cases

Court of Justice of the European Union

Domestic cases

Australia

High Court of Australia

Austria

Asylgerichtshof (Asylum Court)

Canada

Supreme Court of Canada

Federal Court of Canada

Czech Republic

Finland

France

Germany

The Netherlands

Dutch District Courts

Provisional Measures Judge

New-Zealand

Norway

Poland

South Africa

Constitutional Court of South Africa

United Kingdom

Supreme Court

Court of Appeal

High Court

House of Lords

Upper Tribunal (Immigration and Asylum Chamber),

United States

Court of Appeals

United States Board of Immigration Appeals

1 Introduction

Fleeing homophobia, asylum claims related to sexual orientation and gender identity in Europe

*Sabine Jansen**

Thousands of lesbian, gay, bisexual, transgender and intersex[1] (LGBTI) asylum seekers apply for asylum in Europe each year.[2] In principle they can find safety in Europe as recognised refugees or through other forms of international protection. According to Article 1-A of the 1951 United Nations Convention Relating to the Status of Refugees (Refugee Convention) a refugee is a person with a well-founded fear of being persecuted on account of one of the five persecution grounds: race, religion, nationality, membership of a particular social group and political opinion. For a long time sexual orientation and gender identity[3] were not considered as relevant persecution grounds, but this major stumbling block for LGBTI asylum seekers has gradually been taken away.

In 1981, the Dutch Raad van State (Council of State) was the first court to recognise sexual orientation as a relevant persecution ground.[4] This development has culminated in the 2004 EU Qualification Directive (Council Directive 2004/83/EC) which provides in Article 10 that 'a particular social group might include a group based on a common characteristic of sexual orientation'.[5 6] In 2011, 'gender identity' was added into Article 10 of the EU Qualification Directive and this way it has also been recognised as a relevant persecution ground.[7]

Although this constitutes an important step forward, both symbolically (see on the importance of symbolical change, Jenni Millbank's contribution to this volume) as well as practically (many LGBTI asylum applicants have been granted protection as a refugee), the acknowledgement of sexual orientation and gender identity as a persecution ground has only created the condition for protecting persecuted LGBTI asylum applicants. Many legal problems still remain to be addressed: What is the relevance of laws in the country of origin criminalising consensual same sex sexual acts or the expression of non-standard sexual or gender identities? Can asylum applicants be required to return to their country of origin and conceal their sexual orientation or gender identity in order not to 'provoke' violence and discrimination? Can asylum authorities expect LGBTI asylum seekers to seek protection from homo- or transphobic state authorities in the country of origin? How to assess claims of applicants who did not disclose their sexual orientation or gender identity right away? (See on the invisibility of LGBTI refugee families in family reunification law, the contribution of Petra Sußner to this volume.) Apart from these legal issues, there is a host of difficulties in LGBTI asylum practice related to their non-standard sexual or gender identity. Credibility assessment seems to be riddled with stereotypes. In reception facilities LGBTI applicants face specific hazards. Human rights information about LGBTIs in countries of origin is not always available, which makes the assessment of LGBTI asylum claims a formidable task.

In this chapter I present the main outcomes of the Fleeing Homophobia research project (Jansen and Spijkerboer 2011).[8] This was the first comprehensive study ever on the handling of LGBTI asylum claims in Europe. It contributed to closing the existing research gap, identified by the European Union Agency for Fundamental Rights (2009: 129) by providing a more extensive and qualitative research with data from lawyers, governments, academics and non-governmental organisations (NGOs) on policy and practice concerning LGBTI asylum seekers.[9]

A general research finding is that considerable differences occur in the way in which European States deal with the specific problems in LGBTI cases. From a point of view of European harmonisation this divergence is problematic. For example the Dublin system presumes a common European standard, which we can conclude does not exist. If the interpretation and application of asylum law in one or more European States is below the level required by European law, this is not only in itself a violation of European law, but this may also make the transfer of asylum seekers to such States a violation of European law.[10] Also in LGBTI cases, divergence between Member States may interfere with transfer of an asylum seeker to the Member State which is responsible for the examination of the claim.[11]

A second general conclusion is that European State practice is on a number of points below the standards required by international and European human rights and refugee law. Furthermore, the fundamental character of the relevant human rights for LGBTI individuals is frequently denied in the asylum practice of European States.

1.1 Discretion

In large parts of the world people feel compelled to hide or conceal their sexual orientation or gender identity. They stay 'in the closet', because they fear harm from others: their family members, friends, neighbours, society in general or state authorities. The reactions to disclosure ('coming out') can take the form of abuse, discrimination, forced marriage, torture, rape, murder, etc.

LGBTI people who flee their country and apply for international protection in Europe are still often rejected, with the reasoning that they have nothing to fear in their country of origin as long as they remain 'discreet'. They are explicitly or implicitly required to conceal or hide their sexual orientation or gender identity in order to avoid persecution. In fact, they are sent back into the closet.

We found examples of this practice in the majority of European States.[12] For instance in Switzerland the asylum application of a gay man from Iran was rejected by the Federal Administrative Court, stating that in practice homosexuality is tolerated by the Iranian authorities, 'when it is not publicly exposed in a way which could be offensive'.[13] In a West-African lesbian's case the Hungarian authority stated: 'Even if the applicant was a lesbian, if she would not make her lesbianism public, she would not have to fear the consequences of her behaviour'. The Bulgarian expert reported a common opinion apparently shared by the State Agency for Refugees' officials, that it is better if a gay man returns to his country of origin and tries to live a more discreet life or even to make an attempt to 'change' his sexual orientation. In cases of LGBTI applicants from countries where same sex sexual acts are a criminal offence it is sometimes stated: the authorities are not aware of your sexual orientation, so you could go back.[14] These cases implicitly rely on discretion reasoning, also when this is not explicitly stated.

Since the early 2000s, several jurisdictions outside Europe have rejected the 'discretion requirement'.[15] In 2003, the High Court of Australia held: 'It would undermine the object of the Convention if the signatory countries required them to modify their beliefs or opinions or to hide their race, nationality or membership of particular social groups before those countries would give them protection under the Convention'. In 2004, the New Zealand Refugee Status Appeals Authority ruled: 'By requiring the refugee applicant to abandon a core right the refugee decision maker is requiring of the refugee claimant the same submissive and compliant behaviour, the same denial of a fundamental human right, which the agent of persecution in the country of origin seeks to achieve by persecutory conduct'.[16] The UN High Commissioner for Refugees (UNHCR) Guidance Note states in this respect: 'There is no duty to be discreet or to take certain steps to avoid persecution, such as living a life of isolation, or refraining from having intimate relationships'. In other words: 'a hidden right is not a right' (UNHCR 2008: paras 25–26).

In some EU countries the requirement has been abandoned, although it sometimes reappears in other forms. The idea that LGBTI persons could or should conceal their sexual orientation or gender identity proves to be very persistent.

Since 2007, the Dutch policy guidelines explicitly state that 'homosexual people are not expected to hide their sexual orientation upon return in the country of origin' (Aliens Circular (Netherlands) C2/2.10.2). However, the Dutch Immigration and Naturalisation Service (IND), supported by the highest Administrative Court, the Council of State, neglects this policy and still tells people to go home and hide in the closet (Jansen 2012). In fact, three cases in which the Dutch asylum authorities relied on discretion reasoning, in seeming contradiction with their own policy, have led to preliminary questions (see below).

In July 2010, the United Kingdom rejected the discretion requirement through abolishing its previously applied UK manifestation, the 'reasonable tolerability' test, which held that it could be reasonably tolerable to require discretion, with the landmark judgment of the Supreme Court in *HJ (Iran) and HT (Cameroon) v Secretary of State for the Home Department* (*HJ/HT*) (UK Supreme Court, 7 July 2010). The Lords explain what the abolishment of discretion would mean for everyday life, to cite Lord Rodger:

> In short, what is protected is the applicant's right to live freely and openly as a gay man. That involves a wide spectrum of conduct, going well beyond conduct designed to attract sexual partners and maintain relationships with them. To illustrate the point with trivial stereotypical examples from British society: just as male heterosexuals are free to enjoy themselves playing rugby, drinking beer and talking about girls with their mates, so male homosexuals are to be free to enjoy themselves going to Kylie concerts, drinking exotically coloured cocktails and talking about boys with their straight female mates. Mutatis mutandis – and in many cases the adaptations would obviously be great – the same must apply to other societies. In other words, gay men are to be as free as their straight equivalents in the society concerned to live their lives in the way that is natural to them as gay men, without the fear of persecution.
>
> (*HJ/HT* at [78])

Scandinavian countries followed the approach of the UK Supreme Court: Sweden by issuing policy rules (*Rättschefens rättsliga* 2011) Finland and Norway through a judgment of their respective Supreme Courts (*Korkein Hallinto-Oikeus* 13 January 2012; *Norges Høyesterett – Dom* 29 March 2012). A UK Asylum Instruction also made the judgment applicable to gender identity claims (UK Border Agency 2011b). In the contributions of Jenni Millbank, Janna Weßels and Hemme Battjes to this volume, the *HJ/HT* judgment is dealt with in detail.

The *HJ/HT* judgment has led to confusion among asylum authorities and academics. On the one hand, most agree that one cannot expect someone to hide his or her protected characteristic in order to prevent persecution. On the other hand, there is no *communis opinio* on questions like: How far should this go? Are there any limits? Could we expect LGBTI people to hide a little bit or to behave with some restraint? Should we distinguish between private and public conduct? The *HJ/HT* judgment has been criticised from two different angles. Hathaway and Pobjoy argue that the judgment leads to the protection of trivial behaviour, like drinking exotically coloured cocktails. They argue that a distinction should be made between protected and unprotected activities in the refugee context. Only expressions of sexual identity that belong to the core of sexual orientation, and that may trigger persecution, are to lead to recognition as a refugee (Hathaway and Pobjoy 2012: 515).[17] While this criticism holds that the UK Supreme Court went too far in granting refugee protection, Janna Weßels to the contrary argues that the Supreme Court went not far enough, because it has in fact not abolished discretion reasoning. In Weßels' analysis in this volume, the new test proposed in the judgment is still constructed around discretion, as is demonstrated by the distinction between open and discreet gay and lesbian conduct, and the distinction between different types of discretion: out of fear for persecution on the one hand, and out of family or societal pressure on the other hand. In the eyes of the Lords, the latter should not lead to asylum. Weßels criticises the idea that lesbians and gays in a persecutory environment hide their sexual orientation out of 'free choice', which has also been labelled as 'voluntary' or – even – 'natural' discretion.[18]

Possibly, the Court of Justice of the European Union (CJEU) will provide guidance in the near future. Previously, the German Oberverwaltungsgericht (High Administrative Court) of Nordrhein-Westfalen attempted to find this guidance by submitting preliminary questions to the CJEU in the case of an Iranian gay asylum seeker. However, after the full name of the applicant was published by the CJEU, the questions were withdrawn and the applicant was granted refugee status.[19] The German Bundesverwaltungsgericht (Federal Administrative Court) was more successful: in a case of two Pakistani Ahmadiyyas preliminary questions were issued at the CJEU. In these cases the central question was whether the applicants could 'reasonably be expected to abstain from certain religious practices'.[20] The CJEU has not judged this case yet, but the advocate-general concludes that:

> it seems to be contrary to the respect due to human dignity enshrined in Article 1 of the Charter [of Fundamental Rights of the European Union]. By requiring the asylum-seeker to conceal, amend or forego the public demonstration of his faith, we are asking him to change what is a fundamental element of his identity, that is to say, in a certain sense to deny himself. However, no one has the right to require that. (. . .) we cannot reasonably expect an asylum-seeker to forego manifesting his faith *or to conceal any other constituent element of his identity* to avoid persecution without putting at risk the rights that the Directive aims to protect and the objectives it seeks to pursue.
>
> (Advocate-General Bot 2012, *Federal Republic of Germany v Y and Z*; emphasis added)

Although the fundamental right at stake in this case is freedom of religion, by the reference the advocate-general makes to sexual orientation and to identity,[21] there is no doubt that this reasoning also applies to sexual orientation, as well as to gender identity.

Recently, the Dutch Council of State submitted preliminary questions to the CJEU, specifically on sexual orientation, in the cases of three gay men from Senegal, Sierra Leone and Uganda (CJEU – Reference for a preliminary ruling from the Raad van State lodged on 27 April 2012 – *Minister voor Immigratie en Asiel v X Y Z*). The first two questions are modelled on the German questions about Pakistani Ahmadiyyas, and concern: (1) sexual orientation as a possible persecution ground in the sense of Article 10(1)(d) of the EU Qualification Directive; and (2) the possibility of requiring discretion. Specific questions concern whether more discretion may be expected from homosexuals than from heterosexuals; and whether a distinction can be made between the core and the periphery of sexual orientation.

In my analysis, it seems contrary to human rights and refugee law to require lesbians, gays and bisexuals to conceal their sexual orientation in order to prevent persecution. First, it is part of the core of the refugee concept that a well-founded fear of being persecuted on account of a legitimate exercise of a human right is to be remedied by recognition as a refugee, and not by renouncing the legitimate exercise of the human right. This is underscored by the fact that, in defining lesbians, gays and bisexuals as a social group, sexual orientation is considered to be so fundamental that a person cannot be required to change it. But that is precisely what discretion reasoning does: it requires lesbians, gays and bisexuals not to live openly and freely, and in doing so assumes that sexual orientation is not fundamental and that people can be required to renounce it. Second, requiring people to conceal their sexual identity in fact introduces an implicit limitation ground for the exercise of human rights.[22] As there is no basis for such limitations in the 1951 Convention, in my opinion a distinction between core and peripheral aspects of sexual orientation cannot be made, nor can a distinction be applied between the level of discretion required from gay or straight persons, for that would be clearly discriminatory. Third, discretion reasoning assumes that the closet is a safe place for lesbians, gays and bisexuals, while there is overwhelming evidence both from the countries of origin and from our own societies that lesbian, gay and bisexual people who try to conceal their identity are at permanent risk of exposure, extortion and the violence that comes with it.

I argue that instead of focusing on what applicants are entitled to do in expressing their sexual orientation, we need a future-oriented approach, based on the well-foundedness of the fear once the sexual orientation becomes known in the country of origin, as well as on equal treatment vis-à-vis straight people in that society.

1.2 Criminalisation of consensual same sex sexual acts

There are still 78 countries in the world where one risks being arrested and detained, or even sentenced to death, for expressing a sexual orientation or gender identity which is not mainstream (Itaborahy 2012).[23] Criminal provisions prohibit for example 'acts against the order of nature' or sexual acts between males. In several of these 78 states lesbian sex is not explicitly outlawed, and neither is transgender identity. However, it is not very bold to assume that in countries explicitly prohibiting consensual male–male sexual acts, thus reflecting the homophobic attitude of the authorities, lesbians, bisexual women, as well as trans and intersex people will also risk persecution by the state. In other words: the issue of criminalisation is of particular importance for asylum claims based on sexual orientation, but we also think it affects gender identity claims. As an LGBTI person living in such a country, one always risks being arrested by the state authorities, and at the same time violence and discrimination by fellow citizens, family, neighbours, in the street, in the workplace, at school, in hospital, etc. will go unpunished.

In most European States the existence of criminalisation of non-straight sexualities in the country of origin as such is not sufficient for granting refugee status: in addition, proof of prosecution or 'active enforcement' of the criminal provision is needed. We found this situation in Austria, Belgium, France, Germany, Italy, Ireland, Lithuania, the Netherlands, Poland, Sweden and the United Kingdom. In some other countries (Bulgaria, Denmark, Finland, Norway, Spain) the research shows that even the existence of enforced criminalisation in the country of origin seems to be insufficient for recognition as a refugee. For recognition, it is required that applicants show that there are indications that prosecution will take place in their specific case.

In Italy the circumstance that a lesbian, gay or bisexual person originates from a – what we call – 'criminalising country' is regarded as sufficient evidence to grant this person international protection.[24] Whether or not the criminal law is enforced is not an issue in Italian practice: authorities and courts do not carry out an enquiry about the enforcement of criminal law (Jansen and Spijkerboer 2011: 23–24).[25]

In my analysis this Italian State practice is based on a correct interpretation of the refugee definition: the existence of criminal laws concerning consensual same sex sexual acts should, even in absence of information about enforcement, be considered sufficient for refugee status. Although in the Refugee Convention persecution has not been defined, the UNHCR *Handbook* states that from Article 33 of the Convention it may be inferred that a threat to life or freedom on account of one of the five persecution grounds is always persecution, while other serious violations of human rights would also constitute persecution (UNHCR 1992: para 51; Hathaway 1991: 108). As criminalisation constitutes a permanent threat to the freedom – and in some cases also to the lives – of lesbians, gays and bisexuals, criminalisation in itself is to be considered as persecution.

The third question submitted by the Dutch Council of State to the CJEU (see above) is whether 'mere criminalisation of homosexual activities' constitutes persecution in the sense of Article 9 of the EU Qualification Directive. I think this question should be answered affirmatively, on the following grounds.

First, a proper interpretation of the definition of persecution in the EU Qualification Directive leads to the conclusion that criminalisation of consensual same sex sexual activity as such constitutes persecution for lesbians, gays and bisexuals. Article 9 of the EU Qualification Directive qualifies as acts of persecution: 9(1)(a): an act that is sufficiently serious by nature or repetition as to constitute a severe violation of basic human rights, in particular (but not exclusively) non derogable rights: life, torture, inhuman and degrading treatment, slavery or servitude; 9(1)(b): an accumulation of various measures, including violations of human rights, sufficiently severe as to affect in a similar manner. According to Article 9(2)(b) of the EU Qualification Directive these acts can take the form of 'legal, administrative, police, and/or judicial measures which are in themselves discriminatory or which are implemented in a discriminatory manner'.

This is clearly applicable to the issue of criminalisation, because these provisions criminalise same sex sexual acts as opposed to different sex sexual acts, hence they are discriminatory in themselves. Article 9(2)(c) of the EU Qualification Directive, qualifying 'prosecution or punishment, which is disproportionate or discriminatory' as an act of persecution, is applicable here for the same reason, because a prison sentence or corporal punishment on account of a non-standard sexual orientation is inherently discriminatory.

Second, it should be noted that the sole fact that no information on enforcement or 'active prosecution' in a given country is available, does not mean the provisions are not being used in practice or the threat of prosecution has disappeared. The Committee Against Torture considered in a Swedish case that 'the State party's argument that Bangladeshi authorities are not actively persecuting homosexuals does not rule out that such prosecution can occur' (CAT, 23 May 2011, *Uttal Mondal v Sweden*). The scarcity of country of origin information on LGBTIs, including information on enforcement of criminalisation, should also be taken into account here. It will often not be in the interest of the authorities concerned to show statistics on prosecution of LGBTIs. In addition, formal prosecution is not the only way in which criminal provisions are being used. Many examples can be given of situations in which, without formal prosecution, police officers and other authorities detain, abuse, or blackmail LGBTIs based on the criminal provisions (see IGLHRC 2011; HRW 2010a; HRW 2010b).

Third, as UNHCR states in its guidance note on sexual orientation and gender identity: 'the very existence of such laws, irrespective of whether they are enforced, may have far-reaching effects on LGBT persons' enjoyment of fundamental human rights' (UNHCR 2008: para 20). The European Court of Human Rights has considered in several cases that an inhuman and degrading treatment includes acts that 'arouse in [its] victims feelings of fear, anguish and inferiority capable of humiliating and debasing them' (ECtHR, 7 July 1989, *Soering v United Kingdom*, para 100; ECtHR, 8 November 2005, *Bader and others v Sweden*, para 47; ECtHR, 22 June 2006, *D and others v Turkey*, para 56).

In its *Norris* judgment, concerning the criminal provisions against consensual same sex conduct in Ireland, the European Court of Human Rights referred to 'the detrimental effects which the very existence of legislative provisions in question can have on the life of a person of homosexual orientation' (ECtHR, 26 October 1988, *Norris v Ireland*).[26] However, in its first gay asylum (admissibility) decision, the Court decided that the fact that the country to which the alien is to be removed will violate his right to respect to private life by criminalisation does not imply that he cannot be expelled to that country (ECtHR, 22 June 2004, *F v United Kingdom*).[27] I argue that, in the context of criminalisation of non-standard sexual orientation or gender identity, the violation of the right to privacy constitutes an inhuman or degrading treatment because of its foreseeable psychologically harmful effects. Such a violation of the right not to be subjected to an inhuman or degrading treatment constitutes persecution in the sense of Article 9(1)(a) of the EU Qualification Directive. Moreover, Hathaway and Pobjoy have argued that the psychological harm that follows from self-repression or concealment of sexual identity is an endogonous form of persecution (Hathaway and Pobjoy 2012: 36–46). Returning people to a criminalising State would compel them to conceal their sexual identity.

Fourth, criminalisation reinforces a general climate of homophobia (presumably accompanied by transphobia) which enables State agents as well as non-State agents to persecute or harm LGB(TI)s with impunity. Hence, criminalisation makes lesbians, gays and bisexuals into outlaws, at risk of persecution or serious harm at any time. By establishing these type of criminal provisions the state authorities formalise homophobia and sponsor the idea that it is fine to discriminate, attack, beat, harm or persecute LGBTIs. This close relationship between criminalisation and everyday homophobia by non-State agents is illustrated by several Country of Origin reports on the situation of LGBTIs in specific countries. One of the conclusions of the report *Nowhere to Turn* refers to:

> the fact that sodomy laws encourage criminality by implicitly placing LGBT people outside the scope of the law's protection. They serve as license to perpetrators to commit not only blackmail, but theft, assault, rape, and even murder with impunity. They discourage victims from coming forward, and foster corruption in the justice system. So long as these provisions remain in place, unscrupulous individuals are likely to take the law into their own hands, making life intolerable for LGBT people and weakening the rule of law.
>
> (IGLHRC 2011)

A Human Rights Watch report on Cameroon states:

> Though arrests remain relatively rare, they create a climate of fear. Family members have reported other family members to police. Landlords have reported their tenants. Friends have reported friends. Thieves and other perpetrators of crimes have simply accused their victims of homosexuality

> to deflect police attention and escape justice. Others have used the threat of reporting homosexuality to extort money or favors. The consequence is that people are punished for a homosexual identity, not for the specific outlawed practice of homosexual sex. (. . .) Even if a person is not arrested, the climate of prosecution can demand a personal secrecy that can be psychologically devastating and may amount to persecution. (. . .) criminalization leads to stigma, and stigma places people at a higher risk of violence by non-state actors.
>
> (HRW 2010a: 4–5)[28]

These arguments taken together should lead to the conclusion that mere criminalisation of consensual same sex conduct should, indeed, lead to international protection.

Receiving states might fear that following this conclusion (criminalisation should lead to international protection of LGBTI persons), if adopted by, for example, the CJEU, could lead to large amounts of claims from LGBTIs originating from the 78 criminalising countries. However, this did not occur in Italy, nor did the Dutch special policy for Iranian LGBTs lead to vast amounts of Iranian LGBT claims. And even if this were the case, the fact that in theory a measure could concern large numbers is in itself not relevant in refugee law.

Meanwhile, some courts in the Netherlands have acknowledged that gay and lesbian applicants cannot be rejected, while the preliminary questions on the handling of these type of cases are still pending at the CJEU.[29]

1.2.1 Safe countries of origin

Closely connected to the issue of criminalisation is the practice in some European countries to apply lists of so-called 'safe countries of origin'. The safe country of origin concept allows states to deny refugees access to the asylum system on the grounds that human rights are so well protected in their country of origin that persecution severe enough to cause people to flee never occurs. Applicants fleeing those countries have a lesser chance of a positive decision, because they often find their claims fast-tracked and their rights of defence restricted. In drafting these lists no reference is made to the specific risks involved for LGBTI applicants. Some of the lists contain countries of origin where a non-straight sexual orientation is criminalised, mostly African countries. This is practice in France (Ghana, Mauritius, Senegal, Tanzania), Germany (Ghana), Malta (Botswana, Ghana, Jamaica, Senegal), Slovakia (Ghana, Kenya, Mauritius, Seychelles), Switzerland (Ghana, Senegal), the United Kingdom (Ghana, Jamaica, Nigeria).[30]

Article 33 of the Amended Proposal of the EU Procedures Directive states that 'where an applicant shows that there are valid reasons to consider the country not to be safe in his/her particular circumstances, the designation of the country as safe can no longer be considered relevant for him/her'.[31]

Criminalisation of consensual same sex sexual activity in the country of origin would make a clear reason not to consider a country a safe place for an LGBTI applicant from such a country. The country is clearly not safe, so that the presumption of safety is rebutted by the mere fact that an applicant is a lesbian, gay or bisexual person. It seems reasonable to hold the same conclusion for trans and intersex persons. Criminalisation of same sex sexual acts is conclusive of a social system characterised by violent versions of heteronormativity and strict gender norms that rebuts the presumptions of safety, not only for those explicitly targeted by criminal law, but also for others who do not conform to mainstream sexual norms.

Apart from criminalising countries, homo- and transphobic countries appear in the lists of safe countries of origin, like Kosovo, Mongolia and Ukraine.[32] I am of the opinion that these countries are equally unsafe places for LGBTI applicants and therefore cannot be regarded as safe countries.

1.3 State protection

Many LGBTI persons flee their country not because they are prosecuted or persecuted by the state authorities, but because they fear persecution from other citizens: for example their family, neighbours or gangs. In this situation questions may arise, like: Did you seek protection from the police? Could your own state authorities protect you? Because if that is the case, there is no need for international protection. This primacy of national protection over international protection is expressed in Article 7(2) of the EU Qualification Directive (see below).

From an LGBTI rights perspective this general principle of refugee law is to be applauded, because it expresses the obligation of national authorities to protect their LGBTI citizens against homo- and transphobic violence. However, at the same time this notion can be problematic in an LGBTI context, especially when the state authorities criminalise sexual orientation or gender identity or when the state authorities are known to be homophobic or transphobic. In these situations it is perfectly understandable that LGBTI people do not turn to the police for protection, for this would be pointless or even dangerous. In a Dutch case a Ugandan bisexual man stated that, while visiting a night club, he and his male partner were attacked by a group of fellow-citizens. When the police arrived, they assumed they would be protected, but they were arrested instead.[33]

Since July 2009, the Dutch policy rules state that: 'Whenever homosexual acts are criminalised in the country of origin, the applicant is not required to have invoked the protection of the authorities there' (Aliens Circular (Netherlands) C2/2.10.2). Also from France, Germany and Italy it was reported that seeking state protection against non-state actors is not required from LGBTIs originating from criminalising countries.

However, in many other European states we found that claims of applicants from criminalising countries were rejected because they did not report the persecution to the police in the country of origin. For instance in Austria a gay man from Zimbabwe was rejected for not seeking police protection, and in Portugal a lesbian from Senegal was refused for the same reason. In Norway, an Ethiopian man was required to seek protection from the state. In Finland protection was withheld from applicants from Iran and Nigeria on this ground.[34]

In addition, LGBTI applicants also flee countries where the criminal provisions have been abandoned, but where the authorities are still homophobic or transphobic. When they are expected to turn to these authorities for protection against persecution or harassment by non-State actors, this may lead to the person being subjected to further homo- or transphobia, this time from the police. Even when the authorities might not engage in anti-LGBTI-violence themselves, homo- and transphobic authorities are not likely to provide effective protection against this type of violence.

Concerning these applicants there is divergent State practice. For instance in Denmark there was the case of a Russian transwoman. She was humiliated, beaten and sexually abused by the police and she was also raped. She did not report these events out of fear. The Danish Refugee Board decided she could seek the protection of higher authorities in Russia and suggested she move to a larger city, where it would be less likely she would be victim of abuse by the police. In contrast, in France homophobia is taken into account when it comes to the requirement of invoking State protection. In a case of an applicant from Kosovo who had not sought police protection, the French National Asylum Law Court stated that 'Although homosexuality is not criminalised in Kosovo, homosexuals can be the victim of grave discrimination and violence; individuals who have been the victim of such facts mostly refrain from filing a complaint; the attitude of the Kosovo authorities can be perceived as encouraging homophobic acts' (Jansen and Spijkerboer 2011: 31). The man received refugee status. Also, in Germany it is generally not expected that LGBTI applicants seek State protection in countries where the authorities are homophobic.

According to Article 7(2) of the EU Qualification Directive protection is generally provided when the state actors operate an 'effective legal system for the detection, prosecution and punishment of acts constituting persecution or serious harm'. In the case of LGBTI applicants this Article should be applied in such a way that they are only required to turn to the authorities for protection if, first, it has been established that effective protection would generally be available for LGBTI people in that country. In criminalising countries State protection will not be available. In countries where the authorities are homo- or transphobic, State protection will not be available either. Because of the homo- and transphobic nature of the legal and administrative systems in those countries, there cannot be an 'effective legal system for the detection, prosecution and punishment of acts constituting persecution or serious harm', because the legal and administrative system in those countries itself is part of the persecution or serious harm, instead of a source of protection.

Therefore, LGBTI claimants originating from countries where same sex sexual acts are a criminal offence, or where the authorities are homo- or transphobic, who have experienced problems from fellow-citizens or from authorities, cannot be expected to turn to the authorities for protection.

1.4 Internal protection

In asylum cases it may be possible that the threat of persecution is only present in one part of the country of origin and the applicant could move to another region, where it is safe and where protection is available – when needed – the so-called 'internal protection alternative' (also known as internal flight alternative or internal relocation alternative).

LGBTI applications are rejected on the basis of a supposed availability of an internal protection alternative in at least 16 European countries. Many decisions and judgments rely on the presumption that the mere existence of gay bars, gay meeting places or LGBT NGOs in larger cities in the country of origin would be sufficient to provide a safe place for LGBTIs, instead of carefully assessing whether the authorities would offer protection against anti-gay or anti-trans violence in these cities. Furthermore, rejections based on internal protection alternatives are often accompanied by discretion reasoning: for instance the Irish Tribunal decided that a lesbian from Uganda could relocate in that country, as long as she kept her sexual orientation a secret.[35] At least seven European countries still reject LGBTI applications from criminalising countries arguing that an internal protection alternative would be available there.[36] For instance, in Finland the asylum authorities decided a gay man could easily move to another part of Iran. Similarly, the Romanian Immigration Office thought it was reasonable and relevant to send a gay man to another part of Afghanistan because he had no problems with the Afghan authorities.

Obviously, in situations where LGBTI applicants can actually obtain State protection elsewhere in their country of origin, refugee protection can be denied on legitimate grounds. However, apart from exceptions, asylum cannot be denied relying on an internal protection alternative where state organs are the agents of persecution (UNHCR 2008: para 33; UNHCR 2003; Hathaway and Foster 2003; *Michigan Guidelines* 1999). From Article 7(2) of the EU Qualification Directive, it follows that protection is normally provided by state actors operating an effective legal system for the detection, prosecution and punishment of acts constituting persecution or serious harm – in this case serious harm for which the applicant has a well-founded fear in one part of the country.

In case of criminalisation, the legal system cannot be effective for them, for the same reason as why they cannot turn to the authorities for protection. Even if my proposition that criminalisation in itself already constitutes persecution is not accepted: criminalising states cannot be a source of protection for LGBTIs. The – more limited – position put forward here is that in criminalising countries no state protection is available for people with a well-founded fear of being persecuted on account of their sexual orientation or gender identity. This is so neither in the place where they originally came from (see above, paragraph on State protection), nor elsewhere in the country of origin. In both places, an 'effective legal system for the detection, prosecution and punishment of acts constituting persecution or serious harm' (as Article 7(2) of the EU Qualification Directive defines protection) is clearly lacking. Hence, internal protection cannot be available for them.

Whenever LGBTI persons originated from other (non-criminalising) countries, an internal protection alternative can only be considered after it has been established that the State authorities in that part of the country are not homophobic or transphobic, but are instead willing and able to offer protection to LGBTIs, when needed.

As to the idea that gay bars or other meeting places could constitute an internal protection alternative, this seems a violation of the current Article 8(2) of the EU Qualification Directive which states that the assessment of a possible internal protection alternative should be done having regard to the general circumstances in that part of the country and to the personal circumstances of the applicant.[37] The mere fact that there are locations where LGB(TI) people are tolerated or succeed in evading homo- or transphobia is insufficient to conclude that they are protected there. The existence of such localities is insufficient for establishing 'an effective legal system for the detection, prosecution and punishment of acts constituting persecution or serious harm'.

Likewise, if LGBTIs with a well-founded fear of being persecuted in one part of the country can only be safe in another part of the country if they conceal their sexual orientation, then internal protection is not available, both because discretion cannot be required and because the fact that concealment is necessary in order to prevent more trouble is a strong indication that the authorities do not operate a legal system that is effective for LGBTI people. Millbank has noted: 'Discretion reasoning clouded the consideration of internal relocation by implicitly or explicitly assuming that the purpose of relocation was to achieve (re)concealment rather than to move to a place of actual safety and sufficiency of state protection' (Millbank 2009: 394).

My conclusion is that an internal protection alternative can exist only where LGBTI people can live openly and freely, without fear of being persecuted for their sexual orientation or gender identity, and where they have effective access to the legal system for protection against the violence they fear in another part of the country.

1.5 Credibility

An issue that seems to be of growing importance is that of credibility, in particular the answer to the question whether the person who states that she or he fears persecution for reasons of sexual orientation or gender identity, really is an LGBTI individual.

There is huge diversity in the way sexual orientation or gender identity is established in asylum cases in European States. In some States self-identification is the general means by which sexual orientation or gender identity is assessed. But in other States various members of the medical profession are consulted, in order to provide proof of the matter: sexologists, psychiatrists, psychologists. There is the highly controversial practice of phallometry, a method that has been applied in the Czech Republic in asylum cases to 'prove' sexual orientation, by measuring the claimants' physical reactions while watching different types of pornographic material. This kind of testing is intrusive and degrading and constitutes an interference with the person's private sphere and sense of dignity, and is therefore not in line with Articles 3 and 8 of the European Convention on Human Rights. It is especially inappropriate for asylum seekers who have been persecuted due to their sexual orientation. The criticism of the Fundamental Rights Agency, the European Commission, NGOs and UNHCR led to the suspension of this practice in the Czech Republic in 2009 (Verwaltungsgericht Schleswig-Holstein, 7 September 2009; European Union Agency for Fundamental Rights 2010: 56–80; ORAM 2011; UNHCR 2011). However, in Slovakia phallometry is still being applied (Letter of the Human Rights League Slovakia and ILGA-Europe, 19 July 2012). In addition, there are other medical examinations by psychologists, psychiatrists and sexologists, that are being used for the assessment of sexual orientation in Austria, Bulgaria, the Czech Republic, Germany, Hungary, Romania and probably also in Poland and Slovakia (Jansen and Spijkerboer 2011: 49–53). These examinations do not test the physical reactions as phallometry does, but they test the psychological reactions of the asylum seekers in order to 'prove' their sexual orientation. These examinations are sometimes required by the asylum authorities and sometimes they are submitted at the initiative of the applicants or their legal advisors. However, to assess an LGBTI identity these type of medical investigations are inadequate and inappropriate. Sexual orientation is not a medical category and should therefore not be treated as such, and in our opinion the same should apply to gender identity, although we only found one example in which someone's gender identity was not believed (Jansen and Spijkerboer 2011: 51). These medical examinations can be emotionally painful and humiliating and should be considered a violation of the right to privacy of Article 8 of the European Convention on Human Rights. Instead, sexual orientation and gender identity should be regarded as a matter of self-identification, as fortunately happens in several countries.

Another problem connected to credibility is the finding that many decisions contain stereotypes about LGBTI persons and assumptions on how a 'true' LGBTI person behaves or what he or she looks like. For instance, in Cyprus a man was not believed to be gay because he joined the army, in Ireland a man was rejected because he was not familiar with a famous gay bar in Dublin, in several countries lesbians and bisexuals are not believed because they have children or they are or have been married. And in other countries applicants were rejected because they were not aware of the exact criminal provision against homosexual acts in their country. Also, people might be found to be not credible because they give 'evasive' answers to sexually explicit questions, or because their stated same sex sexual conduct was considered too risky to be true (Jansen and Spijkerboer 2011: 53–63).

Credibility seems to become more of an issue in countries where practice becomes more sensitive towards LGBTI applicants (Millbank 2009). There is a trend that, when discretion reasoning is abolished or when LGBTI applicants from particular countries of origin are being protected as a group,[38] the reasons for rejecting asylum claims shift from arguments based on discretion or the situation in the country of origin not being bad enough, to arguments based on not believing that the applicant is an LGBTI person. For this reason, credibility issues are increasingly important.

Although credibility is notoriously hard to establish, the stereotypes which are routinely used in most European countries are problematic. They rely on notions about LGBTI people that are empirically incorrect. Also, they reflect debatable normative ideas about what are acceptable deviations from hetero norms, and they may be culturalistic: Is it as obvious as is commonly assumed that LGBTIs from other parts of the world share the mindset and behaviour that is considered characteristic for LGBTI people living in Europe? Louis Middelkoop's contribution in this volume addresses some of these issues further. There is no uniform way in which people express their sexual orientation or gender identity. The only way in which sexual orientation or gender identity can be established in asylum cases is by an interview which allows the applicant to tell her or his story, freely and in a safe space. People working with LGBTI (and other) asylum seekers should be very much aware of how difficult it is to establish credibility, especially when it concerns intimate and culturally specific issues such as sexual orientation and gender identity. They should be very hesitant to rely on stereotypical notions.

People taking asylum decisions should be professionally trained to better understand that there are many ways in which sexual orientations or gender identities can be expressed. Nicole LaViolette elaborates on this subject in her contribution to this volume. She points out that it is important to reflect on the exact nature and content of the training and she suggests to develop an LGBT Cultural Competency Training, which, in order to encompass all aspects that play a role in a fair determination process, should consist of a training trilogy: awareness and attitudes (focussing on the preconceived notions people working with LGBTI asylum seekers have), knowledge (about LGBTI relevant country of origin information and applicable legal norms) and skills (mainly focussing on interaction with LGBTI asylum seekers).

1.6 Late disclosure

LGBTI asylum seekers sometimes tell about the reasons for fleeing their country only later in the procedure. They may have many reasons for not disclosing their narrative of sexual orientation or gender identity right away: they may have never talked about it before, they may not have fully been aware of their sexual orientation or gender identity at the moment of their first asylum interview, they may be ashamed, they may suffer from internalised homo- or transphobia, they may be afraid that other people from their community learn about it, they may fear the repercussions if their sexual orientation or gender identity becomes known in the reception facility where they are staying, they may not be aware of the fact that a well-founded fear of persecution based on sexual orientation or gender identity is a ground for asylum, or they may have been advised to make up an 'easier' story.

Some countries apply a strict *res judicata* system, which means that the case is considered to be already decided upon, and therefore information which the asylum seeker submits later is not taken into account, nor are the reasons for this late submission. This happens for instance in the Netherlands and this could easily lead to rejection of LGBTI asylum seekers who need protection, thus violating Article 3 of the European Convention on Human Rights. An Iraqi gay spoke in his third procedure for the first time about the real reasons why he fled, which were related to his sexual orientation. He also submitted a declaration of a psychologist, stating that he suffered from post-traumatic stress disorder and that he went through a complicated process of self-acceptance, all of which had made it impossible to speak about this subject with a stranger in the earlier interviews. In addition, he feared aggression and violence from other Iraqis and he was insecure and ignorant regarding the attitude of Dutch society towards homosexuality. The Court did not qualify his statement on his sexual orientation and the problems resulting from it as new facts because they dated from before the decision. The psychological report did not show that he could not declare, even summarily, on his sexual orientation in the previous procedures, nor that he could not declare on his inability to declare (Provisional Measures Judge District Court Zwolle, 27 March 2012).

From Austria a much more flexible approach to a late disclosure of sexual orientation within a *res judicata* system was reported. A gay Iranian mentioned his homosexual orientation two years after he became aware of it. The Appeal Court considered:

> [T]hat for answering the question whether in the present case there is a new fact, relevant is not only that the applicant had purportedly already become aware of his homosexual orientation at a moment at which the previous procedure had not yet been formally ended; it should be considered as more decisive to clarify when the applicant disclosed his homosexuality to others for the first time, whether and at which

> moment the applicant has become homosexually active for the first time, or when the sexual inclination of the applicant has become publicly known.
>
> (Asylum Court, 10 February 2010)

Another problem connected to a later coming out to the asylum authorities is that it will often affect the credibility: the sexual orientation or gender identity is considered to be fabricated after the previous rejection. However, a late disclosure should never be the sole reason for rejection of a claim based on sexual orientation or gender identity. The reasons why sexual orientation or gender identity are disclosed later should always be considered carefully.[39]

In a case of a bisexual man from Afghanistan, who was expelled by Sweden, the Human Rights Committee observed that:

> the State party's migration authorities rejected the author's application, not on the ground of the author's unchallenged sexual orientation and its impact on the author in the particular circumstances in Afghanistan, but rather on the ground that the sexual orientation claim had been invoked at a late stage in the asylum process which, in the view of the State party, substantially undermined his credibility, notwithstanding the reasons given by the author for the late disclosure of his claim – namely stigma associated with bisexuality and homosexuality, feelings of shame, fear of reprisal, as well as lack of knowledge that sexual orientation would be a valid claim for refugee status and asylum – and considered that he failed to meet the standard of 'valid excuse' within the meaning of the [Swedish] Aliens Act. (. . .) The Committee is of the view that insufficient weight was given to the author's allegations on the real risk he might face in Afghanistan in view of his sexual orientation. Accordingly, the Committee considers that, in the circumstances, the author's deportation to Afghanistan constitutes a violation of articles 6 and 7 of the Covenant.
>
> (Human Rights Committee, 8 November 2011, *X v Sweden*)

It follows from both common sense and the case law of the European Court of Human Rights that the late moment of disclosure cannot be the sole reason to dismiss an asylum application. There are many plausible reasons for asylum applicants not to inform the asylum authorities of their sexual orientation or gender identity. Therefore, a strict *res judicata* system such as applied in the Netherlands is unacceptable. But it is equally unacceptable to base credibility findings merely on the fact that an asylum seeker informed the asylum authorities only at a later stage that he or she is LGBTI. The authorities must always inquire into the reasons for late disclosure, and make an overall credibility assessment which is not based exclusively on the late stage at which information was submitted.

1.7 Country of origin information

Objective, complete and reliable Country of Origin Information (COI) is crucial for the determination of all asylum claims. COI enables decision makers to relate a purported fear of persecution to the human rights situation of LGBTIs in the country of origin, and to answer questions, such as: Are non-dominant sexual identities criminalised in the country of origin? What is the general attitude of the authorities towards LGBTIs? What is the legal and social position of LGBTI people? Is effective State protection against non-State persecution available for LGBTIs? How is the situation in different parts of the country?

We found two main problems connected to COI in LGBTI cases. First, the information on LGBTIs in countries of origin that is available is incomplete: often COI just states whether sexual orientation is criminalised, and if so, what is the penalty. Furthermore, COI mostly deals with gay men, while information on lesbians and trans people is scarce and information on bisexuals and intersex people is practically non-existent.

Second, the existing information is not always used appropriately. For example the fact that there is a gay meeting place in a specific area in the country of origin cannot be taken to prove that this area is a suitable protection alternative for lesbians. Also, a lack of information on, for instance, enforcement of criminal provisions or on the situation of trans people, only means there is no information: it should not be taken to mean that the applicant does not risk persecution or discrimination there.

There follows two examples of trans cases in which a combination of these two problems, incomplete COI which is not used in the right way, seems to play a role.

In Sweden applications from Iranian trans asylum seekers have been rejected because in Iran it is possible to undergo a sex reassignment operation. However, the situation of trans persons seems far more complex than that. As is noted in the report *Unknown people*: 'People who transgress gender norms in Iran are given the choice of living as criminals or go through sex reassignment surgery' (Grandin and Sörberg 2010: 31–34).[40]

The Czech Supreme Administrative Court concluded that there is no difference between homosexuality and transsexuality for the purposes of assessment of the claim of a Ukrainian asylum seeker. The Court based this conclusion on COI, stating that 'Ukrainian society is tolerant towards homosexuality. Therefore, it can be reasonably inferred that it is tolerant towards transsexuality, as well' (Supreme Administrative Court, 14 November 2007).[41]

The Czech Court does not realise that information about one subgroup should not automatically be presumed to be applicable to the other subgroups as well, unless there are good reasons to make this presumption. At the same time, the absence of information on one subgroup should not be understood as evidence that there is no risk.

A more sensitive approach is propagated by the Asylum Instruction of the UK Border Agency, which states:

> It is very important, however, to note that there may be very little evidence on ill-treatment of lesbians in the country of origin. It may be the case that if gay men are found to face persecution, then lesbians, as a corresponding group which does not conform to an established gender role, may also be at risk.
>
> (UK Border Agency 2011a)

Article 4(3)(a) of the EU Qualification Directive states that the assessment should take into account 'all relevant facts as they relate to the country of origin at the time of taking a decision on the application; including laws and regulations of the country of origin and the manner in which they are applied'. The Procedures Directive adds that in order to carry out an appropriate examination 'member states shall ensure that precise and up-to-date information is obtained from various sources, such as UNHCR, as to the general situation prevailing in the countries of origin of applicants for asylum'.[42] Furthermore, UNHCR's gender guidelines acknowledge that it is important 'to recognise that in relation to gender-related claims, the usual types of evidence used in other refugee claims may not be as readily available' and propose in such cases to use alternative sources of information (UNHCR 2002: para 37).

Taking into account the current scarcity of country of origin information on LGBTIs, including information on enforcement of criminalisation, it is risky to conclude that it is safe to return LGBTI people to the country of origin, when such a conclusion is only based on a lack of information. In such cases, more information must be gathered, for instance from local LGBT organisations in the country of origin or, if that is impossible, decisions should take into account the lack of accurate information, in particular by relying on the principle of 'the benefit of the doubt'.[43]

Considering countries where gay sexual orientation is criminalised, while lesbian, bisexual, trans and intersex persons are not mentioned explicitly in criminal law, it should be assumed that lesbian, bisexual, trans and intersex persons risk persecution too, until it has been established that this is not the case. It is important to know whether a given country has criminal law provisions which might be applied specifically against LGBTI persons, but it is equally important that all country reports cover more aspects of the human rights situation of LGBTIs, like the attitude of the police towards LGBTIs and the availability of effective protection against discrimination and homo- and transphobic violence. Furthermore, information is needed on the situation of lesbians, bisexuals, trans and intersex individuals. The European Asylum Support Office could play an important role here.

1.8 Reception

Although the focus of the present study was not on reception conditions, it is clear that harassment and violence against LGBTI asylum seekers in reception facilities is a widespread and serious issue in Europe. From most EU countries examples were reported of homophobic and transphobic incidents in reception centres, in accommodation centres and also in alien detention. Often there is social exclusion, verbal and physical harassment, and sometimes even sexual abuse, mostly by other asylum seekers, in particular people from the same country of origin. Also incidents by staff members and by guards and police officers in detention are reported (Jansen and Spijkerboer 2011: 77–78).

In some countries asylum seekers are housed in the countryside, were the local inhabitants have a low tolerance towards LGBTIs and from where it is not possible to reach LGBTI NGOs in the capital. Sometimes LGBTI asylum seekers are so afraid of other asylum seekers that they do not dare to mention their sexual orientation or gender identity to the asylum authorities; as a consequence they cannot be granted refugee or subsidiary protection on that ground (see on the impact of problematic living conditions of LGBT asylum seekers, Giulia Cragnolini's contribution to this volume). Whenever a complaint system exists, in the majority of countries this does not work effectively, partly because LGBTI asylum seekers often fear disclosure of their sexual orientation or gender identity.[44]

It is therefore important that proper complaint systems will be installed in order to prevent and protect people against homophobic and transphobic incidents. In addition, the possibility must be created of moving LGBTI persons to another location, or – even better – relocate the perpetrators in another reception facility, as for instance happens in Finland and Belgium.

Reception authorities in Member States should pay particular attention to the special needs of LGBTI asylum seekers in reception, accommodation and detention centres, and should develop appropriate procedures, guidelines and training modules in order to address their special needs.[45]

1.9 Conclusion

The Fleeing Homophobia research identified several issues that specifically affect LGBTI asylum seekers. Regarding most of these issues there are divergent European state practices, while some practices are below the minimum level required by human rights and refugee norms, including those which are codified in the EU Qualification Directive. In order to solve this divergence, the European Asylum Support Office should promote and coordinate the dissemination of good practices.

The research provides several clear outcomes:

1 Refugee status should be granted to LGBTI applicants originating from countries where sexual orientation or gender identity are criminalised.

2 LGBTI applicants should not be required to invoke State protection against non-State actors of persecution when in the country of origin sexual orientation or gender identity are criminalised, or when the authorities are homo- or transphobic.
3 LGBTI applicants should not be required or presumed to conceal their sexual orientation or gender identity in the country of origin.
4 An internal protection alternative should not be raised in cases of LGBTI applicants from those countries which criminalise sexual orientation or gender identity, or where the state authorites are homo- or transphobic.
5 Late disclosure of sexual orientation or gender identity as such should not lead to denial of asylum. This should happen neither by inflexible application of a *res judicata* principle, nor by considering a 'late coming out' per se as an indication of non-credibility of an applicant's sexual orientation or gender identity.

Concerning the issues of credibility, COI and reception conditions, concrete proposals for legal solutions did not arise. However, the Fleeing Homophobia report gives many examples of pitfalls that should be avoided, like for instance the one-to-one use of COI on the situation of gay men in cases of LBTIs, the non-effectiveness of complaint systems in reception facilities and the regular occurrence of stereotypes and prejudices.

More research is clearly needed. As the vast majority of LGBTI cases are about gay men, the danger exists that specific problems of lesbians, bisexuals, trans and intersex persons are overlooked. The contribution of Laurie Berg and Jenni Millbank to this volume provides a very welcome start for the investigation of trans cases. In addition, more research is needed on the exact nature of the problems LGBTI persons experience in reception, accommodation and detention centres, and on ways of improving their situation. Lastly, but very importantly, concrete actions should be undertaken to establish more LGBTI sensitive trainings. LaViolette's contribution offers valuable guidance in this respect which could help combat the stereotypes, prejudices and misunderstandings of the lives of LGBTI asylum seekers which were found throughout the research. Although we realise these type of trainings are no panacea, and legal improvements remain necessary, they could contribute to better and fairer future assessments of LGBTI asylum applications.

1.10 Notes

* Sabine Jansen (LLM in Law from the University of Amsterdam) is the initiator and the main researcher of the Fleeing Homophobia research, as well as the co-author of the final report. I am very grateful to Thomas Spijkerboer for his generous support and co-operation, and for his invaluable enthusiasm throughout this research. In addition, I would like to thank everyone who played a role in making this project successful, especially the national experts and the advisory panel (S. Chelvan, Joël Le Déroff, Maria Hennessy, Borbála Ivány, Simone Rossi,

Gisela Thäter), and – last but not least – Caco Verhees and Louis Middelkoop, who solved numerous practical problems.

1 'Intersex' refers to a condition of having sexual anatomy that is not considered standard for a male or female. Intersex can be used as an umbrella term covering differences of sexual development, which can consist of diagnosable congenital conditions in which development of chromosomal, gonadal or anatomic sex is atypical. The term 'intersex' is not interchangeable or a synonym for *transgender*. See on trans and intersex also, Agius and Tobler (2012). Our experts reported a total number of 67 trans and only 12 intersex applicants in Europe. We include the category intersex to be as inclusive as we can.

2 As European statistics regarding this issue do not exist, this number is based on an estimate, see Jansen and Spijkerboer (2011: 15–16).

3 'Sexual orientation' is understood to refer to each person's capacity for profound emotional, affectional and sexual attraction to, and intimate and sexual relations with, individuals of a different gender or the same gender or more than one gender. 'Gender identity' is understood to refer to each person's deeply felt internal and individual experience of gender, which may or may not correspond with the sex assigned at birth, including the personal sense of the body (which may involve, if freely chosen, modification of bodily appearance or function by medical, surgical or other means) and other expressions of gender, including dress, speech and mannerisms. Definitions from the *Yogyakarta Principles on the Application of International Human Rights Law in Relation to Sexual Orientation and Gender Identity* (International Commission of Jurists 2007). 'Gender' refers to the socially constructed roles, behaviours, activities, and attributes that a given society considers appropriate for men and women.

4 Afdeling Rechtspraak van de Raad van State (Judicial Division of the Council of State), 13 August 1981.

5 Article 10(1)(d) of Council Directive 2004/83/EC of 29 April 2004. The line in Article 10(1)(d) which states: 'Sexual orientation cannot be understood to include acts considered to be criminal in accordance with national law of the Member States' should in my opinion be removed, for this type of reservation seems to imply that sexual orientation and criminality are somehow related, while such reservations do not occur regarding the other persecution grounds. From Article 10(2) follows that persecution based on an attributed (= imputed or perceived) sexual orientation or gender identity is included as well.

6 Most European States have implemented this provision in their national legislation. However, according to the Bulgarian expert of Fleeing Homophobia, Bulgaria has not implemented the definition in Article 10(1)(d) of Directive 2004/83/EC of sexual orientation as a persecution ground into the national Law on Asylum and Refugees.

7 Directive 2011/95/EU of the European Parliament and of the Council of 13 December 2011. Even before then, Portugal and Spain mentioned 'gender identity' as a persecution ground in the Asylum Law; Austria and the United Kingdom mentioned 'gender identity' in other legally binding documents.

8 Translations of the report into Finnish, French, German, Greek, Hungarian, Italian, Polish, Slovak, Spanish and Swedish are available on the website.

9 In order to map existing practices in the EU Member States a questionnaire was sent to national experts in all Member States, except Estonia, Latvia and Luxemburg, where the experts we contacted informed us they were unable to

report about LGBTI applicants. We included Norway (not an EU Member State, but participating in the EU asylum *acquis* in some ways) and Denmark (an EU Member State presently not participating in the asylum *acquis*). Switzerland answered our questionnaire partially. Israel, an associated state, was also included in order to show the situation in a State with a refugee determination system which is not influenced in any way by EU Directives and Regulations. Most questionnaires are available on the website.

10 See ECtHR, 21 January 2011, *MSS v Belgium and Greece*; CJEU, 21 December 2011, *NS v Secretary of State for the Home Department (United Kingdom) and ME and others v Refugee Applications Commissioner (Ireland)*.

11 See the Belgian questionnaire (Chechenyan asylum seeker not removed to Poland because of great influx of homophobic Chechenyans); the German questionnaire, Verwaltungsgericht (Administrative Court) Schleswig-Holstein, 7 September 2009: interim measure staying the transfer of an Iranian gay applicant because of the risk he would have to undergo phallometric testing 'the conformity of which with human rights standards seems at least very much in doubt'; the Dutch questionnaire (litigation about the physical safety of two gay applicants in Slovenia), Rechtbank (District Court) Zwolle, 15 December 2008; Afdeling bestuursrechtspraak van de Raad van State (Administrative Jurisdiction Division of the Council of State), 7 September 2009; an Iranian gay applicant was rejected in the United Kingdom, the Netherlands did not assume responsibility, decision upheld by courts, Rechtbank (District Court) Zwolle, 14 December 2007, Afdeling bestuursrechtspraak van de Raad van State (Judicial Division of the Council of State), 11 March 2008. The applicant was granted asylum in the United Kingdom after subsequent re-examination, after pressure of the European Parliament, see European Parliament resolution 2008. In a Finnish intersex case, the applicant was not transferred for health reasons; the applicant was in need of hormonal and psychological treatment, which had already been started in Finland; this seems unrelated to the (non)availability of treatment in Italy.

12 This was reported from Austria, Belgium, Bulgaria, Cyprus, Denmark, Finland, France, Germany, Hungary, Ireland, the Netherlands, Malta, Poland, Romania, Spain, Norway and Switzerland.

13 Bundesverwaltungsgericht (Federal Administrative Court), 18 January 2011, *T v Bundesamt für Migration*; see also Nufer and Lipp (2011).

14 Afdeling Bestuursrechtspraak Raad van State (Judicial Division of the Council of State of the Netherlands), 17 August 2011.

15 High Court of Australia, 9 December 2003, *Appellant S396/2002 v Minister for Immigration and Multicultural Affairs* [2003] HCA 71.

16 Refugee Appeal no. 74665/03, 7 July 2004; cf. for similar rulings: United States Court of Appeals for the Ninth Circuit 7 March 2005, *Karouni v Gonzales*, Attorney General; Federal Court of Canada, 8 October 2008, *Atta Fosu v the Minister of Citizenship and Immigration*.

17 See also Millbank (2012: 515).

18 See Upper Tribunal (Immigration and Asylum Chamber), 24 June 2011, *SW (lesbians – HJ and HT applied) Jamaica*.

19 Reference for a preliminary ruling from the Oberverwaltungsgericht (High Administrative Court) Nordrhein-Westfalen, 1 December 2010. The central questions in this case were: (a) To what extent is homosexual activity protected? (b) Can a homosexual person be told to live with his or her sexual orientation in his

or her home country in secret and not allow it to become known to others? (c) Are specific prohibitions for the protection of public order and morals relevant when interpreting and applying Article 10(1)(d) of Directive 2004/83/EC or should homosexual activity be protected in the same way as for heterosexual people?

20 See the questions in para 18, per Advocate-General Bot, Opinion, 2012.

21 For instance in para 56: Persecution is an act of the utmost gravity, because it sets out flagrantly and persistently to deny the most essential rights of the human person, on the basis of skin colour, nationality, gender, sexual orientation, political beliefs or religious convictions. Regardless of the form that it takes, and aside from its discriminatory effect, persecution entails the denial of the human person and seeks to exclude that person from society. Persecution is based on prohibition, prohibiting a person from living in society with others on account of his or her gender, prohibiting a person from being treated equally on account of his beliefs, or from having access to health care and education on account of his race. These prohibitions penalise the individual for what he is or represents.

22 Compare the Opinion of Advocate-General Bot, 2012, *Federal Republic of Germany v Y and Z*.

23 Same sex sexual acts are threatened with the death penalty in Iran, the northern states of Nigeria, Mauritania, Saudi-Arabia, southern parts of Somalia, Sudan and Yemen.

24 The existence of this Italian practice was confirmed by the Dutch Ministry: Letter of the Minister of Immigration, Integration and Asylum, 21 March 2012.

25 See also, the Italian questionnaire on the project's website.

26 See also, ECtHR, 22 October 1981, *Dudgeon v United Kingdom*; ECtHR, 22 April 1993, *Modinos v Cyprus*; UN Human Rights Committee, 4 April 1994, *Toonen v Australia*.

27 In addition, the Court found there was not sufficient proof of active prosecution by the Iranian authorities and the claim was rejected. See also ECtHR (Dec), 20 December 2004, *IIN v the Netherlands*.

28 See also, Human Rights Watch (2010b: 131–132).

29 District Court Haarlem, 8 May 2012, nr. 12/10465 (lesbian from Gambia); similar judgments were based on the questions of the Bundesverwaltungsgericht on religion: District Court Rotterdam, 2 April 2012, nr. 12/7785 (gay from Guinea); District Court Den Bosch, 26 April 2012, 12/10858 (Iranian convert) and Council of State (ABRvS) 11 May 2012, 201203335/2/V2 (Afghan convert).

30 Some of our experts informed us that their country did in fact apply a list of safe countries, but they could not tell whether there were criminalising countries involved, because the list was not publicly available.

31 Brussels, 1 June 2011, COM(2011) 319 final, full text of Article 33: The designation of a third country as a safe country of origin for the purposes of this Directive cannot establish an absolute guarantee of safety for nationals of that country. By its very nature, the assessment underlying the designation can only take into account the general civil, legal and political circumstances in that country and whether actors of persecution, torture or inhuman or degrading treatment or punishment are subject to sanction in practice when found liable in the country concerned. For this reason, it is important that, where an applicant shows that there are valid reasons to consider the country not to be safe in his or her particular circumstances, the designation of the country as safe can no longer be considered relevant for him/her.

32 Kosovo is on the list of safe countries in France and Switzerland, Mongolia is on the list of the Czech Republic and France, Ukraine is listed as safe in France and Switzerland. Although Finland does officially not apply such a list, the Finnish expert has the impression that Russia is considered a safe country of origin.

33 District Court of Haarlem, 22 September 2009. He later received refugee status.

34 We found that seeking State protection in criminalising countries is also required in Denmark, Ireland, Malta, Romania, Spain and Sweden, see Jansen and Spijkerboer (2011: 27–28).

35 Examples of discretion reasoning in relation to an internal protection alternative were found in Denmark, Finland, Germany, Ireland, Malta, the Netherlands, Norway, Poland and Romania.

36 We found examples in Austria, Finland, Ireland, Italy, the Netherlands, Norway and Romania (see Jansen and Spijkerboer 2011: 43). However, it must be noted that in the Italian example the main reason for the rejection was that the sexual orientation of the applicant was not found credible (Jansen and Spijkerboer 2011: 23, note 68).

37 The most recent version of the Recast proposal added to Article 8 that 'to this end, Member states shall ensure that precise and up-to-date information is obtained from relevant sources, such as the UNHCR and the European Asylum Support Office'.

38 For instance the Dutch government in principle grants protection to all LGBTs from Iran and Iraq. See on Iran, WBV2006/38, 17 November 2006 and on Iraq: Letter of Minister Leers to the President of the Second Chamber on the policy regarding Iraqi LGBTs, 11 July 2012.

39 See about the possibility of special circumstances which might set aside national law: ECtHR, 19 February 1998, *Bahaddar v the Netherlands*, para 45.

40 See on homosexuals turning to sex reassignment surgery only to conform to the demands of Iranian society, the documentary-film *Be like others* (Eshaghian 2008).

41 I am not familiar with any COI on 'Ukrainian tolerance towards homosexuality', as referred to in this case.

42 Article 8(2)(b) of Council Directive 2005/85/EC.

43 See for instance UNHCR 2008: para 35: 'Where the applicant is unable to provide evidence as to his or her sexual orientation, and/or there is a lack of sufficiently specific country of origin information, the decision-maker will have to rely on that person's testimony alone. If the applicant's account appears credible, he or she should, unless there are good reasons to the contrary, be given the benefit of the doubt', and para 41: 'Given the difficulties of providing proof in sexual orientation claims, the assessment of such claims often rests on the credibility of the applicant. In these circumstances, decision-makers must lean towards giving the applicant the benefit of the doubt'.

44 A Dutch report (Deloitte 2011) on the willingness of reporting incidents related to religion and sexual orientation in reception facilities concludes that homosexual asylum seekers do not feel safe in reception centres, while the possibility of filing a complaint is not sufficiently known among them.

45 Compare Article 18 of Council Directive 2003/9/EC of 27 January 2003; Article 22 European Commission, Amended proposal for a Directive of the European Parliament and of the Council (Recast) 1 June 2011. See also, ILGA Europe (2011).

1.11 References

Advocate-General Bot, Opinion, 19 April 2012, *Federal Republic of Germany v Y* (C-71/11) *and Z* (C-99/11).

Agius, S. and Tobler, C. (2012) *Trans and Intersex People, Discrimination on the Grounds of Sex, Gender Identity and Gender Expression*, Belgium: European Commission, available at http://www.ilga-europe.org/home/issues/trans_and_intersex (accessed 2 August 2012).

Aliens Circular (Netherlands) C2/2.10.2: *Vervolging van homoseksuelen* (persecution of homosexuals).

Council Directive 2005/85/EC of 1 December 2005 on minimum standards on procedures in Member States for granting and withdrawing refugee status, [2005] OJ L 326, 13 December 2005, pp. 13–34. (See also, Commission's Amended Proposal, COM (2011) 319 final, Brussels, 1 June 2011.)

Council Directive 2004/83/EC of 29 April 2004 on minimum standards for the qualification and status of third country nationals or stateless persons as refugees or as persons who otherwise need international protection and the content of the protection granted, [2004] OJ L 304, 30 September 2004.

Council Directive 2003/9/EC of 27 January 2003 laying down minimum standards for the reception of asylum seekers. (See also, Amended proposal for a Directive of the European Parliament and of the Council, laying down standards for the reception of asylum seekers (Recast) COM (2011)320, 2008/0244 (COD) 1 June 2011.)

Deloitte (2011) *Rapport inzake een kwalitatief onderzoek onder (oud) bewoners van asielzoekerscentra, naar mogelijkheden ter verhoging van de meldingsbereidheid van incidenten op gebied van geloofsovertuiging en seksuele geaardheid*, Report on the willingness of reporting incidents related to religion and sexual orientation in reception facilities, 20 December 2011.

Directive 2011/95/EU of the European Parliament and of the Council of 13 December 2011 on standards for the qualification of third-country nationals or stateless persons as beneficiaries of international protection, for a uniform status for refugees or for persons eligible for subsidiary protection, and for the content of the protection granted (recast) [2011] OJ L 337/9, 20 December 2011.

Eshaghian, T. (2008) *Be Like Others*, documentary film, available at http://www.belikeothers.com (accessed 8 August 2012).

European Parliament resolution on the case of the Iranian citizen Sayyed Mehdi Kazemi, 13 March 2008, P6_TA(2008)0107, available at http://www.unhcr.org/refworld/docid/47da75002.html (accessed 2 August 2012).

European Union Agency for Fundamental Rights (2010) *Homophobia, Transphobia and Discrimination on Grounds of Sexual Orientation and Gender Identity – 2010 Update*, 10 December 2010, Vienna: European Union Agency for Fundamental Rights.

— (2009) *Homophobia and Discrimination on Grounds of Sexual Orientation in the EU Member States Part II – The Social Situation* (updated version), Vienna: European Union Agency for Fundamental Rights.

Grandin, E. and Sörberg, A.M. (2010) *Unknown People, The Vulnerability of Sexual and Gender Identity Minorities and the Swedish Migration Board's Country of Origin Information System*, Migrationsverket, January 2010, available at http://www.migrationsverket.se (accessed 8 August 2012).

Hathaway, J. (1991) *The Law of Refugee Status*, Toronto: Butterworths.

Hathaway, J. and Foster, M. (2003) 'Internal protection/relocation/flight alternative as an aspect of refugee status determination', in E. Feller, V. Türk and F. Nicholson (eds), *Refugee Protection in International Law: UNHCR's Global Consultations on International Protection*, Cambridge: Cambridge University Press.

Hathaway, J.C. and Pobjoy, J. (2012) 'Queer cases make bad law', *New York Journal of International Law and Politics*, 44(2): 315–388.

Human Rights League Slovakia and ILGA-Europe, Letter to Cecilia Malmström, European Commissioner for Home Affairs and others, 19 July 2012.

Human Rights Watch (HRW) (2010a) *Criminalizing Identities, Rights Abuses in Cameroon Based on Sexual Orientation and Gender Identity*, New York, NY: HRW.

— (2010b) *Fear for Life, Violence Against Gay Men and Men Perceived as Gay in Senegal*, New York, NY: HRW.

ILGA Europe (2011) *Policy Paper: The Recast of the EU Asylum Procedure and Reception Directives*, July 2011, Belgium: ILGA Europe, available at http://www.ilga-europe.org/home/publications/policy_papers/the_recast_of_the_eu_asylum_procedure_and_reception_directives_july_2011 (accessed 2 August 2012).

International Commission of Jurists (2007) *Yogyakarta Principles on the Application of International Human Rights Law in Relation to Sexual Orientation and Gender Identity*, 6 March 2007, available at http://www.yogyakartaprinciples.org/principles_en.pdf (accessed 2 August 2012).

International Gay and Lesbian Human Rights Commission (IGLHRC) (2011) *Nowhere to Turn, Blackmail and Extortion of LGBT People in Sub-Saharan Africa*, New York, NY: IGLHRC, available at http://www.iglhrc.org/cgi-bin/iowa/article/publications/reportsandpublications/1328.html (accessed 8 August 2012).

Itaborahy, L.P. (2012) *State-sponsored Homophobia, A World Survey of Laws Prohibiting Same-sex Sexual Acts between Consenting Adults*, Belgium: International Lesbian, Gay, Bisexual, Trans and Intersex Association (ILGA), available at http://old.ilga.org/Statehomophobia/ILGA_State_Sponsored_Homophobia_2012.pdf (accessed 2 August 2012).

Jansen, S. (2012) 'Discretion in the Netherlands: Sabine Jansen responds to Jenni Millbank and Guglielmo Verdirame', Online Symposium, *New York Journal of International Law and Politics*, 44 (2), available at http://opiniojuris.org/2012/03/09/discretion-in-the-netherlands-sabine-jansen-responds-to-jenni-millbank-guglielmo-verdirame/ (accessed 2 August 2012).

Jansen, S. and Spijkerboer, T. (2011) *Fleeing Homophobia, Asylum Claims Related to Sexual Orientation and Gender Identity in Europe*, COC Netherlands and VU University Amsterdam, available at http://www.rechten.vu.nl/nl/onderzoek/conferenties-en-projecten/onderzoeksproject-fleeing-homophobia/index.asp (accessed 2 August 2012).

Michigan Guidelines on the Internal Protection Alternative (1999), First Colloquium on Challenges in International Refugee Law, 9–11 April 1999.

Millbank, J. (2012) 'The right of lesbians and gay men to live freely, openly and on equal terms is not bad law: a reply to Hathaway and Pobjoy', *New York Journal of International Law and Politics*, 44: 497–527.

— (2009) 'From discretion to disbelief: recent trends in refugee determinations on the basis of sexual orientation in Australia and the United Kingdom', *The International Journal of Human Rights*, 13 (2–3): 391–414.

Minister of Immigration, Integration and Asylum (Netherlands), *Letter in Reaction to the Recommendations of the Report Fleeing Homophobia and the Letter of COC Netherlands*, 21 March 2012, TK 19 637, nr. 1510.

Minister Leers (Netherlands), *Letter to the President of the Second Chamber on the Policy Regarding Iraqi LGBTs*, 11 July 2012.

Nufer, S. and Lipp, M. (2011) 'Zulässigkeit der Wegweisung eines homosexuellen Iraners', *Jusletter*, 30 May 2011, available at http://www.jusletter.ch (accessed 8 August 2012).

Organization for Refuge, Asylum and Migration (ORAM) (2011) *Testing Sexual Orientation: A Scientific and Legal Analysis of Plethysmography in Asylum and Refugee Status Proceedings*, February 2011, San Francisco, CA: ORAM.

Rättschefens rättsliga ställningstagande angaende metod för utredning och prövning av den framatsyftande risken för personer som aberopar skyddsskäl pa grund av sexuell läggning (RCI 03/2011) (Sweden), 13 January 2011, available at http://www.migrationsverket.se/lifos (accessed 8 August 2012).

UK Border Agency (2011a) *Sexual Orientation Issues in the Asylum Claim*, 6 October 2010, revised 13 June 2011, London: UK Border Agency, available at http://www.ukba.homeoffice.gov.uk/sitecontent/documents/policyandlaw/asylumpolicyinstructions/apis/sexual-orientation-gender-ident?view=Binary (accessed 2 August 2012).

UK Border Agency (2011b) *Asylum Instruction, Gender Identity in the Asylum Claim*, 13 June 2011, London: UK Border Agency, available at http://www.ukba.homeoffice.gov.uk/sitecontent/documents/policyandlaw/asylumpolicyinstructions/apis/genderissueintheasylum.pdf?view=Binary (accessed 2 August 2012).

UNHCR (2011) *UNHCR's Comments on the Practice of Phallometry in the Czech Republic to Determine the Credibility of Asylum Claims based on Persecution due to Sexual Orientation*, April 2011, Geneva: UNHCR.

— (2008) *Guidance Note on Refugee Claims Relating to Sexual Orientation and Gender Identity*, 21 November 2008, Geneva: UNHCR, available at http://www.unhcr.org/refworld/docid/48abd5660.html (accessed 2 August 2012).

— (2003) *Guidelines on International Protection No.4: 'Internal Flight or Relocation Alternative' within the Context of Article 1A(2) of the 1951 Convention and/or 1967 Protocol relating to the Status of Refugees*, 23 July 2003, Geneva: UNHCR.

— (2002) *Guidelines on International Protection: Gender-Related Persecution within the context of Article 1A(2) of the 1951 Convention and/or its 1967 Protocol relating to the Status of Refugees*, 7 May 2002, Geneva: UNHCR.

— (1992) *Handbook on Procedures and Criteria for Determining Refugee Status under the 1951 Convention and the 1967 Protocol relating to the Status of Refugees*, HCR/IP/4/Eng/REV.1, September 1979, re-edited January 1992, Geneva: UNHCR.

1.12 Cases

1.12.1 International courts

Court of Justice of the European Union (CJEU) – Reference for a preliminary ruling from the Raad van State (Netherlands) lodged on 27 April 2012 – *Minister voor Immigratie en Asiel v X Y Z* (Cases C-199/12, C-200/12 and C-201/12) [2012]

OJ C 217/7, 21 July 2012, (English translation of Afdeling bestuursrechtspraak Raad van State (Judicial Division of the Council of State), 18 April 2012: 201109928/1/T1.)

CJEU, 21 December 2011, *N.S. v Secretary of State for the Home Department (United Kingdom) and M.E. and others v Refugee Applications Commissioner (Ireland)*, Joined Cases C-411/10 and C-493/10.

CJEU, 1 December 2010, Reference for a preliminary ruling from the Oberverwaltungsgericht (High Administrative Court) Nordrhein-Westfalen, *Kashayar Khavand v Federal Republic of Germany* (Case C-563/10) [2011] OJ C 38/7, 2011/C 38/09, 5 February 2011.

Committee Against Torture (Decision), 23 May 2011, *Uttal Mondal v Sweden*, Communication No. 338/2008.

European Court on Human rights (EctHR) 21 January 2011, *MSS v Belgium and Greece*, Appl. No. 30696/09.

ECtHR, 22 June 2006, *D and others v Turkey*, Appl. No. 24245/03.

ECtHR, 8 November 2005, *Bader and others v Sweden*, Appl. No. 13284/04.

ECtHR (Dec), 20 December 2004, *IIN v the Netherlands*, Appl. No. 2035/04.

ECtHR (Dec), 22 June 2004, *F v United Kingdom*, Appl. No. 17431/03.

ECtHR, 19 February 1998, *Bahaddar v the Netherlands*, Appl. No. 25894/94.

ECtHR, 22 April 1993, *Modinos v Cyprus*, Appl. No. 15070/89.

ECtHR, 7 July 1989, *Soering v United Kingdom*, Appl. No 14038/88.

ECtHR, 26 October 1988, *Norris v Ireland*, Appl. No. 10581/83.

ECtHR, 22 October 1981, *Dudgeon v United Kingdom*, Appl. No. 7525/76.

Human Rights Committee, 8 November 2011, *X v Sweden*, Communication No. 1833/2008.

UN Human Rights Committee, 4 April 1994, *Toonen v Australia*, CCPR/C/50/D/488/1992.

1.12.2 National courts

Australia

High Court of Australia, 9 December 2003, *Appellant S396/2002 v Minister for Immigration and Multicultural Affairs* [2003] HCA 71, S395/2002 and S396/2002.

Austria

Asylgerichtshof (Asylum Court), 10 February 2010, E1 217.905-4/2010.

Canada

Federal Court of Canada, 8 October 2008, *Atta Fosu v the Minister of Citizenship and Immigration*, 2008 FC 1135.

Czech Republic

Supreme Administrative Court, 14 November 2007, No. 6 Azs 102/2007.

Finland

Korkein Hallinto-Oikeus (Finnish Supreme Administrative Court), 13 January 2012, KHO:2012:1, 1750/1/11, English summary available at http://www.unhcr.org/refworld/docid/4f3cdf7e2.html (accessed 10 August 2012).

Germany

Bundesverwaltungsgericht (Federal Administrative Court), 18 January 2011, *T v Bundesamt für Migration*, C-2107/2010.

Verwaltungsgericht (Administrative Court) Schleswig-Holstein, 7 September 2009, 6 B 32/09.

The Netherlands

Afdeling bestuursrechtspraak van de Raad van State (Judicial Division of the Council of State), 11 May 2012, 201203335/2/V2.

Afdeling bestuursrechtspraak van de Raad van State (Judicial Division of the Council of State), 17 August 2011, 201012865/1/V2, JV 2011/424.

Afdeling bestuursrechtspraak van de Raad van State (Administrative Jurisdiction Division of the Council of State), 7 September 2009, 200809455/1/V3.

Afdeling bestuursrechtspraak van de Raad van State (Judicial Division of the Council of State), 11 March 2008, 200800250/1.

Afdeling Rechtspraak van de Raad van State (Judicial Division of the Council of State), 13 August 1981, *Rechtspraak Vreemdelingenrecht* 1981, 5, *Gids Vreemdelingenrecht (oud)* D12-51.

Rechtbank (District Court) Haarlem, 8 May 2012, 12/10465.

Rechtbank (District Court) Den Bosch, 26 April 2012, 12/10858.

Rechtbank (District Court) Rotterdam, 2 April 2012, 12/7785.

Rechtbank (District Court) Haarlem, 22 September 2009, 09/31503; 09/31502.

Rechtbank (District Court) Zwolle, 15 December 2008, 08/27847; 08/27850.

Rechtbank (District Court) Zwolle, 14 December 2007, 07/38475.

Voorzieningenrechter Rechtbank Zwolle (Provisional Measures Judge District Court Zwolle), 27 March 2012, 12/7040; 12/7039.

New Zealand

Refugee Appeal no. 74665/03, 7 July 2004.

Norway

Norges Høyesterett – Dom (Norwegian Supreme Court), 29 March 2012, HR-2012-667-A, case no. 2011/1688, English summary available at http://www.unhcr.org/refworld/country,LEGAL,NOR_SC,,NOR,,50084d772,0.html (accessed 10 August 2012).

United Kingdom

Upper Tribunal (Immigration and Asylum Chamber), 24 June 2011, *SW (lesbians – HJ and HT applied) Jamaica CG* [2011] UKUT 00251.

UK Supreme Court, 7 July 2010, *HJ (Iran) and HT (Cameroon) v Secretary of State for the Home Department* [2010] UKSC 31.

United States

United States Court of Appeals for the Ninth Circuit 7 March 2005, *Karouni v Gonzales*, Attorney General, No. 02-72651, 399 F.3d 1163 (2005).

2 Sexual orientation and refugee status determination over the past 20 years

Unsteady progress through standard sequences?

Jenni Millbank[*]

2.1 Introduction

In this chapter, I sketch a framework for analysis of sexual orientation based asylum claims that aims to accommodate both common themes *and* divergent outcomes (Jansen and Spijkerboer 2011: 14; O'Dwyer 2008; and more generally Ramji-Nogales *et al.* 2009) across the range of jurisdictions grappling with these issues to date. I take as my starting point Kees Waaldijk's work from the late 1990s, in which he claimed a discernible trend of 'steady progress' through 'standard sequences' in the development of sexual orientation rights across the European Union in the last third of the twentieth century (Waaldijk 2001b). Waaldijk suggested that within these trends there were two 'laws' or preconditions to reform, which he titled the 'law of small change' and the 'law of symbolic preparation'. I suggest that progress in sexuality rights in refugee status determination (RSD) has in fact been rather *unsteady*, with significant informal resistance springing up to take the place of doctrinal obstacles as these are dismantled.[1]

I believe that 'small change' and 'symbolic preparation' are useful tools to understand existing variations of approach across receiving nations and, more importantly, as signposts for the framing of policy and litigation action in the future. Waaldijk's analysis was developed in the markedly different context of family and relationship recognition claims (Waaldijk 2001a). Yet it draws attention to the ways in which sexual orientation rights have evolved within general human rights frameworks despite not being specified within founding documents such as the International Covenant on Civil and Political Rights (ICCPR) and the European Convention on Human Rights (ECHR). In the same way the potentiality of sexual orientation claims was latent within the 1951 United Nations Convention Relating to the Status of Refugees (the Convention), until 'discovered' quite recently. Using Waaldijk's framework draws our minds back to the critical inter-relation between the development of refugee law, broader human rights norms and the specific step-by-step process of articulating and applying sexuality rights as human rights within adjudication processes.

It is only by starting with the expectation that lesbian, gay, bisexual and transgender (LGBT) people are entitled to enjoy the full range of fundamental human rights and freedoms that their refugee claims can be properly assessed as a failure of state protection, rather than, say, an irrational or improbable violation of prevailing cultural norms. Take the premise that sexual minorities are simply behaving appropriately by concealing their sexuality from neighbours, families and employers. This will lead to the conclusion that a lesbian who pretends to live with a female 'flatmate', because she could not acknowledge her partner without fear, is acting 'naturally'. It is the understanding that lesbians and gay men have human rights rights-claims – to family life, to freedom of association and expression, in addition to privacy and protection from torture – which transforms the whole spectrum of violence and oppression on the basis of sexual orientation *into* a cognisable wrong under the Convention. A deep seated, nuanced and context-sensitive equality analysis is required to transform judicial understandings of minority sexual identities that go beyond (very) private gay sex from being understood as 'flaunting', 'provoking', 'parading' or 'publically proclaiming' (Dauvergne and Millbank 2003b; Millbank 2009a: 393), into what is really being claimed: the right to live an ordinary everyday normal gay life, *openly*.

The place of refugee law within an international human rights framework is, of course, contested. Catherine Dauvergne, Patricia Tuitt, Michelle Foster and many others have contended that refugee law functions more to keep people out than to let them in, and operates as a form of exceptionalism, through its limited categories of claimants and avenues of claim (Dauvergne 2008; Foster 2007; Tuitt 1997). Moreover, much day-to-day refugee decision making lacks any explicit consideration of human rights standards. The counter argument is that international human rights norms underpins refugee law; for example through informing 'persecution' analysis (Hathaway 1991: 105–112), and the development of particular social group analysis (PSG), most especially with regard to gender (Daley and Kelley 2000; Anker 2002; Haines 2003: 46–80; Musalo 2003). I begin here from the premise that refugee law is a distinct but concretely applied manifestation of international human rights law; one which is simultaneously informed by, and inseparable from, the norms and institutional practices of the receiving country. This is why I believe that Waaldijk's framework is so helpful, as his insights of small change and symbolic preparation alert us to the dynamic interplay of national conditions with international standards and 'universal' rights (Billings 2000; Tobin 2012).

2.2 Progress?

Between 1955 and 1967 there were at least nine complaints made under the ECHR by men in Germany and Austria, all designated 'X' in their communications, who had been imprisoned for terms between 15 months and six years for the crime of consensual gay sex. Each one of these applications was declared inadmissible as 'manifestly ill-founded' on the basis that 'the Convention allows a . . . Party to punish homosexuality since the right to respect for private life may, in a democratic society, be subject to interference . . . for the protection of health and morals . . .' (*X v Germany* (No 530/59) 1960 at 194; discussed in Wintemute 1997: 92).[2] Today such men would be eligible to claim asylum in most refugee receiving nations in the world on the basis that such sanctions were persecutory.

The Netherlands was the first country to accept sexuality as a PSG in 1981 (Waaldijk *et al.* 2010: 27; *Afdeling Rechtspraak Raad van State (ARRvS)* no A-21113, *Rechtspraak Vreemdelingenrecht* 1981); others followed haltingly.[3] Sexual orientation was increasingly accepted in principle as eligible under the PSG ground by the mid to late 1990s as major courts in countries such as Canada, Australia and the United Kingdom made such observations largely in *obiter* (*Canada (Attorney General) v Ward* [1993]; *Applicant A v MIEA* (1997); *Reg v IAT ex p Shah* (1999)). However, in practice at lower levels sexuality claims continued to be challenged, and sometimes dismissed, on the basis that no Convention ground had been engaged (Millbank 2009b: 15; *MK v SSHD* (2009) at [351]). Non-government organisations which specifically campaign for sexual orientation rights, such as the International Lesbian and Gay Human Rights Commission and International Gay and Lesbian Association, were crucial in raising the profile of sexuality in human rights and refugee law spheres. The activism and lobbying of these organisations led to a fundamental shift in the focus of a number of mainstream human rights organisations such as Amnesty International, which resolved in 1991 that people imprisoned for their homosexuality were prisoners of conscience. Since then generalist human rights groups such as Human Rights Watch and Amnesty, in addition to specialist LGBT organisations and, more recently UNHCR, have played a major role through documenting abuse in sending countries (Human Rights Watch and International Lesbian and Gay Human Rights Commission 1998, 2003; Amnesty International 2001; Human Rights Watch 2009a, 2009b, 2010, 2012), intervening in key cases (for example *Hernandez-Montiel* (2000), International Lesbian and Gay Human Rights Commission among others; *Appellant S395/2002 v Minister for Immigration and Multicultural Affairs* (2003), Amnesty International Australia; *HJ (Iran) and HT (Cameroon) v Secretary of State for the Home Department* [2010] UKSC 31 (*HJ and HT v SSHD* [2010]), UNHCR and the UK Equality Commission), as well as lobbying, providing policy guidance and participating in decision maker training in receiving countries (see Gray 2011; UK Lesbian and Gay Immigration Group 2010a: 2–3; Wolf-Watz *et al.* 2010).

In the past decade, developments have been rapid, including but not limited to the following milestones:

- 2002: UNHCR issued a guideline on gender-based persecution explicitly noting sexual orientation and gender identity (UNHCR Gender Guidelines) (UNHCR 2002b: [5], [16]);

- 2004: EU Member States adopted a Council Directive on minimum standards for the qualification of refugees, (Council Directive 2004/83/EC) (the EU Qualification Directive), which spelt out that sexual orientation is covered by the particular social group (PSG) Convention ground (article 10(1)(d));
- 2008: UNHCR issued a guidance note on sexual orientation and gender identity claims, followed in 2009 by an additional resource document, and ongoing work including an expert roundtable in 2010 as part of a process of examining ongoing challenges in RSD, resettlement and processing. The guidance note was upgraded into the more authoritative guideline in 2012 (UNHCR 2009, 2010, 2011, 2012);
- 2010: the UN Secretary General gave a speech expressly affirming human rights protection on the basis of sexual orientation and gender identity (Ban 2010);
- 2011: the UN Human Rights Council *finally*, and narrowly, passed a resolution expressing grave concern at acts of violence and discrimination on the basis of sexual orientation and gender identity and commissioned a study documenting such violence and how international human rights law can be used to end it (UN Human Rights Council 2011a, 2011b).[4]

These advances have been hard won and evidence real progress.

2.3 Standard sequences?

While there are now thousands of written decisions on sexual orientation available worldwide in English alone, there remains very little reliable data on outcomes or reasoning in most receiving nations. In recent years Belgium and Norway have collected and made available information on the number and success rates of claims (Jansen and Spijkerboer 2011: 15; Hojem 2009), but they remain the exception as most countries do not release – and many do not even collect – such data.[5] In the few instances where raw figures are available, there is rarely a breakdown on the proportions of claims by women and men, countries of origin of claimants or on the most common reasons for failure of claims. Lack of public access to written reasons for low level decisions (e.g. immigration courts, administrative tribunals and internal government decision makers) makes it extraordinarily difficult to gain an understanding of how the law on sexual orientation and refugee status is being developed and applied at the levels where it has the greatest impact. Access to *both* broad data on trends and outcomes and to the specific reasoning from determined cases is necessary in order to effectively advocate for LGBT asylum seekers on an individual and collective basis.

Some advocacy organisations have pioneered research drawn from client experiences. For example the Lesbian and Gay Immigration Group and Asylum Aid in the United Kingdom have both initiated valuable small scale studies of reasons for refusal letters issued at the lowest levels, which help build a picture of how appellate level jurisprudence and policy about gender, sexuality and PSG is (mis)understood and applied on the ground (Asylum Aid 2011; UK Lesbian and Gay Immigration Group 2010b). Recent multi-jurisdictional research projects such as Fleeing Homophobia and GENSEN in Europe are enormously valuable in identifying relevant case law, policy and trends within and across countries (GENSEN 2012). The *Fleeing Homophobia* report identifies several common themes across the European Union which reflect the findings of my own comparative longitudinal research on RSD in the United Kingdom, Canada, Australia and New Zealand. To pose these as a standard sequence I suggest that we see:

1 Acceptance of sexual orientation as an eligible PSG (see, for example UNHCR 2002b; EU Qualification Directive, article 10(1)(d)),[6] followed by;[7]
2 Evolving Persecution Analysis – involving:
   a recognition that criminalisation of gay sex is persecutory (UNHCR 2002b; EU Qualification Directive; UNHCR 2008: [17–8]),[8] and further, the related but distinct recognition that criminal sanctions may generate a persecutory environment, even in the absence of evidence of recent or systematic enforcement (Jansen and Spijkerboer 2011: 21–26);
   b acceptance that non-state actors are often the primary agents of harm (Jansen and Spijkerboer 2011; UNHCR 2012);
   c development of detailed and appropriately targeted country of origin information (see Dauvergne and Millbank 2003b; LaViolette 2009; Jansen and Spijkerboer 2011);
   d acknowledgement and rejection of the role of 'discretion reasoning';
   e recognition of multiple and intersecting forms of harm as persecution, not 'mere' discrimination or 'social pressure'.

The progress through these sequences appears far from steady. Indeed, a close analysis of the case law from a single jurisdiction will often reveal that there are different decision makers taking contrary interpretations on any number of the above issues over a period of years before they are 'resolved' by an appellate court or legislative directive. Such 'resolution' is in my view frequently also unstable, as lower level decision makers subsequently misunderstand, restrictively interpret, actively reinvent – and on some occasions continue in complete ignorance of – precedents and policy guidance. This resistance, which I refer to here as 'backsliding' (without meaning to suggest that it is necessarily intentional), in combination with other informal barriers such as poor quality credibility assessment to establish whether the applicant is indeed a member of the PSG (see for example Millbank 2009b; Jansen and Spijkerboer 2011: chapter 6), means that each step almost always needs to be taken more than once. While there are many possible illustrations of this argument, for reasons of space I address just one: discretion reasoning.

2.4 Confronting discretion reasoning

While variously expressed, the universalised assumption of natural (and rightful) closetedness for gay men and lesbians provides the conceptual underpinning of persecution analysis in sexual orientation claims across dozens of jurisdictions worldwide.[9] Through 'discretion reasoning' claimants may be required, expected or assumed to be capable of (re)concealing, or relocating and thereby reconcealing, their sexuality in their home country order in order to avoid persecution. This has been expressed as a 'reasonable expectation that persons should, to the extent that it is possible, cooperate in their own protection' (RRT Reference *V95/03527* (1996)), and thus as a normative standard or requirement of 'reasonableness' but is often embedded as an assumption or factual finding that behavioural 'modification', 'restraint' or 'adaptation' will simply 'happen'. So a gay applicant from Uganda will 'be mindful of his society's concepts of good manners and the general social mores' in concealing his sexuality (*JM v SSHD* (2008) at [149]). Discretion logic is a particularly invidious form of victim-blaming because it affirms the perspective, if not the conduct, of the persecutor. In the words of Pill LJ at Court of Appeal level in *HJ and HT v SSHD* [2009] at [32]), according:

> . . . a degree of respect for social norms and religious beliefs in other states is in my view appropriate. Both in Muslim Iran and Roman Catholic Cameroon, strong views are genuinely held about homosexual practices. In considering what is reasonably tolerable in a particular society, the fact-finding Tribunal is in my view entitled to have regard to the beliefs held there.[10]

The content of 'discretion' is rarely spelt out. Expressed as a matter of good manners, it implicitly encompasses lifelong secrecy and all-encompassing strategies of concealment, which time and again decision makers have held 'will not cause significant detriment to [the] right to respect for private life, nor will it involve suppression of many aspects of . . . sexual identity' (*HJ and HT v SSHD* [2009] at [44]).

Discretion reasoning has generated a plethora of legal errors in persecution analysis, including: reversing the onus of Convention protection, treating the scope of protection offered by the Convention grounds inequitably, failing to undertake a future-focused analysis of the risk of harm and construing internal flight alternatives as opportunities for re-concealment rather than safety (see *Atta Fosu v Canada* (2008) at [17]; *Okoli v Canada* (2009) at [37]). It also leads to errors in defining the PSG, by treating 'discreet' and 'open' homosexuals as if they are two completely distinct, stable and mutually exclusive groups (see Weßels 2012; Dauvergne and Millbank 2003a: 117–123; Millbank 2009a: 393–395). This also misleads a future focused analysis of persecution risk for the fundamental reason that there is no such thing as a complete and lifelong closet: a person may be closeted for some purposes or in certain spheres (work but not family, family but not friends, some friends but not all), and even those assiduously committed to concealment are always at risk of exposure through the disclosures of others, or surveillance, and through their own lack of conformity to heterosexual norms over time, for example if they do not marry and raise children by a certain age (*SW v SSHD* (*SW Lesbians*) (2011) at [95]; Chelvan 2011). Discretion reasoning has been associated with very high failure rates for lesbian, gay and bisexual refugee claimants (Millbank 2009a: 393; UK Lesbian and Gay Immigration Group 2010b).

The 2000s saw increasingly high level rejections of discretion approaches in both judicial and policy spheres across multiple jurisdictions.[11] The issue was first considered by an ultimate appellate court in December 2003 when the High Court of Australia, by a slim majority of four judges to three in the case of *S395*, rejected discretion reasoning, stating that, 'It would undermine the object of the Convention if the signatory countries required them to modify their beliefs or to hide' and holding it was incorrect in law to require or expect someone to 'take reasonable steps to avoid persecutory harm' (*Appellant S395/2002 v Minister for Immigration and Multicultural Affairs* (2003) at [41], [50] per Kirby and McHugh J, see also [82]–[83] per Gummow and Hayne JJ). The majority judgments also affirmed that the experience of sexual identity involves more than mere private sexual conduct (*S395* (2003) at [51]–[53] per Kirby and McHugh J, [81]–[82] per Gummow and Hayne JJ). In 2010, the Supreme Court of the United Kingdom issued a unanimous five opinion judgment approving the majority approach in *S395* and condemning discretion reasoning in even stronger terms.

2.5 Backsliding on discretion: reasonableness, choice and other 'perfectly natural' responses to social and family pressure

Discretion logic has shown itself to be extraordinarily resilient. It has appeared, and been challenged, since the very first cases on sexual orientation. In cases from Germany in the 1980s and in Canada, Australia and New Zealand in the 1990s, low level decision makers rejected discretion in forceful terms (Dauvergne and Millbank 2003a: 115–116). It is notable that while such reasoning rarely appeared again in Canada and New Zealand, it remained prevalent in German and Australian cases. Even in countries such as Canada where it was rejected very early, and in the Netherlands where it has been expressly disapproved in policy directives, it continues to resurface at lower levels.[12] The 2011 *Fleeing Homophobia* report found discretion reasoning still occurring in Austria, Belgium, Bulgaria, Cyprus, Denmark, Finland, France, Germany, Hungary, Ireland, the Netherlands, Malta, Poland, Romania, Spain, Norway and Switzerland (Jansen and Spijkerboer 2011: 34).

The interlinked history of the *S395* and *HJ* cases neatly illustrates the adaptive properties of discretion logic, as the themes of reasonableness, the natural and the social appear throughout both, not least of all in the way that

S395 was twisted and misapplied to perpetuate a normative standard of discretion in UK jurisprudence for several years. Mr HJ actually took his claim to the UK Court of Appeal on two occasions and challenged discretion in both. In the first judgment in 2006, the Court expressly followed the majority of the High Court of Australia in *S395* (*J v SSHD* [2006] at [16], [20]). However, Maurice Kay LJ referred to a general definition of persecution from *S395* (as something which one could not 'reasonably tolerate') in a way which suggested that it was relevant to assessing the specific impact of discretion on a gay applicant (*J v SSHD* [2006] at [16], [20]). Several later cases, including the adjudicator rehearing J's claim, reframed the persecution inquiry as whether the applicant could be 'expected to tolerate' a life of secrecy for fear of harm such as imprisonment or death (*HJ v SSHD* [2008] at [31]). In the absence of evidence of past persecution, and regardless of the testimony of applicant's themselves about how intolerable such a situation was, decision makers found without fail that lifelong concealment was indeed something that could be 'reasonably tolerated' (see e.g. *OO (Sudan) v SSHD* (2009) at [9], [17]); *XY (Iran) v SSHD* (2008) at [13]); *HJ (Iran) v SSHD* (2008) at [44]. In addition, *AJ v SSHD* (2009) at [65] and *SB (Uganda) v SSHD* (2010) at [51] both quashed similar tribunal determinations on judicial review because there had been past persecution such that future discretion was not possible).

Related to, and informing, 'reasonableness' is the ubiquity of social forms of expression of heterosexuality and acceptance of the invisibility – or at least the vastly lesser visibility – of expressions of homosexuality within a trope of individualised choice. Heterosexual people just happen to 'choose' to marry while gay men and lesbians often 'choose' not to tell people that they are in a same sex relationship, but this is not for any reason, they just like to keep such things private, or to keep themselves to themselves. Thus, in *S395*, the Minister argued, and Callinan and Heydon JJ in dissent accepted that:

> The appellants had in fact, and would in all likelihood continue to live, as a matter of choice, quietly without flaunting their homosexuality. They were not men who wished to proclaim their homosexuality. Living as they did, they were not oppressed. Discretion . . . was *purely a matter of choice* and not of external imposition. No one required them . . . ever to modify their behaviour.
>
> (*S395* (2003) at [106], emphasis added)[13]

It is alarming that the two more empathic and detailed judgments affirming the 'right to live freely and openly as a gay man' in *HJ* also continue to assume the existence of a naturally secretive gay person who is exercising *free choice* in no way related to persecutory conditions by never disclosing their sexuality. Lord Hope imagines the possibility of someone who is 'naturally reticent' and who conceals his sexuality 'in reaction to family and social pressure' 'or for cultural or religious reasons *of his own choosing*' and states that such person would not have a well founded fear of persecution (*HJ and HT v SSHD* [2010] at [22], [35]). Likewise, Lord Rodger hypothesises a '*perfectly natural* wish to avoid harming his relationships with his family, friends and colleagues' as a reason for concealment and repeatedly uses the word 'choice' in contrasting persecution with 'social pressures' (*HJ and HT v SSHD* [2010] at [61]–[62] emphasis added). Janna Weßels notes that, in addition to being an untenable distinction in any persecutory environment, this may lead later decision makers to place the burden on applicants to demonstrate that the 'material reason' for their concealment is fear – which was also a distinctive feature of the UK discretion approach prior to *HJ* (Weßels 2011: section 7; Millbank 2009a: 397; Johnson 2007) and a feature of the dissents in *S395*.

Through the creeping glosses of reasonableness[14] and choice and the unreflexive dismissal of 'social and family pressure', the very concealment which cannot be 'required' or 'expected' by decision makers may once again become a state that is assumed as chosen, commonplace and natural, and thereby viewed as a complete defence to persecution rather than *prima facie* evidence of its real risk.

Lack of progress through the stage I identify above as (e) 'recognition of multiple and intersecting forms of harm as persecution', may therefore inhibit or even cause a return to stage (d), discretion reasoning. Considering this unsteady progress, exemplified by the Supreme Court decision in *HJ and HT v SSHD* [2010], which is at once so progressive and yet arguably still founded on an untenable dichotomy of 'open' and 'discreet' gay people (Weßels 2012), I argue that the laws of small change and symbolic preparation help us to see a path through. Symbolic change is directed towards the abstract level of rights pronouncements and small change to the concrete application of rights claims to specific experiences. Both of these are necessary elements to a progressive jurisprudence in sexuality claims, and both make each other possible.

2.6 Symbolic preparation

Waaldijk argues that before equality rights were actually granted in practice there had to be a period of 'symbolic preparation' in each nation, whereby some formal legislation or proclamation paved the way for later change. These acts could be relatively abstract – such as repealing criminal provisions that had not been enforced for decades, passing anti-discrimination guarantees that covered only a small sector of civic life or other forms of equality laws of limited scope or practical utility. The symbolism itself was the significant aspect, in marking recognition of lesbians and gay men as subjects within a shifting frame of reference, from outsiders/objects to insiders/subject of rights. The law of symbolic preparation also draws our attention closely to the need for *preparation* – as new ways of thinking about LGBT are integrated into the polity and the collective imaginary.

The more *familiar* and *engaged* a receiving nation is with sexual orientation rights claims across a wide range of areas, the better equipped its decision makers will be to engage in a contextual and sensitive way with sexuality asylum claims. Formal legislative equality guarantees or high profile litigation across a diverse range of rights help to trigger this familiarity and engagement – even in unrelated areas by different legal actors. Thus, receiving countries which have only recently engaged with formal guarantees of sexual orientation rights (including those undertaken with some reluctance as part of the process of entering the Council of Europe, see Stychin (2003)), or which have resisted introducing measures to correct birth documentation for trans people, are likely to have both harsher formal barriers to LGBT claims *and* a weaker understanding of them at a conceptual level. Put plainly, these countries are simply less likely to 'see' persecution when it happens to LGBTs.

The United Kingdom is an interesting example of this phenomenon. Despite being a liberal democratic nation with fairly low levels of homophobic violence, the United Kingdom has had quite a poor history on LGBT asylum claims through eras overseen by both conservative and centre left political governments. The United Kingdom was slow to accept sexuality as a PSG, very resistant to seeing criminalisation as persecution and applied discretion reasoning widely and persistently (see Millbank 2009a; UK Lesbian and Gay Immigration Group 2010b; Miles 2011). This arguably reflects a legal context in which gay sexuality was stigmatised through regimes of privacy and bare 'tolerance'. Although gay sex in private was 'decriminalised' in 1967 in England and Wales, an unequal age of consent remained until 2001, and right through to the early 2000s sweeping and discriminatory laws on public indecency for gay sex continued to be enforced. There was also a rarely utilised but chilling anti-proselytising provision concerning the 'promotion' of homosexuality and 'pretended families' ('Clause 28' of the Local Government Act 1988, which applied to local councils and public education). Affirmative rights such as anti-discrimination protections in employment and same sex relationship recognition came belatedly, in 2003 and 2004, respectively (see the Employment Equality (Sexual Orientation) Regulations 2003 (SI 2003/1661) (UK); the Civil Partnership Act 2004 (UK), followed by more comprehensive rights through the Equality Act 2006 (UK)).

How the question of risk of persecution is answered depends very much on decision makers' pre-existing understandings of what is proper or tolerable behaviour on the part of sexual minorities *and* on the part of the state. These understandings in turn hinge upon implicit conceptions of both human rights and sexual norms – and these reflect the domestic social and political context in which the decision maker lives. Symbolic preparation is part of the process of transforming those norms.

2.7 Small change

Few, if any, receiving countries have managed to progress through all of the steps posed in the 'standard' sequences, and many have faltered on one particular step. Even receiving nations which are generally positive on LGBT claims have tended to address each step separately and have not been capable of moving through several simultaneously. Consideration of the law of small change brings a greater optimism to an examination of the chaos of inconsistent state practice, with the knowledge that each step needs to be taken more than once, and must be taken *in tandem* with the process of symbolic preparation.

The law of small change reminds us that progress will, indeed must, be incremental. Given the highly individualistic nature of RSD, this may mean issues being addressed one case at a time as opportunities present themselves. It is the steps at lower levels, as claims are framed and understood, that build to larger change at institutional and precedential levels. The above discussion on backsliding suggests that the 'trickle down' effect of jurisprudence from higher courts may be muted or undermined and so must be accompanied by an 'educating up' effect. Equality interventions are therefore critical at lower levels in decision making within domestic systems, as is sensitivity and credibility training and other forms of engagement with early stage decision making, such as provision of country evidence, expert evidence, and critical assessment of government compiled country evidence.

HJ and HT v SSHD [2010] illustrates the ongoing inter-relation of symbolic preparation and small change. The death of discretion as a 'reasonable expectation' and the embrace of equality affirming language is a major victory, even as there are suggestions that discretion may yet come back to haunt us in another guise through the approved process of dividing applicants into those who 'live openly' and those who do not prior to undertaking a persecution analysis (*HJ and HT v SSHD* [2010] at [82]).

Lord Hope stated that '[gay people] are as much entitled to freedom of association with others of the same sexual orientation, and to freedom of self-expression in matters that affect their sexuality, as people who are straight' (*HJ and HT v SSHD* [2010] at [14]). Lord Rodger held that:

> the Convention offers protection to gay and lesbian people – and, I would add, bisexuals and everyone else on a broad spectrum of sexual behaviour – because they are entitled to have the same freedom from fear of persecution as their straight counterparts. No-one would proceed on the basis that a straight man or woman could find it reasonably tolerable to conceal his or her sexual identity indefinitely to avoid suffering persecution. Nor would anyone proceed on the basis that a man or woman could find it reasonably tolerable to conceal his or her race indefinitely to avoid suffering persecution. Such an assumption about gay men and lesbian women is equally unacceptable.[15]
>
> (*HJ and HT v SSHD* [2010] at [76])

These clear statements about the importance of equality analysis in determining sexual orientation asylum claims are accompanied by a number of other discursive elements which signal a transformation in English jurisprudence concerning sexuality. The framing of the issues in the case in the opening paragraphs of Lord Hope's opinion, itself the first placed in the judgment, is enormously significant. In place of the usual specific and flat relaying of factual and legal claim – typically expressed in the form: 'This case concerns X person from Y country who claims to have experienced Z, made an application for refugee status on <date>, had a decision made by A, reaffirmed by B and C <on date/s>, which decision is now under appeal on grounds of D' – the judgment opens with a broad foundation of policy and principle. Lord Hope refers to historical, legal and political context in a manner that establishes homophobic violence on a global scale as a matter of deep concern, and moreover as something for which 'we' ('our time', 'our own government' 'remain with us') must take responsibility:

> The need for reliable guidance on this issue is growing day by day. Persecution for reasons of homosexuality was not perceived as a problem by the High Contracting Parties when the Convention was being drafted. For many years the risk of persecution in countries where it now exists seemed remote. It was the practice for leaders in these countries simply to insist that homosexuality did not exist. This was manifest nonsense, but at least it avoided the evil of persecution. More recently, fanned by misguided but vigorous religious doctrine, the situation has changed dramatically. The ultra-conservative interpretation of Islamic law that prevails in Iran is one example. The rampant homophobic teaching that right-wing evangelical Christian churches indulge in throughout much of Sub-Saharan Africa is another. The death penalty has just been proposed in Uganda for persons who engage in homosexual practices. Two gay men who had celebrated their relationship in a public engagement ceremony were recently sentenced to 14 years' imprisonment in Malawi. They were later pardoned in response to international pressure by President Mutharika, but he made it clear that he would not otherwise have done this as they had committed a crime against the country's culture, its religion and its laws. Objections to these developments have been greeted locally with derision and disbelief.
>
> The fact is that a huge gulf has opened up in attitudes to and understanding of gay persons between societies on either side of the divide. It is one of the most demanding social issues of our time. Our own government has pledged to do what it can to resolve the problem, but it seems likely to grow and to remain with us for many years. In the meantime more and more gays and lesbians are likely to have to seek protection here, as protection is being denied to them by the state in their home countries. It is crucially important that they are provided with the protection that they are entitled to under the Convention — no more, if I may be permitted to coin a well known phrase, but certainly no less.
>
> (*HJ and HT v SSHD* [2010] at [2]–[3])[16]

In and of itself this is one of the strongest statements in support of the importance of lesbian and gay equality rights from any English court. But its significance is immeasurably greater when set against the trivialisation and indifference to homophobic persecution evident in so many judgments of English courts and tribunals on sexuality refugee claims in the preceding decade (Chelvan 2011).

Just as Lord Hope makes a large gesture towards homophobic violence as a global phenomenon with national impact at the outset of his opinion, Lord Rodger makes the more intimate gesture, detailing what such violence actually means as a lived experience. It is striking that Lord Rodger is the only judge in any of the available decisions in Mr HT's litigation to actually record the extent of HT's victimisation and his injuries. In a short paragraph Lord Rodger notes that HT was beaten by a mob who tore off his clothes and threatened to kill him, struck him with fists, sticks and stones, cut towards his penis with a knife wounding him in the stomach; that the police on arrival punched him in the face and kicked him repeatedly, and that as a result of this violence HT spent two months in hospital (*HJ and HT v SSHD* [2010] at [44]). Understated as this narration is, it provides a breathtaking contrast to the preceding Court of Appeal decision which, after detailing the procedural history of HT's case, beginning with his arrest and custodial sentence in the United Kingdom for using a false passport, recorded in two sentences the existence and exposure of his relationship in Cameroon, concluding merely: 'Later HT was attacked' (*HJ and HT v SSHD* [2009] at [5], [6]).

2.8 Small symbolic change, symbolic of larger changes

Perhaps the most enduring impact of *HJ and HT* will be in elements that appear at first glance to be its most trivial asides. There appears a multitude of apparently minor elements within the judgment which signify a shifting understanding of sexual orientation. I suggest that these discursive elements could be seen as small symbolic change, altering and opening a frame of reference for larger change in the future.

At a number of key junctures the judges self-consciously reflect on language choice: discretion is repeatedly framed in quotation marks, described as a 'euphemistic expression' which 'does not tell the whole truth' and renamed variously as 'concealment', 'lying', 'denying', 'hiding' and 'suppressing' (Lord Hope at [21], [22], [33], [35] (b), [38]; Lord Rodger at [72], [75], and also spelling out the practical implications of concealment, at [63]; Lord Collins at [101], [104]; Sir John Dyson at [116], [121]).[17] Concealment is also expressly characterised by Lord Rodger and Sir John Dyson as a state *endured* rather than 'tolerated' (*HJ and HT v SSHD* [2010] at [80], [122]).

The judgments refer to 'lesbians' and 'gay men' (and Lord Rodger adds bisexuals) rather than using the traditional terminology of 'homosexuals' so favoured in law. Note by contrast that the two joint majority judgments and both dissents in *S395* (2003) continued to utilise 'homosexual' despite submissions from *amicus curiae* urging them to do otherwise. Moreover, both Lord Hope and Lord Rodger reference heterosexual men and women *as* heterosexual and as 'straight', specifically locating majority sexualities. On first reading the Supreme Court judgment in *HJ and HT* what struck me was a pleasant tone of warmth in the opinions, and also a somewhat surprising note of informality. I cannot recall another judgment from a superior court which called heterosexual people 'straight', nor which referred to one's 'mates' – can you? How nice. But on reflection I concluded that these were not merely incidental colloquialisms; rather, such variations in language reflect the sustained efforts of critical, feminist and queer scholarship to alter the paradigms in which sexuality, identity and perspective are framed within mainstream jurisprudence (West 1990; Brooks 2006; Delgado 1989; Fajer 1991–1992, 1994; Graycar 2008).

First, naming lesbians and gay men separately paves the way for recognition of gendered difference in the experience of sexuality. Lesbians have been routinely disadvantaged in refugee adjudication (as elsewhere) by being subsumed under a male paradigm of experience (Millbank 2003; Neilson 2005). Stepping away from 'homosexuals', or even 'gay people' as a facially neutral but actually male-normative category renders it possible (although certainly not inevitable) for adjudicators to identify and recognise lesbians as women and to take account of their experiences of persecution in the context of gendered vulnerabilities. Naming heterosexual people *as* heterosexual – rather than as, say, 'people', 'normal people' or 'society' – also challenges the pervasive and invisible 'point-of-viewlessness' (MacKinnon 1989: 213) that is heterosexual hegemony. Naming heterosexuals helps us to see how 'general social mores' involve assumptions about the widespread and naturalised *display* of heterosexual identification and relationships (including what Lord Rodger calls the 'small tokens and gestures of affection which are *taken for granted* between men and women': *HJ and HT v SSHD* [2010] at [77], emphasis added). This is a great help in undoing discretion reasoning based on expectations of conformity implicitly entailing concealment. It is a powerful point directed to heterosexual readers when Lord Rodger says, 'No one would proceed on the basis that a straight man or woman could find it reasonably tolerable to conceal his or her sexual identity indefinitely to avoid persecution' (*HJ and HT v SSHD* [2010] at [76]). Naming and locating heterosexuality also makes it possible to unpack, for example, the common finding made in sexuality based refugee claims that it is a 'general social expectation that all people marry'. Such findings inform conclusions that marriage cannot be persecution and that there is no nexus to sexuality in forced marriage claims (Dauvergne and Millbank 2010). Seeing and naming heterosexuality assists us to realise that such a 'general social expectation' is in fact an expectation that people be (or act as if they are) heterosexual and go on to prove, or enact, it by entering into a heterosexual marriage (often with attendant legal disabilities for women) such that coercion to marry may indeed be persecutory on the basis of sexual orientation or gender.

There is a clarity of acceptance across all five judgments that sexual orientation entails a wide range of self expression, that one's erotic life is critical to self identity and that it can and must encompass a social and emotional life. When Lord Rodger affirms that the Convention is there to protect the right 'to live freely and openly as a gay man', he specifies that such a life includes the ability to show affection, have friendships, socialise, be spontaneous, chat and flirt (*HJ and HT v SSHD* [2010] at [82]). Lord Rodger's reference to 'male heterosexuals' playing rugby and drinking beer and gay men 'going to Kylie concerts, drinking exotically coloured cocktails and talking about boys with their straight female mates' (*HJ and HT v SSHD* [2010] at [78]) has been a controversial sticking point (Hathaway and Pobjoy 2012). While I admit to finding this passage grating on first reading, I believe it deserves closer attention, and, given the balance of Lord Rodger's opinion, the benefit of the doubt – not least of all because he concludes the 'Kylie passage' with a finding of *equality* (stating that 'gay men are to be as free as their straight equivalents in the society concerned to live their lives in the way that is natural to them as gay men, without fear of persecution': *HJ and HT v SSHD* [2010] at [78]). Notably, Lord Rodger himself characterises his references to football and cocktails as 'trivial stereotypical examples' and makes it clear that they are intended to illustrate the point that a wide range of un-sexual social behaviour is inextricably engaged by sexuality. In addition, his notation of '*mutatis mutandis* – and in many cases the adaptations would obviously be great – the same must apply to other societies' (*HJ and HT v SSHD* [2010] at [78]) makes it apparent that – unlike some refugee adjudicators – Lord Rodger is *not* unthinkingly seeking to impose a westernised or narrowly stereotyped view onto the wide range of sexual identifications and practices around the world (Millbank 2009b). While I may be alone in being left personally untouched by the enduring allure of Kylie Minogue (Chelvan 2011), there is nonetheless a charming insider *knowingness* to Lord Rodger's 'Kylie'. There are, after all, quite a lot of women in the world called Kylie, but we all know who he means, don't we? This reference, linking to a vision of straight and gay mates drinking and gossiping companionably together, along with Lord Hope's use of 'our' and 'we', paints a discursive community in which gay men belong as insiders, not outsiders.

In the paragraph of the judgment directly following on from the one discussed above, Lord Rodger continues that he does not mean to 'give any false or undue prominence to the applicant's sexuality or to say that an individual is defined by his sexuality' (*HJ and HT v SSHD* [2010] at 79). In what appears to be a response to Callinan and Heydon's dissent in *S395* which held that the applicants in question were naturally discreet and not engaged in 'politics to secure greater toleration of homosexuality in the society in which they lived' (*S395* (2003) at [108]), Lord Rodger held that 'an applicant for asylum does not need to show that his homosexuality plays a particularly prominent part in his life' (*HJ and HT v SSHD* [2010] at 79). To make this point he refers to two English men of 'genius', poet A.E. Housman and mathematician Alan Turing, whose 'talents may have been at least as significant to their identity as their homosexuality' (*HJ and HT v SSHD* [2010] at 79). Alan Turing is a fascinating choice of example, given that he was prosecuted in 1952 for gross indecency after acknowledging a gay relationship in the course of making a statement to police about his home having been burgled. In order to avoid gaol, Turing was forced to undertake so-called 'chemical castration', involving a series of oestrogen injections while he served out a year of probation, following which there was further police surveillance of his activities. In 1954 Turing committed suicide. Recently, this aspect of Turing's history has gained more prominence. In 2009, then Prime Minister Gordon Brown issued a statement of apology, acknowledging that Turing and many thousands of other British men convicted for gay sex under 'homophobic laws' were 'treated terribly' and that 'Over the years millions more lived in fear of conviction' (Davies 2009). Past and current governments have refused to consider a posthumous pardon for Turing, which is still the subject of a public campaign (Northerner Blog 2012). Had Turing lived to challenge his conviction under the ECHR, like the Misters X from Germany and Austria through the 1950s and 1960s, his communication would most likely have been dismissed as manifestly ill-founded. Even the additional violation of chemical 'treatment' may not have been judged cruel and inhumane treatment under the human rights law of the time, given that this was (to use the words of Callinan and Heydon JJ) 'freely chosen' in order to avoid gaol, and goal was a legitimate deterrent. Perhaps Lord Rodger did not intend to evoke the shadow of human rights violations embedded just below the surface of modern human rights law, and the violence in the law of Britain's own recent past. But then again, perhaps he did.

2.9 Conclusion

The application of human rights norms in the assessment of sexuality-based refugee claims continues to come down to subconscious or semi-conscious understandings of what it is to be a normal person living an ordinary life. There can be no wholesale or unmediated application of human rights standards, even if such standards were stable artefacts, because of the embedded role of distinctive domestic 'interpretative communities' in doing the work of refugee adjudication (Tobin 2012).

Challenging and actively reconstituting understandings of human rights norms, sexuality and of 'normal life' requires both big rights claims and the little details of life lived. In the face of pervasive lack of transparency at lower levels of decision making, lack of information about overall trends in RSD outcomes, apparently inconsistent state practice and resilient informal barriers in refugee adjudication, Waaldijk's ideas of small change and symbolic preparation give us a *practical* and *optimistic* framework to work within. Symbolic preparation brings to light the human rights norms that are at stake, while small change entails the process of day to day application of these norms to the specific fact situation of each applicant. Small change and symbolic change are in constant inter-play. Within even apparently small changes such as use of language and choice of facts we may find symbolic dimensions indicative of, and contributing to, much greater change.

2.10 Notes

* Professor of Law, University of Technology Sydney. This chapter arises from a paper delivered to the Fleeing Homophobia Conference, VU University Amsterdam, September 2011. Many thanks to Sabine Jansen and Thomas Spijkerboer for the invitation, VU and UTS for financial support to attend, to Anthea Vogl for research assistance and to Thomas Spijkerboer for comments on an earlier draft. This research is supported by grant DP 120102025 from the Australian Research Council.

1 My work to date has largely focused on Australia, the United Kingdom, Canada and New Zealand, with less systematic consideration of case law from the United States. While this research addresses only written decisions from English-speaking jurisdictions (and a handful of decisions in French from the Canadian set), I contend that the same broad themes appear across several countries in Europe, even if there are differences in emphasis. I acknowledge that there are also many major structural and procedural barriers, including fast-tracking procedures, safe country designations, the use of detention, reduced avenues of appeal and grounds of appeal, the interdiction of boats, excision of territory and attempts to expel applicants to non-signatory countries for processing. Here I focus on barriers arising *within* the RSD process, limited though that is.

2 *X v Germany* No 104/55 (1955) 1 YB 228; *X v Germany* No 167/56 (1956) 1 YB 235; *X v Germany* No 261/57 (1957) 1 YB 255; (196); *X v Germany* No 530/59 (1960) 3 YB 184; *X v Germany* No 600/59 (2 April 1960); *X v Germany* No 704/60 (1960) 3 Coll Dec; *X v Austria* No 1138/61 (1963) 11 Coll Dec 9; (196); *X v Germany* No 1307/61 (1962) 5 YB 230; *X v Germany* No 2566/65 (1967) 22 Coll Dec 35.

3 In Germany, for example, there were contradictory decisions through the 1980s and early 1990s (discussed in European Council on Refugees and Exiles 1997: 9). Janna Weßels argues that international jurisprudence on sexuality and PSG remains 'confused' (Weßels 2011: 12).

4 There were 23 votes in favour, 19 against and three abstentions.

5 Sean Rehaag unearthed outcome statistics for 2006 in Canada through freedom of information claims (Rehaag 2008). Rehaag has since made this data publically available at http://ccrweb.ca/documents/rehaagdata.htm (accessed 17 January 2012), under the link 'Raw data'. Unfortunately such access to information laws cannot be used if the government does not in fact *collect* this information in the first place.

6 As of June 2011, 33 member states within the European Union explicitly recognized sexual orientation as a PSG in either their national legislation or case law (Council of Europe Commissioner for Human Rights 2011).

7 It should be noted that a number of European countries, such as Sweden, Denmark and Norway, did *not* in fact begin here as they addressed sexual orientation and gender claims only under subsidiary or complementary protection regimes

(Denmark continues to do so). While this afforded important protections to individual claimants it arguably perpetuates an inequitable status more broadly, by reinforcing the idea that LGBT are less entitled to Convention protections. For this reason I argue that accepting the PSG is *still* a necessary step before developing an equitable persecution analysis.

8 A further difficulty is that decision makers may then uncritically accept that the repeal of criminal sanctions means there is no further risk of persecution (see Dauvergne and Millbank 2003b). This approach was recently critiqued in the United States: *Rojo v Holder* (2011).

9 In the United States, these issues are more often considered through the frame of 'visibility.' In one sense, this concerns whether the applicant will be 'visible' or identifiable to potential persecutors: Millbank (2003); Hanna (2005). Visibility also increasingly appears in U.S. jurisprudence requiring collective 'social visibility' in order to define a PSG. This may lead to the finding that there is no PSG at all in sending countries where the entire class of applicants are closeted and the broader society disclaims their existence (Marouf 2008: 79–88). See also Soucek (2011). The BIA requirement of 'social visibility' was stringently criticised by the Court of Appeal in the Seventh Circuit (*Ramos v Holder* (2009)). However the 'social visibility' approach was recently upheld by the Court of Appeals in the Tenth Circuit (*Rivera-Barrientos v Holder* (2011)), despite being contrary to UNHCR policy guidance and to the submissions of UNHCR intervening in that case (see UNHCR 2002a; Brief for the United Nations High Commissioner for Refugees 2002: 1222). The 'visibility' approach has also been taken in France, with troubling results for GLB (Jansen and Spijkerboer 2011: 36).

10 This was expressly disapproved by Sir John Dyson (*HJ and HT v SSHD* [2010] at [129]).

11 In 2005 and 2007, respectively, Sweden and the Netherlands amended administrative policy guidance for adjudicators to instruct that lesbians and gay men could not be required or expected to hide their sexuality in their countries of origin (Hojem 2009: 15; Jansen and Spijkerboer 2011: 35). Note that these and other sources also indicate ongoing difficulties putting such guidance into practice (see Wolf-Watz *et al.* 2010)

12 See a recent Canadian case involving pre-removal risk assessment of a gay Guyanan national in which the officer stated, 'While the applicant may feel constrained to exercise discretion with respect to his sexual orientation in some settings, evidence that he need not always feel constrained to do so causes me to find that the sometime exercise of discretion does not constitute cruel and unusual treatment or punishment' (quoted on review in *AB v Minister for Citizenship and Immigration* (2010) – in which the decision was overturned). See also the mixed policy messages and confusion in the decision making process reported in Sweden (Wolf-Watz *et al.* 2010: 3.4.1, 4.4).

13 Callinan and Heydon JJ reinscribe discretion as the 'choice' of applicants but go further to contend that it is in fact not only a 'natural' but a neutral state of social grace encompassing all people in a manner 'by no means unusual. In many societies, both heterosexual and homosexual couples regard their domestic and sexual arrangements and activities as entirely private' (*S395* (2003) at [110]).

14 James Hathaway and Jason Pobjoy's recent critique of the Supreme Court decision in *HJ and HT* involves a proposal that refugee protections ought to be limited to

behaviour which is 'reasonably necessary' to express one's sexuality (Hathaway and Pobjoy 2012). This is a testament to the enduring intuitive appeal of external judgments of 'reasonableness'. Elsewhere I have argued that this suggestion is dangerously retrograde because 'reasonableness' in refugee case law to date has been a by-word for lesser, not equal, protections, for gay and lesbian applicants (Millbank 2012; see also Goodman 2012); through it discretion has lived a second life in English case law, and it would be loathsome to see it revived for a third.

15 See also *HJ and HT v SSHD* [2010] at [53], [65] (stressing that the underlying rationale of the Convention is to ensure that people are free to live openly without fear of persecution).

16 The contrast with *S395* could not be more stark; Gleeson CJ in dissent opens with a statement about the process of judicial review of administrative action which stresses the utmost importance of confining review to the case as originally made out.

17 The exchange of concealment for discretion reflects the submissions of the Equality and Human Rights Commission as second intervenor: see e.g. *HJ and HT v SSHD* [2010] at [4], [44].

2.11 References

Amnesty International (2001) *Crimes of Hate, Conspiracy of Silence: Torture and Ill Treatment Based on Sexual Identity*, London: Amnesty International.

Anker, D. (2002) 'Refugee law, gender, and the human rights paradigm', *Harvard Human Rights Journal*, 15: 133–154.

Asylum Aid (2011) *Unsustainable: The Quality of Decision Making in Women's Asylum Claims*, London: Asylum Aid.

Ban, K.M. (2010) 'Confront Prejudice, Speak Out against Violence, Secretary-General Says at Event on Ending Sanctions Based on Sexual Orientation, Gender Identity', Press Release, available at http://www.un.org/News/Press/docs/2010/sgsm13311.doc.htm (accessed 7 February 2013).

Billings, P. (2000) 'A comparative analysis of administrative and adjudicative systems for determining asylum claims', *Administrative Law Review*, 52: 253–303.

Brooks, P. (2006) *Law's Stories: Narrative and Rhetoric in the Law*, New Haven, CT: Yale University Press.

Council of Europe Commissioner for Human Rights (2011) *Discrimination on Grounds of Sexual Orientation and Gender Identity in Europe*, 2nd edn, Strasbourg: Council of Europe Publishing.

Chelvan, S. (2011) 'Put your hands up (if you feel love)', *Journal of Immigration, Asylum and Nationality Law*, 25: 56–66.

Davies, C. (2009) 'PM's apology to codebreaker Alan Turing: we were inhumane' (2009) *The Guardian*, 11 September 2009.

Daley, K. and Kelley, N. (2000) 'Particular social group: a human rights based approach to Canadian jurisprudence', *International Journal of Refugee Law*, 12: 148–174.

Dauvergne, C. (2008) *Making People Illegal: What Globalisation Means for Migration and Law*, Cambridge: Cambridge University Press.

Dauvergne, C. and Millbank, J. (2003a) 'Before the High Court: *Applicants S396/2002 and S395/2002*, a gay refugee couple from Bangladesh', *Sydney Law Review*, 25: 97–124.

— (2003b) 'Burdened by proof: how the Australian Refugee Review Tribunal has failed lesbian and gay asylum seekers', *Federal Law Review*, 31: 299–342.

— (2010) 'Forced marriage as a harm in domestic and international law', *Modern Law Review*, 73: 57–88.

Delgado, R. (1989) 'Storytelling for oppositionists and others: a plea for narrative', *Michigan Law Review*, 87: 2411.

European Council on Refugees and Exiles (1997) *ELENA Research Paper on Sexual Orientation as a Ground for Refugee Status*, available at http://www.ecre.org/topics/areas-of-work/protection-in-europe/161.html (accessed 7 February 2013).

Fajer, M. (1991–1992) 'Can two real men eat quiche together – storytelling, gender-role stereotypes, and legal protection for lesbians and gay men', *University of Miami Law Review*, 46: 511.

— (1994) 'Authority, credibility, and pre-understanding: a defense of outsider narratives in legal scholarship', *Georgetown Law Journal*, 82: 1845.

Foster, M. (2007) *International Refugee Law and Socio-Economic Rights: Refuge from Deprivation*, Cambridge: Cambridge University Press.

Gender Related Asylum Claims in Europe (GENSEN) (2012) *A Comparative Analysis of Law Policies and Practice Focusing on Women in Nine EU Member States*, available at http://helsinki.hu/wp-content/uploads/GENSEN-Report-FINAL.pdf (accessed 11 December 2012).

Goodman, R. (2012) 'Asylum and the concealment of sexual orientation', *New York University Journal of International Law and Politics*, 44(2): 407–446.

Gray, A. (2011) 'Credibility assessment in LGB cases: the case of the UK', paper given at the Fleeing Homophobia Conference, 5 September 2011, available at http://madikazemi.blogspot.com.au/2011/09/paper-credibility-assessment-in-lgb.html (accessed 19 December 2012).

Graycar, R. (2008) 'Gender, race, bias and perspective: or, how otherness colours your judgment', *International Journal of the Legal Profession*, 15: 73–86.

Haines, R. (2003) 'Gender persecution', in E. Feller, V. Turk and F. Nicholson (eds), *Refugee Protection in International Law: UNHCR's Global Consultations on International Protection*, Cambridge: Cambridge University Press.

Hanna, F. (2005) 'Punishing masculinity in gay asylum claims', *Yale Law Journal*, 114: 913–920.

Hathaway, J. (1991) *The Law of Refugee Status*, Toronto: Butterworths.

Hathaway, J.C. and Pobjoy, J. (2012) 'Queer cases make bad law', *New York Journal of International Law and Politics*, 44(2): 315–388.

Hojem, P. (2009) 'Fleeing for love', *UNHCR Research Paper No. 181*, Geneva: UNHCR.

Human Rights Watch and International Lesbian and Gay Human Rights Commission (1998) *Public Scandals: Sexual Orientation and Criminal Law in Romania*, New York, NY and London: Human Rights Watch and International Lesbian and Gay Human Rights Commission.

— (2003) *More Than a Name: State-Sponsored Homophobia and its Consequences in Southern Africa*, New York, NY and London: Human Rights Watch and International Lesbian and Gay Human Rights Commission.

Human Rights Watch (2009a) *Together, Apart: Organizing around Sexual Orientation and Gender Identity Worldwide*, New York, NY and London: Human Rights Watch.

— (2009b) *'Not Worth a Penny': Human Rights Abuses against Transgender People in Honduras*, New York, NY and London: Human Rights Watch.

— (2010) *'We Are a Buried Generation': Discrimination and Violence against Sexual Minorities in Iran*, New York, NY and London: Human Rights Watch.

— (2012) *'They Hunt Us Down for Fun': Discrimination and Police Violence Against Transgender Women in Kuwait*, New York, NY and London: Human Rights Watch.

Jansen, S. and Spijkerboer, T. (2011) *Fleeing Homophobia, Asylum Claims Related to Sexual Orientation and Gender Identity in Europe*, COC Netherlands and VU University Amsterdam, available at http://www.rechten.vu.nl/nl/Images/Fleeing%20Homophobia%20report%20EN_tcm22-232205.pdf (accessed 7 February 2013).

Johnson, T. (2007) 'Flamers, flaunters and permissible persecution', *Feminist Legal Studies*, 15: 99–111.

LaViolette, N. (2009) 'Independent Human Rights Documentation and sexual minorities: an ongoing challenge for the Canadian refugee determination process', *International Journal of Human Rights*, 13: 437–476.

MacKinnon, C. (1989) *Feminism Unmodified: Discourses on Life and Law*, Cambridge, MA: Harvard University Press.

Marouf, F. (2008) 'The emerging importance of "social visibility" in defining a "particular social group" and its potential impact on asylum claims related to sexual orientation and gender', *Yale Law and Policy Review*, 27: 47–106.

Miles, N. (2011) *No Going Back: Lesbian and Gay People and the Asylum System*, London: Stonewall.

Millbank, J. (2003) 'Gender, sex and visibility in refugee decisions on sexual orientation', *Georgetown Immigration Law Journal*, 18: 71–110.

— (2004) 'The role of rights in asylum claims on the basis of sexual orientation', *Human Rights Law Review*, 4: 193–228.

— (2005) 'A preoccupation with perversion: the British response to refugee claims on the basis of sexual orientation 1989–2003', *Social and Legal Studies*, 14: 115–138.

— (2009a) 'From discretion to disbelief: recent trends in refugee determinations on the basis of sexual orientation in Australia and the United Kingdom', *International Journal of Human Rights*, 13: 391–414.

— (2009b) 'The "Ring of Truth": a case study of credibility assessment in particular social group refugee determinations', *International Journal of Refugee Law*, 21: 1–33.

— (2012) 'The right of lesbians and gay men to live freely, openly and on equal terms is not bad law: a reply to Hathaway and Pobjoy', *New York Journal of International Law and Politics*, 44(2): 497–527.

Musalo, K. (2003) 'Revisiting social group and nexus in gender asylum claims: a unifying rationale for evolving jurisprudence', *DePaul Law Review*, 52: 777–808.

Neilson, V. (2005) 'Homosexual or female? Applying gender-based asylum jurisprudence to lesbian asylum claims', *Stanford Law & Policy Review*, 16: 417.

Northerner Blog (2012) 'Government rejects a pardon for computer genius Alan Turing', *The Guardian*, 7 February 2012.

O'Dwyer, P. (2008) 'A well-founded fear of having my sexual orientation asylum claim heard in the wrong court', *New York School Law Review*, 52(2): 195–212.

Ramji-Nogales J. *et al.* (2009) *Refugee Roulette: Disparities in Asylum Adjudication and Proposals for Reform*, New York, NY: New York University Press.

Rehaag S. (2008) 'Patrolling the borders of sexual orientation: bisexual refugee claims in Canada', *McGill Law Journal*, 53: 59 –102.

Soucek, B. (2011) 'Social group asylum claims: a second look at the new visibility requirement', *Yale Law and Policy Review*, 29: 337–345.

Stychin, C. (2003) *Governing Sexuality: The Changing Politics of Citizenship and Law Reform*, Portland, OR: Hart Publishing.

Tobin, J. (2012) 'Assessing LGBTI refugee claims: Using human rights law to shift the narrative of persecution within refugee law', *New York Journal of International Law and Politics*, 44: 447–484.

Tuitt, P. (1997) 'Human rights and refugees', *International Journal of Human Rights*, 1: 66–80.

UK Lesbian and Gay Immigration Group (2010a) *Annual Report*, London: UK Lesbian and Gay Immigration Group.

— (2010b) *Failing the Grade*, London: UK Lesbian and Gay Immigration Group.

United Nations High Commissioner for Refugees, Brief as Amicus Curiae in Support of Petitioner (2010) *Rivera-Barrientos v. Holder* 658 F.3d (2011) 1222.

UNHCR (2002a) *Guidelines on International Protection No 2: 'Membership of a Particular Social Group' Within the Context of Article 1A(2) of the 1951 Convention and/or its 1967 Protocol Relating to the Status of Refugees*, UN Doc, HCR/GIP/02/02, Geneva: UNHCR.

— (2002b) *Guidelines on Gender-Related Persecution Within the Context of Article 1A(2) of the 1951 Convention and/or its 1967 Protocol Relating to the Status of Refugees*, 30 UN Doc HCR/GIP/02/01, Geneva: UNHCR.

— (2008) *UNHCR Guidance Note on Refugee Claims Relating to Sexual Orientation and Gender Identity*, 21 November 2008, Geneva: UNHCR.

— (2009) *Selected Documents Relating to Sexual Orientation and Gender Identity Relevant to International Refugee Protection*, Geneva: UNHCR.

— (2010) *Summary Conclusions: Asylum-Seekers and Refugees Seeking Protection on Account of their Sexual Orientation and Gender Identity*, Geneva: UNHCR.

— (2011) *Working with Lesbian, Gay, Bisexual, Transgender & Intersex Persons in Forced Displacement*, Geneva: UNHCR.

— (2012) *Guidelines on International Protection No. 9: Claims to Refugee Status based on Sexual Orientation and/or Gender Identity within the context of Article 1A(2) of the 1951 Convention and/or its 1967 Protocol relating to the Status of Refugees*, 23 October 2012, HCR/GIP/12/01, Geneva: UNHCR.

UN Human Rights Council (2011a) *Discriminatory Laws and Practices and Acts of Violence Against Individuals Based on their Sexual Orientation and Gender Identity*, Geneva: UNHRC.

— (2011b) *Human Rights Sexual Orientation and Gender Identity, A/HRC/17/L.9/Rev.1*, Geneva: UNHRC.

Waaldijk, K. (2001a) 'Small change: how the road to same-sex marriage got paved in the Netherlands', in R. Wintemute and M. Andenaes (eds), *Legal Recognition of Same-Sex Partnerships: A Study of National, European and International Law*, Oxford: Hart Publishing.

— (2001b) 'Towards recognition of same-sex partners in European Union law: expectations based on trends in national law', in R. Wintemute and M. Andenaes (eds), *Legal Recognition of Same-Sex Partnerships: A Study of National, European and International Law*, Oxford: Hart Publishing.

Waaldijk, K. *et al.* (2010) *Legal Study on Homophobia and Discrimination on Grounds of Sexual Orientation and Gender Identity: Thematic Study Netherlands*, available at http://fra.europa.eu/fraWebsite/attachments/LGBT-2010_thematic-study_NL.pdf (accessed 23 January 2012).

Weßels, J. (2011) 'Sexual orientation in refugee status determination', *Working Paper No. 74*, Oxford: Refugee Studies Centre.

— (2012) 'HJ (Iran) and Another: reflections on a new test for sexuality based claims in Britain', *International Journal of Refugee* Law, 24(4): 815–839.

West, R. (1990) 'Narrative, responsibility and death: a comment on the death penalty cases from the 1989 term', *Maryland Journal of Contemporary Legal Issues*, 1: 161.

Wintemute, R. (1997) *Sexual Orientation and Human Rights: The United States Constitution, the European Convention and the Canadian Charter*, revised edn, Oxford: Clarendon Press.

Wolf-Watz, O. *et al.* (2010) *Norm-Critical Study of the Swedish Asylum Examination*, available at http://www.migrationsverket.se/download/18.1c1b3f51128bf913da580001304/normkritiskstudie_en.pdf (accessed 19 January 2012).

3 Discretion in sexuality-based asylum cases
An adaptive phenomenon

Janna Weßels[*]

3.1 Introduction

'Discretion' has proven to be very flexible in the context of sexuality-based asylum cases. Although courts have often held it to be incompatible with the objective and purpose of the 1951 United Nations Convention Relating to the Status of Refugees (the Convention), studies such as the *Fleeing Homophobia* report have demonstrated that the idea that lesbian, gay, bisexual and transgender (LGBT) people conceal their protected identity continuously reappears in refugee status determinations in different guises (see Jansen and Spijkerboer 2011).

In spite of declarations by international human rights bodies, decisions from national courts, and the reform of anti-gay legislation in many countries, sexual orientation remains an issue that provokes strong opinions and divides societies. LGBT individuals continue to be oppressed and persecuted in many parts of the world. As a result, gay people often flee their home countries and seek protection abroad. However, there are many hurdles for LGBT individuals connected to receiving that protection, many of which are discussed in other parts of this volume. 'Discretion' is one such obstacle. It consists in the expectation or assumption that claimants would or should hide their sexual orientation and thus avoid a risk of persecution. The idea of concealment is astoundingly persistent. For example, although a German Administrative Court compared 'discretion' in sexuality-based asylum claims to the requirement that someone change their skin colour in order to evade persecution as early as 1983 (IV/IE06244/81 Verwaltungsgericht Wiesbaden 26 April1983), to date, German case law is divided on the subject. In a response to a parliamentary query it was recently argued that 'the outcome of the asylum procedure depends on whether the asylum seeker will *behave* in a manner which will lead to persecution after his/her return' (Bundestags-Drucksache 17/1722). In France, 'discretion' has resurfaced in the form of an '*in*discretion requirement', where those claimants who have not 'exposed their sexual orientation publicly or manifested it by exterior *behaviour*' in their country of origin do not qualify for refugee status (Jansen and Spijkerboer 2011: 36, emphasis added). This reasoning excludes from protection those applicants who have been unable to give expression to their sexual orientation due to the persecution they had good grounds to fear if they had done so. Both these examples illustrate that 'discretion' relies on the *behaviour* of the applicant.

Several authors have addressed the problem of an is/does dichotomy before, such as O'Dwyer, who pointed to the problem of the 'artificial distinction between persecution on account of homosexual *status or identity*, which some circuits hold warrants protection, and punishment for homosexual *acts*, which some circuits hold does not warrant such protection' (O'Dwyer 2008: 136).[1] LaViolette also harshly criticised the distinction between status and conduct as it permits discrimination against people on the basis of their sexual behaviour and public sexual identity (LaViolette 1997: 30). The article by Louis Middelkoop in this volume refers to the difficulties connected to a status/conduct distinction in the different context of credibility.

Interestingly, in their recent work, Hathaway and Pobjoy take the opposite position, arguing *in favour* of a distinction between status and conduct. According to the authors, 'there [is] a duty on the courts to grapple with the scope of activities properly understood to be inherent in, and an integral part of, [the protected] status' (Hathaway and Pobjoy 2012: 335). Such line-drawing to separate protected from unprotected forms of activity is severely criticized by Millbank on the basis that 'activity' associated with a protected status does not cause the persecution nor form the basis of protection, but simply reveals or exposes the protected *identity* (Millbank 2012: 510).

This chapter aims to make a contribution to this debate through a detailed analysis of the 2010 UK case of *HJ (Iran) and HT (Cameroon) v Secretary of State for the Home Department* [2010] UKSC 31 (*HJ (Iran) and HT (Cameroon)*). The case dealt with 'discretion' in sexuality-based asylum claims and has been celebrated as a 'fundamental shift in asylum law' (Law Center (NI) 2011). Indeed, it represents an important achievement: the Supreme Court unanimously held that the so-called 'reasonably tolerable' test is incompatible with the purposes of the Convention. Courts – mainly in the United Kingdom – had previously used this test as a basis on which to decide against asylum claims by finding that claimants could *reasonably be expected to tolerate* being 'discreet' about their sexual identity so as to avoid persecution. In *HJ (Iran) and HT (Cameroon)*, the Justices rightly found that this test is 'wrong in principle, unworkable and inconsistent with the way that Article 1A(2) of the Convention has been interpreted and applied in other authorities' (per Lord Rodger at [82]). However, as is demonstrated, they fail to rule out 'discretion' as a whole. Instead, in the new 'approach to be followed by tribunals' they propose (per Lord Rodger at [82]), through the continuation of a distinction between 'openly' and 'discreetly' gay people, they reinstate a discriminating 'discretion logic' in sexuality-based asylum cases which is based on an is/does dichotomy.

This chapter first describes and critically analyses the new test proposed by the Supreme Court in *HJ (Iran) and HT (Cameroon)* with a view to a distinction between status and acts by putting the legal reasoning of the Justices into perspective as well as by drawing on other relevant cases and forced migration literature. In particular, it looks at the implications of distinguishing between gay people who 'live openly' vs. those who conceal[2] their sexual orientation on the one hand and the procedural difficulties of determining for which reasons a person may be concealing his or her sexual orientation on the other hand. It is argued that while the decision can be seen as an important step forwards in the 'work-in-progress', which is the role of sexuality-based asylum cases in international refugee law, because it is clearly based on an is/does dichotomy, *HJ (Iran) and HT (Cameroon)* fails to reject 'discretion' as a relevant concept in asylum decisions.[3]

After a short description of the facts and background of the present case, the test to be applied in sexuality-based asylum cases as proposed by the Justices is outlined. It is advanced that this test fails on three grounds. First, it makes a distinction between openly demonstrated sexuality and concealed sexuality and thus clearly focuses on the *conduct* of the applicant. Second, it argues that this distinction in the applicants' behaviour and the underlying choice are relevant for assessing whether an applicant is at risk of persecution. Lastly, the case relies heavily on the subjective element of assessing the 'fear' of persecution which leads to a stricter test than necessary. The concluding chapter summarises how the distinction between *status* or *identity* on the one hand, and *conduct* or *acts* on the other hand, is the underlying basis for the continuing 'discretion reasoning' in this test, which leads to an impermissible discrimination.

3.2 *HJ (Iran) and HT (Cameroon)* – and the 'reasonably tolerable test'

The UK Supreme Court case of *HJ (Iran) and HT (Cameroon)* focused on the so-called 'discretion requirement'. The appellants submitted that the test which had been applied by the tribunal and by the Court of Appeal, namely, whether an applicant could be reasonably expected to tolerate concealment, was misconceived (cf. *HJ (Iran) and HT (Cameroon)* per Lord Hope at [8]). The 'discretion requirement' is a problematic concept that has been widely employed in decisions related to asylum claims based on sexual orientation, particularly in Australia (cf. Kassisieh 2008) and in the UK (cf. Millbank 2005): 'The discretion requirement repeatedly expressed in courts consists of a "reasonable expectation that persons should, to the extent that it is possible, co-operate in their own protection"' (*RRT Case No. V95/03527* [1998] RRTA 246).

This test had also been applied in *HJ (Iran)* and *HT (Cameroon)*.[4] Both appellants were gay men. In the case of the HJ, a 40-year old male, Iranian national, the Tribunal concluded that:

> On the evidence he was able to *conduct* his homosexual *activities* in Iran without serious detriment to his private life and without that causing him to suppress many aspects of his sexual *identity*.
>
> (*HJ (Iran) and HT (Cameroon) v SSHD* [2009] per Lord Justice Pill at [19], citing the Tribunal at [44], emphasis added)

On appeal, the Home Secretary agreed with this finding, stating that the test applied in the judgment complied with the standard required by the Convention:

> It is an appropriate and workable test. . . [The] conclusion that HJ could reasonably be expected to tolerate conditions in Iran was firmly based on the evidence in the case, considered in the context of the in-country evidence.
>
> (*HJ (Iran) and HT (Cameroon) v SSHD* [2009] per Lord Justice Pill at [31])

HT, a 36-year old citizen of Cameroon, had been seen kissing his then male partner in the garden of his home by a neighbour. He was later severely attacked by a crowd of people as he was leaving church (*HJ (Iran) and HT (Cameroon)* per Lord Rodger at [44]). Here, the Home Secretary was satisfied that HT would be discreet on return to Cameroon and that the single attack on HT following a one-off incident in his garden did not establish a real risk of persecution in the future – though he could not go back to his home area, he could internally relocate to another location within his home country and be 'discreet'. Further, it was contended that HT had not asserted sufficient facts on which a finding that he could not reasonably be expected to tolerate a life involving discretion, if he returned to Cameroon, could be based (*HJ (Iran) and HT (Cameroon) v SSHD* [2009] per Lord Justice Pill at [44]–[45]).

Thus, in both cases, the 'reasonably tolerable test' was applied. The Home Secretary claimed that:

> Self-restraint due to fear will be persecution only if it is such that a homosexual person cannot reasonably be expected to tolerate such self-restraint. Where a person does in fact live discreetly to avoid coming to the attention of the authorities he is reasonably tolerating that position.
>
> (*HJ (Iran) v SSHD* [2008] at [10])

The case was appealed and proceeded to the Supreme Court. The appellants contended that the 'reasonably tolerable' test, which Lord Rodger describes as 'fairly well established case law' (*HJ (Iran) and HT (Cameroon)* at [50]), is 'incompatible with the definition of "refugee" in article 1A(2) of the Convention and is based on a misunderstanding of the decision of the High Court of Australia in *Appellant S395/2002 v Minister for Immigration* (2003) 216 CLR 437' (*HJ (Iran) and HT (Cameroon)* at [50]). The Supreme Court unanimously allowed the appeal, holding that the 'reasonably tolerable test' applied by the Court of Appeal was contrary to the Convention and should not be followed in the future (Supreme Court of the United Kingdom 2010).

Instead, the Supreme Court Judges propose a complicated test that attempts to distinguish between 'discretion' arising out of fear of persecution, which would warrant international protection, and 'discretion' for reasons other than fear of persecution, such as a personal choice or social pressures, which would not warrant international protection (*HJ (Iran) and HT (Cameroon)* per Lord Rodger at [82] and Lord Hope at [35]). This test will have to prove itself in courts. However, at this stage it appears to be as problematic as the test applied at first instance, as it reiterates some of the same misconceptions.

3.3 The new test as proposed in *HJ (Iran) and HT (Cameroon)*

In the judgment, Lord Rodger provides detailed guidance in respect of the test to be applied by the lower tribunals and courts in determining claims for asylum based on sexual orientation. Lords Walker and Collins as well as Sir John Dyson SCJ expressly agree with the test as outlined by Lord Rodger at [82] of the judgment, while Lord Hope makes reference to the new test and adds further guidance at [35]. He describes the test as an 'Individual and fact-specific inquiry, . . . directed to what *will happen in the future* if the applicant is returned to his own country. An approach which disregards what is in fact likely to occur there in the case of the particular applicant is wrong and should not be adopted' (*HJ (Iran) and HT (Cameroon)* at [35]–[36]). The test as outlined by Lord Rodger reads as follows (*HJ (Iran) and HT (Cameroon)* at [82]; numbering added):

1 When an applicant applies for asylum on the ground of a well-founded fear of persecution because he is gay, the tribunal must first ask itself whether it is satisfied on the evidence that he is gay, or that he would be treated as gay by potential persecutors in his country of nationality.
2 If so, the tribunal must then ask itself whether it is satisfied on the available evidence that gay people who lived openly would be liable to persecution in the applicant's country of nationality.
3 If so, the tribunal must go on to consider what the individual applicant would do if he were returned to that country.

  a If the applicant would in fact live openly and thereby be exposed to a real risk of persecution, then he has a well-founded fear of persecution – even if he could avoid the risk by living 'discreetly'.
  b If, on the other hand, the tribunal concludes that the applicant would in fact live discreetly and so avoid persecution, it must go on to ask itself why he would do so.

    i If the tribunal concludes that the applicant would choose to live discreetly simply because that was how he himself would wish to live, or because of social pressures, e.g. not wanting to distress his parents or embarrass his friends, then his application should be rejected. Social pressures of that kind do not amount to persecution and the Convention does not offer protection against them. Such a person has no well-founded fear of persecution because, for reasons that have nothing to do with any fear of persecution, he himself chooses to adopt a way of life which means that he is not in fact liable to be persecuted because he is gay.

ii If, on the other hand, the tribunal concludes that a material reason for the applicant living discreetly on his return would be a fear of the persecution which would follow if he were to live openly as a gay man, then, other things being equal, his application should be accepted. Such a person has a well-founded fear of persecution. To reject his application on the ground that he could avoid the persecution by living discreetly would be to defeat the very right which the Convention exists to protect – his right to live freely and openly as a gay man without fear of persecution. By admitting him to asylum and allowing him to live freely and openly as a gay man without fear of persecution, the receiving state gives effect to that right by affording the applicant a surrogate for the protection from persecution which his country of nationality should have afforded him.

Thus, to summarise, in the test mandated by the Supreme Court, the first evidential hurdle for the applicant is to establish that he is indeed gay or would be perceived as gay. As the literature shows, there are substantial difficulties linked to credibility issues in these cases – the use of phallometry until recently in the Czech Republic is just one example (UNHCR 2011). However, the question of credibility was not subject of *HJ (Iran) and HT (Cameroon)* and is not further analysed here, but is discussed in detail in the chapter by Louis Middelkoop in this volume.

The problematic reasoning of the new approach begins in the second step. If the applicant can establish that he is indeed gay, the decision maker must examine conditions in the applicant's country of origin. It is crucial to note that the question of reliability of Country of Origin Information concerning the situation of sexual minorities is an issue that is particularly complicated in sexuality-based cases. However, just as the issue of credibility was not in question in this case neither was Country of Origin Information and, as such, is not further addressed here.[5] Yet the Supreme Court added a further limitation to this second step of its test as it only sought to inquire into whether 'gay people *who lived openly*' would be persecuted in their home country. This small but significant detail indicates the reliance on the *behaviour* of the applicant and is examined in the following section as it is directly linked to the following steps of the test.

If the question of whether gay people 'living openly' risk persecution in their country of origin is answered in the affirmative, the decision maker then proceeds to the 'future-focused question' of what the applicant will *do* on return. This is in fact a different question to the one the decision maker claims to ask: Lord Rodger calls the test an enquiry into what will happen if the applicant were returned – but in fact, the question is how the applicant will *behave* ('will do') on return. For the applicant's behaviour after return, the Justices define three situations:

1 If a person will in fact conceal his sexual identity he is not in fact at risk of persecution.
2 If that factual concealment is due to family or social pressures the consequential avoidance of the risk of persecution is an acceptable positive side-effect.
3 If that factual concealment is due to a well-founded fear of persecution, there is a real risk and the person is entitled to international protection.

While this judgment clearly rejects the 'reasonably tolerable test', there are several potential pitfalls in this reasoning. The first is related to the question of whether a person who conceals his sexual orientation is in fact not at risk of persecution. This is closely linked with step 2 of the test which limits the inquiry to persecution of gay people who live openly. The second pitfall concerns the question of why the applicant will conceal his sexual orientation. If it is established that openly gay people are persecuted in that country, in practice, it is hard to fathom how concealment would be completely unrelated to that fact. Further, it is difficult to imagine how decision makers will assess the state of mind of the applicant in practice. Overall, the 'discretion logic' persists in the new test because the latter relies on an evaluation of the *behaviour* of the claimant. The next sections examine these issues more closely and analyse to what extent, taken together, these points result in an indirect 'discretion requirement'.

3.4 The requirement or expectation to conceal a protected characteristic

The great achievement of the present judgment is the rejection of the 'reasonably tolerable test', which had previously been fairly well established in case law. The 'reasonably tolerable test' is in fact based on a misinterpretation of a judgment of the Australian High Court from 2003. *S395/2002* is one of the most important cases to have dealt with the problematic concept of 'discretion' (*Appellant S395/2002 and Appellant S396/2002 v Minister for Immigration and Multicultural Affairs* [2003] HCA 71, High Court, Australia).[6] In issue was the interpretation of persecution and whether it was lawful to consider whether gay applicants could or even should be 'discreet', i.e. secretive, in their country of origin so as to avoid or lessen the risk of persecution. By a narrow majority (4:3), the Court decided that the tribunal had erred in failing to consider the future-focused question of what would happen if the applicant were in fact discovered to be gay, and whether the need to act 'discreetly' to avoid the threat of serious harm itself constituted persecution (*Appellant S395/2002* per McHugh and Kirby JJ at [18], 6). This is the future-focused analysis that should have also been sought in the UK case of *HJ (Iran) and HT*

(Cameroon) instead of the focus on the behaviour of the applicant. In the Australian S395/2002, the two majority joint judgments given by Gummow and Haynes JJ and McHugh and Kirby JJ, clearly rejected the possibility to 'expect' or 'reasonably require' refugee applicants to 'co-operate in their own protection' by concealing their sexuality (*Appellant S395/2002* at [18], 6).[7]

Although the High Court of Australia 'vociferously and convincingly rejected' both a 'discretion' requirement and any expectation of reasonableness (UNHCR 2010: [36(4)], 22), the UK Court of Appeal in *HJ (Iran)* refers precisely to the case of *S395/2002* when outlining its 'reasonably tolerable' approach. For the Supreme Court, Lord Collins clarifies in *HJ (Iran) and HT (Cameroon)* that this is based on a 'misunderstanding' of the following passage of the judgment:

> Persecution covers many forms of harm ranging from physical harm to the loss of intangibles, from death and torture to State sponsored or condoned discrimination in social life and employment. *Whatever form the harm takes, it will constitute persecution only if, by reason of its intensity or duration, the person persecuted cannot reasonably be expected to tolerate it*. But persecution does not cease to be persecution for the purpose of the Convention because those persecuted can eliminate the harm by taking avoiding action within the country of nationality. The Convention would give no protection from persecution for reasons of religion or political opinion if it was a condition of protection that the person affected must take steps – reasonable or otherwise – to avoid offending the wishes of the persecutors. Nor would it give protection to membership of many a 'particular social group' if it were a condition of protection that its members hide their membership or modify some attribute or characteristic of the group to avoid persecution. Similarly, it would often fail to give protection to people who are persecuted for reasons of race or nationality if it was a condition of protection that they should take steps to conceal their race or nationality.
>
> (*Appellant S395/2002* per McHugh and Kerby JJ at [40], 12, emphasis added)[8]

Lord Collins states that the idea of reasonable toleration was plainly mentioned in the context of what amounts to persecution and not in the context of what is described as 'taking avoiding action' or where members of the group 'hide their membership or modify some attribute or characteristic of the group' to avoid persecution (*HJ (Iran) and HT (Cameroon)* at [103]). Accordingly, the UK Supreme Court unanimously rejected this test as 'wrong in principle, unworkable and inconsistent with the way that article 1A(2) of the Convention has been interpreted and applied in other authorities' (*HJ(Iran) and HT (Cameroon)* per Lord Rodger at [81]). This new judgment of *HJ (Iran) and HT (Cameroon)* can thus be seen as an improvement and a step in the right direction. In fact, the new approach has since been applied to cases unrelated to sexual orientation. The case *TM (Zimbabwe)* reinforced the new approach and stressed that it is not limited to sexuality-based cases but applicable to all grounds covered by the Convention (*TM (Zimbabwe) and Others v Secretary of State for the Home Department* [2010] EWCA Civ 916, Court of Appeal (England and Wales), 15 July 2010). Subsequent cases such as *RT (Zimbabwe) and Others* ([2010] EWCA Civ 1285, Court of Appeal (England and Wales), 18 November 2010) and *KM (Zimbabwe)* ([2011] EWCA Civ 275, Court of Appeal (England and Wales), 17 March 2011) also applied the 'pure HJ (Iran) issue' (meaning an individual found to hold genuine political beliefs cannot be required to modify their behaviour or deny their beliefs in order to avoid persecution) and what was called the 'extended HJ (Iran) issue' (understood as the impossibility to require an appellant to actively profess a loyalty to a regime which he does not possess or otherwise lie to the authorities of the home country or other potential persecutors in order to avoid a condition of persecution) (*RT (Zimbabwe) and Others* per Lord Justice Carnwath at [5]).

However, in their judgment, the Justices failed to reject concealment generally as a concept in asylum cases. A general rejection of concealment can, among others, be reached by an analogy with other Convention grounds. The general position that '[a] hidden right is not a right' (*X (Re), VA5-02751* [2007], Immigration and Refugee Board, Canada, 16 February, 2007) is supported by many Courts.[9] The UNHCR Guidance Note clearly states that '[b]eing compelled to forsake or conceal one's sexual orientation and gender identity, where this is instigated or condoned by the State, may amount to persecution' (UNHCR 2008: 8). This is in accordance with the *Yogyakarta Principles on the Application of International Human Rights Law in Relation to Sexual Orientation and Gender Identity* (International Commission of Jurists 2007), which are a set of 29 international principles and recommendations to governments, regional intergovernmental institutions, civil society, and the United Nations, adopted unanimously by members of the International Commission of Jurists and human rights experts from around the world at a meeting on Java from 6 to 9 November in 2006. *Yogyakarta Principle* 19 states:

> Everyone has the right to freedom of opinion and expression, regardless of sexual orientation or gender identity. This includes the expression of identity or personhood through speech, deportment, dress, bodily characteristics, choice of name, or any other means . . .
>
> (International Commission of Jurists 2007: 24)

UNHCR intervened in the case before the UK Supreme Court, in light of its supervisory responsibility in respect of the Convention (UNHCR 2010). UNHCR does not make submissions on the facts of individual cases but is concerned with the interpretation and application of the Convention as a matter of law and principle (UNHCR 2010: [5], 3). In the submission, by reference to the Australian case *S395/2002*, UNHCR holds that the proposition that a person is not to be required or expected to conceal his identity in order to avoid persecution is uncontroversial. UNHCR further notes that the proposition is clearly endorsed by comparative case law concerning claims based on other protected statuses, citing cases that dealt with race, religion or political opinion by analogy.[10] Moreover, an additional discretion requirement for sexuality-based cases would mean discrimination between the statuses protected by the Convention (UNHCR 2010 at [33], 16–17). The Equality and Human Rights Commission, which also intervened before the Supreme Court, made the same point, finding that protection would be denied on a discriminatory basis as this 'impermissible approach has only (to date) been applied to the interpretation of Article 1A(2) of the Convention where sexual orientation is the ground for seeking protection and not where other grounds such as race or religion is the protected basis' (Equality and Human Rights Commission 2010 at [47(d)], 32).[11]

Accordingly, concealment cannot be a relevant factor for a decision if the applicant would have a real chance of persecution, were it not for the concealment (Kassisieh 2008: 70). Similarly, in the UNHCR intervention it is stated that:

> The essence of persecutory conduct is the harm feared, irrespective of whether the applicant is discreet about his or her sexual orientation. The assessment of the existence of a well-founded fear of persecution in LGBT cases should thus be made without reference to whether or not the applicants would be discreet about their sexual orientation.
>
> (UNHCR 2010 at [25], 13)

However, this advice was not followed by the Justices as the basis for the new test to be applied in sexuality-based cases. On the contrary, the test was constructed around a 'discretion logic'. Millbank, in 2009, had criticised the interpretation of persecution as not having been materially altered by the tribunals following the Australian decision of *S395/2002* (Millbank 2009: 398). Instead, she purports, the question has shifted from asking whether a claimant 'should' be secretive to whether an applicant can 'reasonably be expected to tolerate' secrecy (Millbank 2009: 398). Now, the emphasis seems to have moved from 'reasonably tolerable discretion' to a presumption of 'discretion by choice', as is outlined below, because the new test continues to focus on the applicant's behaviour and separates this from the protected identity.

It should also be noted that the use of the word 'discretion' is harshly criticised by the Equality and Human Rights Commission, which intervened in the present case before the Supreme Court:

> As a preliminary point, the Commission notes that 'discretion' or 'discreet' are inapt to describe what the Appellants were being required to do. 'Discreet' suggests that the individual will be expected to be 'considerate', 'judicious', 'prudent', 'circumspect', 'well-behaved', 'civil'

> and 'polite' and not 'indiscreet', meaning 'injudicious', 'imprudent', 'inconsiderate', 'unadvised', and 'unwary', (*Oxford English Dictionary*, 2nd Ed). What is in fact being expected is that the individual take active steps to 'conceal' and keep concealed, his or her sexual orientation. The Commission suggests that where in fact the Court is talking about a need to conceal sexual identity in order to avoid harm, it is that description that should be used, not the word 'discretion' or 'discreet'.
>
> (Equality and Human Rights Commission 2010 at [44], 29)

However, only Lord Hope addresses the choice of words and actively follows this advice: 'I would prefer not to use the word "discretion", as this euphemistic expression does not tell the whole truth' (*HJ (Iran) and HT (Cameroon)* at [22]). Generally, in their judgment the Justices do not consistently follow the suggestion offered by the Equality and Human Rights Commission and in particular, Lord Rodger, who lays out the majority judgment, continues to nonetheless employ the terms 'discretion' and 'discreet' – strikingly so in the new test he lays out.

3.5 'Living openly' as the counterpart of concealment

The main issue that appears to be problematic is the fact that although the Court clearly states that a requirement or expectation of concealment is unacceptable, it continues to use a distinction between 'open' and 'concealed' as the basis for the proposed test. This reasoning departs from an understanding of the Convention where the 'underlying rationale . . . is that they [the social group of gay people] should be able to *live freely and openly* as gay men and lesbian women, without fearing that they may suffer harm of the requisite intensity or duration because they are gay or lesbian' (*HJ (Iran) and HT (Cameroon)* per Lord Rodger at [65]). Lord Rodger attempts to conceive the meaning of 'discretion' at [63],[12] and again at [77],[13] concluding that 'what is protected is the applicant's right to *live feely and openly* as a gay man' (*HJ (Iran) and HT (Cameroon)* per Lord Rodger at [78]).[14] He buttresses this interpretation by reference to the passage of the Australian case of *S395/2002* cited above, where McHugh and Kirby JJ explain that 'persecution does not cease to be persecution . . . because those persecuted can eliminate the harm by taking avoiding action' (*Appellant S395/2002* per McHugh and Kirby JJ at [40] 12). Lord Rodger then states his interpretation of this passage in the following words:

> In the remainder of para 40 they point out that, if the position were otherwise, the Convention would not protect those who *chose to exercise their right*, say, to express their political opinion *openly*. Similarly the Convention would not protect those who chose to live openly as gay men rather than take the option of living discretely.
>
> (*HJ (Iran) and HT (Cameroon)* at [55])

However, nowhere in this passage of *S395/2002* is there a reference to 'choice', 'choosing' or 'openly'. Rather, McHugh and Kirby JJ refer to the obligation to conceal protected characteristics. These words are clearly added by Lord Rodger's reading of the passage. As a result, the whole test is based on the question of whether the applicant would 'in fact live openly' and thus actually wish to make use of this right. Accordingly, in the second stage of the test, the Justices propose to ask only whether 'gay people *who lived openly* would be liable to persecution [. . .]' (*HJ (Iran) and HT (Cameroon)* per Lord Rodger at [82], emphasis added). The term 'living openly' contains a limitation that seems to assume that only those 'living openly' will be liable to persecution. This is even clearer in the last stage of the test:

> If, on the other hand, the tribunal concludes that a material reason for the applicant living discreetly on his return would be a fear of the *persecution which would follow if he were to live openly* as a gay man, then, other things being equal, his application should be accepted.
>
> (*HJ (Iran) and HT (Cameroon)* per Lord Rodger at [82])

However, persecution is clearly not generally restricted to gay people 'who live openly'. In persecutory environments, gay people will be persecuted once their sexual orientation comes to the knowledge of the persecutors, regardless of whether they made efforts to conceal their sexual orientation or not.

In fact, 'living openly' can be seen as the direct counterpart of 'discretion'. Whenever reference is made to 'living openly' or 'openly gay', this must be understood as an indirect reference to 'discretion' or 'concealment'. The way the test is framed, there appears to be a risk of a situation where those applicants for whom the Court is satisfied would live 'openly', i.e. act in a way that makes their sexual orientation publicly known will clearly receive protection. In contrast, those whom decision makers find will in fact conceal their sexual orientation must prove concealment of their identity is in response to their fear of persecution. This qualification in the question seems to re-inscribe the issue of concealment into the test, though more in the form of an '*in*discretion requirement' like that which is applied in France (Jansen and Spijkerboer 2011: 36): Those who have 'lived openly' would have much better chances to convince the decision makers than those who have been compelled to conceal their identity and would continue to do so on return. The test depends on the expected future behaviour of the applicant.

The question of a distinction between 'open' and 'discreet' behaviour was also an issue in *NABD Minister for Immigration and Multicultural and Indigenous Affairs*, a decision by the High Court of Australia on the question of whether the Refugee Review Tribunal made a jurisdictional error as a result of categorising Iranian Christians as 'aggressive proselytisers' – who would be persecuted for religious beliefs – in contrast to 'quiet evangelists' – who would not be persecuted for their beliefs (HCA 29, High Court, Australia, 26 May 2005 per McHugh J at [12], 4).[15] The High Court decided by a close majority (3:2) that the Tribunal had not committed jurisdictional error and thus did not allow the appeal. The majority judgments of Gleeson CJ and of Hayne and Heydon JJ jointly, are kept relatively brief. However, the dissenting opinions by McHugh J and Kirby J (who were both also involved in *S395/2002*) are very instructive here (*Applicant NABD of 2002*). McHugh clearly rejects such classifications as described above: 'There are no recognised sub-groups in Iran of "proselytising Christians" and "quietly evangelising Christians"' (*Applicant NABD of 2002* per McHugh J at [12], 4). He further argues that categorisations of any kind can only be 'relevant and appropriate if there is evidence that *the potential persecutors also make that distinction*' (*Applicant NABD of 2002* per McHugh J at [35], 12, emphasis in original). A test that only inquires into whether a subgroup of 'gay people living openly' is persecuted, thus postulating that there exists such a subgroup in the eyes of potential persecutors generally appears to be in the very least, questionable – in particular for countries where sexual orientation is criminalised. In fact, as Kirby J outlines in his speech:

> Having accepted that a 'quiet' [equivalent to 'discreet'] practice of religious beliefs was imperative for safety in Iran, the second Tribunal effectively *imposed* the requirement of 'quiet sharing of one's faith' on the appellant, were he to be returned to Iran. Its prediction of what he would do was necessarily dependent upon its assessment of what alone it would be safe for him to do in Iran.
> (*Applicant NABD of 2002* per Kirby J at [106], 34, emphasis in original)

Thus, by maintaining 'discretion' as a relevant variable in the new test through the reliance on the actions of the claimant, it can be argued that the Justices continue to effectively impose a 'discretion requirement' on applicants – albeit in an indirect manner.

3.6 The divided social group and the reliability of concealment

It is argued that this continuation of a factual distinction between those gay applicants who will live 'openly' and those who will live 'discreetly' is problematic. To understand this dilemma, it is necessary to look at the 'particular social group' that was the basis for this decision.

The plain words used by both Lord Hope and Lord Rodger on membership of a particular social group are a merit of this judgment: the Secretary of State in *HJ (Iran)* only accepted that '*practising* homosexuals are a particular social group for the purposes of article 1A of the Convention' (*HJ (Iran) and HT (Cameroon) v SSHD* [2009] EWCA Civ 172 per Lord Justice Pill at [7]). This limitation to a sub-group of 'practising' gay people is not repeated on Appeal before the Supreme Court. Although this difference is not addressed or further discussed, Lord Hope holds, by reference to *Islam and Shah*

(*Islam (AP) v Secretary of State for the Home Department; R v Immigration Appeal Tribunal and Another, Ex Parte Shah (AP)*, Session 1998–1999, House of Lords, United Kingdom, 25 March 1999: 8), that 'there is no doubt that *gay men and women* may be considered to be a particular social group for this purpose', as 'to a large extent the meaning of the definition of article 1A(2) is common ground' (*HJ (Iran) and HT (Cameroon)* at [10]). Equally, Lord Rodger states that the debate as to whether gay people constitute a 'particular social group' belongs to the past (*HJ (Iran) and HT (Cameroon)* at [42]). Thus, the relevant particular social group is that of 'gay people' without any further qualifications or limitations. In the words of McHugh and Kirby JJ in the Australian case of *S395/2002*, to hold otherwise 'would arguably have been perverse' (*Appellant S395/2002* at [55], 17). These clear words by the UK Supreme Court thus reduces the discretion of decision makers in sexual orientation cases to use the interpretation of the particular social group to exclude gay refugees from protection, and provides lower-level decision makers with legal guidance on the matter (Weßels 2011: 14).

However, the new test effectively breaks down the genus of 'gay people' into two groups – those 'living openly' and those 'living discretely'. On a similar finding in *S395/2002*, the Australian High Court stated that 'this inevitably invited error' (*Appellant S395/2002* at [55], 18). The High Court of Australia elaborated:

> Similarly, in this case, consciously or unconsciously, the Tribunal directed its mind principally to the consequences of the sexual behaviour of the nondiscreet members of the particular social group. . . . If the Tribunal had placed the appellants in the non-discreet group, it appears that it would have found that they were likely to be persecuted by reason of their membership of that group. Conversely, by placing the appellants in the discreet group, the Tribunal automatically assumed that they would not suffer persecution. But to attempt to resolve the case by this kind of classification was erroneous.
>
> (*Appellant S395/2002* at [56–58], 18)

The UK Supreme Court in *HJ (Iran) and HT (Cameroon)* correctly insists that the central question is always whether the applicant has a well-founded fear of persecution. However, by reverting to the categories of 'open' and 'discreet' in the new test, the Justices risk falling into error in the same way as is criticised by the Australian High Court. Kirby J convincingly explains the inter-connectedness of the classification applied and the prediction of how the appellant *would* conduct himself on return in the Australian case of *NABD*: 'Without the *a priori* classification ("quiet sharing of one's faith" against "aggressive outreach through proselytizing"), the second Tribunal would not have asked, and decided, the second question of what the appellant *would* do if returned to Iran' (*Applicant NABD of 2002* at [139], 44). In fact, this argument can be taken further in the sense that any question on the applicant's conduct is misleading as it immediately results in 'discretion reasoning'. Rather, the relevant question is whether the applicant – by virtue of his identity – is at risk of persecution irrespective of his own actions.

Particularly problematic is the assumption that persecution exists only for gay people who 'live openly'. This omits the possibility of discovery by accident or against a person's will, i.e. what McHugh and Kirby refer to as the 'future-focused question of what would happen if the applicant were in fact discovered to be gay' (*Appellant S395/2002* per McHugh and Kirby JJ at [18], 6) – and not what the applicant would *do*. Even in those cases where applicants have made great efforts to conceal their sexuality over many years, they are often outed against their will, be it by accident or growing suspicion (Kassisieh 2008: 69). The decision of whether or not to conceal is sometimes out of the applicants' control when friends betray their trust or rumours are circulated (Kassisieh 2008: 70). The High Court of Australia similarly criticised in *S395/2002* that the lower court: '. . . failed to consider whether the appellants might suffer harm if for one reason or another police, hustlers, employers or other persons became aware of their homosexual identity. The perils faced by the appellants were not necessarily confined to their own *conduct*, discreet or otherwise' (*Appellant S395/2002* at [56–58], 18, emphasis added). Accordingly, Kassisieh argues that the chance of disclosure will almost always be real and not remote (Kassisieh 2008: 70). Thus, even where an applicant states that his concealment is due to family or societal pressures, he is as much in risk of persecution when his sexual orientation comes to the knowledge of potential persecutors as someone who had stated that his concealment was partly due to a risk of persecution. The Equality and Human Rights Commission also stresses this point in its intervention: '. . . it would nevertheless be necessary . . . to consider the risks of the individual's same-sex sexual orientation becoming public by some other means, such that persecution would ensue' (Equality and Human Rights Commission 2010: [59 (b)], 37, citing *Appellant S395/2002*). This is also clearly illustrated in the case of HT who had been in a relationship for five years. During this time he had been able to conceal his sexual orientation – until neighbours spotted him kissing his partner in his own garden (*HJ (Iran) and HT (Cameroon)* per Lord Hope at [38]). He was then victim of serious violence by way of mob justice (he was beaten with sticks, stones were thrown at him, his clothes were pulled off and the mob tried to cut off his penis with a knife), and police officers joined in when they arrived at the scene (*HJ (Iran) and HT (Cameroon)* per Lord Rodger at [44]). Hence, the distinction between 'openly' and 'discreetly' gay people is unhelpful. Rather, as UNHCR stated in its intervention, the assessment of the existence of a well-founded fear of persecution in sexuality-based cases 'should be made *without reference* to whether or not the applicants would be discreet about their sexual orientation' (UNHCR 2010 at [25], 13, emphasis added).

3.7 A 'choice' of concealment?

Similarly, the introduction of a further theoretical distinction between 'fear of persecution' and 'fear of some sort of social pressure' is questionable as it forces decision makers to decide on an issue that remains blurry (see Battjes in this volume). Lord Rodger correctly asserts that in a society where gay men are persecuted, it is quite likely that the prevailing culture will be such that some of an applicant's friends, relatives and colleagues would react negatively if they discovered that he was gay. Lord Rodger himself notes that 'unless he were minded to swell the ranks of gay martyrs, when faced with a real threat of persecution, the applicant would have *no real choice*: he would be compelled to act discreetly' (*HJ (Iran) and HT (Cameroon)* per Lord Rodger at [59], emphasis added). He then continues with a leap in his logic that is hard to follow:

> In these circumstances it is *at least possible* that the only real reason for an applicant behaving discreetly would be his *perfectly natural* wish to avoid harming his relationships with his family, friends and colleagues. The Convention does not afford protection against these social pressures, however, and so an applicant cannot claim asylum in order to avoid them. So if, having considered the facts of any individual case, the Secretary of State or a tribunal concluded that the applicant would *choose to behave discreetly* on his return simply to avoid these social pressures, his application for asylum would fall to be rejected. He would not be a refugee within the terms of article 1A(2) of the Convention because, by *choosing to behave discreetly* in order to avoid these social pressures, the applicant would simultaneously *choose to live a life* in which he would have no well-founded fear of being persecuted for reasons of his homosexuality.
> (*HJ (Iran) and HT (Cameroon)* per Lord Rodger at [61], emphasis added)

In this paragraph, although he admits that this is unlikely ('at least possible'), Lord Rodger introduces a scenario of 'natural discretion', which – as a positive side-effect – would also effectively protect the applicant from his risk of persecution. Contrary to the submissions by the Equality and Human Rights Commission, he omits the consequential question of whether there is a real likelihood that the individual's sexual orientation be otherwise exposed (Equality and Human Rights Commission 2010 at [60], 37). Furthermore, Lord Rodger disregards the submission on 'voluntary concealment' provided by the Equality and Human Rights Commission:

> Such cases will be extremely rarely (if ever) encountered in the asylum system since where a claim is made on grounds of sexual orientation that will in itself require a person to 'out' him or herself, at least to a limited extent and in any event a person who voluntarily wants to conceal their same-sex sexual orientation in circumstances where there was no real

likelihood of it being otherwise exposed is self-evidently unlikely to claim asylum on grounds of sexual orientation.

(Equality and Human Rights Commission 2010 at [60], 37–38)

Thus, the assumed 'voluntary choice of discretion' is given a far more prominent role in the new test than such an extremely rare exception would require.

This blurry distinction can be attributed to the correct and necessary attempt by the Supreme Court to distinguish those applicants who are in genuine need for protection from those who are not. However, arguably, the test proposed by the Supreme Court appears contradictory in that it first requires decision makers to be satisfied that 'gay people who lived openly would be liable to persecution in the applicant's country of nationality' and thereafter to determine whether or not concealment may be a personal choice or a reaction to social pressures, even though it was already established that openly gay people are persecuted in that country (*HJ (Iran) and HT (Cameroon)* per Lord Rodger at [82]). Other factors may also play a role in concealment; however, in a country where gay people are persecuted, this fact will always be one decisive element for secrecy.[16] Although it is indisputable that discrimination is not automatically protected by the Convention unless it passes the threshold of persecution, and understandable that the Supreme Court would seek to make that distinction, the manner in which persecution is determined is problematic, as it lends itself to misinterpretations. By assuming that some may 'choose' to live 'discreetly', the Justices follow a similar reasoning as Callinan and Haydon JJ in the Australian case of *Appellant S395/2002*. In their joint dissenting opinion, they present concealment as a 'naturally' occurring state:

On the tribunal's findings, no fear of such harm as could fairly be characterised as persecution imposed a need for any particular discretion on the part of the appellants: such 'discretion' as they exercised, was exercised as a matter of *free choice*. The outcome of these proceedings might have been different – it is unnecessary to decide whether that is so – if that position were different.

(*Appellant S395/2002* at [110], emphasis added)

Lord Rodger does the same in the new UK test as outlined at [82]:

If the tribunal concludes that the applicant would *choose* to live discreetly simply because that was how he himself would wish to live, or because of social pressures, e g, not wanting to distress his parents or embarrass his friends, then his application should be rejected.

(*HJ (Iran) and HT (Cameroon)* at [82], emphasis added)

In the Australian case of *S395/2002*, Callinan and Heydon JJ found that the appellants were not oppressed as their modes of *conduct* were voluntarily chosen (*Appellant S395/2002* at [110]). The Justices placed the burden of responsibility on applicants to claim at first instance, that their lives of secrecy were motivated largely, or even exclusively, by fear of harm.[17] The problem with such reasoning is that if a claimant admits to a 'choice' of discretion, the tribunal may not consider the way this may be a conscious or unconscious reaction to a persecutory environment (Kassisieh 2008: 68). The decision to conceal one's sexual identity may be made out of fear or for more subtle reasons (Kassisieh 2008: 70). These may certainly often include those reasons cited by the Justices, such as 'social pressures, e.g. not wanting to distress his parents or embarrass his friends'. However, this 'decision' is hardly really freely decided, rather it is impelled by the constraints of an actual or perceived homophobic environment (Kassisieh 2008: 70). This point is supported by Kirby J, who draws attention to the 'error of postulating self-censorship' in the Australian case of *NABD*:

> The fundamental error of the second Tribunal in this case is similar to that identified by this Court in *Appellant S395*. It lay in the second Tribunal's conclusion that 'a distinction can be drawn' between 'the quiet sharing of one's faith' and aggressive proselytising and in its stated belief that, if returned to Iran, the appellant would adhere to the former classification and avoid the latter, not because of fear of persecution by the Iranian authorities but because that was the kind of Christianity he had accepted.
>
> (*Applicant NABD of 2002* at [139], 44)

Arguably, the same error is bound to be committed in the application of the new test as suggested by the Justices in *HJ (Iran) and HT (Cameroon)*. Kirby J further elaborates that the 'choice' is given meaning by reference to the peril the appellant would face if he were to 'choose' any other course. Viewed within the context of the new test, the prediction of what would in fact occur in the future is clearly based on the immediately preceding acknowledgement that any hope that a gay person would be let alone is dependent on a willingness to *behave* 'discreetly' (*Applicant NABD of 2002* at [103–104], 33, emphasis added). Instead, as was submitted by the Equality and Human Rights Commission in its intervention, the focus should rather be on the question of whether the person seeking refuge will on return continue to be part of the relevant protected class, i.e. *identity* (Equality and Human Rights Commission 2010 at [70], 41).

Thus, in practice, although under the new test the fear of harm need no longer be the only or even main reason for concealment, applicants will have to convince decision makers that 'a material reason' for their concealment will be their fear of persecution – unless decision makers are satisfied that the appellant will in fact 'live openly' (*HJ (Iran) and HT (Cameroon)* per Lord Rodger at [62] and at [82]). According to Lord Rodger, the central question will be whether the reality is that, if he were returned to his country of nationality, in addition to any other reasons for behaving discreetly, he would have to behave 'discreetly' in order to avoid persecution because of being gay (*HJ (Iran) and HT (Cameroon)* at [62]) (after it was found that 'openly gay' people would be persecuted in his country of origin). While this appears to respond to the criticism voiced in the earlier Australian case of *S395/2002*, as it now considers the reason which motivates concealment, it effectively changes little. The test continues to place the burden on applicants to claim at first instance that their concealment is motivated – if only in part – by fear of persecution. In the recent UK case of *SW Jamaica*, the applicant was in fact able to convince the court, which was 'impressed' by the 'calm and credible witness', that she 'would not return to living discreetly, whatever the risk' (*SW Jamaica v Secretary of State for the Home Department*, CG [2011] UKUT 00251(IAC), Upper Tribunal (Immigration and Asylum Chamber), United Kingdom, 24 June 2011 at [120]). The court further found that if this finding were wrong and the following question of the test had to be considered, the appellant was not 'naturally discreet' and any return to 'discreet living' would be by reason of her fear of persecution rather than by reason of social pressures (*SW Jamaica* at [121]). This application of the test shows that while this applicant was found to be a credible witness and able to convince the court that she would in fact not conceal her sexual orientation in spite of the existing risk, the new test continues to be centred on 'discretion logic' and the activities the decision makers expect the applicant to conduct.

3.8 The state of mind: the role of the subjective element

The test goes even a step further. Not only does it focus on the expected future conduct of the applicant, but it also requires decision makers to inquire into the reasons for this expected behaviour. The proposed distinction between 'discretion out of fear' and 'discretion for social pressures' relies wholly on an evaluation of the state of mind, or the so-called 'subjective element', of the applicant. However, the relevance of the 'subjective element' in the refugee definition is disputed. Lord Hope began his examination of the case *HJ (Iran) and HT (Cameroon)* by considering whether the case before him was based on a 'well-founded fear of being persecuted for reasons of sexual orientation'. This, in the view of Lord Hope, includes an assessment of the situation in the country of origin of the applicant as well as of the 'state of mind' of the individual: 'It is the fear which that person has that must be examined and shown to be well-founded' (*HJ (Iran) and HT (Cameroon)* per Lord Hope at [17]).

Indeed, the concept of 'fear' is the relevant motive for defining refugees (UNHCR 1992: 37). The UNHCR *Handbook* as well as the academic debate and case law commonly distinguish between a subjective and an objective element of 'well-founded fear'. However, this separation is contested. Several authors have pointed out that the distinction is never clearly made. Gregor

Noll harshly criticises the division of 'well-founded fear' into a subjective fear and an objective well-foundedness element, drawing attention to the risks and confusion caused by this language (Noll 2005). He argues that 'fear' pure and simple is inaccessible in the procedure. Correctly, according to Noll, the protection seeker will provide evidence on his or her 'well-founded fear' as a totality (Noll 2005: 146). A fragmentation augments the total burden of proof and burden of persuasion (Noll 2005: 148). Moreover, Noll holds that the separation of 'subjective' and 'objective' credibility transforms the assessment of fear into an assessment of trepidation, which will typically lead to an exercise of parapsychology. This has also been criticised by Hathaway and Hicks: 'there is simply no principled way for decision makers to evaluate an applicant's state of mind for evidence of trepidation' (Hathaway and Hicks 2005: 509). As Grahl-Madsen puts it: 'Every person claiming . . . to be a refugee has "fear" ("well-founded" or otherwise) of being persecuted . . . irrespective of whether he jitters at the very thought of his return to his home country, is prepared to brave all hazards, or is simply apathetic or even unconscious of the possible dangers' (Grahl-Madsen 1966: 174). Noll concludes that the UNHCR *Handbook* approach to well-founded fear 'succeeds merely in augmenting the range of state discretion rather than the force of law' (Noll 2005: 151). The introduction of a break-down into an 'open' and a 'discreet' group and then again, and particularly, into a subgroup of those 'discreet out of fear' and those 'discreet for other reasons' does precisely that: it requires an exercise of parapsychology which effectively augments the range of personal discretion of the decision maker.

It is in this line that Hathaway and Hicks argue that while there is general agreement that a fear is 'well-founded' only if the refugee claimant faces an actual, forward-looking risk of being persecuted in her country of origin, it is less clear whether the well-founded fear standard also requires a showing of that the applicant is not only genuinely at risk, but also stands in trepidation of being persecuted (Hathaway and Hicks 2005: 506). 'Under such an approach, persons whose fear is readily recognised as such by decision makers, as well as those who are simply more demonstrative, will be advantaged in securing refugee status for reasons that have nothing to do with the actual risk faced' (Hathaway and Hicks 2005: 509). Kagan makes a similar point when he suggests that a Tutsi fleeing Rwanda in 1994, with an invented and entirely false refugee claim, could still establish a well-founded fear of being persecuted due to independent evidence of her ethnic identity combined with evidence of ongoing ethnic genocide (Kagan 2003: 370). He states that allowing a central part of refugee status determination to be essentially subjective generates serious doubts about the fairness and effectiveness of the adjudication system (Kagan 2003: 377). Grahl-Madsen equally argues that 'the adjective "well-founded" suggests that it is not the frame of mind of the person concerned which is decisive for his claim to refugeehood, but that his claim should be measured with a more objective yardstick. . . . In fact. . . the frame of mind of the individual hardly matters at all' (Grahl-Madsen 1966: 174).

Thus, while the term 'fear' in Article 1A(2) clearly imposes an obligation on states to include the applicant's own risk assessment into the evidence (Noll 2005: 158), the emphasis on the state of mind of the applicant concerning his motives for concealment in the test proposed in *HJ (Iran) and HT (Cameroon)* implies an impractical approach and really only appears to increase the range of discretion for decision makers. Hence, this test offers a sort of 'loophole' that lends itself to abuse as a basis for negative asylum decisions.

3.9 Concluding remarks

The case *HJ (Iran) and HT (Cameroon)* was received as a fundamental shift in refugee law. Indeed, this decision represents a great achievement in the development of refugee law with relation to sexual orientation: it abolishes 'discretion reasoning' in the form of a 'reasonably tolerable' test, which was long overdue. Upon closer examination, however, it becomes clear that in fact the change contained in the new test may not be quite as radical as it first seems: 'Discretion' slips in again through the back door of 'voluntary discretion', based on the continuation of an is/does dichotomy.

In this chapter, after an overview of the cases of *HJ (Iran)* and *HT (Cameroon)* and the application of the 'reasonably tolerable test', the new test as proposed by the Justices in *HJ (Iran) and HT (Cameroon)* was outlined. The consequent analysis of the new test has shown that the main achievement of the case is the rejection of the 'reasonable tolerable reasoning'. However, the examination also showed that the new test does not reject 'discretion' (as it continues to be referred to) as a concept in asylum decisions as a whole. On the contrary, the new test is in fact still based on a 'discretion logic'. By distinguishing between gay people 'living openly' and gay people 'living discreetly', the test is constructed around concealment and thus a distinction between status and acts. This approach relies on the assumption that of two distinguishable behaviours – 'open' vs. 'discreet' – only the former is liable to persecution. The existence of such a distinction in the eyes of potential persecutors remains questionable, and the approach is blind towards the future-focused question of what will happen if the applicant is indeed 'discovered' to be gay. Moreover, the 'discretion logic' of this test assumes that there may be a 'free choice' of concealment, disregarding the constraints that the persecutory environment imposes on the applicant. The problematic assumption that individuals freely exert a 'choice of concealment' results in the decision maker having to evaluate the motivations for concealment. This is not only practically prohibitive but also places an undue emphasis on the so-called subjective element in the form of an assessment of trepidation.

Hence, upon closer examination, the test which the Supreme Court recommends tribunals and Courts of Appeal to apply, risks coming down to a backward return to 'discretion'. By assuming that only 'gay people who lived openly' would be liable to persecution, the Court is able to conclude that those 'choosing' to be 'discreet' are not at risk. However, this 'discretion' by 'choice' is effectively imposed. If returned, the applicant will *be impelled* to conceal his sexual orientation in order to avoid harm. Consequently, the 'discretion logic' entails several complicated issues that distract decision makers from the actual inquiry, which is whether the applicant has a well-founded fear of persecution. Concealment has no place in this inquiry, not even as a 'positive side-effect' that would presumably provide protection from persecution, as was proposed in this case.

Moreover, the new test might lead to a higher standard of proof in sexuality-based asylum cases. Not only will the claimant have to show that he is indeed gay, which is connected to a wide range of obstacles, particularly where the applicant has had to conceal his sexual orientation in the past, but also that precisely this concealment is not voluntarily chosen but constrained by his genuine fear.

Overall, it appears that the Supreme Court continued to revert to 'discretion' as a variable in sexuality-based asylum cases in spite of the advice to the contrary given by numerous authorities. Concealment should play no role. In order to avoid misapplications linked to the distinction between 'discreet' and 'open' behaviour, Kirby J suggests:

> Following the decision in *Appellant S395*, it is necessary to rid this area of decisional discourse of the supposed dichotomy between applicants for protection visas who might be able to avoid or diminish the risks of persecution by conducting themselves 'discreetly' in denial of their fundamental human rights and those who assert those rights or who might deliberately or even accidentally manifest them, or be thought or alleged to have done so.
>
> (*Applicant NABD of 2002* per Kirby J at [143], 45)

Just as Kirby J proposes that 'the most effective way that this Court [the Australian High Court] can ensure that this untextual, irrelevant and undesirable dichotomy is deleted from refugee decisions in Australia is by the insistence that, where it surfaces, the outcome is set aside and the matter remitted for reconsideration, freed from such error' (*Applicant NABD of 2002* per Kirby J at [143], 45), a decision by the Court of Justice of the European Union (CJEU) that clearly rules out any such dichotomy in sexuality-based decisions would be a useful way to prevent misguided negative decisions on these grounds. While one reference to the CJEU by a German High Administrative Court in the case of *Kashayar Khavand* on the interpretation of sexual orientation in the EU Qualification Directive (Council Directive 2004/83/EC) had been withdrawn in 2011[18], the Dutch Raad van State lodged a similar reference in the case of *Z v Minister voor Immigratie en Asiel* on 27 April 2012.[19] This case provides a great opportunity for the CJEU to take a clear stance against any requirement or acceptance of concealment as an effective protection from persecution.

Thus, while it is yet unclear how the new test will be applied, lower courts must be encouraged to read it in a way that adheres to the Convention. This includes an awareness of the several pitfalls it contains, in particular linked to the impermissible and artificial classification of 'open' and 'discreet' claimants. While concealment remains a defining variable in this test, when assessing the well-founded fear of a claimant, decision makers should undertake a very careful analysis of the case, and keep in mind that not only does concealment vis-à-vis sexual orientation not provide reliable protection from persecution but also that concealment for reasons completely unrelated to fear of persecution in persecutory environments will be extremely rare and should rather be treated as hypothetical.

In the meantime, this new test demonstrates that there is a need for further reflection on the relationship between and the role of status and acts in refugee determination. The question of what the claimant will do on return, that is, whether the claimant will *behave* secretively or openly, touches on the much broader question of the scope of protection in refugee law, as Hathaway and Pobjoy demonstrate in their piece. In their view, the approach put forward by the Australian High Court in *S395* and the UK Supreme Court in *HJ (Iran) and HT (Cameroon)*, looking at the question of what a claimant will do on return 'risks fracturing the normative consensus upon which the Refugee Convention is based' (Hathaway and Pobjoy 2012: 335). The analysis in the present chapter supports this position though in a substantially different way than that intended by the authors: Whereas Hathaway and Pobjoy conclude that in order to interpret the nexus clause in line with the scope of international non-discrimination law, there is a need to make a distinction between protected and unprotected activities, this chapter comes to the opposite conclusion, finding that the question of what the applicant will *do* on return indeed fractures the normative consensus of the Convention because it discriminates between Convention grounds and entails a series of impermissible distinctions. The case of *HJ (Iran) and HT (Cameroon)* thus underlines the need for further debate on the role of the is/does dichotomy in order to finally overcome 'discretion' in refugee status determinations.

3.10 Notes

* Janna Weßels is a Quentin Bryce Scholar, University of Technology, Sydney. She holds an MSc in Forced Migration from the Refugee Studies Centre, University of Oxford and is co-founder and Vice Chair of the Oxford Monitor of Forced Migration. The author is grateful to Paul Weßels, Tai Sayarath, Clara Straimer and S. Chelvan as well as the participants of the Fleeing Homophobia Conference that took place in Amsterdam on 5–6 September 2011 for their helpful comments on earlier drafts of this chapter.

Another version of this chapter has been published by Oxford University Press: Weßels, J., '*HJ (Iran) and HT (Cameroon)* – Reflections on a new test for sexuality-based asylum claims in Britain' (2012) 24 *International Journal of Refugee Law* 815–839

1 This was especially true for early decisions, such as in *Matter of Toboso-Alfonso*, A-23220644, United States Board of Immigration Appeals, 12 March 1990: 'The government's actions against him were not in response to specific conduct on his part (e.g. for engaging in homosexual acts); rather, they resulted simply from his status as a homosexual'.

2 In this chapter, the terms 'to conceal', 'concealment' or 'secretive' will be used rather than the euphemistic expression of 'discretion' when referring to the hiding of a protected characteristic. The term 'discretion' is only used in quotation marks when referring precisely to its euphemistic character. Also, see the discussion of terms below.

3 See also the chapter by Hemme Battjes in this volume, who analyses 'discretion' in a more general context.

4 *Cf HJ (Iran) v Secretary of State for the Home Department; HT (Cameroon) v Secretary of State for the Home Department* [2009] EWCA Civ 172, Court of Appeal (England and Wales), 10 March 2009; *HJ (Iran) v Secretary of State for the Home Department;* [2008] UKAIT 00044, United Kingdom: Asylum and Immigration Tribunal/ Immigration Appellate Authority, 10 May 2008, *J v Secretary of State for the Home Department* [2006] EWCA Civ 1238, Court of Appeal (England and Wales), 26 July 2006; On Appeal from the Asylum and Immigration Tribunal (AIT NO. HX/44557/2002).

5 Note, however, that the complexities of this new test cannot be fully grasped without considering the procedural difficulties that both credibility assessment and Country of Origin Information imply. For a discussion, see for example Thomas (2006: 79–96); Macklin (1998); McGhee (2000: 29–50); Coffey (2003: 377–417); Dauvergne and Millbank (2003b: 299–342); Weßels (2011).

6 See on this case, Dauvergne and Millbank (2003a: 97–124).

7 Note that in *Appeal No 74665/03*, a case in New Zealand from 2004, Haines QC agrees with this rejection, arguing: 'By requiring the refugee applicant to abandon a core right the refugee decision maker is requiring of the refugee claimant the same submissive and compliant behaviour, the same denial of a fundamental human right, which the agent of persecution in the country of origin seeks to achieve by persecutory conduct', *Refugee Appeal No. 74665*, Refugee Status Appeals Authority, New Zealand, 7 July 2004.

8 See also *HJ (Iran) and HT (Cameroon)* at [102].

9 For example, Sachs J of the Constitutional Court of South Africa in *National Coalition for Gay and Lesbian Equality and Another v Minister of Justice and Others*, Case CCT 11/98, Constitutional Court, South Africa, 9 October 1998; the German Bundesverwaltungsgericht compared sexual orientation with 'race' and 'nationality' in an early case: *Bundesverwaltungsgericht, Urteil vom 15.03.1988 –* BVerwG 9 C 278.86, Bundesverwaltungsgericht, Germany, 15 March 1988, at 11–12; in Canada a comparison was found with the request to practise the official state religion in public and one's own faith only in private or carrying false identification and 'passing' for someone of another race or nationality in: XMU (Re), T94-06899 [1995] C.R.D.D. 146, IRB Canada, 23 January 1995. Note that even the UNHCR *Handbook* rejects discretion in the case of political opinion (UNHCR 1992: para. 82).

10 E.g. 'no one would suggest a racial minority should bleach their skin to avoid the threat of serious harm, or otherwise hide their ethnic origins by ceasing contact with loved ones or denying language and history' (*Hysi v Secretary of Stat for the*

Home Department [2005] EWCA Civ 711, United Kingdom, Court of Appeal (England and Wales), 15 June 2005 at [33]–[34]).

11 Note, however, that 'discretion' was in issue in relation to religion in: *Applicant NABD of 2002 v Minister for Immigration and Multicultural and Indigenous Affairs* [2005] HCA 29 High Court, Australia, 26 May 2005. The case is referred to below.

12 'It is convenient to use a phrase such as "acting" or "behaving" "discreetly" to describe what the applicant would do to avoid persecution. But in truth he could do various things. To take a few examples. At the most extreme, the applicant might live a life of complete celibacy. Alternatively, he might form relationships only within a circle of acquaintances whom he could trust not to reveal to others that he had gay relationships. Or, he might have a gay partner, but never live with him or have him to stay overnight or indulge in any display of affection in public. Or the applicant might have only fleeting anonymous sexual contacts, as a safe opportunity presented itself. The gradations are infinite' (*HJ (Iran) and HT (Cameroon)* per Lord Rodger at [63]).

13 'At the most basic level, if a male applicant were to live discreetly, he would in practice have to avoid any open expression of affection for another man which went beyond what would be acceptable behaviour on the part of a straight man. He would have to be cautious about the friendships he formed, the circle of friends in which he moved, the places where he socialised. He would have constantly to restrain himself in an area where powerful emotions and physical attraction are involved and a straight man could be spontaneous, impulsive even. Not only would he not be able to indulge openly in the mild flirtations which are an enjoyable part of heterosexual life, but he would have to think twice before revealing that he was attracted to another man. Similarly, the small tokens and gestures of affection which are taken for granted between men and women could well be dangerous. In short, his potential for finding happiness in some sexual relationship would be profoundly affected. It is objectionable to assume that any gay man can be supposed to find even these restrictions on his life and happiness reasonably tolerable' (*HJ (Iran) and HT (Cameroon)* per Lord Rodger at [77]).

14 Note, however, that when outlining the new test in his own words, Lord Hope states that 'it would be wrong to approach the issue on the basis that the purpose of the Convention is to guarantee to an applicant who is gay that he can live *as freely and as openly as a gay person* as he would be able to do if he were not returned' (*HJ (Iran) and HT (Cameroon)* per Lord Hope at [35] (c)).

15 Note that jurisdictional error has a particular location in Australian constitutional law: 'If . . . an administrative tribunal falls into an error of law which causes it to identify a wrong issue, to ask itself a wrong question, to ignore relevant material, to rely on irrelevant material or, at least in some circumstances, to make an erroneous finding or to reach a mistaken conclusion, and the tribunal's exercise or purported exercise of power is thereby affected, it exceeds its authority or powers. Such an error of law is jurisdictional error which will invalidate any order or decision of the tribunal which reflects it', Australian High Court in *Craig v South Australia* (1995) 184 CLR 163 at [179].

16 Except, maybe, in very particular cases as suggested by the Equality and Human Rights Commission (see above).

17 This position was also adopted in *Z v Secretary of State for the Home Department* [2004] EWCA Civ 1578, Court of Appeal (England and Wales), 2 December 2004,

where the Court of Appeal found that the applicant had not provided evidence to support discretion out of fear. See also, Millbank 2009: 396.

18 Case C-563/10, [2011] OJ C 38/7, 2011/C 38/09, 5 February 2011. The claimant was granted refugee status because his full name had been published.

19 Minister voor Immigratee en Asiel v XYZ (Cases C-199/12, C-200/12 and C-201/12) [2012] OJ C 217/7, 21 July 2012.

3.11 References

Battjes, H. (2011) 'Accommodation. Sur place claims and the accommodation requirement in Dutch asylum policy', papers for the Fleeing Homophobia Conference VU University Amsterdam, 5 and 6 September 2011.

Bundestags-Drucksache 17/1722. Response to a parliamentary query from 18 May 2010, available at: http://dip21.bundestag.de/dip21/btd/17/017/1701722.pdf (accessed 11 March 2012).

Coffey, G. (2003) 'The credibility of credibility evidence at the Refugee Review Tribunal', *International Journal of Refugee Law*, 15: 377–417.

Dauvergne, C. and Millbank, J. (2003a) 'Before the High Court: applicants S396/2002 and S395/2002, a gay refugee couple from Bangladesh', *Sydney Law Review*, 25: 97–124.

Dauvergne, C. and Millbank, J. (2003b) 'Burdened by proof – how the Australian Refugee Review Tribunal has failed lesbian and gay asylum seekers', *Federal Law Review*, 31: 299–342.

Equality and Human Rights Commission (2010) *HJ (Iran) and HT (Cameroon) v Secretary of State for the Home Department – Case for the Equality and Human Rights Commission.*

Grahl-Madsen, Atle (1966) *The Status of Refugees in International Law* (Foreword by Felix Schnyder), Leyden: A. W. Sijthoff.

Hathaway, J.C. and Pobjoy, J. (2012) 'Queer cases make bad law', *New York Journal of International Law and Politics*, 44(2): 315–388.

Hathaway, J.C. and Hicks, W. (2005) 'Is there a subjective element in the Refugee Convention's requirement of well-founded fear?', *Michigan Journal of International Law*, 26: 505–562.

International Commission of Jurists (2007) *Yogyakarta Principles on the Application of International Human Rights Law in Relation to Sexual Orientation and Gender Identity*, 6 March 2007, available at http://www.yogyakartaprinciples.org/principles_en.pdf (accessed 7 April 2010).

Jansen, S. and Spijkerboer, T. (2011) *Fleeing Homophobia, Asylum Claims Related to Sexual Orientation and Gender Identity in Europe*, COC Netherlands and VU University Amsterdam, available at http://www.rechten.vu.nl/nl/onderzoek/conferenties-en-projecten/onderzoeksproject-fleeing-homophobia/index.asp (accessed 9 December 2012).

Kagan, M. (2003) 'Is truth in the eye of the beholder? Objective credibility assessment in refugee status determination', *Georgetown Immigration Law Journal*, 17: 367–415.

Kassisieh, G. (2008) *From Lives of Fear to Lives of Freedom: A Review of Australian Refugee Decisions on the Basis of Sexual Orientation*, Glebe: Gay & Lesbian Rights Lobby.

LaViolette, N. (1997) 'The immutable refugees: sexual orientation in Canada (A.G.) v. Ward', *University of Toronto Faculty Law Review*, 55(1): 1–42.

Law Center (NI) (2011) Information Briefing, March 2011: 'HJ (Iran): A fundamental shift in asylum law', available at http://www.lawcentreni.org/Publications/Law Centre Information Briefings/HJIranMarch2011.pdf (accessed 12 August 2011).

Macklin, A. (1998) 'Truth and consequences: credibility determination in the refugee context', paper for the conference, *International Association of Refugee Law Judges*, Ottawa, Canada, 14–16 October 1998.

McGhee, D. (2000) 'Accessing homosexuality: truth, evidence and the legal practices for determining refugee status – the case of Ioan Vraciu', *Body and Society*, 6(1): 29–50.

Millbank, J. (2012) 'The right of lesbians and gay men to live freely and openly is not bad law: a reply to Hathaway and Pobjoy', *New York Journal of International Law and Politics*, 44(2): 497–529.

Millbank, J. (2009) 'From discretion to disbelief: recent trends in refugee determinations on the basis of sexual orientation in Australia and the United Kingdom', *The International Journal of Human Rights*, 13(2/3): 391–414.

Millbank, J. (2005) 'A preoccupation with perversion: the British response to refugee claims on the basis of sexual orientation 1989–2003', *Social Legal Studies*, 14(1): 115–138.

Noll, G. (2005) 'Evidentiary assessment under the Refugee Convention: risk, pain and the intersubjectivity of fear', in G. Noll (ed.) *Proof, Evidentiary Assessment and Credibility in Asylum Procedures*, Leiden: Martinus Nijhoff.

O'Dwyer, P. (2008) 'A well-founded fear of having my sexual orientation claim heard in the wrong court', *New York School Law Review*, 52: 185–212.

Supreme Court of the United Kingdom (2010) *Press Summary. HJ (Iran) and HT (Cameroon) v Secretary of State for the Home Department {2010} UKSC 31. On Appeal from: {2009} EWCA Civ 172.*

Thomas, R. (2006) 'Assessing the credibility of asylum claims: EU and UK approaches examined', *European Journal of Migration and Law*, 8: 79–96.

UN High Commissioner for Refugees (UNHCR) (2011) *UNHCR's Comments on the Practice of Phallometry in the Czech Republic to Determine the Credibility of Asylum Claims based on Persecution due to Sexual Orientation*, April 2011, available at http://www.unhcr.org/refworld/docid/4daeb07b2.html (accessed 15 August 2011).

UN High Commissioner for Refugees (UNHCR) (2010) *HJ (Iran) and HT (Cameroon) v. Secretary of State for the Home Department – Case for the first intervener (the United Nations High Commissioner for Refugees)*, 19 April 2010.

UN High Commissioner for Refugees (UNHCR) (2008) *UNHCR Guidance Note on Refugee Claims Relating to Sexual Orientation and Gender Identity*, Geneva: Protection Policy and Legal Advice Section.

UN High Commissioner for Refugees (UNHCR) (1992) *Handbook on Procedures and Criteria for Determining Refugee Status under the 1951 Convention and the 1967 Protocol relating to the Status of Refugees*, HCR/IP/4/Eng/REV.1, September 1979, re-edited January 1992, Geneva: UNHCR.

Weßels, J. (2011) 'Sexual orientation in refugee status determination', *RSC Working Paper series No. 74*, Oxford: Refugee Studies Centre.

4 Accommodation

Sur place claims and the accommodation requirement in Dutch asylum policy

*Hemme Battjes**

4.1 Introduction

In many jurisdictions, applications for asylum by persons who state they fear persecution or risk ill-treatment because of their sexual orientation are refused on the ground that these persons should accommodate, hide their orientation, in order to escape persecution or ill-treatment. At first sight, Dutch asylum policy is different. The Aliens Circular states that as far as appeal to the 1951 United Nations Convention Relating to the Status of Refugees (the Refugee Convention) is concerned, 'persons with a homosexual orientation are not required to hide this orientation after return'.[1] On a closer look, it appears that accommodation is being required, in case of *sur place* claims. A *sur place* claim is an appeal to (for present purposes) the Refugee Convention or Article 3 of the European Convention on Human Rights (ECHR) based on events or circumstances that came up after the applicant left the country of origin. Thus, it concerns new events: either some new event in the country of origin, or a new protected characteristic dating from after the flight (for example, a conversion talking place in the Netherlands). In such cases, accommodation is being required. Obviously, the sexual orientation or gender of the asylum seeker usually is not a new event that occurred after arrival; rather, it is the public expression of the orientation there after having hidden it in the country of origin. But as we see, in cases where lesbian, gay, bisexual or transgender (LGBT) asylum seekers had to hide their orientation in the country of origin, their wish to live in the open is also assessed as a *sur place* event. There may be much to say against this practice of treating public expression of a previously hidden protected characteristic as a new, *sur place* event. But as this practice exists in the Netherlands (and elsewhere), I discuss how such cases should be dealt with if they are framed as *sur place* cases.

I address the assessment of *sur place* claims in Dutch asylum policy and case law, and discuss whether it is in accordance with the Refugee Convention and with the ECHR. As the number of Dutch cases on *sur place* claims by LGBT people is relatively small, I address also other *sur place* claims where accommodation is discussed, in particular claims by Afghan women who adopted a so-called westernized lifestyle in the Netherlands, and by Muslims who converted in the Netherlands to a Christian denomination that requires them to convert others. To these categories, more or less the same applies: the Aliens Circular states that applicants are not required to hide their westernized lifestyle or affiliation to a minority religion, but at the same time accommodation is required if it concerns *sur place* claims.[2]

When interpreting the Refugee Convention, I apply (next to the rules laid down in the Vienna Convention on the Law of Treaties) both the UNHCR *Handbook* and Guidelines and the EU Qualification Directive as authoritative, hence not necessarily correct interpretations.[3] Apart from Dutch case law, I discuss a few foreign cases – not pretending to present a comparative overview, but because those cases present valuable arguments for discussing the Refugee Convention. As to the ECHR, I simply follow the European Court of Human Rights.

I first discuss whether the Refugee Convention or Article 3 of the ECHR state special requirements as to *sur place* claims (para. 4.2). Then I address the accommodation requirement in Dutch asylum law (para. 4.3). This requirement is then tested to Article 3 of the ECHR and the Refugee Convention (paras 4.4 and 4.5). I end with a number of concluding observations (para. 4.6).

4.2 *Sur place* refugees

According to Article 1A(2) of the Refugee Convention, a person is a refugee who has 'well founded fear of being persecuted for reasons of . . . religion . . . membership of a particular social group or political opinion, is outside the country of his nationality and is unable or, owing to such fear, is unwilling to avail himself of the protection of that country'.[4] By employing the term 'fear' the definition is future-oriented, addressing the chance or risk of future persecution.[5] Past persecution or past threats of persecution are relevant if they support the well-foundedness of the fear,[6] but they are not required by the provision. Hence, the possibility of becoming a refugee *sur place* seems to flow from the refugee definition: whether events took place before or after departure from the state of origin is in itself not relevant for the risk of future harm. Both the UNHCR *Handbook* and the EU Qualification Directive confirm that a person may become a refugee *sur place*.[7]

It is useful to distinguish two types of *sur place* situations. First, events in the country of origin take place after the alien departed. The classic example is the revolution or coup causing well-founded fear with the ambassador abroad of the old regime of being persecuted by the new regime.[8] Second, the fear of being persecuted is due to activities employed by the alien after he or she arrived in the country of refuge. A classic example is participation in an oppositional meeting before the embassy of the country of origin, thus attracting negative attention from the authorities of the country of origin.[9] This second type of *sur place* claim is more common, at least in the Netherlands, and is looked upon with much more suspicion than the first situation.

A radical expression of this suspicion can be found in an *obiter dictum* in a case decided by the *Bundesverwaltungsgericht*, the highest German instance on asylum, from 2008. Interestingly, the *Bundesverwaltungsgericht* suggests that the refugee definition itself excludes the second type of claim:

> First of all, it already appears doubtful whether fear of persecution within the meaning of Art. 1A of the GC can exist at all in cases of risk-free provocation of persecution in a host country. [. . .; I]t does not appear that one must necessarily conclude [. . .] that, without legal limitation, post-flight reasons created by the individual himself can [. . .] provide grounds for refugee status – albeit subject to the proviso of a careful examination of the circumstances [. . .]. Against this position, it is argued that the 'events' within the meaning of Art. 1A (2) of the GC always pertain to events within the home country, not actions by the concerned individual in the host country [. . .]. Moreover, at the time when the Convention was signed, the treaty states did not wish to forgo the ability to regulate the political activities of foreigners, and to expel foreigners if such activity nevertheless took place; yet Art. 33 of the GC would have deprived them of this option if even post-flight reasons created by the individual himself could provide grounds for refugee status. Nor does the practice of nations provide any indication to the contrary [. . .]. There is even less of an argument that postflight reasons created by the individual himself should be incorporated within the scope of protection of Art. 1A GC if the circumstances represent an abusive claim on the protection provided under the Convention.[10]

Is the *Bundesverwaltungsgericht* right and should we conclude that both the UNHCR *Handbook* and the EU Qualification Directive offer an incorrect, or at least overly wide reading of the refugee definition? Arguably, the approach to treaty interpretation in the German case is flawed. Treaty interpretation must be based on the text of the provision, changes included, read in the light of purpose and objective. In the original version of the Refugee Convention, Article 1A(2) defined as a refugee any person who '[a]s a result of events occurring before 1 January 1951 and owing to well-founded fear' of persecution was unable or unwilling to avail himself of the protection of the country of origin. The states party to the Protocol of New York of 1967, including Germany and all other member states of the EU, agreed that 'the term "refugee" shall [. . .] mean any person within the definition of article 1 of the Convention as if the words "As a result of events occurring before 1 January 1951 and . . ." "and the words" . . . "a result of such events", in article 1 A (2) were omitted'.[11] Hence, the term 'events' is no longer part of the text that must be interpreted; accordingly, the refugee definition in the EU Qualification Directive does not mention it.[12] The text of the refugee definition therefore does not offer any ground for a temporal restriction on events relevant for status determination, as suggested by the *Bundesverwaltungsgericht*.

The intention of the contracting parties to regulate political activities of foreigners assumed by the *Bundesverwaltungsgericht* has not been expressed in the text of the Refugee Convention, so this assumption is presumably based on the *travaux preparatoirs*. These play no role here, as they can at best confirm a reading based on text and context.[13] The reference to state practice is not substantiated with empirical evidence. On the contrary, if we take the EU Qualification Directive as (partial) codification of state practice, Article 5(2) of this instrument shows that the assumption is simply wrong.[14] In sum, there is no reason to conclude that the Refugee Convention excludes *sur place* claims.

But in a somewhat diluted form the position of the *Bundesverwaltungsgericht*, (no refugee status in case of 'abusive claims' based on activities in the country of refuge), can indeed be traced in the EU Qualification Directive. It states that refugee status can be denied, or alternatively benefits for recognised refugees can be reduced, 'if the risk of persecution is based on circumstances which the applicant has created by his own decision since leaving the country of origin'.[15] Arguably, application of these provisions would be at variance with the Refugee Convention. Those who qualify for refugee status pursuant to Article 1 are entitled to the benefits set out in Articles 2–34 under the conditions mentioned in those provisions. Neither creating refugee status nor abuse are among those conditions (Battjes 2006: 448–466; Hathaway 2005).

Like the refugee definition, the prohibition on refoulement in Article 3 of the ECHR is future oriented: it prohibits expulsion in case of real risk that the alien will be submitted to ill-treatment after expulsion. Temporal limitations to risk assessment do not fit in. The case law by the European Court of Human Rights confirms this. An example is *N v Sweden*, which concerned a second application for asylum by an Afghan woman for the most part based on the consequences of a petition for a divorce submitted in Sweden.[16] The Court deemed this *sur place* event (i.e. the marriage in Sweden) relevant for the assessment of the claim of violation of Article 3; expulsion turned out to be a violation of Article 3 (see further para. 4.4). In another case the Court did not deem relevant that the applicant had deliberately tried to bring his *sur place* activities to the attention of the authorities of the country of origin.[17]

So, neither the Refugee Convention nor the ECHR gives reason to deny relevance to events or activities that occurred or were engaged in after departure from the country of origin when assessing an application for asylum. Neither the moment the event took place nor the intention for engaging in the activity is relevant. Arguably, assessment of *sur place* cases and those of others may still differ for other reasons. To begin with, the applicant cannot invoke the rule of Article 4(4) of the EU Qualification Directive, which states that past persecution or harm warrants the assumption of future persecution or harm. And the credibility of *sur place* claims may beg its own questions (Van Halder 2010; Musalo 2004). But if the sexual orientation or conversion to Christianity or the adaptation to a western lifestyle has been established, there is no reason to state further requirements on credibility or otherwise because of the *sur place* character.

Still, Dutch asylum law did so until recently by requiring 'continuity'. *Sur place* activities could, according to the Aliens Circular, only provide grounds for recognition of refugee status if they were a continuation of activities performed in the country of origin.[18] This requirement did not apply to claims to Article 3 of the ECHR. As a consequence, it is the latter provision that has been mostly invoked in *sur place* claims over the last few years.[19]

But in January 2010 the Council of State (the highest judicial authority in asylum cases) ruled that requiring continuity was at variance with Article 5(2) of the EU Qualification Directive, which states that well-founded fear (or real risk) can be based on *sur place* activities, 'in particular', if these activities are the continuation of beliefs held before departure from the country of origin.[20] The requirement of continuity hence no longer applies its old form. But the Council of State addressed in its ruling only the text of Article 5(2) of the EU Qualification Directive; it did not address object and purpose of Article 1 of the Refugee Convention. The ruling therefore does not mean that a temporal exclusion clause in some other context would be at odds with the refugee definition.

4.3 Accommodation in Dutch case law

And indeed a requirement with effects comparable to the old continuity requirement is being applied: the accommodation requirement. This requirement has been applied in policy rules and in case law to LGBT persons, westernized Afghan women and converts to Christianity.

We saw above that according to the Aliens Circular, LGBT people cannot be expected to hide their orientation. But this requirement is not observed in *sur place* cases. Cases of LGBT people are often not *sur place* cases, in the sense that the sexual orientation has not changed after departure from the country of origin.[21] But in many cases there is a *sur place* element, insofar as the applicant could not practice the sexual orientation in public in the country of origin, can do so in the country of refuge and is unwilling to give that up after expulsion. In such cases, the application is rejected as 'discretion' ('*terughoudendheid*') may be expected from the applicant.

In the case of a Sierra Leonese lesbian woman, asylum was denied because the applicant could be expected to accommodate, i.e. hide the orientation after return as she had done so before leaving Sierra Leone. The district court quashed the negative decision because the minister had not stated reasons why she could accommodate; the judgment concerns the applicant's appeal to the refugee definition and to Article 3 of the ECHR. The Council of State then quashed the district court's decision: the accommodation requirement was not at variance with Articles 3 and 8 of the ECHR. The refugee definition and therefore the statement in the Aliens Circular mentioned above were not addressed (para. 4.1).[22] Another case concerned a young man from Syria, where homosexuality can be punished with three years of imprisonment. He was spotted by a neighbour when having a homosexual affair, stayed one month with his parents and then fled to the Netherlands. The application was rejected, as there was no reason to suppose that the Syrian authorities knew of his sexual orientation (he had not been harassed by the police during the month he stayed with his parents). The district court quashed the decision, as return would imply that the man would have to hide his orientation. But the Council of State upheld the decision, because the Syrian had not invoked the policy rule stating that accommodation cannot be required. But it did assess the well-foundedness of the fear, hence implicitly allowing for the accommodation requirement as Spijkerboer argues in his comment on the case.[23]

The Aliens Circular states that 'westernized' Afghan women cannot continue their lifestyle if they lack the protection of some influential male patron, but have nothing to fear if they accommodate.[24] One would say that women with a western lifestyle who lack such protection have a well-founded fear. But if those women adopted a western lifestyle in the Netherlands, it can be expected that they would revert to a non-western lifestyle in Afghanistan,[25] hence the fear will not be well-founded (or the risk not real).

Iranian ex-Muslim converts to Christianity have nothing to fear when they return, so the Aliens Circular states.[26] The situation is different if they were to try to convert Muslims; but they can again be expected not to do so.[27]

The presupposition that in all these instances the applicant will, indeed, be able to accommodate raises questions which I choose to neglect as they are connected with empirical issues outside the scope of this chapter.[28] However, the compatibility of the accommodation requirement with the Refugee Convention and the ECHR is a legal question I discuss in paras 4.4 and 4.5. Before doing so, I first assess under which circumstances accommodation is to be required according to Dutch asylum law and policy.

In several cases it was argued that the accommodation requirement is not in accordance with the ECHR. It was implicitly assumed that accommodation could in itself be required, but that in this special case the applicant would be brought in a situation also addressed by a prohibition of refoulement (what has been referred to in UK case law as the Anne Frank principle).[29] The reference is to the Jewish girl who in order to escape deportation, had no choice but to go into hiding in most distressing, inhuman circumstances. This type of reasoning can be found in a number of Dutch court decisions. For example, the Amsterdam district court (first instance) stated that as a consequence of the accommodation requirement 'westernized women must give up their rights under Article 8 ECHR (to respect for private life) in order to preclude a violation of their rights under Article 3 ECHR'; therefore, the requirement was not in accordance with the ECHR.[30] In the appeal against this decision the Council of State confirmed that Article 8 of the ECHR can be invoked together with Article 3, but stated that the minister had sufficiently addressed the appeal to Article 8, hence the negative decision did not violate the ECHR.[31] We may conclude that Council of State also embraces the Anne Frank principle.

Hence, if a risk of treatment as meant in Article 3 of the ECHR can be avoided by means of an alternative mode of behaviour (hiding sexual orientation, hiding westernized lifestyle, abstaining from conversion), asylum can be denied, unless the alternative is at variance with human rights norms. If I understand the Council of State correctly, this is the case only if living the alternative mode of behaviour would also qualify as being subjected to ill-treatment. The Council seems to follow case law of the European Court of Human Rights according to breaches of prohibitions of the ECHR other than Article 3, for present purposes: breaches of Article 8 (respect for private life) or 9 (freedom of religion), prohibit refoulement only if these breaches are sufficiently serious to qualify as ill-treatment.[32] The mere fact that the alien cannot express sexual orientation, religion or lifestyle in the country of origin in the same way as he or she can in the Netherlands is insufficient ground to assume that expulsion is at odds with the ECHR, so the Council states.[33]

This approach can help to identify cases where an alternative cannot save the alien from persecution or serious harm. In such cases, it is a means of applying the ECHR. But what about cases where the alternative mode of behaviour does not amount to a situation of ill-treatment? Would it be in accordance with international law to expect the alien to accommodate?

4.4 Accommodation and the European Convention on Human Rights

For Article 3 of the ECHR, not the possibility but the probability of accommodation seems relevant. A case in point is the approach taken by the European Court of Human Rights in *N v Sweden*,[34] about an Afghan woman who declared that she wanted to divorce her husband. As a single and divorced woman without male protection, she would end up in a very dire situation in Afghanistan.[35] There was an alternative for her: continuing the marriage. But in that case her husband would (under Afghan law) be fully entitled to beat her and demand sexual favours at will. The Court concluded that in both situations, in divorced and in married state, N would run a real risk of being subjected to ill-treatment.[36] This outcome reminds one of the Council of State's accommodation requirement (only if accommodation also results in ill-treatment, accommodation cannot be required), but in fact the Court's reasoning is different. It does not consider whether accommodation may be expected from N. Rather, it focuses on facts and probabilities: is the husband willing to comply with the petition for divorce? If he does, what would the consequences be? That reasoning is quite different from contemplating steps she could and maybe should take to avoid harm.

Arguably, there is no place for an accommodation requirement in the Court's approach as it would be irrelevant. The reasoning would be the following. Relevant is only what is foreseeable.[37] If it follows from the assessment that the applicant will not accommodate, expulsion is prohibited. If it follows that the applicant will not engage in certain activities because of the danger attached to it and therefore will not risk ill-treatment, expulsion is allowed. In both cases, only risk assessment, and not accommodation, is relevant. Because this assessment is in large part based on the alien's intentions, his or her credibility is of great importance. A case in point is the comparison the Court draws in *N v Sweden* between N's case and *SA v the Netherlands*. SA had stated that she risked ill-treatment in Afghanistan for adultery, as her child was allegedly not her husband's. She had told her husband about the adultery, but not substantiated that he had taken steps to divorce her. Therefore, the Court considered SA's wish to divorce unlikely, in contrast to N's wish.[38] That likelihood was relevant for the Court, not the question whether they could be asked to continue the marriage.

The same approach can be found in *F v UK*, concerning an Iranian homosexual who stated that he ran a risk of being subjected to ill-treatment in Iran as homosexual acts were criminal offences attracting severe punishments such as flogging. The Court, however, ruled that the risk was not real – it was not likely that he would be prosecuted at all. F also invoked Article 8 of the ECHR. In *Dudgeon*, the ECHR had ruled that the mere existence of an Irish law prohibiting certain homosexual acts was a breach of private life, even if the law was in fact never applied. F argued that Article 8 prohibited expulsion on the same ground. But the Court stated that this infringement of private life was not sufficiently severe to reach the threshold of ill-treatment proscribed by Article 3 of the ECHR, and only in the latter case expulsion is prohibited by the ECHR as we saw above. It should be observed that there is no reference to accommodation in the decision; only foreseeable consequences of expulsion are assessed.

The same holds true for the case of *IIN v the Netherlands*, an Iranian homosexual who invoked Article 3 of the ECHR on the basis that homosexuality could lead to capital punishment.[39] The Court considered the case manifestly unfounded, as there was no convincing evidence of trials for homosexuality. It explained this absence by the circumstance that 'Islamic law' is concerned with public, not private acts; it continued to remark that there were known and tolerated public meeting places for homosexuals. Again, the Court did not require accommodation but rather restricted itself to assessing the probabilities of ill-treatment.[40] The same approach was applied in *Z and T v UK*, concerning two Pakistani Christians (not *sur place* converts) who, because of an assumed risk of ill-treatment because of their religious affiliation, feared violation of both Article 3 and Article 9 of the ECHR.[41] The appeal under Article 3 of the ECHR failed, and the appeal under Article 9 was dismissed on similar grounds as in *F v UK*. Again, accommodation is not addressed.

If this reading is correct, Article 3 of the ECHR only to a quite limited degree offers protection in *sur place* cases – provided the empirical assumption underlying the Court's approach, i.e. that LGBT people who hide their sexuality in the country of origin are not at risk, is correct. Most people will not be willing to risk life and limb in order to express their sexual or religious orientation or lifestyle in the open, which means that it will be hard to substantiate real risk in *sur place* cases.

4.5 Accommodation and the Refugee Convention

More precisely than Article 3 of the ECHR, Article 1A(2) of the Refugee Convention defines who is eligible for protection. It requires protection in case of well-founded fear of being persecuted where the state is not able or not willing to provide for protection, for reasons of one of the Convention grounds. The nexus with the Convention grounds is not or not merely an additional requirement in comparison to Article 3 of the ECHR, it also has bearings on the elements of fear, persecution and protection. For these elements taken together define who is eligible for protection; therefore, they must be read in conjunction.

Why does the refugee definition require a nexus with the Convention grounds? Hathaway has shown that the Convention grounds define categories of persons whose position is marginal, and who are excluded from society on discriminatory grounds. It is because of that exclusion that they are eligible for protection whereas others who also have well-founded fear of persecution are not. These other victims of persecution should be able to solve their needs using existing or newly created structures in their country of origin (Hathaway 2005: 135–137). If persecution is being feared for reasons of a Convention ground, the possibility of improving one's situation is absent or at least unlikely (Hathaway 2005: 136). The Refugee Convention serves to offer them the protection their country of origin denies them on discriminatory grounds. In that way, the refugee definition serves the object and purpose of the Convention.

That purpose is explicitly discussed in a judgment by the British Supreme Court, in *HJ (Iran and HT (Cameroon) v Secretary of State for the Home Department* (*HJ and HT*).[42] The case concerned two homosexual men from Iran and Cameroon who said they feared persecution if they would not hide their sexual orientation in their country of origin. The Supreme Court addressed the question whether accommodation could be required. In that connection Rodgers LJ (whose opinion was joined by the majority) described the purpose or rationale of the Refugee Convention as follows:

> The underlying rationale of the Convention is therefore that people should be able to live freely, without fearing that they may suffer harm of the requisite intensity or duration because they are, say, black, or the descendants of some former dictator, or gay. In the absence of any indication to the contrary, the implication is that they must be free to live openly in this way without fear of persecution. By allowing them to live openly and free from that fear, the receiving state affords them protection

> which is a surrogate for the protection which their home state should have afforded them.[43]

This means that accommodation should not be required. For the person who has to hide his sexual orientation because otherwise he would be persecuted, still finds himself in the situation of fear due to a marginalized position as defined by Article 1A(2) of the Refugee Convention. In such a situation, denying refugee protection would be at variance with the Refugee Convention, as its rationale says that members of the particular social group of gay men and lesbian women

> should be able to live freely and openly as gay men and lesbian women, without fearing that they may suffer harm of the requisite intensity or duration because they are gay or lesbian.[44]

If the country of origin does not offer the required protection, the country of refuge should do so.

As we saw above, in Dutch case law in a case like this one the argument would be made that the mere fact that the applicant cannot enjoy freedoms in the country of origin he can enjoy in the country of refuge does not warrant the conclusion that accommodation cannot be required. That kind of reasoning is at odds with the refugee definition:

> In short, what is protected is the applicant's right to live freely and openly as a gay man. That involves a wide spectrum of conduct, going well beyond conduct designed to attract sexual partners and maintain relationships with them. To illustrate the point with trivial stereotypical examples from British society: just as male heterosexuals are free to enjoy themselves playing rugby, drinking beer and talking about girls with their mates, so male homosexuals are to be free to enjoy themselves going to Kylie concerts, drinking exotically coloured cocktails and talking about boys with their straight female mates. *Mutatis mutandis* – and in many cases the adaptations would obviously be great – the same must apply to other societies. In other words, gay men are to be as free as their straight equivalents in the society concerned to live their lives in the way that is natural to them as gay men, without the fear of persecution.[45]

Can the requirement of accommodation never apply? In *HJ and HT* three types of situation are defined. First, the applicant shows that he cannot or will not hide his sexual orientation. If that would result in well-founded fear, he is a refugee (this is the situation also covered by Article 3 of the ECHR). Second, the applicant will hide the orientation because of fear of persecution for reasons of that orientation. In that case, he is a refugee too (the situation discussed above). Third, the applicant will hide the orientation not for fear of persecution, but for fear of some sort of social pressure. In that case he would not qualify as a refugee. Arguably, the third situation can in theory be distinguished from the second one, but in practice the distinction is difficult if not impossible to make as the line between pressure and threat of persecution is blurry.[46]

Hathaway and Pobjoy (2012) stated that the reasoning of the Supreme Court was incorrect, for two reasons. First, if the applicant states he will conceal his sexual orientation, the fear is not objectively well-founded. They argue that the necessity to conceal may constitute a 'violation' of the right to privacy and an amount of psychological harm that could amount to persecution – the Anne Frank principle mentioned above. But this harm can be distinguished from the persecution for reason of belonging to a particular social group: 'if it were found that Anne Frank could have successfully avoided detection by hiding in the attic, then [. . .] she was not at real risk of being sent to the concentration camps. [. . .] The risk of permanent enforced confinement would in itself [. . .] give rise to a risk of being persecuted' (Hathaway and Pobjoy 2012: 349). But who would be the perpetrator of this harm? Not Anne Frank or her family I would say, but the Nazis threatening her with deportation. Thus, the separation of the threat of murder and the violation of privacy is artificial and untenable – the threat of deportation is the risk of permanent confinement. Besides, taking into account that about 80 per cent of the Dutch Jews were murdered during the Nazi occupation of the Netherlands, I wonder what meaning the Refugee Convention could have according to Hathaway and Pobjoy if the fear of a Dutch Jew could possibly not be 'objectively' well-founded, no matter how 'safe' a hiding place he or she found on Dutch territory. Second, Hathaway and Pobjoy argue that the Supreme Court construes the ground 'particular social group' too wide: things such as going to a Kylie concert and so on are not protected characteristics. That is in itself probably true: if merely going to Kylie concerts would be forbidden, there would be no well-founded fear of being persecuted. But if going to such concerts is seen as proof of being gay, causing the person going to the concert to be ill-treated, he is a refugee. Furthermore, the approach advocated by Hathaway and Pobjoy, separating core and fringe aspects of Convention grounds, finds no basis in the Convention or in the EU Qualification Directive. Examples adduced by Hathaway and Pobjoy show that a different approach risks rendering the Convention grounds devoid of all meaning, such as a finding that 'standing up for law and order' in corrupt system would fall outside the ambit of 'political opinion' (Hathaway and Pobjoy 2012: 378).

4.6 Concluding remarks

Dutch asylum policy states that LGBT people cannot be expected to hide their orientation after return, that westernized people cannot be expected to hide their lifestyle, and that members of minority religions cannot be expected to hide this affiliation. That is fully in line with the Refugee Convention and the ECHR.

But these policy rules do not apply if the claim is treated as a *sur place* claim: if an LGBT person states that he wants to live his orientation in the open, even though he did not do so in the country of origin due to well-founded fear of persecution. In such cases, the wish to live without hiding one's orientation is labeled as a circumstance that arose after arrival, *sur place*, and therefore, the accommodation requirement applies: the applicant is expected to be able to accommodate to local rules in the country of origin and hide his or her orientation. The same rule is being applied to Afghan women who adopted a western lifestyle after arrival (or state they want to live a western lifestyle on arrival and did not do so in the past in Afghanistan) and to converted Christians who wish to convert others to their new religion.

This requirement of accommodation is not compatible with Article 3 of the ECHR and the Refugee Convention. If ill-treatment upon return is foreseeable, Article 3 of the ECHR prohibits expulsion. In the risk assessment, accommodation may play a role insofar as it can be established that it will take place. Whether or not it can be expected is not relevant, nor whether the conversion, western lifestyle or open sexual orientation were manifested only after departure.

The Refugee Convention also affords protection in case the applicant will accommodate due to well-founded fear. The Refugee Convention presumes a society where protection against persecution cannot be denied for reasons of one of the persecution grounds. A person who is not able to participate due to fear of being persecuted on one of those grounds is a refugee. Accommodation would not change that and cannot be a ground for denying protection.

The difference in outcome under Article 3 of the ECHR and the Refugee Convention seems to be due to the purpose or rationale of these instruments. Article 3 of the ECHR only serves to afford protection against foreseeable harm, without propagating a particular type of society. It is also neutral regarding the type of person: the prohibition applies in equal measure to persons such as political dissidents who are deemed to make valuable contributions to the country of origin or the country of refuge, and to dangerous terrorists. The Refugee Convention has an ideological basis and supports a particular view on society. This is expressed in, *inter alia*, the exclusion from protection of terrorists, and the inclusion of only those who are being persecuted on discriminatory grounds.

This difference shows in the way accommodation is being addressed. For Article 3 of the ECHR it is only a matter of assessing future risk. For the refugee definition it is also a question about the Convention grounds: does it concern a property the Convention serves to protect?

To what extent Dutch case law complies with this interpretation of the Refugee Convention is as yet hard to say, because the Convention is addressed in very few cases. In most *sur place* cases, only Article 3 of the ECHR is considered. Some of the groups mentioned here enjoy protection on a different, national ground: Iranian homosexuals and certain categories of westernized women.[47] And *sur place* claims to refugee status were, until recently, denied on the basis of the continuity requirement. Now the latter has been abolished, it is time to rediscover the refugee definition. Where it comes to claims by LGBT people who fear persecution if they do not hide their orientation, this means recognition as a refugee.

4.7 Notes

* Hemme Battjes is Professor of European Asylum Law at VU University, Amsterdam, the Netherlands. This chapter is based on his contribution to A.B. Terlouw and K.M. Zwaan (eds), *Tijd en asiel. 60 jaar Vluchtelingenverdrag*, Nijmegen: Kluwer, 2011.

1 Aliens Circular C2/2.10.2. In a letter dating from 21 March 2012 to the Dutch Parliament (letter nr. 5710139/11), the Minister for Asylum and Aliens Affairs responded to the recommendations in *Fleeing Homophobia, Asylum Claims Related to Sexual Orientation and Gender Identity in Europe*. As to the recommendation that LGTB people should not be required or presumed to hide their identity or gender upon return in order to avoid persecution or ill-treatment, he said that the current should be 'clarified' in the following sense: 'If it is to be assumed that there is well-founded fear of being persecuted or real risk of ill-treatment if the surroundings of the asylum seeker are or will be aware of his or her sexual orientation, then the alien is in principle eligible for protection under the Geneva Convention or Article 3 ECHR'. He added that 'The mere fact that the authorities or third parties impose restrictions does not mean in all cases that this restriction amounts to persecution or a breach of Article 3 ECHR'. The text of the Aliens Circular remained unchanged at the time of writing this chapter (20 May 2012). It remains to be seen which consequences this policy change will have in practice.

2 Aliens Circular C2/2.7 and C2/2.8.

3 Vienna Convention on the Law of Treaties of 23 May 1969, UNTS 1155, 331; UNHCR *Handbook* (UNHCR 1992), available at http://www.unhcr.org (accessed 9 December 2012); Council Directive 2004/83/EC of 29 April 2004 on minimum standards for the qualification and status of third country nationals or stateless persons as refugees or as persons who otherwise need international protection and the content of the protection granted, [2004] OJ L 304; EU Qualification Directive. See for a discussion of the interpretation rules, Battjes 2006: 14–24.

4 1951 United Nations Convention Relating to the Status of Refugees (28 July 1951) 189 UNTS 150.

5 Hathaway 1991: 66–69; Spijkerboer and Vermeulen 2005: 28–29.

6 Cf. Article 4(4) of the EU Qualification Directive, which states that past persecution yields a rebuttable presumption of future persecution.

7 UNHCR *Handbook*, paras 83 and 94–96; Article 5(1): 'A well-founded fear of being persecuted or a real risk of suffering serious harm may be based on events which have taken place since the applicant left the country of origin'.

8 Examples are district court The Hague (Breda), AWB 06/32733 VRWET, LJN BA0056, *Jurisprudentie Vreemdelingenrecht* 2007/195 and district court The Hague (Amsterdam), AWB 04/57053 VRWET, LJN AX6515, *Jurisprudentie Vreemdelingenrecht* 2006/291.

9 E.g. district court The Hague (Amsterdam) 6 June 2007, AWB 06/7468 (meeting before embassy), and district court The Hague (Amsterdam) 1 April 2004, AWB 02/59650 (occupation embassy).

10 BVerwG, 18 December 2008, 10 C 27.07, available at http://www.bverwg.de (accessed 9 December 2012), English translation provided by the BVerwG on the website, with references to relevant literature. A reasoning quite similar to that of the Bundesverwaltungsgericht can be found in Hailbronner and Alt 2010: 1038–1039.

11 Protocol Relating to the Status of Refugees of 1967, Article 1(2).

12 Article 2(c) of the EU Qualification Directive.

13 Article 32 of the Vienna Treaty Convention and see Battjes 2006: 14–24.

14 Article 5(2) of the EU Qualification Directive: 'A well-founded fear of being persecuted or a real risk of suffering serious harm may be based on activities which have been engaged in by the applicant since he left the country of origin, in particular where it is established that the activities relied upon constitute the expression and continuation of convictions or orientations held in the country of origin'.

15 Article 5(3) of the EU Qualification Directive; cf. Article 20(7): 'Member States may reduce the benefits of this Chapter, granted to a person eligible for subsidiary protection, whose subsidiary protection status has been obtained on the basis of activities engaged in for the sole or main purpose of creating the necessary conditions for being recognized as a person eligible for subsidiary protection'. Both provisions are optional. Neither of them has been implemented in the Netherlands.

16 European Court of Human Rights, 20 July 2010, *N v Sweden*, appl. no. 23505/09.

17 European Court of Human Rights, 8 July 2008, *AJ v Sweden*, appl. no. 13508/07.

18 Aliens Circular 2000, C1/4.2.2.6 (old).

19 See e.g. the cases mentioned in footnote 8 above.

20 Council of State, 13 January 2010, available at http://www.refugeecaselaw.org/redirectpdf.aspx?caseid=1966 (accessed 9 December 2012), *Jurisprudentie Vreemdelingenrecht* 2010/96; Article 5(2) had been correctly transposed in Article 3.37b Voorschrift Vreemdelingen, a ministerial decree, which apparently had escaped the minister when writing the Aliens Circular.

21 There are exceptions, Council of State, 3 October 2003, nr. 200305027/1, *Jurisprudentie Vreemdelingenrecht* 2004/3 (alien was a young child when entering the Netherlands), President district court The Hague (Haarlem), 12 July 2007, AWB 07/44181, 07/44180 (alien was 15 years old when entering the Netherlands); President district court The Hague (Haarlem), 18 April 2011, AWB 10/36310 (transgender treatment in the Netherlands has visible physical effects).

22 Cf. Council of State, 11 May 2011, 201011782/1/V1, *Jurisprudentie Vreemdelingenrecht* 2011/307.

23 Council of State, 17 August 2011, 201012865/1/V2, LJN BR5419, *Jurisprudentie Vreemdelingenrecht* 2011/424.

24 Aliens Circular 2000, C/24 Afghanistan, 3.2.2.

25 Council of State, 29 September 2009, 200807067/1/V2, *Jurisprudentie Vreemdelingenrecht* 2009/463 and 23 December 2011, 201104178/1/V1, 201104188/1/V1, LJN BV0396, *Jurisprudentie Vreemdelingenrecht* 2012/94.

26 Aliens Circular 2000, C24, Iran, 3.7.

27 Council of State, 4 October 2010, 200902318/1/V2, LJN BN9951, *Jurisprudentie Vreemdelingenrecht* 2010/447, para. 2.2.7.

28 Cf. district court The Hague (Den Bosch), 20 January 2011, AWB 10/41119, AWB 10/42525, AWB 10/42526, LJN BP1516, *Jurisprudentie Vreemdelingenrecht* 2011/105, that concluded that accommodation was not possible (the *Sahar* case, para. 16).

29 UK Supreme Court, 7 July 2010, *HJ (Iran) and HT (Cameroon) v Secretary of State for the Home Department* [2010] UKSC 31 at [96].

30 District court The Hague (Amsterdam), 27 March 2009, AWB 07/12408, AWB 07/12377, LJN BH8923, *Jurisprudentie Vreemdelingenrecht* 2009/218, *NAV* 2009/27, para. 10.

31 Council of State 7 June 2010, *Jurisprudentie Vreemdelingenrecht* 2010/284, paras 2.1.5 and 2.1.7; in a similar vein 11 May 2011, 201011782/1/V1, LJN BQ4610, *Jurisprudentie Vreemdelingenrecht* 2011/307.

32 Cf. Council of State, 19 January 2011, 201007538/1/V1, LJN BP2541, *Jurisprudentie Vreemdelingenrecht* 2011/117, referring to European Court of Human Rights, 28 February 2006, nr. 27034/05, RJ&D ECHR 2006 III, *Jurisprudentie Vreemdelingenrecht* 2006/274.

33 Council of State, 4 October 2010, 200902318/1/V2, LJN BN9951, *Jurisprudentie Vreemdelingenrecht* 2010/447, para. 2.2.6; in the same vein district court The Hague (Den Bosch), 20 January 2011, *Jurisprudentie Vreemdelingenrecht* 2011/105, para. 12.

34 European Court of Human Rights, 20 July 2010, *N v Sweden*, appl. no. 23505/09, *Jurisprudentie Vreemdelingenrecht* 2010/373.

35 Ibid, para. 60.

36 Ibid, para. 61. As indicated in my comment on the case in *Jurisprudentie Vreemdelingenrecht* 2010/373, the judgment is somewhat unclear. In its conclusions the Court mentions 'cumulative risks of reprisals which fall under Article 3 of the Convention from her husband X, his family, her own family and from the Afghan society' (para. 61), whereas the remainder of the case make clear that it concerns alternative risks. It therefore remains unclear whether the position of a divorced woman is in itself sufficient to assume a real risk.

37 E.g. European Court of Human Rights, 28 February 2008, *Saadi v Italy*, appl. no. 37201/06, *Jurisprudentie Vreemdelingenrecht* 2008/131, para. 130.

38 European Court of Human Rights, 20 July 2010, *N v Sweden*, appl. no. 23505/09, *Jurisprudentie Vreemdelingenrecht* 2010/373, para. 56.

39 European Court of Human Rights, 9 December 2004, appl. no. 2035/04.

40 The Committee against Torture applied a similar approach in *KSY v The Netherlands*: it merely addressed the credibility of the applicant and the intensity of prosecution of homosexuality in Iran, not possibilities to preclude torture by being discrete (CAT, 15 May 2003, comm. no. 190/2001).

41 European Court of Human Rights, 28 February 2006, *Z and T v VK*, appl. no. 27034/05, *Jurisprudentie Vreemdelingenrecht* 2006/274.

42 See for a far more thorough and critical discussion of this judgment, Weßels in this volume.

43 UK Supreme Court, 7 July 2010, *HJ (Iran) and HT (Cameroon) v Secretary of State for the Home Department* [2010] UKSC 31 at [53].

44 Ibid.

45 Ibid at [78].

46 The reader is referred to Weßels' well argued criticism of this requirement in this volume, which shows that the requirement may not be as harmless as I suggest here.

47 See WBV 2011/5, para. 3.2.4.

4.8 References

Battjes, H. (2006) *European Asylum Law and International Law*, Leiden/Boston, MA: Nijhoff.

Hailbronner, K. and Alt, S. (2010) 'Article 5 Qualification Directive', in K. Hailbronner, *EU Immigration and Asylum Law – Commentary*, München: Beck.

Hathaway, J.C. (1991) *The Law of Refugee Status*, Toronto/Vancouver: Butterworths.

— (2005), *The Rights of Refugees under International Law*, Cambridge: Cambridge University Press.

Hathaway, J.C. and Pobjoy, J. (2012) 'Queer cases make bad law', *New York Journal of International Law and Politics*, 44(2): 315–388.

Jansen, S. and Spijkerboer, T.P. (2011) *Fleeing Homophobia, Asylum Claims Related to Sexual Orientation and Gender Identity in Europe*, COC Netherlands and VU University Amsterdam, available at http://www.rechten.vu.nl/nl/onderzoek/conferenties-en-projecten/onderzoeksproject-fleeing-homophobia/index.asp (accessed 17 December 2012).

Musalo, K. (2004) 'Claims for protection based on religion or belief', *International Journal of Refugee Law*, 16: 165–226.

Spijkerboer, T.P. and Vermeulen, B.P. (2005), *Vluchtelingenrecht*, Nijmegen: Ars Aequilibri.

UN High Commissioner for Refugees (UNHCR) (1992) *Handbook on Procedures and Criteria for Determining Refugee Status under the 1951 Convention and the 1967 Protocol relating to the Status of Refugees*, HCR/IP/4/Eng/REV.1, September 1979, reedited January 1992, Geneva: UNHCR, available at http://www.unhcr.org (accessed 9 December 2012).

Van Halder, S. (2010) 'De toetsing van de geloofwaardigheid van het bekeringsverhaal bij asielzoekers in Nederland', in *Asiel&Migrantenrecht* (1): 475–482.

5 Lesbian, gay, bisexual and transgender refugees

Challenges in refugee status determination and living conditions in Turkey

Giulia Cragnolini[*]

5.1 Introduction

Lesbian, gay, bisexual and transgender (LGBT) people experience human rights violations all over the world (O'Flaherty and Fisher 2008: 208). In particular, more than 80 countries still criminalize same sex relations between consenting adults and seven impose the death penalty as a punishment[1] (O'Flaherty and Fisher 2008: 208). Also, laws against public scandal, immorality or indecent behaviour are arbitrarily used against LGBT people (Amnesty International 2001: 11). The reason why LGBT people are mistreated worldwide is because they challenge social gender norms assigning particular tasks to males and females at birth. As a consequence, the acceptability of LGBT people is a very delicate issue in every society.

When severe human rights violations occur, some LGBT people feel forced to leave their countries to seek protection in another state. However, the living conditions in the state of asylum are not necessarily safe, as the case of Turkey illustrates. This chapter addresses the challenges faced by LGBT asylum seekers and refugees looking for legal protection as a refugee in order to enjoy human rights, and for safety, in terms of physical and psychological peace outside their countries of origin.

The first part of the chapter presents the main challenges that LGBT asylum seekers face during the asylum procedure. This phase, very delicate in the life of every asylum seeker, may be even more sensitive for LGBT cases due to the particularities characteristic for LGBTs.

The second part of this chapter is related to the challenges that LGBT asylum seekers and refugees encounter in finding protection and safety in Turkey. The refugee status determination process is described in relation to the role of UNHCR in Turkey and the experiences of asylum seekers and refugees. The difficulties that the refugee LGBT community has in Turkey derive from the dual condition of being foreigners seeking asylum and being LGBT. This status implies a double discrimination that results in precarious living conditions, serious security concerns and psychological disorders. These circumstances can have a negative impact on the asylum procedure.

5.2 Methodology

This research about refugee status determination practices derives from a six-month field experience with the Refugee Status Determination Unit of the UNHCR Office in Ankara and through extensive literature reviews of international refugee law. This chapter does not reflect UNHCR views but only the personal findings of the author.

The information regarding the life conditions of asylum seekers and refugees in Turkey was collected by adopting a qualitative approach, conducting interviews with various parties involved in the treatment of LGBT cases in Turkey.[2] I interviewed some members of the Iranian LGBT community located in Kayseri (Central Anatolia), considering that the majority of the LGBT seeking refuge in Turkey reside in this city. Moreover, I exchanged with the representatives of some non-governmental organisations (NGOs) in Turkey, namely the Kaos GL Association (Kaos GL) (the main Turkish LGBT rights organisation) in Ankara, and the Association for Solidarity with Asylum Seekers and Migrants (ASAM) in Ankara and Kayseri. My field research findings are also supported by relevant human rights reports on LGBTs in Turkey.[3]

5.3 LGBTs looking for protection: challenges in the asylum procedure

LGBT people fleeing situations where they already experienced or would be at risk of experiencing serious violations of human rights may seek protection in another country. In the host country the applicants must approach the competent authorities and start the process aimed at examining whether they meet the national or international standards for refugee status.[4] According to Article 1.A-2 of the 1951 United Nations Convention Relating to the Status of Refugees (the Refugee Convention), a refugee is a person who:

> (. . .) owing to well-founded fear of being persecuted for reasons of race, religion, nationality, membership of a particular social group or political opinion, is outside the country of his nationality and is unable or, owing to such fear, is unwilling to avail himself of the protection of that country; or who, not having a nationality and being outside the country of his former habitual residence as a result of such events, is unable or, owing to such fear, is unwilling to return to it.

It is acknowledged that LGBT claims can fall under one of the grounds for persecution (Choi 2010: 2),[5] typically membership of a particular social group[6] but some issues remain critical. Indeed, the immutable characteristic approach that considers some features of the group as fixed is still largely applied to LGBT cases, sometimes along with the social perception approach that implies a certain level of visibility of the group in the society (LaViolette 2010b: 19; see also Hathaway and Foster 2003). This approach is problematic especially for refugees who tried to hide their sexuality in their country of origin. In addition, when immutability is considered as an innate characteristic,[7] it implicitly attaches a social stigma to homosexuality (Rehaag 2009: 6) and does not consider that there is no scientific evidence regarding the mutable or immutable nature of sexuality (Rehaag 2009: 5; see also American Psychological Association). In particular, bisexual claims might be considered in this sense only to the extent that they conform to homosexual standards (Rehaag 2009: 16). As a consequence, the approach to be preferred in order to define an LGBT group is an approach that considers that 'sexual orientation and gender identity are integral to every person's dignity and humanity and must not be the basis for discrimination or abuse' (International Commission of Jurists 2007: introduction and art. 9). In addition, other grounds for persecution such as political and religious conviction need to be further explored to address LGBT claims (UNHCR 2008: para. 30).

Over the years, credibility became one of the main issues in claims based on sexual orientation or gender identity, playing an increasing role in their rejections (Berg and Millbank 2009: 195–196; Millbank 2009b: 1). Due to the intimate nature of LGBT claims, it is very challenging to asses credibility in these cases. As these stories are based on non-visible characteristics, there might be no other evidence apart from the applicants' testimony in support of their claim (Berg and Millbank 2009: 196 ff), especially if the applicants lived hiding their sexual orientation in the country of origin due to fear of persecution. Moreover, the applicants' psychological reactions typically play an important role during the interview as they might not be able to talk linearly and coherently about their experience if, as it is in most of the cases, physical or psychological sufferance exists (Berg and Millbank 2009: 200–203). Also, the attitude and the understanding of the examiners, who might themselves be trapped in prejudices and rigid gender schemas, can have a negative impact on the outcome of the case. Indeed, as sexuality and sexual orientation are at the core of the auto-determination of every society, the interviewers' mind is normally shaped by the societal attitude in their own environment (Choi 2010: 1). As a consequence, adjudicators largely apply stereotypical images and westernized evaluation models when deciding on these claims (Millbank 2009a: 392; see also Berg and Millbank 2009: 197; Jansen and Spijkerboer 2011: 57–63). UNHCR acknowledges these obstacles and suggests that self-identification should be considered as an indicator of sexual orientation (UNHCR 2008: para. 35),[8] underlining the importance of according the benefit of the doubt.[9] However, the issue of credibility in LGBT cases remains open.[10]

As for credibility, problems relating to the assessment of well-founded fear might arise from the interviewer's incapacity to imagine 'otherness',[11] resulting in the application of westernized standards. Some claims were rejected considering a westernized sharp division between private and public conduct. Indeed, lesbians are more likely to face persecution in a private setting, i.e. at home or at work and by members of the family or of the community, whereas gays encounter more frequently persecution in public places, for example in streets and parks, and from public actors, i.e. people linked with the State (Neilson 2005: 4). In the rejection of lesbian cases, their stories were considered as 'too private' and the social and governmental reaction was disregarded. At the same time, gay claims were regarded as 'too public' and prosecution derived from public acts was not considered as persecution, in close comparison with western standards (Millbank 2002: 168). Also, an analysis that ignores the gender perspective might seriously affect the outcome of cases involving sexual orientation (LaViolette 2010b: 9). In addition, a lack of human rights documentation or improper use of it, might lead to the misinterpretation of the applicants' testimony. Indeed, due to the improvement of human rights conditions for sexual minorities in many countries, the examiners might be tempted to decide that the harm does not amount to persecution but simply to discrimination (LaViolette 2010a: 5). Also, the lack of evidence has been sometimes misinterpreted as lack of persecution. Sometimes, claims based on sexual orientation were rejected on the basis of the so-called discretion requirement.[12] The decision was based on the assumption that if a person behaves discreetly or could 'choose' to do so, he or she should not be considered in danger in the country of origin (Millbank 2009a, 2009b; Jansen and Spijkerboer 2011: 34–39). However, as in cases involving other fundamental identity issues, such as political opinions, beliefs or nationality, an applicant cannot be asked to avoid the harm simply by denying his or her identity, as a hidden right cannot be considered a right (UNHCR 2008: para. 25). In addition, UNHCR explicitly states that 'being compelled to forsake or conceal one's sexual orientation and gender identity, where this is instigated or condoned by the State, may amount to persecution' (UNHCR 2008: para. 12; see also LaViolette 2010b; Millbank 2003; Weßels' contribution to this volume). The rationale behind the discretion reasoning implies a homophobic attitude that regards the expression of sexual orientation and gender identity as limited to the private sphere.

In conclusion, because of their particular sensitive nature, LGBT claims are challenging for both the applicants and the examiners. That is also why, as recognized by UNHCR, this is still an 'evolving area of international refugee law' (UNHCR 2008: para. 2).

5.4 LGBT asylum seekers looking for protection and safety in turkey

Turkey hosts a high number of refugees and asylum seekers every year (UNHCR 2011),[13] mainly from Iraq, Iran and Afghanistan but also from different African countries. Among them, the refugees who are fleeing homophobia arrive in a country that is quite hostile towards LGBT people. The precarious living conditions that asylum seekers and refugees face in Turkey are complicated by feelings of frustration and feeling unsafe in the case of LGBTs. The following part of this chapter addresses this issue, presenting the protection system in Turkey and the experiences of LGBT people during the asylum procedure. A final section is devoted to the analysis of the various difficulties that LGBTs have during their stay in Turkey, including security, housing, work and education.

5.4.1 The general procedure in Turkey

Due to its geographical location at a crossroads between Europe, Asia, Africa and the Middle East, Turkey has always been subjected to mixed migration flows of refugees and migrants (UNHCR 2012).

The Republic of Turkey is party to both the Refugee Convention and the 1967 Protocol (UNHCR 2010b: 2)[14] but still maintains the 'geographical limitation' and processes only cases resulting from 'events occurring in Europe' (UNHCR Office in Turkey: 2010).[15] In practice, this results in two different entities responsible for the refugee status determination (RSD) process: the Ministry of Interior for the European asylum seekers and UNHCR for non-European asylum seekers (UNHCR 2009b),[16] which at present constitutes the vast majority of the refugee population in Turkey.[17] Interestingly, UNHCR role in RSD is not explicitly referred to in any law and there is no particular agreement between Turkey and UNHCR determining the operations of the office (UNHCR 2009b: 6).[18]

Non-European asylum seekers are subjected to two parallel procedures: the request for temporary asylum to the Turkish authorities[19] and the application for the recognition of refugee status to UNHCR (Zieck 2010: 1). Even though the process should follow this order, in practice, the asylum seekers mostly approach UNHCR first. The applicants are then referred to the police station to register in the satellite city[20] they are assigned to by the Ministry of Interior[21] (UNHCR 2009a: 2). The applicants have a legal entitlement to remain in Turkey only after a detailed interview with the government authorities, aimed at determining if they meet the Refugee Convention criteria, but resulting only in the declaration of asylum seeker status (Zieck 2010: 3).[22] Indeed, by hosting non-European asylum seekers and refugees on its territory Turkey is bound by the fundamental principle of *non-refoulement*[23] as laid down in the international and regional legal instruments it is a party to, in particular, the European Convention on Human Rights (ECHR).[24]

After registration with the police, the asylum seekers are provided with an identification card. Then, they have to apply for residence permit, *ikamet*, which allows for social assistance, work and in some cases medical assistance (Helsinki Citizens Assembly – Turkey and Organization for Refuge, Asylum and Migration 2011: 11).[25] Once recognized refugees, the applicants are usually granted temporary asylum in Turkey[26] until, with the assistance of

UNHCR, they are offered the possibility of resettlement in a third country (UNHCR 2009b: 4).[27] The applicants remain on average 11 months in Turkey, from registration to resettlement.

5.4.2 LGBT asylum seekers looking for refugee protection

The number of LGBT asylum seekers and refugees in Turkey is, similarly to global trends, limited (compare Jansen and Spijkerboer 2011: 15). Although there are no official statistics from UNHCR it can be estimated that in January 2011 between 110 and 200 LGBT people were residing in Turkey (source: ASAM, oral information). The vast majority of them were Iranian and gay.[28] Fleeing a country where they are very likely to face persecution, LGBTs come to Turkey looking for protection and safety. Even if UNHCR recognition rate is very high for this category,[29] they cannot always find safety during their staying in Turkey. As for other vulnerable cases,[30] UNHCR tries to prioritize these claims, reducing the waiting period between registration and resettlement. Also, in recent years, UNHCR has paid great attention to the simultaneous submission of couples to the resettlement countries (Helsinki Citizens Assembly – Turkey and Organization for Refuge, Asylum and Migration 2011: 15). Still, due to UNHCR limited resources and long procedures of the resettlement countries, LGBTs, as others refugees, are likely to remain in Turkey one or more years (Helsinki Citizens Assembly – Turkey and Organization for Refuge, Asylum and Migration 2011: 3).

5.4.3 The UNHCR procedure

The refugee status determination procedure, located between the rigidity of the laws and the fast mutability of reality, is challenging for both the applicant and the examiner in many ways as it leads to a fundamental decision upon the life of an individual. As mentioned above, the attitude of the examiner plays a significant role in this respect. Until 2009 various complaints were addressed to the UNHCR office concerning improper homophobic attitudes of some of the staff. However, since 2009 considerable improvement has been registered on the UNHCR side and the LGBT refugee community has expressed satisfaction with the treatment received. In particular, the *Unsafe Haven* reports[31] as well as the LGBT people interviewed in Kayseri recognized that UNHCR had adopted a more respectful and sensitive approach. This positive trend derives from an increased awareness of the problems of LGBT asylum seekers acquired through trainings, coaching by supervisors and a closer co-operation with NGOs working with LGBTs.[32] The attention of the UNHCR headquarters to LGBT issues,[33] including new policies relating to Iranian refugees,[34] have also contributed to these improvements (Helsinki Citizens Assembly – Turkey and Organization for Refuge, Asylum and Migration 2011: 14). Still, as is underlined later, some criticism continues to be addressed to the office.

As far as the first step for the determination of refugee status is concerned, i.e. the registration interview, the refugees interviewed in Kayseri did not report any problems. They (LGBT asylum seekers or refugees from Kayseri) did not feel embarassed declaring that the reason for fleeing Iran was related to their sexual orientation or gender identity. Only in one case, a gay claimant asserted that he experienced some embarrassment at the beginning of the interview while disclosing his homosexuality to a male officer. However, he stated that he preferred not to ask for a female officer fearing that this would have resulted in a longer waiting period. It should also be mentioned that UNHCR pays great attention to requests related to the sex of officers.[35]

It is also worth mentioning that the 2009 *Unsafe Haven* report expressed concern at the offensive treatment of LGBT claimants by some fellow asylum seekers while waiting for their UNHCR interview in a common room in the Ankara office (Helsinki Citizens Assembly – Turkey and Organization for Refuge, Asylum and Migration 2009: 15). The same problems were not documented in the 2011 report and were also not revealed to this chapter's author during the interviews in Kayseri.

A general level of satisfaction was registered among the people interviewed in Kayseri in relation to the treatment received during the RSD interviews. They appreciated in particular the professional behaviour of the legal officers and most of the time said they felt at ease to explain their stories. Considering that the interview's atmosphere can have a critical impact on its outcome and given the high emotional charge of many LGBT experiences, it is extremely relevant to create a safe environment and establish trust between the parties from the beginning of the interview (Berg and Millbank 2009: 198). The interviewer should always remember that the applicants are usually very stressed during the interview, being conscious that its outcome is determinant for their future. One gay asylum seeker described his feelings as follows: 'All of my life I had to hide my sexual orientation in Iran and during the interview I had to describe my life as gay in a very limited time. I was very stressed of forgetting some details'.

Refugees as well as Kaos GL acknowledged in general a positive and constructive atmosphere during UNHCR interviews, where the applicants were put at ease and treated respectfully. However, in some cases, the nature of the questions asked was criticized. Even though the applicants admitted that the ideal condition of being believed on the basis of a mere declaration of being LGBT is not always applicable to RSD procedures, they maintained that some questions are unnecessary or offensive. For instance, Kaos GL complained that questions relating to child abuse where misleading when interpreted as a determinant of the applicant's sexual orientation or gender identity. Furthermore, in sporadic cases, Kaos GL and the interviewees in Kayseri referred to very detailed and embarrassing questions regarding sexual activities and preferences. While the asylum seekers criticized the obsessive attention to sexual details, they said they felt at ease to answer questions about their sexual orientation and gender identity. However, some affirmed to be disturbed by queries relating to other aspects of their life. In particular, they complained about an excessive attention to the dates of events, especially when documents were submitted as an evidence.

In one case, a claimant stated to be disturbed by the unpleasant and homophobic attitude of the interpreter, who addressed him using terms with a negative connotation. However, the applicant preferred not to raise the issue during his interview and not to complain afterwards, even if he was aware of the existence of a formal complaint mechanism at UNHCR. Apparently, the fact that UNHCR guarantees a clear separation between the complaint procedure on the one hand, and the RSD procedure on the other,[36] fails to reassure some asylum seekers. In particular, they fear that submitting a complaint can delay their case.

5.4.4 The Turkish authorities' procedure

All the interviewees in Kayseri were registered with the police and went regularly to sign in order to certify their presence in the city they were assigned to live by the Turkish authorities. They affirmed they were treated very respectfully. Similarly, the *Unsafe Haven* reports confirm that the LGBT community usually received satisfactory treatment from the police. However, especially in Kayseri and Nevsheir, some LGBT people were recommended to change their appearance 'for their own safety', in order to reduce the risks of being targeted by the local population. This is a significant indicator of the social attitude towards LGBT people in Turkey. Indeed, LGBT asylum seekers and refugees would be forced to live 'discreetly', in continuous denial of their rights, whereas the police should guarantee that their rights are respected. Not surprisingly, the police attitude did not reassure many of the asylum seekers and refugees, who felt instead that the police would not be able to protect them (Helsinki Citizens Assembly – Turkey and Organization for Refuge, Asylum and Migration 2011: 17).

As far as the asylum interviews with the police are concerned, the refugees in Kayseri were pleased with the treatment received. However, both editions of the *Unsafe Haven* report underlined that the applicants' experiences varied a lot and many of them also felt that their privacy was not respected because excessively invasive questions were asked (Helsinki Citizens Assembly – Turkey and Organization for Refuge, Asylum and Migration 2011: 13). The differences in the author's and in the reports' findings derive from the fact that the reports consider a wider range of cases from different cities where different authorities operate.

5.5 LGBT asylum seekers and refugees looking for safety

The situations of LGBT asylum seekers and refugees in Turkey should be addressed taking into account their double condition of foreigners seeking refuge and of LGBT in Turkey. Indeed, not only do they experience precarious life conditions similar to other asylum seekers and refugee population, but also they suffer the consequence of a general climate of intolerance towards LGBTs in the country. According to Randazzo, the situation of LGBT asylum seekers and refugees is not only the sum of those two characteristics but should be considered in a wider perspective. In this sense, their marginality is 'double', deriving also from the lack of access to traditional support systems and resources to which straight asylum seekers and LGBT citizens may have access (Randazzo 2005: 30). LGBT asylum seekers and refugees are more dependent than other refugees on the state of asylum (Amnesty International 2011: 12) and this is problematic in a country like Turkey, where the support system for refugees is very limited.

LGBTs are among the most vulnerable asylum seekers and refugees in Turkey nowadays (Helsinki Citizens Assembly – Turkey and Organization for Refuge, Asylum and Migration 2011: 29) as they find themselves in an 'unsafe haven'. Some Iranian LGBTs expressed their feeling of insecurity referring to Turkey as 'worse than Iran'.[37]

5.5.1 Feeling unsafe in Turkey

The social context for LGBT people in Turkey is quite hostile. Even though Turkey does not prohibit homosexuality, there is no law protecting LGBTs and morality-based laws are often applied against sexual minorities (Human Rights Watch 2008: 9).[38] The authorities tend to ignore the rights of LGBT people and have repeatedly refused to reform non-discrimination provisions in favour of them. Moreover, important politicians have expressed their homophobic views in public, sometimes maintaining that society is not ready to change (Amnesty International 2011: 9).[39]

Due to the pervasive culture of homophobia and transphobia, LGBT people in Turkey experience tremendous pressures from their families and from society more generally. They are discriminated by state and non-state actors in the workplace, education, housing and health service. LGBT people are also targets of violence, harassment and serious crimes, including violent attacks and murders (Amnesty International 2011: 30).[40] However, the victims do not always find adequate protection from the police and many choose not to approach the police out of fear of being falsely accused of crimes or misdemeanours (Helsinki Citizens Assembly – Turkey and Organization for Refuge, Asylum and Migration 2011: 3). As a consequence, many of them live hiding their sexual orientation and gender identity. This is very complicated in particular for transgenders, who are typically more visible and as a result suffer more violence and discrimination (Amnesty International 2011: 6).

I decided to interview LGBT people in Kayseri because this is one of the satellite cities where LGBT people experience considerable societal pressure. Although being one of the most conservative cities in Turkey, it is also the one that hosts the highest number of LGBT Iranian refugees (source: Kaos GL and ASAM, oral information). Knowing that in this city they would find at least the support of an LGBT community, many LGBT asylum seekers ask to be sent there while others are automatically sent there, sometimes with the same belief (source: ASAM, oral information). However, all the LGBT asylum seekers hosted in Kayseri complain about the fact that members of their community are very likely to be mistreated and harassed by the local population. Some of the people interviewed asserted to feel less free in Turkey than in Iran, observing that while in their country of origin they could eventually live a second hidden life; in the country of asylum they were not able to do it due to the pervasive conservative social attitude, especially in some cities. One interviewee stated: 'Potentially every time you go out you can be mistreated or harassed'. For instance, two of the interviewees recalled being beaten on the street for no clear reason other than their being gay. In addition, they referred to other members of the community being harassed on the street as well as in their private houses. They reported that recently some teenagers threw stones at a lesbian's house. Similar episodes of violence are mentioned in the *Unsafe Haven* reports (Helsinki Citizens Assembly – Turkey and Organization for Refuge, Asylum and Migration 2009, 2011).[41] Fearing to be assaulted or mistreated, LGBT asylum seekers try to hide their sexual orientation or gender identity from the local Turkish population[42] and sometimes also from the refugee population.[43] Indeed, other Iranians seeking refuge in Turkey repeatedly mock and ridicule the LGBT community. The 2009 *Unsafe Haven* report noted the case of a lesbian physically attacked by another asylum seeker while waiting to give a signature in Kayseri (Helsinki Citizens Assembly – Turkey and Organization for Refuge, Asylum and Migration 2009: 19). As a result, the LGBT refugee people in Kayseri try to protect themselves by living in their closed community and staying mainly at home. Also, they do not socialize much with the Turkish LGBTs, who are anyway very reserved.

However, the interviewees in Kayseri as well as ASAM confirmed that the police have been very responsive to their complaints since 2009 (Helsinki Citizens Assembly – Turkey and Organization for Refuge, Asylum and Migration 2011: 18).[44] While recognizing the positive attitude of the police in Kayseri, the *Unsafe Haven* report underlines that the help accorded by the police varies conspicuously from city to city and is usually not very satisfactory (Helsinki Citizens Assembly – Turkey and Organization for Refuge, Asylum and Migration 2011: 18).[45] Also, even though Turkish laws grant everyone the right to initiate legal proceedings on the same basis as normal citizens, in many cases the victims prefer not to report crimes to the police as they do not believe in their assistance and they fear retaliation from local communities or other Iranians (Helsinki Citizens Assembly – Turkey and Organization for Refuge, Asylum and Migration 2009: 20). In addition, some refugees decide not to initiate legal proceedings in order not to delay their resettlement procedures. Indeed, Kaos GL documented the case of a gay refugee who was raped in Turkey and whose resettlement procedure was suspended as a consequence of the trial related to this event. Thus, even if the police's responsiveness is a very positive element, LGBTs do not always seek justice for different reasons and continue to live in constant fear.

5.5.2 Access to work and means of survival

As for other asylum seekers and refugees, it is almost impossible for LGBTs to find a regular job in Turkey. Indeed, the law grants foreigners the possibility to obtain a legal work permit only if a qualified Turkish national cannot be identified (UNHCR Office in Turkey 2010).[46] Also, they must hold a six-month residence permit, the *ikamet*.[47] Usually lacking the language skills to meet these requirements, asylum seekers and refugees frequently resort to illegal jobs. However, even when obtaining illegal jobs they are usually exploited and may have difficulties in getting their salaries. These difficulties are exacerbated if the person is LGBT and the *Unsafe Haven* reports document multiple cases of discrimination in the access to jobs and harassment in the workplace (Helsinki Citizens Assembly – Turkey and Organization for Refuge, Asylum and Migration 2009: 23–25, 2011: 21–22, see also Kaos GL Association 2009).

Seventy per cent of the LGBT refugee population in Kayseri was reported not to be very poor, while the rest was described as living in extremely harsh economic conditions. For instance, a transgender woman explained that her economic condition was so bad on her arrival in Turkey that she had to share her house with a man and accept his sexual proposals. The people interviewed asserted that they were almost never able to work[48] and they experienced discrimination mainly due to their status as refugees, sometimes aggravated by their LGBT identity. They support their lives through their savings and in sporadic cases through money sent from their families.[49] In addition, some LGBT asylum seekers and refugees receive assistance from local churches as well as from the Iranian Railroad for Queer Refugees, an Iranian LGBT association based in Canada.[50] Limited economical assistance is also provided by UNHCR to the most vulnerable cases, in particular after the recognition of the refugee status.

Lastly, some LGBT people turn to sex work as a survival option (Helsinki Citizens Assembly – Turkey and Organization for Refuge, Asylum and Migration 2011: 22). However, getting to know the scope of this phenomenon is very difficult because people doing it tend to avoid speaking about it. The few LGBT Iranian sex workers reported to be working in Kayseri were reputedly already engaged in that type of work in Iran.

5.5.3 Housing

Turkey does not have reception centres for asylum seekers and refugees who are not provided with accommodation (UNHCR 2009b: 6); they must pay for their own expenses. Due to their precarious economic conditions, LGBT refugees often have to share their apartment and live in overcrowded and unhealthy places. Typically, they decide to live with other members of the LGBT community to avoid additional discriminations.[51]

Most of them face discrimination due to their sexual orientation or gender identity when looking for accommodation. They encounter hostility from the local population but also from other refugees. Kaos GL documented the case of a transgender woman who was a victim of physical assault at the hands of her landlord in Ankara (Kaos GL 2009). Similarly, a transgender woman in Kayseri said she was harassed and abused a lot due to her gender identity while trying to find an apartment (Helsinki Citizens Assembly – Turkey and Organization for Refuge, Asylum and Migration 2011: 19–20).

It should be noted that Turkey does not guarantee protection from discrimination in the access to housing on the basis of sexual orientation or gender identity. Refugees and asylum seekers do not usually have a standard contract and thus it might be difficult for them to start legal proceedings against the landlord in case of eviction, even though in theory this is not impossible (Helsinki Citizens Assembly – Turkey and Organization for Refuge, Asylum and Migration 2011: 20).

5.5.4 Education

Turkish law recognizes the right to primary education for both citizens and non-citizens, and grants to foreign adults the opportunity to attend language and vocational classes. However, the students must hold a regular residence permit, which is not always the case (Helsinki 2011: 24–25).

Anyway, these services are not always available, especially in minor satellite cities. Indeed, only a few NGOs in Turkey are able to provide language classes while not all refugees are aware of this facility. Also, in some cases, LGBT people attending those courses decide to quit because of being mistreated by classmates (Helsinki Citizens Assembly – Turkey and Organization for Refuge, Asylum and Migration 2011: 25).

The LGBT asylum seekers and refugees interviewed in Kayseri did not attend any classes. They underlined the importance of learning the language but said that they did not have access to language and vocational classes.

5.5.5 Health care and social assistance

Ninety per cent of the LGBT asylum seekers and refugees in Kayseri were exempted from paying the residential fees.[52] Holding a residence permit, *ikamet*, is fundamental for accessing social assistance and being granted free medical care in particular cases. The people interviewed sought medical assistance and never had problems related to their sexual orientation or gender identity. LGBT people are usually respected by health care providers but some of them are not able to afford some treatments due to financial constraints (Helsinki Citizens Assembly – Turkey and Organization for Refuge, Asylum and Migration 2011: 23).

The LGBT interviewed in Kayseri never sought social assistance. However, cases of discrimination were documented for LGBT seeking social assistance in Kayseri and in other cities (source: ASAM, oral information).

5.5.6 A psychological unsafe haven

Gun stressed the importance of perceiving the living place as a *psychological safe haven,* especially for refugees who have experienced serious trauma (Gun 2011). Indeed, refugees remain in a condition in which their lives are suspended and have feelings of non-existence. If this might be common to all displaced people, the specific situation of LGBT people carries additional concerns.

In the city of Kayseri the precarious life conditions and the frightening environment has led to psychological problems. In addition, being practically forced to live in their closed LGBT community, they develop an extreme feeling of loneliness and helplessness. The transgender woman interviewed said that she became depressed during her staying in Turkey. A gay asylum seeker said that due to the stress resulting from the harsh living conditions and the fact that his status was pending at UNHCR, he started to think about committing suicide for the first time in his life. This case seems not to be isolated as numerous suicides attempts were reported by LGBT asylum seekers and refugees living in Turkey in the last three years (Helsinki Citizens Assembly – Turkey and Organization for Refuge, Asylum and Migration 2011: 23).

The interviewees underlined that the psychological suffering is one of their main concerns and complained that the services offered by the NGOs supporting them, such as ASAM, are not effective.

5.6 Conclusions

This chapter presented the challenges that LGBT asylum seekers and refugees face after fleeing from their countries of origin, while they are looking for protection and safety in another country.

As far as the protection dimension is concerned, it is well-established that LGBT asylum seekers are entitled to international protection if they meet the Refugee Convention requirements. However, different variables contribute to the fact that LGBT asylum seekers who are, in fact, fleeing persecution see their claims rejected. Emotional and psychological problems which are related to their being LGBT asylum seekers can play against the applicants and be considered to undermine their credibility. Moreover, examiners might subconsciously adopt westernized stereotypical positions or homophobic attitudes, as a result of the fact that LGBT issues represent a deviation from the constituted gender roles everywhere in the world.

In order to overcome the impasse that decisions on LGBT can sometimes create, Millbank's statement regarding refugee law in sexuality cases can be helpful. Indeed, more than in other cases, increased 'empathy and imagination' are more crucial than a better application of the law (Millbank 2002: 34). This approach envisages a deeper understanding of the cases that takes duly into account the particular features of LGBT experiences, both in the country of origin as well as in the country of refuge. It is on the latter aspect that this chapter has focussed.

As far as the living conditions of LGBT asylum seekers and refugees in Turkey are concerned, it is evident that the country is not experienced as a safe refuge. Positive trends were registered regarding the treatment by UNHCR staff and the local authorities, in particular in Kayseri. However, training should continue both for UNHCR and for the police in order to increase awareness about LGBT specific concerns. In particular, the police should be warned to support victims of ill-treatment and follow up more actively on their complaints. Indeed, LGBT asylum seekers and refugees are not only discriminated against, but also suffer serious episodes of violence. As they fear attacks from the local or the refugee population, they prefer to hide themselves and try to find peace in their closed LGBT community.

LGBT refugees live a suspended life waiting for the UNHCR decision or for resettlement in a third country. More than other asylum seekers and refugees, they are marginalized from the surrounding context and experience feeling of loneliness and hopelessness that may result in suicide attempts. LGBTs' main concerns derive from precarious living conditions, where psychological and security problems assume great relevance. New solutions aimed at providing effective psychological support to the people in need should be explored. Also, Turkish classes and financial assistance should be ensured. Lastly, LGBT refugees should be allowed to move to bigger and less conservative cities such as Istanbul, Ankara and Izmir (Helsinki Citizens Assembly – Turkey and Organization for Refuge, Asylum and Migration 2011: 26).

It should also be considered that the general negative atmosphere surrounding the LGBT community in Turkey may have an impact on the asylum procedure. Indeed, continuous experiences of exclusion, discrimination and violence influence the psychological well-being of the applicants. Their ability to give coherent statements during the asylum interview can be reduced by the experience of Turkey as an unsafe country of refuge. In addition, they may underestimate the fear they felt they had in the country of origin on account of the fears they experience in the country of refuge. This may impact negatively on the accuracy of their statements during the asylum interview. Thus, the link between living conditions in the country of refuge and asylum procedure should be further explored in order to assure that LGBT asylum seekers receive adequate protection.

Although this chapter has focussed on the situation in Turkey, where the position of both asylum seekers and that of LGBT people is precarious, these findings are relevant for other countries as well. Even in countries where asylum seekers are provided with reception facilities, and in countries where the position of LGBTs is generally good, LGBT asylum seekers face homophobic and transphobic incidents in reception centres, accommodation centres and in alien detention (Jansen and Spijkerboer 2011: 77–79). These incidents may have particularly serious effects on LGBT asylum seekers because many of them feel they cannot turn to asylum seekers from their country of origin for support against negative experiences. The isolation many LGBT asylum seekers experience in countries with high reception standards may cause effects similar to those of LGBT asylum seekers in Turkey. Although this is an under-researched issue, this chapter makes clear that such incidents may have effects on the ability to give statements during asylum interviews, as well as on the perception of the problems LGBT asylum seekers have experienced in their country of origin. As a result, the difficult situation of LGBT asylum seekers in reception facilities is not just a problem in itself; it may also endanger their entitlement to protection as refugees.

5.7 Notes

* This chapter is a revised version of the author's master thesis entitled: 'Lesbian, Gay, Bisexual and Transgender (LGBT) Refugees looking for protection and safety: challenges in refugee status determination and living conditions in Turkey' – Master in Human Rights and Conflict Management (VIII ed.), Sant'Anna School of Advanced Studies, Pisa, Italy, April 2011.

1 These countries are Iran, Mauritania, Saudi Arabia, Sudan, United Arab Emirates, Yemen and Nigeria.

2 The interviews with the Iranian refugees and local NGOs were conducted by the author in March 2011.

3 The reports relating to LGBT in Turkey were produced by Helsinki Citizens Assembly – Turkey and Organization for Refuge, Asylum and Migration; Amnesty International; Human Rights Watch and Kaos GL Association.

4 States party to the Refugee Convention and/or the 1967 Protocol are obliged to apply at a minimum the Convention criteria in determining if a person is eligible for refugee status. In countries that are not party to the Convention and/or the Protocol, and in countries party to these instruments that did not establish the required procedures or have not established them adequately, UNHCR eligibility officers are in charge of the refugee status determination (UNHCR 2005: 9–11).

5 In 1995, UNHCR declared homosexuals eligible for refugee status as members of a particular social group and nowadays around 18 States recognize people persecuted on the basis of sexual orientation and gender identity as a social group in conformity with the Refugee Convention definition (Choi 2010: 2).

6 'A particular social group is a group of persons who share a common characteristic other than their risk of being persecuted, or who are perceived as a group by the society. The characteristic will often be one which is innate, unchangeable, or which is otherwise fundamental to the identity, conscience or exercise of one's human rights' (UNHCR 2002b: para. 11).

7 It is internationally recognized that three social groups may be identified considering the immutability approach. In this sense a group can be identified

by: 'an innate, unchangeable characteristic; a past temporary or voluntary status that is unchangeable because of its historical permanence; a characteristic or association that is so fundamental to human dignity that group members should not be compelled to forsake it' (UNHCR 2002b: para. 3).

8 Interestingly, in part E about credibility, the reference is mainly to sexual orientation and not to gender identity. This is not very appropriate, as not every LGBT person has a claim based on sexual orientation. Still, it is true that sexual orientation claims are more difficult to assess, whereas transgender claims are considered to be more 'visible', thus easier to prove (Swink 2006: 2).

9 The benefit of the doubt principle is quoted from para. 196 of the UNHCR *Handbook*: 'If the applicant's account appears credible, he or she should unless there are good reasons to the contrary, be given the benefit of the doubt' (UNHCR 2008: para. 35).

10 The conclusions of the UNHCR expert roundtable read: 'A superficial understanding of what it means to be LGBTI as well as an absence of cross-cultural understandings of sexuality and gender can lead to negative credibility determinations' (UNHCR 2010b: para. 17).

11 The expression 'imagining otherness' is taken from Millbank (2002).

12 Choi notes that the discretion requirement was applied especially in early cases in the 1990s, but this trend continues also nowadays (Choi 2010: 4). However, according to Walker the majority of the countries in the world do not apply the discretion requirement (Walker 2000: 205).

13 In January 2011 the number of asylum seekers was 6,715 whereas the number of refugees was 10,032. The general recognition rate for refugees in 2010 was 65 per cent.

14 Turkey ratified the Refugee Convention in 1961 (Law n. 10898) and the Protocol in 1967.

15 Events occurring in Europe should be understood as events occurring in a country member of the Council of Europe. Turkey is expected to adopt the first ever asylum law in the next years and lifting the geographical limitation is still under discussion. In the meantime, UNHCR will continue to conduct RSD for non European refugees.

16 UNHCR conducts refugee status determination under its mandate and applies the UNHCR *Procedural Standards for Refugee Status Determination under UNHCR's Mandate*.

17 Between 50 and 60 European refugees were present in Turkey in 2010. Source: ASAM.

18 UNHCR is quoted in the so called '1994 Asylum Regulation' (Regulation No. 94/6169 of 30 November 1994 on the procedures and principles related to population movements and aliens arriving in Turkey either as individuals or in groups wishing to seek asylum either from Turkey or requesting residence permits in order to seek asylum from another country, amended in 2006) only in relation to its role in facilitating resettlement and assisting refugees. The presence of UNHCR in Turkey is determined only by the 1965 Revised Standard Agreement between the United Nations and the Government of Turkey referring to the 1946 Convention on Privileges and Immunities of the United Nations.

19 The application for 'temporary asylum seeker status' is highlighted by the 1994 Asylum Regulation.

20 The RSD interview is not conducted unless the person is registered with the government.

21 Refugees are not allowed to reside in the largest cities in Turkey, i.e. Istanbul, Izmir and Ankara. They are assigned to one of the so-called satellite cities. Their number is decided by the Minister of Interior and varies during the years. In March 2011 there were 51 satellite cities. The cities hosting the highest number of refugees and asylum seekers were Kayseri, Nevşehir, Niğde, Kırşehir, Tokat, Sivas, Yozgat, Konya, Isparta, Burdur, Adana, Hatay, Afyon, Gaziantep, Van, Kastamonu, Amasya, Karaman, Aksaray. Source: ASAM.

22 The applicant is not immediately informed about the positive outcome of the interview granting him or her asylum in Turkey. Indeed, the procedure for temporary asylum is usually completed when the applicant has already been recognized as a refugee by UNHCR and is about to leave the country (Helsinki Citizens Assembly – Turkey and Organization for Refuge, Asylum and Migration 2011: 13).

23 Zieck concludes that Turkey should not be bound by the principle of *non-refoulement* in terms of the Convention as far as non-European refugees are concerned as Turkey is a *persistent objector*. Still, Turkey is bound by Article 3 of the European Convention on Human Rights (ECHR) (Zieck 2010: 12). The idea presented by Zieck is not supported by the author of this chapter, as no evidence was found of Turkey being a persistent objector not accepting *non-refoulement* in relation to ECHR judgments.

24 Turkey signed the ECHR on 4 November 1950 and ratified it on 18 May 1954. The ECHR is available at http://conventions.coe.int/Treaty/Commun/ChercheSig.asp?NT=005&CM=&DF=&CL=ENG (accessed 10 December 2012).

25 The cost of the *ikamet* is decided by the government and varies every year. For 2011, asylum seekers were obliged to pay at a minimum 149 Turkish Lira plus residential fees. These fees are variable according to nationality (for Sudanese, Iranians, Afghans – $25 for the first month and $5 for the following months; for Iraqis, Tunisians and Egyptians $5 for the first month and $0.5 for the following months) and can be waived in case of indigence (Helsinki Citizens Assembly – Turkey and Organization for Refuge, Asylum and Migration 2011: 3).

26 Resettlement countries asses the case and decide to accept the refugee on their territories according to their national criteria. The decisional process includes an interview by consular or immigration staff of the country and security verifications.

27 Even though there is collaboration between the Turkish authorities and UNHCR, UNHCR decisions are not always respected by the Turkish authorities. Thus, a refugee recognized by UNHCR can still be repatriated by the Turkish authorities, as some cases ruled by the European Court of Human Rights demonstrate (Zieck 2010: 4–5).

28 These estimates derive from the unofficial data from UNHCR and ASAM.

29 In 2010, the acceptance rate was almost 100 per cent for this category.

30 Although LGBTs are not considered as vulnerable people *per se*, they can be included in one of the categories of applicants with 'special needs'. For instance, transgenders are commonly considered as vulnerable cases (UNHCR 2003: para. 3.4).

31 I refer to the Helsinki reports (2009 and 2011) in these terms.

32 The allocation of additional resources to the Office created new opportunities for trainings and monitoring by the supervisors (Helsinki Citizens Assembly – Turkey and Organization for Refuge, Asylum and Migration 2011).

33 UNHCR headquarters' concern towards LGBT asylum seekers and refugees is proved by the elaboration of the *Guidance Note* in 2008 and the organization of the workshop held in Geneva in October 2010. On 23 October 2012 UNHCR issued the Guidelines on International Protection No. 9: Claims to Sexual Orientation and/or Gender Identity within the Context of Article 1A (2) of the 1951 Convention and/or its 1967 Protocol relating to the status of Refugees that were not addressed in this chapter.

34 The new policies draw attention to credibility of the applicants' claims, while considering laws criminalizing homosexuality and discriminatory practices as persecutory *per se*.

35 The applicants have the right 'to request that registration and RSD interviews are conducted by UNHCR staff and interpreters of the sex preferred by the Applicant, where available' (UNHCR 2003: 42).

36 'Applicants should be advised that reporting through complaints procedures will not in any way prejudice or positively influence the consideration of their refugee claim or other decisions regarding assistance or services to which the complainant would otherwise be entitled' (UNHCR 2003: para. 2.6).

37 This was the expression used by some of the refugees and asylum seekers interviewed in Kayseri.

38 The three biggest LGBT organizations (Lambda Istanbul, Kaos GL Ankara and Black Pink Triangle Izmir) have repeatedly been taken to Court in recent years with the accusations of 'fuelling immorality', 'going against Turkish identity', 'housing illegal activities' and 'violating values and family structures'. However, the only provisions explicitly discriminating towards LGBT are the one relating to the military service. Indeed, gays are exempted from the service as homosexuality is considered an illness (Human Rights Watch 2008: 80).

39 Some of the examples quoted by Amnesty International are particularly significant. For instance, Aliye Kavaf, the Minister of State responsible for Women and the Family, stated: 'homosexuality is a biological disorder and should be treated'. In 2003 Prime Minister Recep Tayyip Erdoğan's spokesperson held that LGBTs could not be members of his party. Also, Members of Parliament justified the absence of reforms on these issues with the excuse that the population was not ready. The national attitude is mirrored in the international context, where Turkey did not support initiatives aiming at improving LGBT protection. For instance, in May 2010, during the United Nation's Universal Periodic Review process, Turkey rejected the recommendations to adopt non-discrimination provisions relating to sexual orientation and gender identity. In December 2010, Turkey did not support the United Nations General Assembly Resolution that condemns extrajudicial, summary or arbitrary executions with reference to people targeted due to their sexual orientation. Moreover, in March 2011, Turkey did not support a joint statement at the United Nations Human Rights Council on ending acts of violence and human rights violations based on sexual orientation and gender identity.

40 Amnesty International underlines that there are no official statistics relating to the attacks suffered by LGBTs but according to human rights organizations 16 murders were perpetrated in 2010 due to the victims' sexual orientation or gender identity (Amnesty International 2011: 30). The 2011 *Unsafe Haven* report documents instead 45 LGBT murders resulting from hate-motivated crimes (Helsinki Citizens Assembly – Turkey and Organization for Refuge, Asylum and Migration 2011: 4)

41 The vast majority of the 108 people interviewed for both the reports referred to physical safety as one of their main concerns. The vast majority suffered at least one episode of violence during their stay in Turkey. Five violent physical attacks, two sexual assaults and numerous verbal harassments and threats against LGBT asylum seekers and refugees have been documented by the *Unsafe Haven* reports since 2009.
42 Lesbians are specially careful in hiding their sexual orientation in order not be harassed (Helsinki Citizens Assembly – Turkey and Organization for Refuge, Asylum and Migration 2011: 16).
43 In one case mentioned by one interviewee, an asylum seeker kept describing himself as a political refugee while his case was based on sexual orientation.
44 The positive engagement of the police followed an episode of particular hostility towards some Iranian LGBTs living in Kayseri.
45 In many cases the police did not offer adequate support and protection and, instead, dissuade the victims from making complaints.
46 Law on Work permit of Foreigners, n. 4817 of 2003.
47 However, at least for the LGBTs in Kayseri this does not constitute a problem as 90 per cent of them got an exemption.
48 Some of the interviewees said they were able to work only occasionally. The few interviewees who were able to work declared that in some instances it was difficult for them to be paid. These difficulties were related to discrimination for being LGBT or foreigners.
49 Some Iranian families prefer to send their LGBT children out of the country to save them from persecution.
50 See http://www.irqr.net/finaid/fin-aid-application.htm (accessed 3 March 2011).
51 This is true also for the case of Kayseri. Still, while ASAM maintains that all the LGBT refugees live in the same area, this was not confirmed by the interviewees.
52 UNHCR has always criticized the obligation of the payment of a residential fee for asylum seekers. On a more positive note, since 2008 Turkey has started to grant more exceptions to asylum seekers and refugees. Source: ASAM.

5.8 References

American Psychological Association, *Sexual Orientation and Homosexuality. Answers to your questions for a better understanding*, available at http://www.apa.org/topics/sexuality/orientation.aspx (accessed 3 March 2012).

Amnesty International (2001), *Crimes of Hate, Conspiracy of Silence, Torture and Ill-treatment Based on Sexual Identity*, ACT 40/016/2001, London: Amnesty International Publications.

Amnesty International (2011), *Not an Illness nor a Crime: Lesbian, Gay, Bisexual and Transgender People in Turkey Demand Equality*, London: Amnesty International Publications, available at http://www.amnesty.org/en/library/asset/EUR44/001/2011/en/aff47406-89e4-43b4-93ed-ebb6fa107637/eur440012011en.pdf (accessed 3 March 2012).

Berg, L. and Millbank, J. (2009) 'Constructing the personal narratives of lesbian, gay and bisexual asylum claimants', *Journal of Refugee Studies*, 22(2): 195–223, Oxford: Oxford University Press, available at http://jrs.oxfordjournals.org/content/22/2/195.abstract (accessed 3 March 2012).

Choi, V. (2010) 'Living discreetly: a catch 22 in refugee status determinations on the basis of sexual orientation', *Brooklyn Journal of International Law*, 36: 241–263.

Daley, K. and Kelley, N. (2000) 'Particular social group: a human rights based approach in Canadian jurisprudence', *International Journal of Refugee Law*, 12(2): 148–174, Oxford: Oxford University Press, available at http://ijrl.oxfordjournals.org/content/12/2/148.abstract (accessed 3 March 2012).

Davuergne, C. and Millbank, J. (2003) 'Burdened by proof: how the Australian Tribunal system has failed lesbian and gay asylum seekers', *Federal Law Review*, 31(2): 299–243, Canberra: ANU College of Law, available at http://ssrn.com/abstract=700503 (accessed 3 March 2012).

Ettelbrik, P.L. and Zeran, A. T. (2010) *The Impact of the Yogyakarta Principles on International Human Rights Law Development. A study of November 2007 – June 2010*, available at http://www.ypinaction.org/files/02/57/Yogyakarta_Principles_Impact_Tracking_Report.pdf (accessed 3 March 2012).

Gun, Z. (2011) 'From past to present human at the nexus between laws, conventions, and borders: psychological disturbance during asylum application process', UNHCR seminar, Turkey's Historical Tradition of Asylum: Past practice and Future Application in the Context of Developing Legal Frameworks, Ankara, 6–7 January 2011.

Hathaway, J.C. and Foster, M. (2003) 'Membership of a Particular Social Group: Discussion Paper No. 4 Advanced Refugee Law Workshop, International Association of Refugee Law Judges Auckland, New Zealand, 2002', *International Journal Refugee Law*, 15(3): 477–491, Oxford: Oxford University Press, available at http://ijrl.oxfordjournals.org/content/15/3/477.extract (accessed 3 March 2012).

Helsinki Citizens Assembly – Turkey and Organization for Refuge, Asylum and Migration (2009) *Unsafe Haven: The Security Challenges Facing Lesbian, Gay, Bisexual and Transgender Asylum Seekers and Refugees in Turkey*, San Francisco, CA: ORAM.

Helsinki Citizens Assembly – Turkey and Organization for Refuge, Asylum and Migration (2011) *Unsafe Haven: the Security Challenges Facing Lesbian, Gay, Bisexual and Transgender Asylum Seekers and Refugees in Turkey*, updated and revised edition, San Francisco, CA: ORAM, available at http://www.oraminternational.org/images/stories/PDFs/oram-unsafe-haven-2011-web.pdf (accessed 3 March 2012).

Hinger, S. (2010) 'Finding the fundamental: shaping identity in gender and sexual orientation based asylum claims', *Columbia Journal of Gender and Law*, 19(2): 367–408, available at http://law-journals-books.vlex.com/vid/fundamental-shaping-orientation-asylum-202580803 (accessed 3 March 2012).

Human Rights Watch (2008) *We Need a Law for Liberation*, New York, NY: Human Rights Watch Publications, available at http://www.hrw.org/sites/default/files/reports/turkey0508_1.pdf (accessed 3 March 2012).

Human Rights Watch (2009) *Together, Apart. Organizing Around Sexual Orientation and Gender Identity Worldwide*, New York, NY: Human Rights Watch Publications, available at http://www.hrw.org/sites/default/files/reports/lgbt0509web.pdf (accessed 3 March 2012).

Immigration and Refugee Board of Canada (2007) *Turkey: Treatment of Gay, Lesbian and Transgender People by Turkish Society; Treatment by Authorities; Legislation, Protection and Services Available*, TUR102515.E, available at http://www.unhcr.org/refworld/docid/46fa537428.html (accessed 4 March 2012).

International Commission of Jurists (2007) *Yogyakarta Principles on the Application of International Human Rights Law in Relation to Sexual Orientation and Gender Identity*, 6 March 2006, available at http://www.yogyakartaprinciples.org/principles_en.htm (accessed 3 March 2012).

Jansen, S. and Spijkerboer, T. (2011) *Fleeing Homophobia, Asylum Claims Related to Sexual Orientation and Gender Identity in Europe*, COC Netherlands and VU University Amsterdam, available at http://www.rechten.vu.nl/nl/onderzoek/conferenties-en-projecten/onderzoeksproject-fleeing-homophobia/index.asp (accessed 9 December 2012).

Kaos GL Association (2009) *Report on the Problems of the Lesbian, Gay, Bisexual, Transvestite and Transsexual (LGBTT) Refugees*, Ankara: Kaos GL Association.

Landau, J. (2005) '"Soft immutability" and "imputed gay identity": recent developments in transgender and sexual-orientation-based asylum claims', *Fordham Urban Law Journal*, 32: 237–263.

LaViolette, N. (1997) 'The immutable refugees: sexual orientation in Canada (AG) v. Ward', *University of Toronto Faculty of Law Review*, 55(1): 1–42.

LaViolette, N. (2007) 'Gender-related refugee claims: expanding the scope of the Canadian guidelines a critical commentary', *International Journal of Refugee Law*, 19(2): 169–214, Oxford: Oxford University Press, available at http://ijrl.oxfordjournals.org/content/19/2/169.abstract (accessed 4 March 2012).

LaViolette, N. (2009) 'Independent human rights documentation and sexual minorities: an ongoing challenge for the Canadian refugee determination process', *The International Journal of Human Rights*, 13(2/3): 437–467.

LaViolette, N. (2010a), *Sexual Orientation, Gender Identity and the Refugee Status Determination Process*, Immigration and Refugee Board of Canada, Refugee Protection Division.

LaViolette, N. (2010b) 'UNHCR Guidance Note on Refugee Claims Relating to Sexual Orientation and Gender Identity: a Critical Commentary', *International Journal of Refugee Law*, 22(2): 173–208, available at http://ijrl.oxfordjournals.org/content/22/2/173.abstract (accessed 4 March 2012).

Millbank, J. (2002) 'Imagining otherness: refugee claims on the basis of sexuality in Canada and Australia', *Melbourne University Law Review*, 26: 144–177.

Millbank, J. (2003) 'Gender, visibility and public space in refugee claims on the basis of sexual orientation', *Seattle Journal for Social Justice*, 1(3): 725–741.

Millbank, J. (2009a) 'From discretion to disbelief: recent trends in refugee determinations on the basis of sexual orientation in Australia and the United Kingdom', *The International Journal of Human Rights*, 13 (2–3): 391–414.

Millbank, J. (2009b) '"The Ring of Truth": a case study of credibility assessment in particular social group refugee determinations', *International Journal of Refugee Law*, 21(1): 1–33, available at http://ijrl.oxfordjournals.org/content/21/1/1.short (accessed 3 March 2012).

N Kendall, C. (2003) 'Lesbian and gay refugees in Australia: now that "acting discreetly" is no longer an option, will equality be forthcoming?', *International Journal of Refugee Law*, 15(4): 714–749, available at http://ijrl.oxfordjournals.org/content/15/4/715.short (accessed on 4 March 2012).

Neilson, V. (2005) 'Homosexual or female? Applying gender-based asylum jurisprudence to lesbian asylum claims', *Stanford Law and Policy Review*, 16 (2): 417–4441.

O'Flaherty, M. and Fisher, J. (2008) 'Sexual orientation, gender identity and international human rights law: contextualizing the Yogyakarta principles',

Human Rights Law Review, 8(2): 207–248, available at http://www.yogyakartaprinciples.org/yogyakarta-article-human-rights-law-review.pdf (accessed 3 March 2012).

Organization for Refuge, Asylum and Migration (2011) *Testing Sexual Orientation, A Scientific and Legal Analysis of Plethysmography in Asylum & Refugee Status Proceedings*, San Francisco, CA: ORAM, available at http://www.oraminternational.org/images/stories/PDFs/testing%20sexual%20orientation%20feb%202011%20download.pdf (accessed 3 March 2012).

Randazzo, T. (2005) 'Social and legal barriers: sexual orientation and asylum in the United States', in E. Luibhéid and L. Cantu (eds), *Queer Migrations: Sexuality, US Citizenship, and Border Crossing*, Minneapolis, MN: University of Minnesota Press, pp. 30–38.

Regulation No. 1994/6169 on the Procedures and Principles related to Possible Population Movements and Aliens Arriving in Turkey either as Individuals or in Groups Wishing to Seek Asylum either from Turkey or Requesting Residence Permission in order to Seek Asylum From Another Country (last amended 2006) [Turkey], No. 1994/6169, available at http://www.unhcr.org/refworld/docid/49746cc62.html (accessed 4 March 2012).

Rehaag, S. (2009) 'Bisexuals need not apply: a comparative appraisal of refugee law and policy in Canada, the United States, and Australia', *International Journal of Human Rights*, 13(2–3): 415–436.

Saiz, I. (2000) 'Bracketing sexuality: human rights and sexual orientation – a decade of development and denial at the UN', *Health and Human Rights*, 7(2): 48–80; reprinted in Sexuality Policy Watch (2005), Working Papers, n. 2, available at http://www.sxpolitics.org/wp-content/uploads/2009/03/workingpaper2.pdf (accessed 3 March 2012).

Swink, A. (2006) 'Queer refuge: a review of the role of country condition analysis in asylum adjudications for members of sexual minorities', *Hastings International and Comparative Law Review*, 29(2): 25.

UNHCR (1951 and 1967) 1951 Convention and 1967 Protocol Relating to the Status of Refugees, available at http://www.unhcr.org/3b66c2aa10.html (accessed 3 March 2012).

UNHCR (1992) *Handbook on Procedures and Criteria for Determining the Refugee Status under the 1951 Convention and the 1967 Protocol Relating to the Status of Refugees*, HCR/IP/4/Eng/REV.1, September 1979, reedited January 1992, Geneva: UNHCR, available at http://www.unhcr.org/refworld/pdfid/3ae6b3314.pdf (accessed 3 March 2012).

UNHCR (2002a) *Guidelines on International Protection No. 1: Gender-Related Persecution Within the Context of Article 1A(2) of the 1951 Convention and/or its 1967 Protocol Relating to the Status of Refugees*, HCR/GIP/02/01, available at http://www.unhcr.org/refworld/docid/3d36f1c64.html (accessed 3 March 2012).

UNHCR (2002b) *Guidelines on International Protection No. 2: 'Membership of a Particular Social Group' Within the Context of Article 1A(2) of the 1951 Convention and/or its 1967 Protocol Relating to the Status of Refugees*, HCR/GIP/02/02, available at http://www.unhcr.org/refworld/docid/3d36f23f4.html (accessed 3 March 2012).

UNHCR (2003) *Procedural Standards for Refugee Status Determination Under UNHCR's Mandate*, available at http://www.unhcr.org/refworld/docid/42d66dd84.html (accessed 3 March 2012).

UNHCR (2004) *Advisory Opinion by UNHCR to the Tokyo Bar Association Regarding Refugee Claims Based on Sexual Orientation*, available at http://www.unhcr.org/refworld/docid/4551c0d04.html (accessed 3 March 2012).

UNHCR (2005) *Refugee Status Determination, Identifying Who is a Refugee*, self-study module 2, Geneva: UNHCR, available at http://www.unhcr.org/refworld/pdfid/43141f5d4.pdf (accessed 3 March 2012).

UNHCR (2008), *UNHCR Guidance Note on Refugee Claims Relating to Sexual Orientation and Gender Identity*, available at http://www.unhcr.org/refworld/docid/48abd5660.html (accessed 3 March 2012).

UNHCR (2009a) *Information for Non-European Nationals Seeking Asylum in Turkey*, available at http://info.unhcr.org.tr/leaflets/AsylumInTurkey/AsylumInTurkey_English.pdf (accessed 3 March 2011).

UNHCR (2009b) *Written Submission by the Office of the United Nations High Commissioner for Refugees in the Case Abdolkhani and Karimnia v. Turkey (Application No. 30471/08)*, available at http://www.unhcr.org/refworld/docid/4991ad9f2.html (accessed 4 March 2012).

UNHCR (2010a) 'The Protection of Lesbian, Gay, Bisexual, Transgender and Intersex Asylum-Seekers and Refugees', discussion paper prepared for a UNHCR Roundtable on Asylum-Seekers and Refugees Seeking Protection on Account of their Sexual Orientation and Gender Identity, 30 September–1 October 2010, Geneva: UNHCR, Division of International Protection, available at http://www.unhcr.org/refworld/pdfid/4cff9a8f2.pdf (accessed 3 March 2012).

UNHCR (2010b), 'Summary Conclusions: Asylum seekers and Refugees Seeking Protection on Account of their Sexual Orientation and Gender Identity', UNHCR Roundtable 30 September–1 October 2010, Geneva: UNHCR, available at http://www.unhcr.org/refworld/pdfid/4cff99a42.pdf (accessed 3 March 2012).

UNHCR (2011), *2011 UNHCR country operations profile – Turkey*, available at http://www.unhcr.org/pages/49e48e0fa7f.html#

UNHCR (2012) *2012 UNHCR country operations profile – Turkey*, available at http://www.unhcr.org/pages/49e48e0fa7f.html# (accessed 3 March 2012).

UNHCR Office in Turkey (2010) *UNHCR in Turkey: Facts and Figures*, Ankara: UNHCR.

Walker, N.L. (2000) 'Sexuality and refugee status in Australia', *International Journal of Refugee Law*, 12(2): 175–211, available at http://ijrl.oxfordjournals.org/content/12/2/175.short (accessed 4 March 2012).

Zieck, M. (2010) 'UNHCR and Turkey, and beyond: of parallel tracks and symptomatic cracks', *International Journal of Refugee Law*, 22(4): 593–622, available at http://ijrl.oxfordjournals.org/content/22/4/593.abstract (accessed 3 March 2012).

5.9 Websites

http://www.irqr.net (accessed 3 March 2011).

http://www.ohchr.org/EN/Issues/Discrimination/Pages/LGBT.aspx (accessed 3 March 2011).

http://conventions.coe.int/Treaty/Commun/ChercheSig.asp?NT=005&CM=&DF=&CL=ENG (accessed 3 March 2011).

6 Developing a jurisprudence of transgender particular social group

*Laurie Berg and Jenni Millbank**

6.1 Introduction

In this chapter, we analyse refugee status determinations (RSD) in claims brought by applicants who articulate a fear of persecution on the basis that they are transgender, broadly defined to include those who are transsexual, cross-dressing, transvestite or who identify strongly with another gender. Our principal focus is on how trans identity and experience is framed within the terms of the Convention ground 'particular social group' (PSG) in the 1951 United Nations Convention Relating to the Status of Refugees (the Convention). In recent years, the protection needs of sexual minorities have received increasing attention (UNHCR 2008, 2011, 2012; Jansen and Spijkerboer 2011). However, to date, there remains a significant gap in the international literature surrounding asylum claims brought by transgender applicants, with the notable exception of the United States (see Neilson 2004; Landau 2004; Hanna 2005; Benson 2008; Mohyuddin 2001).

We seek to unpack how trans identity is understood, claimed and received in RSD, by attending to decision making processes and moments as much as, or even more than, outcomes. At the same time, we acknowledge that it is frequently not possible to discern from written reasons the multiple layers of how identity is articulated by the applicant, expressed by the advocate and understood by the decision maker. RSD is a multistage process in which identities are experienced, articulated, framed and translated – literally and figuratively – for the purposes of making the self intelligible within both the terms of the Convention and the decision maker's own understandings of human sexuality and behaviour (Berg and Millbank 2009).

We argue that the specific issues raised by trans asylum claims must be examined within an overarching analysis of persecution related to gender non-conformity – a framework which allows for complex intersections between sexuality, gender identity and gender (Prosser 1998; Sharpe 2002). The 2002 UNHCR Gender Guidelines make this connection explicit when they note the 'gender element' in claims that 'involve homosexuals, transsexuals or transvestites': 'the claimant has refused to adhere to socially or culturally defined roles or expectations of behaviour attributed to his or her sex'

(UNHCR 2002a: 4). Gender roles and expectations include particular sexual, as well as social, but sexualised, practices – including autonomous female sexuality, homosexual sex and widespread expectations of heterosexual marriage and child rearing. Relatedly, groups which are stigmatised as gender non-conforming are disproportionately likely to suffer sexualised forms of persecution, including 'corrective' rape and forced marriage (Oxford forthcoming; Dauvergne and Millbank 2010). Notably, although all of the jurisdictions in this study except New Zealand had gender guidelines in place at a domestic tribunal or administrative level at the time the cases were determined, only two Canadian decisions referenced such guidance (Immigration and Refugee Board of Canada 1996; Immigration Appellate Authority, UK 2000; UK Border Agency 2004; Coven 1995; Department of Immigration and Multicultural Affairs Australia 1997. The cases are *T98-04159* [2000] and *Montoya Martinez* [2011]).

Attending to the claimant's experience of gender non-conformity requires a careful and flexible process of setting out the PSG. Transgender identities can be extremely confronting for refugee law which evinces a preference for static and concrete identity groupings, preferably with external forms of corroboration. The process of asylum claims is built on an unrealistic ideal of a definitive and revelatory self (Jordan 2009; Berg and Millbank 2009), whereas trans claims necessarily involve fluidity – of sexed status, identification and bodily expression – arising from deeply internal senses of gender and sexuality. We argue that the PSG analysis must begin with a nuanced and validating account of the applicant's evolving gender identities over time with due attention to how this self-perception interacts with external perception of gender non-conformity.

This duality is required because a comprehensive analysis of persecution in any transgender claim must take in not only the self-identity of the applicant but also the imputations about gender and sexuality which are placed upon them. Transgender people subjected to violence, in a range of cultural contexts, frequently report that transphobic violence is expressed in homophobic terms (Moran and Sharpe 2004: 403). The tendency to translate violence against a trans person to homophobia reflects the role of gender in the attribution of homosexuality as well as the fact that hostility connected to homosexuality is often associated with perpetrators' prejudices about particular gender practices and their visibility (Mason 2002). Taken alone, either self perception or social perception (and indeed the US focus upon perpetrator motivation) is liable to mislead. This inter-relation is well captured in the opening paragraph of the recently issued UK Border Agency Asylum Policy Instruction on Gender Identity, which urges primary decision makers to consider claims in conjunction with separate Asylum Policy Instructions on gender and sexual orientation:

> The experiences of discrimination and persecution for transgender people are often distinct, and in addition to those they may experience due to

> other characteristics. For example, a transgender man may be perceived to be a lesbian even after gender reassignment if his 'new' gender is not acknowledged. A transgender woman may be vulnerable as a woman and as a transgender person.
>
> (UK Border Agency 2011a: 2)

A profound challenge of trans claims in the context of RSD, therefore, is to understand applicants' identities both as they are internally felt as well as externally perceived.

Our study indicated that, while trans claims appeared relatively successful (although we state this tentatively given our small sample), the PSG jurisprudence in this area is fundamentally incoherent. We observed an extraordinary diversity of PSGs, referencing transgender or sexual orientation or both. Sometimes the PSGs framed by decision makers were at odds with reported aspects of applicants' own self-identities, rendering invisible the applicants' experience of gender non-conformity. The lack of clarity of PSG in many decisions also misdirected the analysis in other areas of the claim such as persecution and failure of state protection. All too commonly, trans was simply treated as a subset or 'kind' of sexual orientation leading to erroneous comparisons between social groups and inappropriate application of country of origin information in the assessment of risk of persecution. On occasion we also found that trans status was uncritically conflated with either born or chosen gender in the assessment of risk or sufficiency of state protection.

6.2 The study

We gathered all publicly available decisions which concerned a trans applicant made by administrative tribunals and courts in Australia, New Zealand (NZ), Canada, the United Kingdom (UK) and the United States (US). This period covered 17 years, from the first identified case in July 1994 to July 2011. The cases involve applicants who self-describe as transgender, transsexual, cross-dressing or as a transvestite or otherwise strongly identify with another gender.

This yielded a very small pool of 37 publicly available decisions.[1] These cases are therefore only a starting point in the project of understanding the ways in which trans claims are made, heard and assessed in the English speaking countries under review. To this end, we added a further four unpublished tribunal decisions we received from advocates and one Australian tribunal decision accessed through a freedom of information request, a pool we will continue to expand as the study continues in an attempt to gather as much data on lower level adjudication as possible. We also hope to include English translations of decisions from a variety of European jurisdictions. The 42 decisions collected to date fall unevenly across our five receiving countries: with only three decisions from the UK, five from NZ, ten from Australia, 11 from the US[2] and 13 from Canada.[3] These figures vastly under-represent the number of such claims decided and are skewed against the forums in which such claims were likely to have been finally determined (lower level tribunals rather than appellate courts), as well as almost certainly misrepresenting the countries in which they were decided. In 2010, the UK determined more than 70 times as many on-shore asylum claims as NZ, such that NZ deciding more trans cases than the UK over a 17-year period is absurdly unlikely (UNHCR 2011: 18). The available cases are therefore much more a function of writing and release policies in each country. For example, in Australia approximately 40 per cent of tribunal decisions have been released in recent years (MRT/RRT 2006, 2007, 2009); the US is a much larger receiving nation but releases only 1.2 per cent of tribunal decisions (Neilson 2004: 267). As an additional caution, released decisions may not be representative of the determined cases in the countries deciding them, much less of the experiences of transgender applicants. In the US in particular there appears to be a wide schism between the publicly available appellate jurisprudence and lower level practice at Immigration Courts where decisions are rarely released (discussed below). Nonetheless, we believe that a close reading of the trends and divergences in the small pool of trans decisions that are on the public record is important, not least because these are the resources which lawyers and advocates most readily access. Such cases are disproportionately influential on future decisions at all levels because they are public *and* because there are so few of them.

6.3 Categories and terms

Trans terminology and categorisation remains hotly contested within and across trans communities (Broad 2002). Originating in the 1990s, the category 'transgender' sought to reflect the gender identities of those who cross gender boundaries, irrespective of a desire for sex reassignment surgery and/or hormonal treatments (Feinberg 1992; Bornstein 1994; Stryker 2008: 19). As we see in the analysis below, trans categories are porous and unstable; moreover, it was not clear in numerous cases which terms were being invoked by applicants or necessarily what decision makers meant by them. For example, 'transvestite' was used repeatedly in the case law to refer to cross-dressing behaviours with no clear sense of how this related to applicants' gender identity. Here we use the term 'transsexual' to describe a person who has changed, or is in the process of changing, physical sex to conform to gender identity, without predicating this upon any particular hormonal or surgical practice. We use 'MTF' or 'trans woman' to refer to someone born with a male body who has a female gender identity, and 'FTM' to refer to someone born with a female body who has a male gender identity. Of course, trans people, like the general population, are also represented across sexualities: transgender people may identify as straight, gay, bisexual or queer, or move between these. Equally, trans people may have complex gender identities, moving from one trans category to another over time.

When analysing the judgments we occasionally distinguish between 'chosen' gender and born sex if this was relevant to the determination (such as when decision makers compared trans women to 'women' or to 'men' or when they referred to applicants by their born/legal sex). This is not meant to imply that trans people necessarily experience their gender as a choice (indeed, many argue that it is biologically grounded: Wallbank 2004; Sharpe 2012); rather it was selected as the least disrespectful among current language options (for example 'acquired' in section 1(2) of the Gender Recognition Act 2004 (UK)).

6.4 Outcomes

Even with all of the acknowledged limitations about representativeness and absence of transparency, we believe it is still of interest to identify broad trends in order to provide a pathway for future research and advocacy.

Within the case set overall, half were positive decisions (21/42). In keeping with our earlier work on RSD outcomes, we counted 'positive' or 'negative' decisions from the perspective of the applicant, even if (as in the case of judicial review and also some UK tribunal outcomes) the decision involves remitting the claim for reconsideration rather than an actual grant of refugee status. This gives an inflated sense of 'positive' outcomes, as we do not have access to the majority of the remittal determinations and some, perhaps many, of these are ultimately negative to the applicant. Of the 21 positive decisions, only 13 involved a grant of asylum, while eight were remittals for rehearing. Table 6.1 details our case set to date, charting outcomes against countries of asylum and countries of origin.

6.4.1 Gender of claimants

We found that people who were identified as men at birth (MTF trans women) vastly outnumbered people who were identified as women at birth (FTM trans men). Thirty-eight cases concerned MTF trans women (including those labelled 'female identified gay men' and 'transvestites'; one more case concerned an applicant who identified as MTF where the decision contained evidence of an intersex condition). Only three of the 42 cases involved applicants whose born sex was female. This could be seen as a continuation of a trend in which (born) male applicants outnumber female applicants in RSD in ever increasing proportions in marginalised groups. In on-shore claims, men generally outnumber women as principal applicants by an approximate ratio of 2:1 (DIAC 2011: 9). In studies of sexual orientation-related RSD, men outnumber women by a 4:1 ratio (Millbank 2009; Jordan 2009: 169). In trans asylum this arises in our study as a ratio of MTFs versus FTMs of 13:1. At this stage we can only begin to consider reasons why this disparity is so extreme. In addition to possibly being more numerous than FTMs (American Psychiatric Association 2000), MTFs may also have greater mobility and

Table 6.1 Cases by jurisdiction

	Australia (10)	*Canada (13)*	*New Zealand (5)*	*United Kingdom (3)*	*United States (11)*
China (1)	MTF 1 neg				
Costa Rica (1)		MTF 1 neg			
El Salvador (4)		MTF 1 neg			MTF 1 neg MTF 2 pos
Germany (1)		MTF(I) 1 neg			
Guatemala (1)					FTM 1 pos
Honduras (1)					MTF 1 neg
India (1)					MTF 1 pos
Iran (3)		MTF 1 pos		MTF 1 neg MTF 1 pos	
Lebanon (4)	MTF 3 neg	FTM 1 pos			
Malaysia (1)	MTF 1 pos				
Mexico (10)		MTF 1 neg MTF 4 pos FTM 1 neg			MTF 4 pos
Pakistan (1)	MTF 1 pos				
Philippines (3)	MTF 1 neg	MTF 1 neg			MTF 1 pos
South Korea (1)	MTF 1 pos				
Thailand (7)	MTF 2 neg		MTF 5 neg		
Turkish Republic of Northern Cyprus (1)				MTF 1 pos	
Venezuela (1)		MTF 1 pos			

access to resources. Travel for all trans people is risky if official documentation reflects born sex and this is at odds with gender presentation. Options such as closeting chosen gender for the purpose of escape may not be open to FTMs if they come from countries where women cannot travel unaccompanied by men; likewise, business and student visas may be harder to obtain for born women (Jordan 2009: 171). In keeping with Jordan's finding that FTM applicants are likely to travel accompanied by family members, in the three FTM decisions in our pool, two applicants were accompanied by a mother or partner (who were also co-applicants), as opposed to only one of the 39 cases involving claimants who were born men. Mobility and other differences in FTM and MTF trans experience may also reflect an inner sense of safety and danger that remains predicated to a certain degree on born sex and early life experience (Moran and Sharpe 2004: 409).

6.4.2 Countries of origin

The countries of origin of claimants were: Mexico (ten decisions), Thailand (seven), El Salvador and Lebanon (each with four), and Iran and the Philippines (each with three). All of the remaining countries of origin gave rise to a single claim: those concerning South Korea, Malaysia, India, Pakistan, the Turkish Republic of North Cyprus, Venezuela and Guatemala were positive, while those regarding claimants from China, Germany, Costa Rica and Honduras were negative. Within the main countries of origin, success rates were very unevenly distributed: eight of ten claims from Mexico were positive, while all of the seven from Thailand were negative. El Salvador involved two positive and two negative, while two of three from Iran were positive and only one of four from Lebanon and one of three from the Philippines were positive. The positive rate, then, appears very much a function of the success of MTF/'female identified gay male' claimants from Mexico appearing predominantly in the US and Canadian jurisprudence. The positive rate in the US (nine of 11 decisions) is significantly higher than the positive rate in the four other countries under review, which seems paradoxical given that the US is the sole jurisdiction in our study to have not yet set precedent clearly establishing transgender as a PSG. We discuss below in more detail why this anomalous American approach to the PSG is cause for concern, despite the high positive rates it appears to have generated to date.

6.4.3 The meaning of success

While a 50 per cent positive decision rate may appear high, this figure requires some unpacking. First, the sample of cases is small and even a few negative decisions could tilt the figure greatly. Second, it must be recalled that not every 'positive' decision results in a grant of refugee status. In addition, the case set must be placed in a context in which trans people constitute highly visible minorities in many societies and as such experience extraordinarily high rates of discrimination and violence worldwide. It is therefore our view that a relatively high success rate should reflect strong factual bases of claims. Moreover, what is a 'high' success rate cannot only be assessed relative to the success rates of claimants from comparable social groups or countries of origin. Rather, a realistic appraisal of success rates must be relative to the quality of claims within the pool. If 80 or 90 per cent of applicants in a given pool appear to meet the Convention definition but only 50 per cent are granted status then this is in fact a *low* success rate. Evaluating the meaning of success rates must therefore involve a qualitative assessment and, to some extent, a subjective sense of what a result ought to have been (Legomsky 2007). While there were many thorough and well-grounded decisions in this case set, there were nonetheless several negative decisions which in our view were badly made and arguably wrong.

Within our case set, there was acceptance of the genuineness of claimants' trans identities in the majority of cases (although as we see, how those identities were defined was extraordinarily muddled). In fact, the credibility of an applicant on the issue of their gender identity was directly rejected in only a single case. This is strikingly different from claims based on sexual orientation where a significant portion of negative determinations in recent years appear to arise from rejection of applicants' claimed sexual orientation (Millbank 2009; Berg and Millbank 2009; UK Lesbian and Gay Immigration Group 2010; Jansen and Spijkeboer 2011). We considered whether trans identity was relatively uncontentious as a result of corroboration or 'proof' of status by trans claimants, particularly through medical evidence relating to bodily modification through surgery (Jansen and Spijkeboer 2011: 51) in contrast to sexual orientation claims where external verification of the claimed identity is rare (ORAM 2011). Yet on examination the presence of medical gender affirmation treatment through surgery or hormone treatment did not appear to correlate to any real difference in positive rates (eight of 21 positive decisions versus six of 21 negative decisions). Further, it was notable that only a minority of decisions in the case pool actually *recorded* information on whether such treatment had occurred (14 out of 42). This is remarkable given that in many western cultures and legal systems surgery in particular has been a major focus in determining and fixing sexed status (Sharpe 2006: 3, 7; Sabatello 2011: 61; *AB* [2011]) and recent policy guidance has highlighted medical 'corroboration' (or an explanation for its lack) as an expected element in transgender claims (US Citizenship and Immigration Services 2011: 46; UNHCR 2012: [63(iv)]).

We suggest that trans applicants were accepted as credible when their bodies conformed to a visual typology *and* their narratives to accepted western tropes of gender dysphoria. Clinical evidence still played a role but this was not solely medical documentation of surgical practices, rather it also comprised psychological assessment and corroborating accounts of applicants' gender narratives. In the classic transsexual 'wrong body' narrative (Stoller 1975; King 1993), self-perception from an early age is as a member of the opposite gender, evidenced through experiences of childhood play, adolescent behaviour and growing alienation from others (American Psychiatric Association 2000: 577–582). This narrative draws not only on the internal felt sense of gender but also on how gender is manifested externally, and so its emphasis can shift from an assessment of the individual's experience of their gender identity (the psychological) to an assessment of how the individual's gender identity is experienced by others (the social).

Our cases echoed these considerations. Decisions were replete with observations by adjudicators that they were satisfied that claimants genuinely were gender non-conformant with reasoning that drew on the applicant's medical history, their physical expression of gender at the hearing (including deportment and demeanour) and a coherent psychological description of their gender over time. For instance, under the heading 'Is the claimant a transsexual?', the Canadian tribunal stated in relation to a successful MTF applicant from Venezuela:

> The claimant presented herself as a woman. She was dressed as a woman and displayed the characteristics, gestures and behaviour of a woman. Dr. Xxxxxx, in his report, states that the claimant has had breast implant surgery and hormone treatments but also has normal male genitalia. The panel accepts that the claimant is a transsexual.
>
> (*T94-07129* [1995] at 3)

This applicant 'testified that throughout her life she has felt that she was a woman locked in a male body' and that 'she hoped to have a sex change operation shortly'. The decision concluded:

> that the claimant's gender identity is that of a female and is innate. The efforts that she has made to bring her physical characteristics in line with her gender identity is (sic) indicative of the extent to which she identifies with being a woman.
>
> (*T94-07129* [1995] at 4)

The applicant's mixed anatomical sexed characteristics were read in light of her dress, gestures, behaviour and 'wrong body' narrative. We see a desire for coherence in the emphasis placed in this passage not only on the medical evidence but also on the applicant's desire for further surgery to complete her transition. This credibility assessment about the genuineness of the applicant's trans identity becomes an assessment of the applicant's gender performance of femaleness. (Contrast the sole negative finding on claimed trans identity in which the Canadian tribunal held that the presentation of an MTF cross-dresser from El Salvador was characterised as 'a put-on' in which the applicant 'had pulled out no stops', appearing for 'his hearing dressed in a bare shouldered and immaculately coifed manner' (*Rivera* [2007] at [15]).

A further Canadian decision demonstrated concern with the authenticity of transsexual identity as borne out by *consistency* and *corroboration* by others in 'wrong body' narratives that did not centre proof of 'complete' or 'irreversible' surgical change. In a successful claim by an FTM applicant, the tribunal noted with approval that his mother testified that:

> the claimant never wore high heels or wanted to wear dresses like other girls of his age in Lebanon. At the hearing, the claimant presented himself as a man. He was dressed as a man and displayed the characteristic, voice, gestures and behaviour of a man.
>
> (*T94-07963* [1999] at 2)

However, as we see in the analysis below of PSG, many applicants expressed their identities in far more fractured terms, oscillating between terms referencing sexuality and gender identity, such as 'gays/transvestites and sex change people' (see e.g. *N02/41726* [2002] concerning a claim from Thailand) in narratives which lacked a coherent or linear sense of gender transition.

6.5 Articulating the basis of trans identity as a particular social group

Gender and sexual orientation were increasingly accepted as eligible bases for PSG in many receiving nations through the 1990s; trans has often been appended to these categories without additional analysis or explicit articulation.[4] The question of what makes trans people a protected group under the Convention is an incredibly complex one, which to date remains largely unexplored.

In the absence of clear articulation it seems that gender identity has often been characterised as the basis of a PSG through a process of analogy with sexual orientation. In the 2008 Guidance Note on sexual orientation and gender identity, UNHCR stated that many jurisdictions have recognized gay men and lesbians as a PSG before noting '[w]hile claims relating to bisexuals and transgender people have been less common, such groups may also constitute a particular social group' (UNHCR 2008: [32]).[5] The 2008 Guidance Note and 2012 UNHCR Guidelines on sexual orientation and gender identity, as well as domestic Gender Guidelines in Australia, explicitly adopt the formulation of transgender offered in the *Yogyakarta Principles on the Application of International Human Rights Law in Relation to Sexual Orientation and Gender Identity* (International Commission of Jurists 2007) of 'gender identity' as:

> [E]ach person's deeply felt internal and individual experience of gender, which may or may not correspond with the sex assigned at birth, including the personal sense of the body and other expressions of gender, including dress, speech and mannerisms.
>
> (UNHCR 2008, 2012: [9]; MRT and RRT 2010: 2)

Yet the very fluidity of shifting gender and sexuality identification involved in gender transitions poses numerous challenges to norms and requirements of innateness and unchangability enmeshed in the RSD elements of 'well-founded fear' and PSG: a heterosexual born man, once MTF, may 'become' a lesbian. And, as sexual orientation claims may often involve applicants with heterosexual histories or mixed identifications over time (Berg and Millbank 2009), so too may transgender applicants move back and forth between different gender identifications and expressions rather than a binary sex 'change'. Writing in the US context, K.L. Broad describes the work of trans movements as more committed to 'identity-blurring' than 'identity building' (Broad 2002: 244). The diversity of identification involved in gender variance is captured in a US study of 1,229 transgender people in which numerous respondents expressed a continuum of self-categorisation from female to male, such as 'in-between and beyond', 'shemale', 'gender neutral', 'intergendered' and '75% female but no plans on surgery or hormones' (Bockting 2008).

UNHCR defines particular social group in the following terms as a:

> group of persons who share a common characteristic other than their risk of being persecuted, or who are perceived as a group by society. The characteristic will often be one which is innate, unchangeable, or which is otherwise fundamental to identity, conscience or the exercise of one's human rights.
>
> (UNHCR 2002a: [11])

This definition was intended to include, and reconcile, both the 'protected characteristics' and 'social perception' approaches to PSG which had developed in the jurisprudence of different receiving nations (Foster 2012). Michelle Foster notes that there has been a recent trend toward the narrowing of PSG as a result of wording in the EU Qualification Directive (Council Directive 2004/83/EC) suggesting, and US jurisprudence explicitly requiring, the satisfaction of *both* the protected characteristic and social perception elements, rather than treating them as alternative bases as clearly intended by UNHCR (Foster 2012).[6] Writing for UNHCR in a research briefing, Foster argues that requiring both elements, as well as the additional glosses of 'social visibility' and 'particularity' in much US case law (also arising now in France and Germany) is likely to develop into a significant barrier to PSG claims for women and lesbians, gay men and bisexuals (Foster 2012). It is therefore of interest that to date it does not appear that requirements of social perception (and even additional requirements of social visibility) have presented a major barrier to trans claimants. We suggest that this may reflect the emphasis on visual presentation of trans discussed above. If trans claimants are seen by adjudicators as distinctively embodied (unlike women, who are everywhere, and the unencoded gay body which may be 'discrete' and pass as straight, or indeed be straight in a deceptive posture) their very exoticism assuages the implicit floodgates fears in PSG analysis. In this sense the question of 'what is the social group?' and 'does the applicant belong to it?' are collapsed into the same question. The lack of clarity around how the group (or groups) are defined as well as the analytical basis for framing them as PSG have therefore not impeded recognition of transgendered claimants as eligible for Convention protection. However, we argue that this lack of clarity has had negative effects in the consequent analysis of risk of persecution. And we suggest that the US approach in particular may impede the development of analysis in gender and sexuality based claims more broadly.

Australia, Canada and the UK have all established precedent recognising that transsexuals or transgender people may constitute a PSG, as has NZ at the administrative tribunal level (*SZOBR* [2010a]; *Contreras Hernandez* [2007]; *Birdiricin* [2000]; *No. 72005/00* [2000]). Moreover, domestic policy guidance increasingly acknowledges transgender as the basis of a PSG. While the original Australian, UK, US and Canadian gender guidelines did not refer to transgender people, the current Australian and UK Gender Guidelines reflect the wording of the UNHCR Guidance Note on sexual orientation and gender identity in referring to 'gender identity' as a basis for gender-based persecution (MRT and RRT 2010; UK Border Agency 2011a: [2.2], 5; UNHCR 2008). In addition, in 2011 the UK was the first jurisdiction to issue stand alone policy guidance specifically on the assessment of gender identity claims (UK Border Agency 2011b).

The US presents a striking and paradoxical contrast. While there are clear indications of significant numbers of transgender claimants in the US on-shore system (Mohyuddin 2001: 405–410; Neilson 2004: 267), there remains no precedential authority explicitly establishing transgender identity as a PSG. To the contrary, in three major 9th Circuit Court of Appeals decisions, the Court resolutely declined to consider 'whether transsexuals constitute a PSG' (*Hernandez-Montiel* (2000) at 1095; *Reyes-Reyes* (2004); *Ornelas-Chavez* (2006)). Instead, the PSG accepted was of 'gay men with female sexual identities' (*Hernandez-Montiel* (2000) at 1095). Confusingly, *Hernandez-Montiel* is frequently cited as a precedential transgender case (US Citizenship and Immigration Services 2011: 15; UNHCR 2012).

US case law on trans asylum claimants has been lauded by commentators for recognising the social expressions and performative dimensions of gender non-conformity in a manner that has lessened focus on clinical diagnosis or medical treatment. The Court of Appeal's judgment in *Hernandez-Montiel* focused primarily on the appellant's social presentation and made only a passing footnote reference to medical treatment when it recorded an occasion when the applicant's sister required attendance at a re-education programme which 'forced him to stop taking female hormones' (*Hernandez-Montiel* (2000) at 10470). This 'relaxed' (Landau 2004: 238) approach of looking beyond biology and anatomy is viewed by some as a flexible and progressive step, rather than medicalising or essentialising trans through an identity-based PSG (Kirkland 2003: 31). The US approach is also helpful in drawing attention to the role that gender non-conformity more broadly plays in transgender claims, as well as those by gender and sexual orientation claimants, and the potential inter-relation of such claims. So, for example, the US Training Module notes that:

> Most persecutors may not have been making the distinction between gay, lesbian, bisexual, transgender, intersex or HIV-positive. They may simply have harmed or want to harm the applicant based on their perception that the applicant is gay or a sexual minority that is "outside the norm."
> (US Citizenship and Immigration Services 2011: 18)

Nevertheless, we believe that the US approach to PSG is incorrect and, whether or not it has been largely successful for claimants, has potentially high collateral costs. We believe that presenting transgender as a subset of sexual orientation rather than its own unique group mischaracterises claims made by transgender applicants.

The 'flexible' and 'performative' descriptor 'gay men with female sexual identities' has in fact crystallised into a PSG that is more rigidly fixed (and far more frequently adopted) than PSG formulations in any other jurisdiction (*Hernandez-Montiel* (2000); *Reyes-Reyes* (2004); *Ornelas-Chavez* (2006); *Morales* (2009); Untitled [2009]; Untitled [2010a]. The dominance of this unitary PSG characterisation may act formally to exclude trans claimants who are perceived as, or self identify as, heterosexual, from the PSG analysis in the US (Jenkins 2009: 88–89, 94). It may also confuse the analysis in sexual orientation claims, for example by marginalising gay claimants who present a gender-conforming appearance (LaViolette 2007; Hanna 2005).

Not acknowledging trans claimants *as* trans in refugee claims contributes to the erasure of trans identity in legal texts and lawmaking. Landau, who represented Reyes-Reyes, later noted that his client did in fact identify as transgender, but chose tactically to rely on 'uncontested membership in [the] previously established PSG' rather than centring transgender identity (although he did pose this as an alternate formulation: Landau 2004: 249, n 71). Successful decisions about gay men which could be seen as claims by MTF trans people act to deprive future trans claimants of reliable and useful precedent through which their claims could be framed. This is a major issue when one recollects that there are so few publicly available cases to begin with. Moreover, these cases contribute to both mainstream cultural erasure of trans identity and gay cultural appropriation of trans experiences of victimisation and resistance to violence (Minter 2000; Hazeldean 2011: 388–389; Jenkins 2009). Thus, for example, media around the world, and Lord Hope's opinion in the landmark judgment of *HJ (Iran) and HT* [2010], refer to 'two gay men' who were sentenced to 14 years' imprisonment in Malawi in 2010 for engaging in a same sex marriage ceremony, with no acknowledgement that one of the participants self-identified and publicly presented as a woman (Smith 2010, 2011; *HJ (Iran) and HT* at [2]).

Also of concern is the characterisation of transgender, not just as a subset of gay sexual orientation, but as a *manifestation* of it. It is a little remarked point that in *Reyes-Reyes* the 9th Circuit noted that the applicant's 'sexual *orientation*, for which he was targeted, and his transsexual *behaviour* are intimately connected' (*Reyes-Reyes* 2004 at 785, n 1, emphasis added). Simplistic identity/behaviour binary distinctions have plagued US jurisprudence on sexuality in general in the past, and have also appeared with disturbing implications for narrowed protection in some recent case law and scholarship on RSD (Hathaway and Pobjoy 2012; Millbank 2012). It is of concern that the current formulation of PSG for transgendered people reinscribes the artificial identity/behaviour distinction both implicitly and explicitly, and does so in such a manner that trans is characterised as (what it viewed as chosen and therefore dispensable or circumscribable) 'behaviour' and not as (immutable and protected characteristic) 'identity'. By way of example, at the lower levels of *Hernandez-Montiel*, a focus on 'cross dressing' behaviour profoundly misled the persecution analysis. The US Immigration Court and Board of Immigration Appeals rejected the claims of Hernandez-Montiel because they characterised him as a gay man who was 'choosing' to cross dress socially, rather than, for example, seeing her as an MTF trans woman who as a response to persecutory conditions had been coerced into hiding her trans identity at work and in many other aspects of the public realm over a period of many years.[7] While trans identities, like lesbian and gay identities, are expressed through an infinitely wide range of outward behaviours, we argue that it is important that they also be acknowledged in the foundations of refugee analysis *as* identities.

Yet there appears to be a stark difference in the approach of lower level courts and tribunals in the US. We found one recent unpublished Board of Immigration Appeals decision in our pool, Untitled [2010b], which accepted a PSG of either transgender females or effeminate gay men from El Salvador. In addition, the first official Training Module for Immigration Officers in the US to address sexual orientation and gender identity strongly implies the recognition of a distinct PSG in several remarks, for example that, '[t]ransgender is a gender identity, not a sexual orientation' (US Citizenship and Immigration Services 2011: 13). The module refers to examples of sexual minority claimants who may qualify under PSG category, including those who 'are transgender' and provides examples of how to frame a PSG including: '[g]ay, lesbian, transgender, or HIV-positive (choose one)/men or women (choose one) from Country X (choose one)' (US Citizenship and Immigration Services 2011: 17–18). Immigration Equality in New York reports that in the past four years it routinely claimed transgender as a PSG at Immigration Court and Board of Immigration Appeals level, with very high levels of success (Neilson, personal communication, 12 May 2012).[8] In this light it is perhaps only a matter of time until the issue of transgender PSG in the US is settled in a precedential case.

6.6 Defining the parameters of the relevant PSG

Both gender (Foster 2012; Dauvergne and Millbank 2010; GENSEN 2012) and sexual orientation (Weßels 2011) jurisprudence on PSG has been critiqued elsewhere as unpredictable and inconsistent in the breadth and narrowness of the definitions chosen. In keeping with these findings, we found significant variability in the framing of PSG in trans claims. In four of the five NZ cases, decision makers did not articulate a PSG ground at all. In addition, there was also one UK decision, two US decisions and two Canadian decisions which failed to identify a PSG in their written reasons (*AK (Iran)* 2008; *Pangilinan* [2009]; *N-A-M* (2009); *T97-03025* [1998]; *TA5-08019* [2005]). Given that eight of these nine cases were negative determinations, this is a particularly disturbing finding.

In the remaining cases decision makers formulated an extraordinary diversity of particular social groups based on a combination of gender identities, gender expressions, sexualities and imputations of gender identity and sexuality. The PSG ranged from broad, such as 'transsexuals' (*N96/12268* [1997]; *T94-07129* [1995]; *No. 72005/00* [2000]) to extremely narrow, such as 'transgender women in Malaysia without familial or financial support or protection' (*0903346* 2010) or 'bisexual man who prefers men and being a transvestite' (*T98-04159* 2000). On occasion, multiple PSGs were accepted as alternative or cumulative bases. Imputations were accepted with respect to both gender and sexuality – that is, homosexuality with imputed trans (*0805932* 2008) as well as trans with imputed homosexuality (*Montoya Martinez* [2011]; Untitled [2010b].

Only one case, the first public trans decision in our pool, entailed a claim for a protection decided not on the basis of PSG but on imputed political opinion:

> there is a good possibility that the claimant, as a transsexual, would come to the attention of the Iranian authorities should he be returned to Iran. . . Such behaviour and expression is perceived by the authorities as being a defiant demonstration of political opposition to the current regime.
>
> (*V93-01711* [1994])

This reflects trends in gender and sexual orientation RSD, where despite repeated calls by UNHCR and scholarly commentary (UNHCR 2002a, 2008; LaViolette 2010; Wilets 1997) to address political and religious grounds implicated in gender related persecution, the overwhelming majority of cases concerning gender related persecution are marshalled into PSG.

The full list of PSGs accepted by adjudicators is listed below: divided broadly into groupings which centre transgender, followed by those which centre sexual orientation, and finally those which articulate them as alternatives or as intersecting groups. Numerous others were articulated by applicants but were either rejected or overlooked.[9]

1 Trans specific:

- Transsexuals
  (*N96/12268* [1997]; *T94-07129* [1995]; *Miranda* [1995]; *Reyes-Reyes* [2004])
- Transgender people
  (*0903346* [2010] at initial determination)
- Transgender identity
  (*Doe* [2005])
- FTM transsexual
  (*T94-07963* [1999])
- Transsexuals or transvestites
  (*No. 72005/00* [2000])
- Transsexual in country of origin
  (*0902671* [2009])
- Transgender women in Malaysia without familial or financial support or protection
  (*0903346* [2010])

2 Sexual orientation:

- Gay man
  (*T98-03951* [1995])
- Homosexual in country of origin
  (*V02/14696* [2004]; *Hernandez* [2003]; *Contreras Hernandez* [2007]; *Untitled* [1999])

3 Interrelated or alternative formulations:

- Homosexual or transgender
  (*SZOBR* [2010a]; *SZOBR* [2010b]; *S* [2009])
- Homosexuals and transvestites
  (*VA1-00875* [2002])
- Homosexuality and imputed transgender
  (*0805932* [2008])
- Gay men with female sexual identities in country of origin
  (*Hernandez-Montiel* (2000); *Reyes-Reyes* (2004); *Ornelas-Chavez* (2006); *Morales* (2009))
- Homosexual individuals in country of origin who have a female identity and are HIV positive
  (*Untitled* [2009])
- Homosexual woman with a male sexual identity
  (*Untitled* [2010a])
- Sexual orientation as a gay cross-dresser
  (*Wilfredo Guerra Rivera* [2007])

- Homosexual, transvestite and Muslim, individually and cumulatively (*N03/46498* [2003])
- Bisexual man who prefers men and being a transvestite (*T98-04159* [2000])
- Transsexual woman or easily perceived as an effeminate gay male (*Untitled* [2010b])
- Women facing domestic violence or lesbians facing homophobic violence or transgender people (*Montoya Martinez* [2011])

Within our small case set we could see no clear correlation between the positive rate and either the narrowness of the group or the use of multiple or cumulative grounds.[10] However it is clear at a glance through this listing that PSG groupings were predominantly framed within and by reference to sexual orientation and we believe that this is cause for concern.

We do not consider that the text of decisions should necessarily be taken as an accurate representation of identity categorisations that applicants are 'comfortable' with (Southam 2011: 1386) – even if the applicant's submissions or testimony relied on or included such terminology. We concur with Sharalyn Jordan that '[c]laimants are being asked to give a narrative account of a sexuality or gender identity that they have had limited experience articulating' and 'may inhabit only uneasily' (Jordan 2009: 175). Transgendered claimants may find it difficult to articulate stable identities within expected tropes of 'coming out' (US Citizenship and Immigration Services 2011: 45; UNHCR 2012) and 'gender dysphoria' established in the RSD process (Jordan 2009: 167, 173–177). This is in part because such expectations may not be culturally appropriate but also because applicants themselves struggle to 'form an identity under conditions of erasure' (Jordan 2009: 170). Jordan quotes Miriam, a trans woman refugee speaking about experiences several years earlier in her country of origin:

> I remember visiting an internet site for gay men – and they were all muscular, all manly. *If they are gay, what am I?* I started to ask myself. I thought *I am nothing. I am nothing in this world – not even gay. So what am I?*
> (Jordan 2009: 170)

This confusion and unease was reflected in a number of cases in our pool where the applicants' claimed PSG was either focused on sexual orientation or was not clearly articulated, and was contradicted or destabilised by their written and oral evidence. So for example in one case the applicant asserted a PSG of 'homosexuals in the Philippines' but also self-described in the course of evidence as a 'transsexual' and expressed the desire 'to live freely as a woman' (*Untitled* [1999] at 7).

Trans elements to claims may be obliquely raised in such a way that both advocates and decision makers marginalise them or overlook them altogether.

In a 2009 Australian case, a Lebanese applicant made a claim which did not specify transgender as a PSG but which clearly raised the issue. In the original documentation, the applicant stated:

> I, [..] tell the story of my life.
>
> Since I was 12 years old I used to like playing with my sisters and like to play girl games. I used to dress like my sisters.
>
> My dad is very conservative, he used to hit me because of my behaviour as a gay, he used to hit me brutally.
>
> When I was at school my friends used to hit me and call me gay.
>
> All my school friends used to hit me and used to say that I am not a boy and I should be a girl.
>
> I had a very hard times in my life because I wasn't like all the boys in my area. I did not like the girls as they used to like them.
>
> I wish I was born a girl.
>
> There was only one person who could understand me, this person is [A]. We were very close friends because he used to feel the same way as me and he is gay like me. This friendship became a relationship that last for 6 years, we used to spend all day together in the mountains in Lebanon where no one can see us and I used to love him and have a feeling that he is all my life.
>
> Some times I used to sleep in the mountain because my dad did not let me sleep in the house.
>
> My dad used to take my money and did not let me get in the house because he used to say that I bring shame to the family. Once my dad hit me with a knife and cut my left hand following an argument in which he accused me of being gay.
>
> Some times I used to think of suicide and finish all this pain but the only person who kept me alive is [A] because he used to help me through all these problems.
>
> None of my family members know that I can't love girls I used to feel that I should be born as a girl. I was not comfortable with my situation with the boys.
>
> Especially, I am a Muslim and my family would kill me if they know that I am gay and I had a relationship with a Muslim gay too, the Authorities and the Muslim sharia will support them in this. I think being gay is something normal and I was born like that.
>
> I was happy because I left Lebanon and came to Australia where I can say that I am gay and have the right to say that I love boys and I can't love girls.
>
> (quoted in *S* [2009] at [17])

The original decision was made on the basis of sexuality alone, and protection denied because internal relocation was held to be possible (*S* [2009] at [24]). On review at tribunal level the claim again was principally framed and discussed on the basis of homosexuality (*SZOBR* [2010a], [2010b]) with 'transgender' not mentioned at all until page 11 of the 15-page decision, despite legal submissions at tribunal level that 'treating psychologists have both indicated that there is a gender identity issue and that a sexual reassignment operation may be an option' (*SZOBR* [2010a] at [16]). The tribunal concluded that the applicant was not gay and *by extension* did not accept any claim relevant to transgender. Two judicial review claims, arguing that the tribunal had not properly ventilated the distinct aspects of transvestism, transgenderism and homosexuality, failed (*SZOBR* [2010a], [2010b]). The Federal Magistrates' Court concluded that 'the behaviour of dressing in women's clothing was a manifestation of his homosexual orientation. The tribunal therefore did not fail to deal with this aspect of the applicant's claims' (*SZOBR* [2010a] at [65]). On review, the Federal Court emphasised that this reflected the applicant's case having not distinguished trans and sexual orientation as distinct grounds: '[h]is behaviour of wearing women's clothes, and even his feelings of being a woman, were all presented as part of, integral to, and *behavioural examples of* his homosexual orientation' (*SZOBR* [2010a] at [37] emphasis added).

We contend that the burden of formulating a PSG cannot rest on applicants alone, and urge adjudicators to be proactive in exploring the evidence to consider appropriately tailored categories. An example of where this was well done occurred in another Australian decision (*0805932* [2008]). Apparently asserting the PSG of 'homosexual', the claimant explained that 'he has only had sexual encounters with men' (*0805932* [2008] at [50]), that 'his body has female characteristics' (*0805932* [2008] at [49]), and also that he 'received female hormones for some time' (*0805932* [2008] at [49]). The tribunal observed, '[h]e considers himself to be a transgender person; "that is, although I am predominantly male, I feel that I have a lot of female characteristics. I considered undergoing an operation to become female but felt that it was too medically risky"' (*0805932* [2008] at [27]). Elsewhere, the tribunal noted that the applicant had 'given up the life of a transgender' but added that '[t] he applicant stated that in South Korea there is a misunderstanding that a homosexual is considered to be transgender' (*0805932* [2008] at [50]). The tribunal itself formulated the PSG of 'homosexuality and imputed transgender' (*0805932* [2008] at [99]) which enabled it to explore not only country of origin information on gay men but the broader dimensions of gender-related persecution in South Korea.

It is possible that PSG categories often centre sexual orientation because the evidence of persecution or the country evidence of a persecutory environment is expressed in relation to homosexuality or same sex activity. Many cultures do not have words for transphobia or transgender identity. Indeed, it seems clear that some people have no substantial comprehension of what a transgender person is or what transgender means (Moran and Sharpe 2004). Applicants may focus on, or be directed by their advocates towards, terminology reflecting homophobic language used by persecutors

(Landau 2004: 260–261; Neilson 2004: 288). There may be occasions in which gender identity claims are framed as actual or imputed sexual orientation in order to make the evidence of persecution 'consistent', or in order to make use of available country of origin information if this is sparse, or indeed, as in the US, because the category is better accepted and appears as a less risky advocacy strategy (Landau 2004: 113; Neilson 2004: 284–288). Further, the anomalous emphasis upon perpetrator motivation in US asylum law exacerbates the trend of looking to sexual orientation imputations (US Citizenship and Immigration Services 2011: [3.2.1])

Centring sexual orientation may also reflect institutional practices. It is notable that Canada, the largest receiving nation in our study, recorded the sole trans case in the 2003 'Compendium of decisions' under its gender guidelines below the heading 'sexual orientation' (Immigration and Refugee Board of Canada 2003: Section III) and did not appear to separately code for trans claims in 2006 tribunal data recording sexual orientation and gender claims.[11] If decision makers are more familiar with sexual orientation claims and have better country of origin information on the relevant country they too may be tempted to erase or de-emphasise gender identity aspects within claims. Alternatively, adjudicators may simply not 'see' the trans aspects of claims if these are not clearly articulated from the outset, or at worst, actually assume that sexuality and gender identity are interchangeable. We stress that, while related, violence against trans people is not simply reducible to the category of homophobia. Gender bias produces distinct effects in the transgender context. To miscategorise all transphobia as homophobia is to misunderstand not only the nature of trans identities but also the nature of the dangers faced by trans people.

6.7 Locating trans persecution in relation to gender and sexuality

We pose that a key challenge of trans RSD is the simultaneous holding in mind of related *and* distinct aspects of sexuality, gender and gender identity.

The interaction between sexuality and gender is particularly fraught in RSD because of the dearth of country information available on human rights abuses perpetrated against transgender people. Around the world, including in Western countries, high levels of violence experienced by trans people are not reflected in official crime statistics (Liddicoat 2008: 43). Trans people remain largely invisible as victims of crime because they tend to under-report violence or attribute it to factors other than their trans status. Under-reporting of violence against trans men (FTMs) may be even more pronounced because of the specific perceptions of the nature and meaning of violence informed by their previous experiences of living as women.

The cases take highly divergent approaches to the questions of the relationship between gender and sexuality in the claimants' identities and how this plays out in their experiences of persecution and state protection. We observed a handful of decisions which showed a strong appreciation for the ways in which violence informed by gender bias and violence related to prejudice against particular sexualities 'co-exist and are co-implicated' (Moran and Sharpe 2004: 403; see *0903346* [2010]; *0902671* [2009]; *T94-07129* [1995]). However, several decisions suggested a troubling blurring in the analysis of gendered status, sexuality and mainstream understandings of gender which require critical attention. The paucity of detailed and trans-specific country of origin information exacerbated decision makers' inappropriate conflation of gender identity and sexuality-related aspects of applicants' claims.

6.7.1 *Confusing or conflating transgender and sexual orientation*

Several decisions in our study cited no country of origin information that was specific to trans people and some made no reference whatsoever to this deficiency (e.g. *N96/12268* [1997]; *N02/41726* [2002]). In these and other cases, decision makers misapplied information about country conditions regarding gay people to trans applicants. A 1999 Canadian case justified using sexual orientation information as proxy for trans in the following terms:

> While there is a lack of documentary evidence before us which specifically addresses the situation of the transgendered in the Philippines, the panel takes judicial notice of the fact that, as between communities in society, gay communities tend to be among the most tolerant of the transgendered and the communities within which the transgendered often choose to lead their lives, as the claimant has in Toronto. If gay life is tolerated in the Philippines, as the panel finds, the panel infers that the claimant could live a transgendered existence going to gay institutions such as bars and theatres without facing a serious possibility of persecution.
>
> (*Untitled* [1999])

The Canadian tribunal engaged in no detailed analysis of trans identity as a PSG that might expose the applicant to risks quite different from a gay man. In extrapolating from the country of origin information on sexuality, the tribunal did not even attempt to reflect on the sort of trans-specific persecution that might be missing from this account, nor indeed what the *absence* of any country of origin information on trans people in this country might say about the robustness of state protection. Indeed, the approach taken in the extract is extremely reductive of both 'gay life' and the experiences of gender minorities, inferring safety from an asserted ability to attend certain entertainment venues.

In a 1998 Canadian decision (*T97-03025* [1998]), the tribunal reviewed country of origin information which addressed protections for lesbians and gay men and human rights broadly but included none on gender identity, and then observed:

> [a]dmittedly, most of the above noted documentary evidence pertains to gay men and lesbians without any mention of transsexuals. Nevertheless, since the claimant now identifies her sexual orientation as lesbian, we find that the situation as described in the documentary evidence adequately applies also to her particular situation.
>
> (*T97-03025* [1998] at [7])

The applicant articulated her PSG as that 'of a person who has undergone a sex change and a person who fears mistreatment because of her sexual orientation' (*T97-03025* [1998] at [1]) but the trans aspect of her claim was completely erased in the adjudicator's analysis.

These decisions appear superficially to treat sexual orientation and gender identity as *similar*; others appear to collapse homosexuality and minority gender identities as *the same*, as in the following statements from two Australian tribunal decisions:

> While there is a social stigma attached to blatant expression of one's sexual preferences, homosexuals and transsexuals are generally tolerated in Thai society and the pursuit of sexual partners is regarded as essentially a private matter.
>
> (*N02/41726* [2002] at 5)

> Societal prejudice against transsexuals and hijras in Pakistan indicates that not only do they share a certain characteristic – their sexual orientation – but this element makes them a cognisable group within Pakistan society.
>
> (*0902671* [2009] at [99])

6.7.2 *Conflating transgender with chosen sex*

Writing in the context of violence against lesbians, Gail Mason has argued for a complex understanding of the interrelationships between gender and sexuality (Mason 2002). She observes that in some circumstances common experiences of gender-related violence can connect the subjectivities of lesbians with those of women more generally. In other contexts, though, sexuality can inform gender, separating out the lesbian experience from that of other women. We contend that persecution analysis which only looks to chosen gender can lead to error. A straightforward correlation of the identity of an MTF trans woman to the subject position of 'woman' will likely conceal the specific needs and experiences of trans women, as well as misapprehend social responses to those needs or vulnerabilities.

Two early decisions in our case set overtly characterised trans women as 'women', rejecting their claims on the basis of findings that 'women' in their situations would not have a well-founded fear of persecution for a Convention ground. In the first reported decision in Australia to recognise transsexuals as a PSG (*N96/12268* [1997]), the claim was rejected for lack of nexus. The Australian tribunal held that the violence which the MTF applicant from the Philippines feared from her ex-boyfriend was motivated by revenge rather than a Convention reason (a common barrier in gender claims brought by women who have experienced domestic violence: Musalo and Knight 2001; Oxford 2005). After noting in the first paragraph that the applicant is 'a transsexual and identifies as a woman', the decision does not address her transsexualism at all in the reasons until the conclusion regarding absence of nexus. In the intervening paragraphs, the tribunal noted the history of violence by her ex-boyfriend (including physical assaults, ongoing threats and harassment), the police refusal to provide support or protection, and the applicant's struggles to complete tertiary education and to gain employment, all without reference to her trans identity – except for one passing comment that these experiences may have been influenced by 'prejudice against her sexuality' (*N96/12268* [1997] at 3). Likewise, the Canadian Federal Court upheld a decision rejecting the claims of an MTF trans woman from Germany (who may have been intersex) on the basis that state protection was available for women who had been subjected to the mistreatment she has experienced: 'violence against women, though probably underreported, is prohibited by laws that are effectively enforced' (*T97-03025* [1998] at [7]).

By conflating the subject positions of 'trans women' and 'women', these decision makers in our view committed serious errors in the persecution analysis. The Australian tribunal did this by construing the domestic violence as 'personal' without any inquiry into the significance of the applicant's identity as a trans woman in terms of sufficiency of state protection. The Canadian court erred both by presuming that the applicant's fear of violence was comparable to that of other women in her country of origin and also by assuming that trans women had equal access to services which address the needs of female victims of gender-related violence.

6.7.3 Ignoring trans and centring born sex

Legal decisions betray the view that trans people are, or remain, their birth sex, through apparently minor discursive elements such as the use of pronouns; thus, it is not uncommon to see judgments referring to an MTF trans person as 'he' or 'Mr' on the basis that other legal documents also do so (Hazeldean 2011). In the asylum context this is of particular concern since upsetting or intimidating applicants who do not perceive themselves in such terms may interfere with their ability to present their claim (Jordan 2009). The UK

Asylum Policy Instruction explicitly addresses this issue as one of respectful treatment when instructing border staff that:

> a transgender applicant should be given respect and referred to by their chosen name. If in any doubt, an applicant should be asked which personal pronoun and salutation he or she would like used.
>
> (UK Border Agency 2011a: 2, repeated at 12)

We would go further and suggest that any refusal to address applicants in their chosen gender could interfere with both the quality of evidence obtained and the ability to properly assess it if it infuses the analysis of the claim, that is, as 'really' about a man rather than a trans woman. In a 1999 case concerning an applicant from the Philippines, the Canadian tribunal noted:

> The claimant, although legally male, presented at both hearings dressed as a female, and he possessed a female alias. In advance of both sittings, he was asked how he would prefer to be addressed. He indicated to the panel that he had no preference. He presented his documentation in the name of his male persona.
>
> (*Untitled* [1999] at [11])

The tribunal proceeded to use the male pronoun throughout. This case is troubling because of the lack of reflection of what this applicant's lack of expressed preference as to pronoun might actually mean. This decision is recorded as though the applicant were ambivalent about gender or placed no great importance in it. There was no appreciation of how speaking *to* someone in a gender may affect someone's testimony, nor of how speaking *about* someone affects the PSG categorisation. Indeed, this decision considered the applicant's claim in the context of a PSG of 'homosexuals in the Philippines' even as it recorded that the applicant 'fears that if he were to return to the Philippines, he would not be able to live freely as a woman' (*Untitled* [1999] at [7]). The tribunal made no effort at all to assess the failure of state protection of the applicant as a trans woman.

In most of the cases in our pool, adjudicators did indeed refer to applicants by their legal sex, which was overwhelmingly their birth sex. However, it was not clear from the face of the decisions whether the applicants had actually presented their chosen sex or preferred mode of address in written and oral submissions, so it was not possible to determine if the text of the decisions reflected the adjudicators' views or the materials put to them. For instance, in *Reyes-Reyes* the PSG claimed was 'a homosexual male with a female sexual identity' and the court referred to the applicant consistently as 'he' even while describing a feminine identification:

> He dresses and looks like a woman, wearing makeup and a woman's hairstyle. Although Reyes has not undergone sex reassignment surgery,

> he has had a characteristically female appearance, mannerisms, and gestures for the past sixteen years. He has a 'deep female identity' and has gone by female names such as Josephine, Linda and Cukita.
>
> (*Reyes-Reyes* (2004) at 13547)

Similarly, in an English case concerning an MTF applicant from Iran, the decision says 'he' is 'a transsexual and in need of gender reassignment' (*AK (Iran)* [2008]).

There were only 15 cases in which it was clear that the applicant's chosen sex was presented as other than their legal sex. Interestingly, in 14 of those cases the decision makers consciously used language reflecting the applicants' chosen sex but there was no apparent correlation with success rates (seven positive and seven negative). In only one case did the decision maker explicitly reject language reflecting the applicant's chosen sex, but this was nonetheless a positive decision for the applicant (*0902671* [2009]). (In a further case, the decision maker used no pronouns at all, leaving the decision entirely gender-neutral (*Doe* [2005]). The outcome of this case was also positive.)

We found a much clearer trend when examining the ways in which country of origin information relating to gender was utilised. In several cases, decision makers assessed claims by using the birth gender as the relevant group in assessing both the likelihood of persecution and availability of state protection. We argue that this fundamentally misconceives the nature of the risk. For example, a recent Canadian decision assessed the claims of an FTM trans man and his girlfriend from Mexico as lesbians, using female pronouns throughout, and made findings by reference to 'women facing domestic violence' (*Montoya Martinez* [2011], upheld on review). In a 2000 NZ decision, an MTF transsexual from Thailand, who had undergone 'hormone treatment for many years', claimed that she had been sexually assaulted in military training. She asserted a fear of conscription or a gaol sentence if it was discovered that she had attempted to bribe officials to avoid military training. The tribunal rejected the claim on the basis that:

> [t]he government does not discriminate against transsexuals by differentially enforcing military conscriptions to transsexuals as opposed to any other Thai men. The penalties for delinquency to military service are similarly universally enforced. These penalties in themselves are not so extreme as to amount to persecution.
>
> (*No. 71790/99* [2000] at 7)

This conclusion failed to appreciate that, under Thai law, this trans woman is treated as a *man*. Her claim, therefore, concerned the possibility of conscription in a military unit, or imprisonment, in male facilities. It is not clear that she asserted that she feared a disproportionately heavy penalty but rather that any gaol term would be extremely dangerous for her as a trans woman.

6.8 Conclusion

Our hope is that this chapter will prompt wider comment and reflection about trans asylum claims in a broader comparative context which includes non-English speaking receiving countries and inquiries into even less transparent aspects of lower level RSD, through methods such as observation and interview (Oxford 2005; Oxford forthcoming; Jordan 2009). We propose that an examination of common issues and barriers across nations is a useful starting point in developing a more sophisticated jurisprudence of transgender asylum. In particular, we are concerned that the distinctive approach to trans PSG in the US context, and the dominance of US literature on these issues, may in fact mislead rather than illuminate international dialogue on trans asylum.

Transgender refugee claims pose complex challenges for advocates and decision makers in framing an appropriate and workable PSG and thereby undertaking persecution and nexus analysis in ways which capture the nuance of claimants' past experience of persecution and risk of future harm through a shifting embodied self. A 2007 Canadian case presents an example of how this can be accomplished, even at the far more truncated judicial review stage. The Minister argued that a Mexican applicant's written submissions about transgender identity should be discredited due to inconsistencies between paragraphs which used the descriptor 'transgender' and 'transvestite' and an oral submission where the applicant self-described as a 'cross-dresser' (*Contreras Hernandez* [2007] at [20]). The Federal Court rejected this argument. The applicant in this case had framed the PSG as 'homosexual men living in Mexico', but also stated that when kidnapped outside a nightclub, 'he was dressed as a woman' (*Contreras Hernandez* [2007] at [28]). The Federal Court overturned the decision on the basis that there was ample evidence before the tribunal to alert it to the fact that the applicant identified as a cross-dresser and transgender, thus it erred in failing to assess absence of state protection on each of these grounds (*Contreras Hernandez* [2007] at [27], [29]).

The task of framing PSG in trans claims involves awareness of the multiplicity of gendered experience taking into account the born and once-was sex, the now-is gender identity and the in-between-ness of felt and outwardly perceived sex and gender relations. This forces a deeper appreciation of the experience of gender transitioning as involving not only 'sex change' processes but ever-evolving gendered expressions of the self, including the social experience of 'passing' (or not) in the chosen gender.

We argue that attending to the uniquely embodied specificity of an applicant's trans identity is central to defining the PSG in each case. At the same time, it is critical that the framing and understanding of trans RSD are grounded within a broader framework of gender-related persecution which illuminates the interrelation between gender non-conformity and sexuality (LaViolette 2010). We suggest that persecution analysis may be most attuned to applicants' claims when it takes place within analysis which is alert to their felt self-identification *as well as* the gender-identity or sexual orientation imputed to them. To focus only on self-identity without social imputations can fundamentally misunderstand the hazards of being a trans body in a persecutory environment. To focus only on imputations of gender or sexual orientation within a persecutory environment and not the applicant's gender identity (as in much of the American case law) contributes to a further erasure of trans experience. At worst, it may result in the rejection of atypical transgender applicants with valid claims and contribute to the ossification of PSG analysis, with negative consequences for a variety of other social groupings.

6.9 Notes

* This research was supported by funding from the UTS Law Public Purpose Fund and Australian Research Council, DP 12010205. Thanks to Victoria Neilson and Thomas Spijkerboer for their thoughtful comments on an earlier version, to Senthorun Sunil Raj, Anthea Vogl and Simon Levett for research assistance and to S. Chelvan and Victoria Neilson for assisting us with access to decisions. We plan to make deindentified unreleased decisions public through our project website in the near future.

1 We used the following search terms: gender identity, trans*, transgender, transsexual, transvestite, FTM, MTF, sex change, transitioning, cross dress*, gender divers* and intersex. Searches were conducted using the following databases: Refword (global), Worldlii (global), Michigan Casebase (global), Austlii (Australia), LexisNexisAu (Australia), Canlii (Canada), QuickLaw (Canada), Electronic Immigration Network (UK), Immigration and Asylum Chamber (UK), Hastings Centre (US), Board of Immigration Appeals (US), LexisNexis (US) and RefNZ (NZ). Note that a few cases teetered on the edge of categories. We did not include claims on the basis of sexual orientation that involved gender non-conformity if trans did not appear on the face of the record to be a distinct aspect of the claimant's identity and/or cognisable in the claim. Thus cases involving lesbians described as butch or 'effeminate' gay men were not included without further trans-related descriptors. In contrast, cases involving a born woman who self identified as a lesbian trans man and a number of men who identified themselves in their claims as gay but whose testimony established that they had 'always wanted to be a girl' or cross dressed from an early age, were included. Further, three cases involved two applicants (two were the primary applicants' mothers, and one involved a partner).

2 Of the US cases, many involved combined claims for asylum, withholding of removal and relief under the 1984 Convention against Torture and Other Cruel, Inhuman or Degrading Treatment or Punishment (the Convention against Torture). Two cases involved only a claim to suspension of removal (*Miranda* (1995)) or relief under the Convention against Torture (*Doe* [2005]). For a discussion of the differences involved in these forms of claim in US law, see Neilson and Morris 2005.

3 The breakdown of tribunal versus judicial review decisions in each jurisdiction was as follows: NZ all tribunal; UK one tribunal, two judicial review; Australia eight tribunal, two judicial review; US four tribunal, seven judicial review; Canada nine tribunal, four judicial review.

4 The 2004 European Qualification Directive (Council Directive 2004/83/EC) added to, rather than resolved, confusion, by specifically noting sexual orientation as an example of a PSG but stating that 'Gender related aspects might be considered, without by themselves alone creating a presumption for the applicability of this Article' (article 10(1)(d)). This was resolved in the Recast EU Qualification Directive in 2011 (Directive 2011/95/EU) (article 10(1)(d)) which expressly includes 'due consideration' of gender identity within gender.

5 Victoria Neilson has posed the relevant PSG for trans claims as 'individuals born with one anatomical sex who believe their anatomical sex does not match their gender' arguing that this meets the protected characteristic ground as there is 'scarcely any characteristic more fundamental to identity than a person's gender' (Neilson 2004: 277). The US Citizenship and Immigration Services Training Module 2011 states that gender identity should be regarded as either innate or fundamental, 'In the case of a transgender person, he or she either cannot change or should not be required to ignore the inner feelings that his or her gender identity does not match his or her biological sex at birth. Even if these traits could somehow be changed, they are traits that are so fundamental to a person's identity that he or she should not be required to change them' (US Citizenship and Immigration Services 2011: 16).

6 The receiving countries in our study represent all variations of these approaches to PSG: Canada and New Zealand having emphatically adopted the protected characteristics approach while Australia adopts the social perception approach. The US requires both (Foster 2012; Marouf 2008). UK case law has a longstanding preference for the protected characteristics approach (*Shah* [1999]; *SSHD and Fornah* [2006]) – yet strikingly this appears to have narrowed to a suggestion in recent policy documents that both elements are required, reflecting the wording of legislative implementation of the Qualification Directive (see e.g. UK Border Agency 2004, [revised 2006, 2010]). Thus the Asylum Policy Instruction on *Gender Identity Issues in the Asylum Claim* issued by the UK Border Agency in 2011 states that both innate or fundamental characteristics *and* 'a distinct identity in the relevant country, because it is perceived as being different by the surrounding society' is necessary to find a PSG (UK Border Agency 2011a: 11). This is directly contrary to UNHCR Guidance (UNHCR 2002b, 2012).

7 The 9th Circuit articulated the relationship between identity and behaviour in a more complex manner (finding that gay men with female sexual identities were targeted for persecution because they were perceived to undertake receptive anal sex: see *Hernandez-Montiel* (2000) at 10482), but still arguably one which erased trans identity.

8 These cases from 1 January 2008 to May 2012 comprise 24 asylum claims and four withholding of removal claims, all successful, and one Convention against Torture claim (from Cuba) which failed. The asylum claims involved four FTM trans men, from Belize, Brazil, Egypt and Venezuela, respectively, and MTF trans women from El Salvador and Mexico (four each); Honduras (three), Ecuador (two) and one each from Colombia, Grenada, Jamaica, Panama, Peru, Sri Lanka and Trinidad. The withholding of removal cases involved MTF applicants from Brazil, Ivory Coast, Mexico and Peru respectively (Neilson, personal communication, 12 May 2012).

9 Further claimed PSGs included 'gays/transvestites and sex change people' (*N02/41726* 2002), 'practising homosexuals' (*V02/1496* [2004]), 'homosexuality,

transgender identification and practice of transvestitism' (*SZOBR* [2010a], [2010b]), 'person who has undergone a sex change and a person who fears mistreatment because of her sexual orientation' (*T97-03025* [1998]), 'transvestite-homosexuals who are HIV positive' (*TA5-08019* [2005]), 'biological women in transgender relationships who may be perceived as lesbians or as transgressing gender-presentation roles as transgender men and who are dealing with male familial violence and discrimination but as a transgender couple and as lesbians' (*Montoya Martinez* [2011]), 'imputed homosexuality' (*AK(Iran)* [2008]). In *0903346* [2010], seven alternative PSGs were asserted: 'Post-operative transgender women in Malaysia', 'heterosexual transgender women in Malaysia', 'members of the Aravani', 'transgender women in Malaysia who are mistaken for prostitutes', 'transgender women in Malaysia who are deemed by the authorities to be prostitutes', 'people in Malaysia who are deemed by the authorities to be homosexuals' and 'transgender women in Malaysia without familial or financial support or protection'. The last was accepted by the RRT.

10 Of the broadly framed groups, 15 of 24 arose in positive decisions; of the narrow formulations, four of six decisions were positive. Comparing single as opposed to multiple/cumulative formulations: single formulations arose in 14 of 20 positive decisions; multiple/cumulative arose in 5 of 10 positives.

11 Sean Rehaag released a 2006 Access to Information request, in which the Canadian Immigration and Refugee Board listed every claim by category of claim as well as key issues in each claim: 'sexual orientation' (broken down to gay, bisexual or lesbians) and 'gender' (broken down to domestic violence, rape, female genital mutilation) but no listing under any of them for transsexuality or gender identity: see http://ccrweb.ca/documents/rehaagdata.htm (accessed 10 December 2012) under the link 'Raw data'.

6.10 References

American Psychiatric Association (2000), *Diagnostic and Statistical Manual of Mental Disorders DSM-IV-TR*, 4th edn, Washington, DC: American Psychiatric Association.

Amnesty International (2006) *Stonewalled – Still Demanding Respect!: Police Abuses Against Lesbian, Gay, Bisexual and Transgender People in the USA*, Oxford: Alden Press.

Benson, C.J. (2008) 'Crossing borders: a focus on treatment of transgender individuals in US asylum law and society', *Whittier Law Review*, 30: 41–66.

Berg, L. and Millbank, J. (2009) 'Constructing the personal narratives of lesbian, gay and bisexual claimants', *Journal of Refugee Studies*, 22(2): 195–223.

Bockting, W. (2008) 'Psychotherapy and the real-life experience: from gender dichotomy to gender diversity', *Sexologies*, 17: 211–224.

Bornstein, K. (1994) *Gender Outlaw: On Men, Women and the Rest of Us*, New York, NY: Routledge.

Broad, K.L. (2002) 'GLB+T?: gender/sexuality movements and transgender collective identity (de)constructions', *International Journal of Sexuality and Gender Studies*, 7: 241–264.

Coven, P. (1995) 'Office int'l aff. memorandum on considerations for asylum officers adjudicating asylum claims from women to all INS asylum officers and HQASM coordinators' *International Journal of Refugee Law* 7(4): 700.

Dauvergne, C. and Millbank, J. (2010) 'Forced marriage as a harm in domestic and international law', *Modern Law Review*, 73: 57–88.

Department of Immigration and Multicultural Affairs, Australia (1997) 'Guidelines on gender issues for decision makers (1996)', *International Journal of Refugee Law* (Special Issue) 9: 195.

Department of Immigration and Citizenship, Australia (DIAC) (2011) *Asylum Trends Australia 2010–11: Annual Publication*, available at http://www.immi.gov.au/media/publications/statistics/asylum/_files/asylum-trends-aus-annual-2010-11.pdf (accessed 20 February 2012).

Feinberg, L. (1992) *Transgender Liberation: A Movement Whose Time has Come*, New York, NY: World View Forum.

Foster, M. (2012) *The 'Ground with the Least Clarity': A Comparative Study of Jurisprudential Developments Relating to Membership of a Particular Social Group*, Geneva: UNHCR.

Gender Related Asylum Claims in Europe (GENSEN) (2012) *A Comparative Analysis of Law Policies and Practice Focusing on Women in Nine EU Member States*, available at http://helsinki.hu/wp-content/uploads/GENSEN-Report-FINAL.pdf (accessed 10 December 2012).

Hanna, F. (2005) 'Punishing masculinity in gay asylum claims', *Yale Law Journal*, 114: 913–920.

Hathaway, J.C. and Pobjoy, J. (2012) 'Queer cases make bad law', *New York Journal of International Law and Politics*, 44(2): 315–390.

Hazeldean, S. (2011) 'Confounding identities: the paradox of LGBT children under Asylum Law', *University of California Davis Law Review*, 45: 373–443.

Immigration and Refugee Board of Canada (1996) *Women Refugee Claimants Fleeing Gender-Related Persecution, Guideline 4*, Immigration and Refugee Board of Canada.

Immigration and Refugee Board of Canada (2003) *Compendium of Decisions, Guideline 4, Women Refugee Claimants Fleeing Gender-Related Persecution*, Immigration and Refugee Board of Canada.

Immigration Appellate Authority, UK (2000) *Asylum Gender Guidelines*, London: Immigration Appellate Authority.

International Commission of Jurists (2007), *Yogyakarta Principles on the Application of International Human Rights Law in Relation to Sexual Orientation and Gender Identity*, 6 March 2007, available at http://www.yogyakartaprinciples.org/principles_en.pdf (accessed 9 December 2012).

Jansen, S. and Spijkerboer, T. (2011) *Fleeing Homophobia, Asylum Claims Related to Sexual Orientation and Gender Identity in Europe*, COC Netherlands and VU University Amsterdam, available at http://www.rechten.vu.nl/nl/onderzoek/conferenties-en-projecten/onderzoeksproject-fleeing-homophobia/index.asp (accessed 9 December 2012).

Jenkins, E. (2009) 'Taking the square peg out of the round hole: addressing the misclassification of transgender asylum seekers', *Golden Gate University Law Review*, 40: 67–95.

Jordan, S. (2009) 'Un/convention(al) refugees: contextualizing the accounts of refugees facing homophobic or transphobic persecution', *Refuge*, 26: 165–182.

King, D. (1993) *The Transvestite and the Transsexual: Public Categories and Private Identities*, Avebury: University of California Press.

Kirkland, A. (2003) 'Victorious transsexuals in the courtroom: a challenge for feminist legal theory', *Law & Social Inquiry*, 28: 1–38.

LaViolette, N. (1997) 'The immutable refugee: sexual orientation in Canada (AG) v Ward', *University of Toronto Faculty of Law Review*, 55: 1–41.

LaViolette N. (2007) 'Gender-related refugee claims: expanding the scope of the Canadian guidelines', *International Journal of Refugee Law*, 19: 169–214.

— (2010) 'UNHCR Guidance Note on Refugee Claims Relating to Sexual Orientation and Gender Identity: a critical commentary', *International Journal of Refugee Law*, (22): 173–208.

Landau, J. (2004) 'Soft immutability and imputed gay identity: recent developments in transgender and sexual-orientation-based asylum law', *Fordham Urban Law Journal*, 32: 237–263.

Legomsky, S. (2007) 'Learning to live with unequal justice: asylum and the limits to consistency', *Stanford Law Review*, 60: 413–474.

Liddicoat, J. (2008) *To Be Who I Am: Report of the inquiry into discrimination experienced by transgender people, He Purongo mot e Uiutanga mo Aukaitanga e Pangia nan e nga Tangata Whakawhitiira*, Auckland: New Zealand Human Rights Commission.

Marouf, F. (2008) 'The emerging importance of "social visibility" in defining a "particular social group" and its potential impact on asylum claims related to sexual orientation and gender', *Yale Law and Policy Review*, 27: 47–106.

Mason, G. (2002) *The Spectacle of Violence: Homophobia, Gender & Knowledge*, London: Routledge.

Migration Review Tribunal and Refugee Review Tribunal (MRT and RRT) (2006) *Annual Report 2005–2006*, Sydney: MRT and RRT.

— (2007) *Annual Report 2006-2007*, Sydney: MRT and RRT.

— (2009) *Annual Report 2008–2009*, Sydney: MRT and RRT.

— (2010) *Gender Guidelines* (revised 2012), Sydney: MRT and RRT.

Millbank, J. (2002) 'Imagining otherness: refugee claims on the basis of sexuality in Canada and Australia', *Melbourne University Law Review*, 26: 144–177.

— (2009) 'From discretion to disbelief: recent trends in refugee determinations on the basis of sexual orientation in Australia and the United Kingdom', *International Journal of Human Rights*, 13: 391–414.

— (2012) 'The right of lesbians and gay men to live freely, openly and on equal terms is not bad law: a reply to Hathaway and Pobjoy', *New York Journal of International Law and Politics*, 44: 497–527.

Minter, S. (2000) 'Do transsexuals dream of gay rights? Getting real about transgender inclusion in the gay rights movement', *New York Law School Journal of Human Rights*, 17: 589–621.

Mohyuddin, F. (2001) 'United States asylum law in the context of sexual orientation and gender identity: justice for the transgendered', *Hastings Women's Law Journal*, 12: 387–410.

Moran, L. and Sharpe, A. (2004) 'Violence, identity and policing: the case of violence against transgender people', *Criminology & Criminal Justice*, 4: 395 –417.

Musalo, K. and Knight, S. (2001) 'Steps forward and steps back: uneven progress in the law of social group and gender-based claims in the United States', *International Journal of Refugee Law*, 13: 51–70.

Neilson, V. (2004) 'Uncharted territory: choosing an effective approach in transgender-based asylum claims', *Fordham Urban Law Journal*, 32: 266–289.

Neilson,V. and Morris, A. (2005) 'The gay bar: the effect of the one-year filing deadline on lesbian, gay, bisexual transgender, and HIV positive foreign nationals seeking asylum or withholding of removal', *New York City Law Review*, 8: 233–282.

Organization for Refugee Asylum & Migration (ORAM) (2011) *Testing Sexual Orientation: A Scientific and Legal Analysis of Plethysmography in Asylum and Refugee Status Proceedings*, San Francisco, CA: ORAM.

Oxford, C. (2005) 'Protectors and victims in the gender regime of asylum', *NWSA Journal*, 17(3): 18–38.

— (forthcoming), 'Queer asylum: US policies and responses to sexual orientation and transgendered persecution' in M. Schrover and D. Moloney, *Shifting Control: Gender and Migration Policy, 1917–2010*.

Prosser, J. (1998) *Second Skins: The Body Narrative of Transsexuality*, New York, NY: Columbia University Press.

Sabatello, M. (2011) 'Advancing transgender family rights through science: a proposal for an alternative framework', *Human Rights Quarterly*, 33: 43–75.

Sharpe, A. (2002) 'Thinking critically in moments of transgender law reform', *Griffith Law Review*, 11: 309–331.

— (2006) *Transgender Jurisprudence Dysphoric Bodies of Law*, 2nd edn, New York, NY: Routledge-Cavendish.

— (2012) 'Transgender marriage and the legal obligation to disclose gender history', *Modern Law Review*, 75: 33–53.

Smith D. (2010) 'Malawi gay couple who "married" face harsh prison sentences', *The Guardian*, 14 May 2010.

— (2011) 'Malawi to review homosexuality ban after US aid threat', *The Guardian*, 9 December 2011.

Southam, K. (2011) 'Who am I and who do you want me to be? Effectively defining a lesbian, gay, bisexual and transgender social group in asylum applications', *Chicago–Kent Law Review*, 86: 1363–1387.

Stoller, R. (1975) *The Transsexual Experiment*, London: Hogarth.

Stryker, S. (2008) *Transgender History*, Berkeley, CA: Seal Press.

UK Border Agency (2004) *Gender Issues in the Asylum Claim* (revised 2006, 2010), Asylum Policy Instruction, UK Border Agency.

— (2011a) *Gender Identity Issues in the Asylum Claim*, Asylum Policy Instruction, UK Border Agency.

— (2011b) *Sexual Orientation Issues in the Asylum Claim*, Asylum Policy Instruction, UK Border Agency.

UK Lesbian and Gay Immigration Group (2010) *Failing the Grade*, London: UK Lesbian and Gay Immigration Group.

UNHCR (2002a) *Guidelines on International Protection No. 1: Gender-Related Persecution within the Context of Article 1A(2) of the 1951 Convention and/or its 1967 Protocol relating to the Status of Refugees*, UN Doc HCR/GIP/02/01 (7 May 2002), Geneva: UNHCR.

— (2002b) *Guidelines on International Protection No. 2: 'Membership of a Particular Social Group' within the context of Article 1A(2) of the 1951 Convention and/or its 1967 Protocol Relating to the Status of Refugees*, UN Doc HCR/GIP/02/02 (7 May 2002), Geneva: UNHCR.

— (2008) *UNHCR Guidance Note on Refugee Claims Relating to Sexual Orientation and Gender Identity*, 21 November 2008, Geneva: UNHCR, available at http://www.unhcr.org/refworld/docid/48abd5660.html (accessed 7 February 2012).

— (2011) *Asylum Levels and Trends in Industrialized Countries: Statistical overview of asylum applications lodged in Europe and selected non-European countries*, Geneva: UNHCR.

— (2012) *Guidelines on International Protection No 9: Claims to Refugee Status Based on Sexual Orientation and/or Gender Identity within the context of Article 1A(2) of the 1951 Convention and/or its 1967 Protocol Relating to the Status of Refugees*, UN Doc HCR/GIP/12/09, Geneva: UNHCR.

US Citizenship and Immigration Services (2011) *Guidance for Adjudicating Lesbian, Gay, Bisexual, Transgender and Intersex (LGBTI) Refugee and Asylum Claims*, Training Module, November 2011.

Vade, D. (2005) 'Expanding gender and expanding the law: toward a social and legal conceptualization of gender that is more inclusive of transgender people', *Michigan Journal of Gender and Law*, 11: 253–316.

Wallbank, R. (2004) '*Re Kevin* in perspective', *Deakin Law Review*, 9: 461–502.

Weßels, J. (2011) *Sexual Orientation in Refugee Status Determination*, RSC Working Paper series No. 74, Oxford: Refugee Studies Centre.

Wilets, J. (1997) 'Conceptualizing private violence against sexual minorities as gendered violence: an international and comparative law perspective', *Albany Law Review*, 60: 989–1050.

Whittle, S., Turner, L. and Al-Alami, M. (2007) 'Engendered penalties: transgender and transsexual people's experiences of inequality and discrimination', West Yorkshire, Communities and Local Government Publications, available at http://www.pfc.org.uk/pdf/EngenderedPenalties.pdf (accessed 18 December 2012).

7 Normativity and credibility of sexual orientation in asylum decision making

*Louis Middelkoop**

7.1 Protection of gay and lesbian asylum seekers

In 1981 the Council of State, the highest Dutch immigration court, held that a reasonable interpretation of persecution on account of membership of a particular social group may entail persecution on account of sexual orientation.[1] This judgment introduced refugee protection for some gays and lesbians coming to the Netherlands. Some, because refugee status is only granted to members of this group under certain conditions. Under the government's current policy, criminal prosecution on account of homosexuality may be considered an act of persecution. However, such prosecution alone is not sufficient to award refugee status. The applicant must make credible that he or she has a well-founded fear of being targeted personally and that the inflicted sentence caries a 'certain weight.' A mere fine would not lead to the conclusion that the applicant is a refugee.[2]

In 2007, the requirement that an asylum seeker conceals his or her sexual orientation to avoid persecution was repealed under parliamentary pressure.[3] However, Millbank (2009) observed that in Australia and the United Kingdom the end of the so-called 'discretion requirement' meant a shift in focus of credibility assessments from alleged acts of persecution to whether the person concerned is gay at all.

In this chapter, 13 cases adjudicated in the Netherlands are studied. The results indicate that credibility of the asylum seeker's sexual orientation is also relevant for status determination in the Netherlands. This warrants an evaluation of how the particular social group is defined and how the credibility of an asylum seeker's sexual orientation is assessed in practice. Accordingly, this chapter addresses three corresponding questions. First, how does the Immigration and Naturalisation Service (IND) define the particular social group of homosexuals? Second, how is this definition applied in practice? Third, how should definition and practice be evaluated?

7.2 Defining the particular social group

7.2.1 Manifestations of sexual orientation

This chapter assumes that sexual orientation may be present within an individual in three different ways: behavioural, emotional and self-identification. In this chapter, same sex behaviours are defined as sexual activities with the same sex.[4] Same sex emotions are understood to be feelings of sexual attraction or love that an individual experiences, whether expressed or not, towards a member of the same sex. By self-identification this chapter refers to the phenomenon of considering one's orientation a part of their personal identity. In other words, whether a person refers to oneself as hetero- or homosexual. Self-identification can be overt and communicated to others, but can also occur only privately or internally. In other words, one can self-identify as gay, regardless whether one is 'out or in the closet'.

Self-identification issues may complicate matters in an asylum context in at least four different situations. First, a person could feel occasionally attracted to the same sex, even engage in sexual relations with a person of the same sex, but still not identify as gay or bisexual, because that person is predominantly orientated towards the other sex. We see below that the IND does not consider that these people fall within the definition of the particular social group of gays.

Second, an individual might experience a conflict between his or her values on the one hand and his or her behaviour or feelings on the other hand. Homosexuality may carry a large stigma for a person who at the same time is attracted to the same sex. They thus experience two opposing thoughts or cognitions. In psychology this phenomenon is called cognitive dissonance (Festinger 1957). To lessen this dissonance or discrepancy, the person may employ ego-defence mechanisms, such as denial, repression or disassociation (Freud 1920; Festinger 1957). If an individual is not able to reduce the feelings of discomfort, he or she may develop severe stress, which eventually may lead to, for example, the manifestation of a depersonalization disorder.[5] This chapter considers such an apparent case in para. 7.3.5 below.

Third, anthropological research suggests that sexual behaviour is not always connected with personal identity issues. Verkaaik (2010) argues that modern societies link sexual behaviour to notions of masculinity and femininity, which as a consequence allows feelings and behaviour to bring the personal identity in crisis. He bases his argument on a survey by Agha (2002: 199) of Pakistani truck drivers of whom 55 per cent voluntarily report homosexual contacts to the researchers.

According to Verkaaik (2010), same sex behaviour is frowned upon in Pakistani society because Islam prohibits it, not because it affects one's manhood. Having sex with a member of the same sex is considered a form of religious rebellion; sinful, like smoking cigarettes or drinking alcohol, but at the same time more innocent than behaviour that challenges personal identity and masculinity. In more modern societies, like Western countries, but also Iran, same sex activities have broader implications for one's identity and are therefore more problematized (Verkaaik 2010). It appears that this cultural disagreement is in play in a case discussed in paras 7.3.3 and 7.3.7.2 below.

The fourth and last situation is a reversal of the previous ones. One could self-identify as gay, without ever having engaged in same sex relationships, for example because the opportunity has not (yet) arisen or certain internalized values inhibit the person from pursuing his feelings.[6]

In sum, although behaviours and emotions are more or less straightforward dimensions of sexual orientation, self-identification can complicate matters considerably. Having sketched out these parameters in which sexual orientation may be manifest within a person, the following sections discuss how sexual orientation is understood in an asylum context.

7.2.2 *Actual and perceived membership*

Dutch law and policy documents do not indicate in a general way which persons fall within the scope of the particular social group of gays and lesbians. However, the Alien Circular, a publicly disclosed policy guideline, does contain the remark that if an asylum seeker is not actually gay, but it is nevertheless credible that the authorities consider him to be so and persecution is likely to have happened or to happen, the asylum seeker shall be considered a refugee.[7] UNHCR (2008: para. 3) and the EU Qualification Directive[8] adopt similar viewpoints.

Thus, two types of persons are to be distinguished in determining the scope of a particular social group: the 'actual' members and the 'perceived' members. The first type of asylum seeker needs to make it plausible he is gay, the second type that he is perceived to be gay. The obvious questions then are: when is one considered 'actually' gay? And how is perceived homosexuality made plausible?

The IND uses an internal policy document for guidance in answering these questions in practice. Contrary to the Alien Circular this document is confidential and was not made available to the author. However, the IND agreed to an interview between the author and a senior decision maker on this issue. The interview primarily focused on what the relevant parts of a refugee narrative are and to what degree the IND is open to cultural differences in understanding sexuality. The following paragraphs are a summary of the conversation.[9]

7.2.3 *Interview summary*

The decision maker first explained that gays and lesbians constitute a particular social group because their persecution pertains to their lifestyle. A person should be free to be who he or she is, and sexual orientation is part of that. By identifying gays and lesbians as making up a particular social group, the Netherlands expresses its conviction that gay asylum seekers should be able to be who they are.

According to the official, a gay person under the 1951 United Nations Convention Relating to the Status of Refugees (the Refugee Convention) is someone who experiences sexual or romantic feelings towards members of the same sex. This explicitly means that homosexual behaviour alone does not suffice to say that somebody is protected by the Refugee Convention. A person who only engages in same sex activities without experiencing feelings of attraction is not persecuted for who he or she is. And, according to the decision maker, the Refugee Convention principally protects people against persecution for who they are, not for what they do.

Typical examples of situational homosexuality, such as forced prostitution or homosexuality in communities without access to heterosexual sex, like prisons, thus fall outside the scope of the particular social group. Sexual behaviour is not considered a primary trait of homosexuality by the IND. Instead, the applicant needs to explain what it means to him or her to be gay. The feelings of the applicant, the way he or her experiences his or her sexuality and what events have occurred in relation to his or her sexuality are central to the credibility assessment. In this respect, elements regarding becoming aware of these feelings, a coming out, entering into relationships, etc. are important for the credibility of the narrative.

Although it is true that homosexual behaviour is generally the cause for persecution, rather than internal feelings or experiences, the IND official pointed out that if a person merely displays homosexual behaviour or is perceived to be gay, he or she only is entitled to protection under Article 3 of the European Convention on Human Rights (the ECHR), provided he or she faces a real risk accordingly. Thus, the Refugee Convention and the ECHR are to be seen complementary to each other to protect both forms of sexuality, according to the official.

The interview turned to the third manifestation of homosexuality: self-identification. The official indicated that whether or not a person identifies him- or herself as gay is immaterial to the case. In the official's opinion, feelings are essential in assessing membership of the particular social group. On the other hand, the official made the caveat that her colleagues might reject an application if an asylum seeker denies being gay after being straightforwardly asked. To prevent arbitrariness however, the official pointed out that all cases are reviewed by a second official, before the decision is handed down. Moreover, when in doubt a policy department safeguarding the uniformity and quality of decisions is always consulted.

7.2.4 Discussion

The particular social group of gays and lesbians is thus defined by the decision maker as a group of people who experience sexual or romantic feelings towards members of the same sex. Accordingly, the central elements of the credibility assessment are the feelings, experiences and past events relating to sexuality that the applicant describes in the hearing.

It appears that the IND considers that a person who only engages in same sex behaviour does not fall under the category of perceived gays. Nevertheless, the official believes that such persons may invoke the protection of Article 3 of the ECHR. This is contrary to what the EU Qualification Directive and Dutch legislation and policy documents stipulate on the point of an attributed persecution ground.[10]

Moreover, contrary to what the official purports, Article 3 of the ECHR does not offer complementary protection in all situations of persecution, as it only protects people from a real risk of torture or inhuman or degrading treatment or punishment. Other acts of persecution fall outside the scope of Article 3. The Refugee Convention, on the other hand, may also provide protection against violations of fundamental freedoms or against systematic discrimination.[11] In sum, the interview gave an indication as to how the particular social group is conceptualized, i.e. defined in abstract terms. The next section studies how this definition is operationalized in individual cases.

7.3 Credibility assessment in practice

7.3.1 Method

This section presents the results of an analysis of sexual orientation credibility assessment conducted in a selection of 13 cases of gay asylum seekers whose applications were decided and adjudicated upon between the period of 2006 and 2010. This study is not a representation of the full practice concerning credibility assessment of sexual orientation. Such a full analysis turned out to be impossible to do within the limited time available.

The first obstacle to obtaining a complete picture is that asylum claims are not registered in categories of motives or persecution grounds. Therefore, the IND could not provide a list of relevant cases it has had under its review. Instead, legal search engines, but most importantly, the co-operation of lawyers, staff of the refugee council and asylum seekers themselves were called upon to discover relevant cases. The results of the query were thus heavily dependent upon the network of the author.

In principle, the IND does not motivate decisions if it has a positive outcome for the asylum seeker, in other words, if the application for protection is accepted.[12] Consequently, this research excludes an evaluation of any such positive decisions. However, the bias that ensues from this is not a fundamental problem to this research, as this study does not aim to assess to what extent the overall decision making practice is sound. Rather, it only aims to asses to what extent lines of argumentation to reject asylum applications are valid.

Unfortunately, the search for cases did not return usable cases of lesbian or transgender applicants, thus there is an exclusive focus on men. Accordingly, the study presented below should be understood as a preliminary survey of what practical aspects might be problematic in assessing the sexual orientation of asylum seekers.

In analyzing the cases, the present research relies on Berg and Millbank (2009) who drew upon psychological and sociological literature to 'explore the particular issues that arise in eliciting and presenting a refugee narrative when the claim is based upon sexual orientation' in the Canadian, British, Australian and New Zealand context. The following sections explore to what extent their critique might be applicable to the 13 selected cases decided and adjudicated in the period between 2006 and 2010 in the Netherlands.

7.3.2 Appearance, demeanour and body language

No cases were encountered in which criteria such as 'does not look gay', 'not effeminate' or 'too masculine' were used to assess the credibility of sexual orientation. Yet, the IND does pay attention to demeanour and non-verbal expressions by an asylum seeker, such as sighing or long pauses before answering. Indeed, this could be a useful tool in interpreting the honesty of an answer. Yet, the possible negative consequences of including this in credibility assessments are illustrated by the following excerpt from the interview transcript of the case of 'Amir':[13]

Question:	Did you have full physical contact with that guy, or was it limited to touching only?
Answer:	I do not know what to say.
Observation by interviewing officer:	Mr [Amir] is silent.
Comment by interpreter:	I asked Mr [Amir] whether it would be easier for him to talk about this subject if I do not look him in the face. He replied that this is not the problem.
A:	I do not know what to say.
Q:	That father of that guy found you with that guy in bed. How did he find you?
A:	We were naked; I do not know how to explain this.
Q:	At that moment, were you engaged in sexual activities?
A:	We were naked, we were having sex. The father came. He found us.
Q:	What do you mean by sex? This might be a strange question to you, but it is a word with many different meanings.
A:	I do not know what to say, we were just sitting. I do not really remember. He was my boyfriend.

	I do not know what to say, it was like someone else with his girlfriend.
Observation interviewing officer:	Mr [Amir] sighs after every question and pauses before he answers.
Q:	Why did the father respond in such a way if you were just sitting?
A:	That guy and I were always together. He found us that day. He saw the scene. It happened. I do not know what to say.
Q:	Where you touching each other?
A:	Yes.
Q:	On erotic body parts?
A:	Yes, I do not know how to explain. For him, this was unacceptable of course. He saw me and his son touching each other.[14]

The decision maker subsequently determined that:

> Generally, the applicant gave very evasive answers to all questions that related to actual homosexual contacts, or actual homosexual interests. For example, he could not, not even after persisting questioning, explain in what *position* he was found with his neighbour by his father.[15]

This was used as one of the arguments to conclude that Amir is not credible and that his application has to be rejected. Certainly, this way of answering questions could indicate Amir was lying, yet it could also mean that he feels embarrassed to talk about this or even despises himself for it (see Berg and Millbank 2009: 200).

The court indeed held that 'the plaintiff indeed frequently gave evasive answers at first, yet it can be established from plaintiff's answers and the observations of the interviewing officer that the plaintiff was clearly ashamed to talk about his orientation'.[16] The decision was quashed and remanded to the IND for reconsideration.

7.3.3 *Expectations about homosexual feelings and emotions*

The above case is not only remarkable for the decision maker's interpretation of the behaviour of the asylum seeker during the interview. The interviewing officer's very intrusive questions into sexual contacts are in itself disturbing. The applicant is apparently expected to share his most intimate experiences during the interview.

UNHCR (2008, para. 17) advises against queries into sexual acts and prefers a focus on 'realization and experiences of sexual identity'. Although far more proper, the way such 'realization and experiences' are described need to conform to the decision maker's ideas of how one realizes and experiences sexual identity. If the applicant does not talk about his emotions and feelings in a way the decision maker can comprehend, a negative status determination might follow.[17]

In 1979, Australian psychologist Cass developed a model for homosexual identity formation (Cass 1979; Berg and Millbank 2009: 206). According to this model, identity is developed in a number of stages: initial confusion about sexual identity, comparison of sexual identity with others, tolerance of own identity, acceptance of it, and pride and integration of the sexual identity with the overall personal identity. It appears from the present research that IND officials understand sexual identity development similarly to this model. A good example is provided by the case of the 18-year-old Pakistani asylum seeker 'Sarmed':

Q: Can you tell me how you realized you are gay?
A: I liked boys. I wanted to have sex with them.
Q: Can you tell me more?
A: Like I said, I like boys and I wanted to have sex with them.
Q: Can you tell me more on the process of finding out that you are gay?
A: I did not fancy girls. I liked boys more. The girls did not appear attractive to me. The boys did. The boy has become my good friend. I had good contact with him. I was happy that he became my boyfriend.

. . .

Q: How did it psychologically affect you, that you are gay?
A: I wanted a boyfriend.[18]

Despite being insightful, Berg and Millbank (2009: 207) criticize Cass's model for being linear and for being culturally blind. They argue that the model is orientated towards western conceptions of sexuality and fails to explain deviance or alternative development. Not all gays and lesbians go through the same process, and particular people from non-western cultures may experience their identity development wholly differently from this model.

Yet, the sexual discovery process of Sarmed is brought up at least another five times during the interview. On each question, the 18-year-old applicant persists in answering that he likes boys and likes to sleep with them. The decision maker then concludes that the applicant 'at no time immersed himself into the question what it means to be homosexual' and that 'at no time he experienced an inner struggle'. This would be particularly odd because he was raised 'with the societal notion that homosexuality is bad'. The decision maker bases all this on the, for several reasons debatable, suggestion that 'even in a tolerant society as the Netherlands, the discovery of homosexual feelings will cause an inner struggle'.

In other words, the IND expects that the normal gay person goes through a period of internal confusion before he comes to terms with his sexuality.

Immediate self-acceptance or not considering the implications of one's feelings for one's identity is unlikely to the decision maker. Jansen (2010) remarked on this point that Sarmed 'is not believed to be gay *because* he is attracted to men'. The District Court indeed reversed the decision, holding that 'nothing was adduced to support the contention that from homosexuals from a society like Pakistan may be expected to go through a phase of inner struggle'.[19]

7.3.4 Belated coming out

Irrespective of the value of Cass's model for developing sexual identity, the applicant might be in an intermediate stage upon arrival, in other words he might still be uncertain about his sexual orientation. This uncertainty, particularly on the possible implications for his identity, might lead to contradictory statements about his sexuality or a complete withholding of this part of his narrative. To expect that an asylum seeker will always be ready for a coming out is therefore wrong.

If an applicant reveals his sexual orientation in a late stage or after the initial procedure, this may be repaired by reapplying and bringing it as a new element.[20] In Dutch law, new elements, also called *nova*, are facts or circumstances that occurred after the initial decision and therefore could not and did not have to be brought forward.[21] If the decision maker accepts the elements as new, a new assessment of the application will follow. If the element is not considered new in the sense that they technically could have been mentioned by the applicant earlier, the decision maker may reject the application with a referral to the initial decision.[22] If accepted as admissible, each *novum* is then tested on its credibility.

In reapplications of cases concerning homosexuality, the contested issue regularly is whether the applicant could and should have mentioned his sexual orientation earlier. In the case of the Angolan asylum seeker 'Kwame' the court held that, in principle, an applicant should mention his sexual orientation once he is conscious of it.[23] Thus, homosexuality in itself is not considered a *novum*, yet a realization of these experiences after the initial application may be considered to be so. In the case of Kwame, the court held that the IND erred in not believing that the applicant, who came to the Netherlands when he was aged 15 and even had a girlfriend at first, only became aware of his sexual orientation during his adolescence. The decision was quashed accordingly. *En passant*, the court found opportunity to note that it is to be assumed that 'sexuality is determined genetically'.[24]

Yet, if an applicant is aware of his sexual orientation he is expected to be open about this immediately. Iraqi born 'Rasul' and his family were granted temporary protection on account of the general situation in Iraq in 1998. This was revoked after some time and many reapplications and appeals followed. Eventually, Rasul reapplied again and argued that he fled Iraq in part because of his sexual orientation. The court was sceptical as to whether this was really true, but principally focused on the question whether this should have been mentioned earlier and thus was inadmissible as a new element. The court held: 'the applicant was aware that his family would not accept his sexual orientation straight away, and therefore should have told this during his initial application'.[25]

The court thereby disregarded the fact that precisely because he knew that his family would not accept his sexual orientation, it was not unreasonable to believe that this made him afraid of disclosing it when he did not have to in order to be granted asylum and avoid persecution. In this way, Rasul was punished for being discrete for eight years, while at that time the Dutch government still required discretion from him in order to avoid persecution.[26]

Recourse to Article 3 of the ECHR, the absolute prohibition of torture, was denied, because the court held that 'an application pursuant to article 4:6 of the Awb must be made in accordance with national procedure and only extraordinary facts or circumstances pertaining to the case at hand may require that these rules are not held against the applicant'.[27] Such circumstances were not believed to exist in the present case.[28] Rasul thus was made subject to deportation to Iraq in 2006. It appears from the case that, by then, Rasul's family had learned that he was gay.

The rigidity of the asylum procedure led to an amendment to the Aliens Act of 2000 which came into force on 1 July 2010. The amendment expanded the possibilities to argue new facts or circumstances on appeal. Pursuant to the new article 83 of the Aliens Act of 2000, facts, circumstances and evidence shall be considered by the court even if the alien could have submitted them earlier during the procedure. Yet, the *nova* system pertaining to renewed applications remained unchanged.

7.3.5 *Internalized homophobia*

A particular category of applicants who disclose their sexual orientation at a late stage are those who suffer from internalized homophobia. Amir suffered from this to such a degree that it led to a 'psychological blockade'. Only years after his initial application could Amir discuss for the first time his problems that were caused by his sexual orientation.

During the interview, it become clear that Amir still found it difficult to talk about this. He said that 'Thank god, I do not know any books or magazines on homosexuality'.[29] He indicated that he found such questions unpleasant. As mentioned in para. 7.3.2 above, he evaded questions pertaining to his personal sexual experiences. In court a psychologist testified as an expert-witness that Amir suffers from a mental disorder 'that makes it difficult for him to embrace his gay identity, which in turn may lead to a detachment of personality, which means that one may have a certain orientation and even perform certain acts in line with this, but at same time find this repulsive or abnormal'.[30]

Earlier in the procedure Amir's attorney filed a brief explaining that it was likely that Amir was not mentally able to give coherent and consistent answers to questions regarding his sexual orientation. However, the IND argued that Amir was given plenty of time and opportunity to mention his sexual orientation in his initial application in 1998 and dismissed the case for want of facts or circumstances that could not have been raised earlier under article 4:6 of the Awb.[31] The court, however, held that the applicant made it sufficiently plausible to believe that he indeed suffered from a mental disorder and, hence, his homosexuality could not have been raised earlier.[32] Accordingly, the appeal on this point was also allowed.[33] However, in January 2012, the Council of State held that the psychologist had failed to provide information on the condition of the applicant at the time of the initial application in 2006, leaving open the possibility that he did not suffer from this disorder back then. The appellate court accordingly reversed the District Court's judgment.[34] Spijkerboer (2012) criticized the logic of this decision, as it was unlikely that Amir developed his disorder after arrival in the reception country and not in the country of origin. After all, the disorder was directly tied to the problems Amir experienced in Iran.

7.3.6 *Knowledge of 'gay culture'*

In nearly all the cases that were researched for this chapter the IND questioned the applicant on his knowledge of gay culture. Applicants are regularly expected to be able to tell about (inter)national gay rights organizations, local places where gay people meet, gay nightlife, famous gay persons, and movies and books that centre on homosexuality.

The IND official interviewed for this research explained that these questions are asked to give the applicant one final opportunity to convince the decision maker. If applicants relay vague statements about their feelings and experiences, knowledge of gay culture may give them the benefit of the doubt. Yet, from the cases researched it appears this argument is sometimes reversed and a lack of knowledge is deemed to undermine the credibility of the rest of the story. For example, in the case of 'Kamal' the IND held that if his statement that he led 'a sexual life with men' and regularly rented gay-erotic movies from age 19 onwards was to be believed, 'more knowledge on homosexuality in Pakistan may be expected, which is presently not the case'.[35]

At face value, this might not be an unreasonable thought. Yet, as became apparent during the interview, the IND is not very conscious of the difference between sexual attraction and sexual identity. This leads to an inability to distinguish people who experience sexuality as a private matter (attraction) from those who experience sexuality as (part of) their broader social identity. The former group may not take an interest in gay culture, while the latter might. According to Berg and Millbank (2009), the failure to recognize this difference requires asylum seekers to turn their personal preference or experience into a political or societal identity.

Although the IND surely does not expect every gay person to be an activist, the mere expectation that all homosexuals are interested in public manifestations of sexuality, such as media, literature or 'the gay circuit' is stereotypical. Particularly, in countries where being open about sexuality is taboo or even an offence against public decency, this assumption is hard to support. The asylum seeker himself may even agree with the taboo and the offensive nature, and treat his orientation as a private matter. The IND should therefore consider both the availability and accessibility of gay culture in the country of origin as well as the applicant's personal disposition and background. For example, a person from a rural area might have far less access to media than somebody in a city. Moreover, a person who has had the same partner for a long time might find little interest in gay nightlife.[36]

7.3.7 *Social condemnation*

7.3.7.1 *Criminalization*

To continue with the case of Amir. During the interview he was asked about his knowledge of sodomy laws in Iran. He answered that homosexuality is subject to capital punishment. The IND held this was an incorrect answer: homosexuality as such is not criminalized in Iran, only homosexual acts.[37]

There are more cases in which applicants are expected to know the legal position of homosexuals in their country of origin. 'Rashid' from Indonesia did not know whether or not homosexuality (in whatever form) was an offense in his country. The IND argued that it is 'completely reasonable to expect him to be able to tell more about the position of homosexuals in Indonesia'.[38] This assumption probably originates in the idea that a member of a persecuted minority is interested in knowing what persecution might entail. Although a sensible assumption if criminal law enforcement is the type of persecution that the applicant fears, it is nevertheless unreasonable to expect that an applicant knows the exact formulation of the penal code. In the case of Amir, the interpretation of his answer in the negative is malevolent. Moreover, in instances where persecution does not originate from criminal law enforcement, but from relatives, the community or governmental actors who persecute the asylum seeker without putting him on criminal trial, acquiring knowledge on the penal code is not necessarily a priority.

7.3.7.2 *Homosexuality and religion*

Apart from criminalization by the government, homosexuality may also have been prohibited by the prevailing religion. In the cases of Sarmed and Kamal, both from Pakistan, the IND expected them to know what the dominant religion in their country, Islam, has to say on this. Kamal's lack of knowledge about the Quran 'did not give his narrative any more credibility'.[39] Sarmed was expected to examine his religion and his sexual orientation upon (ir)reconcilability:

> Q: How religious are your parents?
> A: Moderate Muslims. [. . .] The important things in Islam, they do them. [. . .] praying five times, fasting, almsgiving.

> [. . .]
> Q: How religious are you yourself?
> A: I do the important things too, like praying five times, fasting.
> Q: The Muslim faith does not allow you to be homophile (sic), am I correct?
> A: No, it is not allowed.
> Q: Can you explain to me how you reconcile being Muslim on the hand and discovering you have homophile feelings at the other hand?
> A: Religion is one side, and personal feelings are the other side. There are many things prohibited in Islam. Drinking alcohol. Each Muslim has to grow a beard. Other things are prohibited too.[40]

In other words: Sarmed believes Islam prohibits a lot and he does not really care. Yet, the IND considered it unlikely that a person like Sarmed would not contemplate his abnormal behaviour.[41] Australian and Canadian courts have considered such reasoning to be stereotypical (Berg and Millbank 2009).

After Sarmed was caught with his boyfriend, he fled the house of his partner. He called his father and confessed the relationship. His father was furious at first, but calmed down after a few minutes. He told his son to leave the city. Sarmed believed his father was worried, now that his boyfriend's family was out to seek revenge. The IND deemed the father's protective advice unlikely in light of 'the way Islamic and Pakistani society thinks about homosexuality'.[42] In other words: all Muslims and Pakistani condemn homosexuality so strongly, they would not want to protect their children from persecution. To the decision maker the father's advice to seek safety was too tolerant and, without any further explanation, not plausible. A questionable assumption.

7.3.8 Diverging definitions

During the interview Amir made several statements indicating that his asylum application was based on persecution on account of his sexual orientation. Yet, when directly asked, he denied he was gay. After some more questions, it appeared that Amir understands somebody to be gay if he has sexual encounters with different men on a regular basis. In other words, he equates homosexuality with promiscuity. Amir, on the other hand, had been with the same man for a long time, hence his negative answer. It appeared from the interview that the interviewing officer realized the misunderstanding and explained to him that in the Netherlands somebody is generally understood to be gay if he feels attracted to the same sex. Amir then said that he supposed that he was gay then. Yet, the eventual decision maker, a different officer than the interviewer, had little consideration for this miscommunication:

> . . . [Amir] then stated he is not attracted to women, but that he is nevertheless not gay. From a person who has reached the age of 40 and

> bases his renewed application on his alleged homosexuality clearer statements as to his sexual orientation may be expected.[43]

The District Court held that the IND erred in making this finding, as it was clear that the asylum seekers and the interviewing officer were using different definitions.[44]

7.4 The problems of deciding upon sexual orientation

The previous paragraphs provided an analysis of the practice of assessing the sexual orientation of gay asylum seekers in the Netherlands over a four-year period. The following paragraphs evaluate this practice more in depth. The following problematic aspects are discussed: first, normative bias in individual assessment; second, normativity in defining sexual orientation; third, the appropriateness of governments deciding what somebody's sexual orientation is.

An important conclusion is that the IND sometimes makes use of flawed lines of argumentation in individual assessments. Although more limited in scope, the present study indicates that Berg and Millbank's (2009) critique of Canadian, British, Australian and New Zealand practice is also applicable to practice in the Netherlands. It is shown that IND decision makers and judges compare the statements made by the asylum seeker to what is known to them about sexual orientation. Questions asked and conclusions based on them occasionally betray preconceptions of homosexuality that are not universal to all gays and lesbians and sometimes they are just plain stereotypical.

However, in determining what is credible the decision maker has little choice but to compare the asylum seeker's narrative to the information about sexual orientation available to him. He is given no other tool: no phallometry nor, insofar this would be valuable, a psychologist's opinion.[45] The decision maker thus has to determine what are expected or 'normal' elements in a narrative of an 'actually' gay person. As Sedgwick (1990) writes, however, the way in which people experience their sexuality differs greatly. Assessment of sexual orientation thus turns out to be inherently problematic as it requires the decision maker to judge how an 'actually' gay person would behave according to his own subjective standards. This study shows that such a method is susceptible to biased and flawed argumentation.

Note, however, that this normative approach is not necessarily detrimental to all gay applicants. As Spijkerboer (2000: 64) noted with regard to female asylum seekers, it works against those who act in contrast to that which is expected of them, but it works in favour of those who fit the mould. Accordingly, applicants who do not adhere to prevailing preconceptions are lying; to the decision maker's mind it does not indicate that they are less stereotypical than expected. The present study is, however, not conclusive as to what number of asylum seekers profit and what number suffers.

The subjective nature of credibility assessment and the problems that ensue from it is not limited to individual case assessment, but also extends to the conceptual level. The discussion as to what manifestations of sexual orientation make a person gay or straight or bisexual is ongoing on a philosophical and theoretical plane; however, as it turns out, it is also a legal discussion relevant to refugee law. Out of the three manifestations of sexual orientation identified in this chapter, namely feelings, behaviour and identification, the IND indicates that it will focus on feelings alone. This is reflected in practice, as is particularly shown in paras 7.3.3 and 7.3.5 above. The IND argues that this is because the Refugee Convention protects 'people for who they are, not primarily for what they do'. Thereby, the IND equates feelings with identity as far as the applicant is open about them.

Only people describing feelings of attraction towards the same sex, insofar as the decision maker appreciates elements of the narrative as being such feelings, are considered 'actual' gays protected by the Refugee Convention. The IND says it does not consider performing same sex acts to mean a gay sexual orientation and such acts can only lead to protection under Article 3 of the ECHR. This is in spite of contrary provisions in EU and Dutch law regarding imputed persecution grounds. The status of people who do not identify as gay because of internalized homophobia, confusion about feelings or because they have a different understanding of the concept, is ambiguous. The IND has refused to award refugee status to these individuals, although courts are more lenient.

By taking this approach, the IND forces itself to take sides in an ontological debate on the nature of sexual orientation in defining the scope of the protected group. According to Segdwick (1990) the question of gay identification has become one of authority and evidence in the twentieth century. Societal resistance towards homosexuality has led to a situation where the subject himself is no longer in control of the definition and must evidence his sexuality in all kinds of contexts. A coming out is not accepted by others if the individual bases this on only a few feelings, but no actions or, conversely, on a few actions, but not feelings. Segdwick writes, however, that the notion of gay identity is complicated and that no single person can take control over all the multiple, often contradictory, codes by which information about sexual identity and activity can seem to be conveyed. Nevertheless, the IND seemingly tries to do this.

In this respect, the case of Amir should be recalled. Amir had a different understanding of the definition of homosexual than the decision maker who rejected his application. The court forgave this and ordered the IND to reconsider its decision. Should the IND then determine on Amir's behalf that he is gay, even if he experiences that as stigmatizing? In that way, the authority of definition is removed from Amir and the government seizes this authority to label him as gay. It might be more appropriate to determine that Amir is likely perceived to be gay by the authorities, because his partner is a man. In other words, the problems identified at the individual case level do not only originate from problems at the conceptual level, but the conceptualization problems also extend to the normative level.

7.5 An alternative approach towards refugee status determination

Apart from the inherent subjectivity of the assessment and the questions as to whether Dutch immigration service officers are equipped to go into the ontology of sexuality and whether it is appropriate for a government agency to determine who is and is not actually gay, it is also unnecessary for the government to assess the sexuality of asylum seekers. This chapter suggests an alternative approach to determine whether an asylum seeker is a refugee because he is persecuted on account of his sexual orientation. This approach has been staring us in the face all the time and does not require any legislative change. At times, it has already been used by courts to arrive at a satisfactory outcome. It entails a shift in focus from assessing whether it is credible that the asylum seeker is gay to whether elements in the narrative indicate that the actors of persecution perceive him to be gay.

This approach has the advantage in that it avoids the problems mentioned in the previous section. That is the theoretical debate on defining homosexuality, the question of appropriateness of a government labelling individuals as gay and the subjective expectations of how an 'actually' gay person behaves. This approach also does not deny that the asylum seeker is gay. Instead, it is a question that becomes irrelevant, because the fear of persecution is equal regardless of whether the persecutors are right in believing that the asylum seeker is or is not gay.

This approach would be supported by article 3.37(2) of the Aliens Regulations of 2000, which reads:

> When assessing whether the fear of the alien for persecution pursuant to the Refugee Convention is well-founded, it is irrelevant whether the alien actually displays the racial, religious, national, social or political features that gave cause for persecution if these features are imputed to him by the actor of persecution.[46]

This alternative has been used by Dutch courts in the past. The case of 'Abdul' from Morocco is a good illustration. The IND reasoned that Abdul is not gay because he is in a relationship with a transgender. Abdul's partner is biologically male, yet self-identifies and dresses as a woman. In addition, Abdul stated he does not feel attracted to men. The IND argued that this relationship between a man and a transgender is therefore heterosexual in nature.[47]

However, the IND failed to recognize that Abdul is persecuted because he did not confirm with mainstream sexual morals in Morocco. This is independent from the label the IND likes to attach to his relationship with a transgender person. Thus, on appeal, the District Court held that 'the determinative question is whether it is credible that the authorities in the country of origin will perceive the asylum seeker as gay or not' and quashed the decision.[48]

In a case concerning political affiliation the Supreme Court held that persecution pursuant to article 1A of the Refugee Convention is to be understood to include persecution on account of political convictions that the persecuting institution believes it should impute to the refugee.[49] The Commission on Equal Treatment (CGB) adopted this interpretation in another ruling concerning a discrimination case.[50] The Council of State itself has also taken over this argumentation from the Supreme Court, although it has not yet pronounced on cases concerning sexual orientation.[51] An exhaustive overview of all case law concerning imputed persecution grounds falls outside the scope of this chapter. The main point is clear, however, Dutch courts have found imputed membership a valid approach in determining instances of persecution and discrimination.

It is suggested that the IND adopts this approach as a point of departure in all cases concerning gay and lesbian asylum seekers. So rather than assessing whether actors of persecution impute a sexual orientation *after* the decision maker failed to establish that the asylum seeker is gay, it should be done *before*. The burden is on the asylum seeker to make plausible that persecutors perceive him to be gay, or any sexual minority for that matter.

In a 1993 Supreme Court case, a Zairian man was persecuted for bringing away a package with video tapes with footage in which then-president Mobutu was insulted. Although he was not personally politically opined, the Supreme Court believed he was in trouble because of perceived political affiliation. Similarly, an Argentinean lifeguard who found bodies washed ashore of the Rio Plata was threatened with his life by agents of the junta. Because he accidentally got involved into politics he was also entitled to protection.[52]

This chapter suggests that in sexual orientation cases a focus should be adopted on what behaviour by the applicant might lead to the perception of persecutors that he is gay. This could be acts of speech, kissing or other displays of affection in public, getting caught in private, possession of gay literature or other media, living with another person of the same sex, wearing certain types of clothes that are a code for an alternative sexual orientation, or gender identity for that matter, and so on. This chapter proposes a refocus on the outward and the visible and whether it attracts persecution.

A caveat is in order. The parliamentary repeal of the discretion requirement means that a refugee cannot be ordered back into the closet. The Council of State has, however, held that this is still permissible if the person concerned is able to have a 'meaningful private life' in the country of origin without the authorities having to know.[53] In this case a Sierra Leonean woman came out in the Netherlands, but already was secretly engaged in a same sex relationship for a long time in Sierra Leone. Spijkerboer (2011) criticized this decision for implying that living in the closet can constitute a meaningful way in living a gay life and for falsely assuming that life in the closet is safe. Some districts courts have followed the line of Spijkerboer and navigated around the Council of State's judgment.[54]

Is the alternative approach useful in cases of applicants whose well-founded fear only developed after departure of their country of origin? A genuine example of such a refugee *sur place* in a sexual orientation case would be a person who came to the reception country as a child and realized he is gay during adolescence. Upon deportation, for example because protection was ultimately denied to his parents, he could then argue a fear of persecution on his own.[55]

The essence of the approach suggested in this chapter is to focus on what the authorities believe to know with regard to the applicant and whether they may persecute him on account of these beliefs. Without perception, thus without outward visibility, persecution cannot occur. In *sur place* cases protection is appropriate if it is plausible that if the asylum seeker would live an openly gay life in the country of origin the authorities will be put on notice and might persecute him. The relevant questions then become whether the asylum seeker is likely to want to live an openly gay life, whether the authorities will therefore perceive him as gay, and whether he will be persecuted.

As to the first question, whether it is likely that the asylum seeker would want to live an openly gay life, the only way to discover the answer is by assessing whether he is, indeed, gay. Except for when the asylum seeker manufactures his fear, thus falsely claiming he is gay in order to receive protection, there would be no other reason to assume why he would do that.[56] Thus, for now it is concluded that assessment of sexual orientation is sometimes inescapable. It is hoped that the pitfalls discussed in this chapter are then borne in mind. As to the other two questions, they may be answered through a normal assessment of reasonable fear, as is done in any other asylum case.

7.6 Conclusion

This chapter analyzed the practice of assessing credibility of sexual orientation in Dutch refugee law through an interview with an IND officer and a study of 13 cases adjudicated between 2006 and 2010. It turns out that determining whether or not an applicant is gay is problematic on three different levels: on the conceptual level the IND forces itself to take sides in a debate on the nature of homosexuality. This translates into problems at the individual application level: assessment of narratives of individual applicants is normative and subjective. Third, by focusing on whether the applicant is actually gay according to its own standards, the government is forcing its definition upon others. This is of questionable appropriateness.

As an alternative approach, a focus on perceived homosexuality is suggested to avoid many of the inherently problematic aspects. Such an approach requires no new legislation and has already been applied by the judiciary in political persecution cases. In *sur place* cases assessment of credible sexual orientation might, however, be inevitable. The hazards that come with this will hopefully be on the radar with decision makers, judges and attorneys alike.

7.7 Notes

* LLB (hons), VU University 2010; LLM, Columbia Law School/University of Amsterdam 2011; MSc, VU University 2012. Presently, lecturer, European Human Rights Protection, VU University Amsterdam. I am very grateful to Thomas Spijkerboer for his support and guidance throughout this research. Additionally, I thank Annemiek van Spanje, the editors at *asiel and migrantenrecht* and the participants of the Fleeing Homophobia Conference at the VU University on 5 and 6 September 2011 for their useful comments on earlier versions of this chapter. This chapter benefited greatly from discussions about the psychological dimensions with Anne Timmerman and Miriam Wijkman. In addition, I thank the Ministry of Justice, the Immigration and Naturalization Service, the Dutch Refugee Council and a number of immigration lawyers for their invaluable co-operation. Lastly, I am highly indebted to the people who allowed me to read their files and use them for my research. I express my sincere gratitude to them.

1 ARRvS (Judicial Division of the Council of State), 13 August 1981, No. A-2.1113, RV 1981, 5.

2 Alien Circular 2000, C1/4.2.10.2.

3 Replies by Minister Verdonk of 28 November 2006 to the Parliamentary questions of Lambrechts of 3 October 2006 (Aanhangsel Handelingen II, 2006/07 nr. 394). For an extensive discussion of the repeal of the discretion requirement and attempts to return it through the back door via the notion of 'voluntary discretion' and a reconceptualization of *sur place* claims, compare both Battjes' and Weßels' contributions to this volume.

4 Thus culturally coded communication, such as the use of certain language, voice intonation, gestures or the manner of clothing, is excluded from this definition.

5 See *International Statistical Classification of Diseases and Related Health Problems*, Geneva: World Health Organization, F48.1.

6 Orthodox Dutch protestant churches have a support network 'refo-anders' (refo-different) run by gays that spreads a message of celibacy, http://www.refoanders.nl (accessed 11 December 2012).

7 Section C2/2.10.2 of the Alien Circular.

8 (Council Directive 2004/83/EC); Article 10(2).

9 Note that the original summary was authorized as accurate by the IND; this translation was not (see Middelkoop 2010 for the original).

10 Article 10(2) of the EU Qualification Directive.

11 See article 3.36(1) and (2) of the Aliens Regulations 2000 (Voorschrift Vreemdelingen 2000); Articles 9 and 15 of the EU Qualification Directive; see also Battjes 2006: 242.

12 According to 4:18(1) of the Awb, motivation may be omitted if a reasonable assumption exists that there is no need for it.

13 All names of individuals who appear in this chapter have been anonymized.

14 Transcript of Second Interview Amir, The Hague District Court, sitting in Haarlem, 8 December 2009, LJN BK7528, on file with author.

15 Decision on the Repeated Application of [Amir] ibid, note 14 (emphasis added).

16 The Hague District Court, sitting in Haarlem, 8 December 2009, LJN BK7528, para. 2.18.

17 See also Spijkerboer (2000: 56–59) who identifies emotion as one of the three axes along which credibility of women asylum seekers is assessed.

18 Transcript of Second Interview Sarmed, The Hague District Court, sitting in Haarlem, 29 September 2009, JV 2010/20, on file with the author.
19 The Hague District Court, sitting in Haarlem, 29 September 2009, JV 2010/20, para. 2.18.
20 Article 32(3) of Council Directive 2005/85/EC.
21 ABRvS (Judicial Division of the Council of State), 4 April 2006, LJN: AF7223.
22 Article 4:6 of the Awb (General Administrative Law Act).
23 The Hague District Court, sitting in Haarlem, 7 December 2007, LJN: BC5647 ('Kwame').
24 Ibid, para. 2.12.
25 The Hague District Court, 28 November 2006, LJN: AZ4539 ('Rasul').
26 As noted in the first paragraph, the discretion requirement was only repealed in 2007.
27 The Hague District Court, 28 November 2006, LJN: AZ4539 ('Rasul') referring to ECtHR, 19 February 1998, JV 1998, 45 (Bahaddar).
28 Ibid, para. 2.7.
29 Transcript of Second Interview Amir.
30 The Hague District Court, sitting in Haarlem, 8 December 2009, LJN BK7528, para. 2.12.
31 Decision on the Repeated Application of Mr [Amir], above, note 14, at 3.
32 The Hague District Court, sitting in Haarlem, 8 December 2009, LJN BK7528, para. 2.13. Note that Amir also had won on the issue raised in para. 8.3.2 above.
33 For more cases in which homosexuality as a 'new fact' was accepted: The Hague District Court, sitting in Zwolle, 26 September 2007, AWB 06/55693, available at https://www.vluchtweb.nl/livelinkvw/llisapi.dll?func=ll&objId=1832690&objAction=download (accessed 18 December 2012); The Hague District Court, sitting in Groningen, 17 September 2006, AWB 06/52448, available at https://www.vluchtweb.nl/livelinkvw/llisapi.dll?func=ll&objId=1587771&objAction=download (accessed 18 December 2012). For a case in which an appeal based on a mental disorder was dismissed, see The Hague District Court, sitting in Amsterdam, 17 October 2008, AWB 08/34324 (dossier and judgment on file with author).
34 ABRvS (Judicial Division of the Council of State), 13 January 2012, JV 2012/118.
35 'Intention to decline the application of Kamal', p. 7 (on file with author) The Hague District Court, sitting in Haarlem, 9 March 2010, AWB 10/6922, available at https://www.vluchtweb.nl/livelinkvw/llisapi.dll?func=ll&objId=2091941&objAction=download(accessed 18 December 2012).
36 *Cf.* The Hague District Court, 11 December 2009, LJN: BK 7528 (Amir).
37 Ibid, para. 2.22.
38 Intention to Decline the Application of 'Rashid' (case on file).
39 Decision the Application of Kamal, The Hague District Court, sitting in Haarlem, 9 March 2010, AWB 10/6922, on file with author.
40 Transcript of Second Interview Sarmed, The Hague District Court, sitting in Haarlem, 29 September 2009, JV 2010/20, on file with the author.
41 Decision on Sarmed, on file with author.
42 Ibid.
43 Decision on the Reapplication of Mr [Amir], on file with author. See The Hague District Court, sitting in Haarlem, 8 December 2009, LJN BK7528.

44 The Hague District Court, sitting in Haarlem, 8 December 2009, LJN BK7528, para. 2.17.
45 Phallometry was practiced in the Czech Republic for some time, but fell into disuse after pressure by the European Commission (see Johnstone 2011).
46 This is an almost verbatim citation of article 10(2) of the EU Qualification Directive.
47 The Hague District Court, 4 November 2009, AWB/09/32210, available at https://www.vluchtweb.nl/livelinkvw/llisapi.dll?func=ll&objId=2056042&objAction=download (accessed 18 December 2012).
48 Ibid, para. 9.
49 Supreme Court of the Netherlands, 26 February 1993, NJ 1993/507, para. 3.3. (Until 1994, the Supreme Court was competent to hear cassation appeals about interim measures suspending the expulsion of aliens during their immigration or asylum procedure.)
50 Commission on Equal Treatment, Opinion, 9 July 2002, No. 02-84, para. 5.6.
51 ARRvS (Judicial Division of the Council of State), 29 June 1982, RV 1982, 3; 23 April 1993, RV 1993, 3; 8 June 1993, GV (old) D12-232; 15 April 1994, RV 1994, 4.
52 ARRvS (Judicial Division of the Council of State), 29 June 1982, RV 1982, 3.
53 ABRvS (Judicial Division of the Council of State), 11 May 2011, JV 2011/307.
54 See e.g. The Hague District Court, sitting in Arnhem, 25 October 2011, JV 2011/513; The Hague District Court, sitting in Amsterdam, 2 November 2011, JV 2012/102.
55 See e.g. The Hague District Court, sitting in Haarlem, 7 December 2007, LJN: BC5647 (Kwame); ABRvS, 3 October 2003, JV 2004/3.
56 Note that the article 5(3) of the EU Qualification Directive contains safeguards against manufactured fear.

7.8 References

American Psychiatric Association (2000), *Diagnostic and Statistical Manual of Mental Disorders DSM-IV-TR*, 4th edn, Washington, DC: American Psychiatric Association.

Agha, S. (2002) 'Sexual behaviour among truck drivers in Pakistan', *Culture, Health & Sexuality*, 4(2): 191–206.

Battjes, H. (2006) *European Asylum Law and International Law*, Leiden: Martinus Nijhoff.

Berg, L. and Millbank, J. (2009) 'Constructing the personal narratives of lesbian, gay and bisexual asylum claimants', *Journal of Refugee Studies*, 20: 195–223.

Cass, V.C. (1979) 'Homosexual identity formation: a theoretical model', *Journal of Sex Research*, (4): 147–153.

Festinger, L. (1957) *A Theory of Cognitive Dissonance*, Evanston, IL: Row, Peterson.

Freud, S. (1920) *A General Introduction to Psychoanalysis*, New York, NY: Boni and Liveright.

Jansen, S. (2010) Annotation of The Hague District Court, sitting in Haarlem, 29 September 2009, JV 2010/20.

Johnstone, C. (2011) *Czechs Deny 'Medieval' Penis Pressure Testing Still in Use*, Czechposition.com, 18 May 2011, available at http://www.ceskapozice.cz/en/

news/society/czechs-deny-%E2%80%98medieval%E2%80%99-penis-pressure-testing-still-use (accessed 18 December 2012).

Middelkoop, L.P. (2010) Geloofwaardigheidskwesties rond homoseksuelen in de Nederlandse asielprocedure, *Asiel en Migrantenrecht*, (1): 508–515.

Millbank, J. (2009) 'From discretion to disbelief: recent trends in refugee determinations on the basis of sexual orientation in Australia and the United Kingdom', *International Journal of Human Rights*, 13(2/3): 391–414.

Sedgwick, E.K. (1990) *Epistemology of the Closet*, Hemel Hempstead: Harvester Wheatsheaf.

Spijkerboer, T.P. (2000) *Gender and Refugee Status*, London: Ashgate.

— (2011) Annotation of ABRvS (Judicial Division of the Council of State), 11 May 2011, JV 2011/307.

— (2012) Annotation of ABRvS (Judicial Division of the Council of State), 13 January 2012, JV 2012/118.

UNHCR (2008) *Guidance Note on Refugee Claims Relating to Sexual Orientation and Gender Identity*, Geneva: UNHCR.

Verkaaik, O. (2010) Waarom hebben Pakistanen geen probleem met homoseks? Omdat ze modern zijn, *NRC Handelsblad*, 29 January 2010.

8 Invisible intersections, queer interventions

Same sex family reunification under the rule of asylum law

*Petra Sußner**

8.1 Introduction

Let me start in 2001. This is when the Life Partnership Act was passed in Germany, thus turning the recognition of same sex partnerships into legal reality. Equal rights activists celebrated. Fatima El Tayeb used this event as an opportunity for raising the issue of the category of race[1] within this discourse around the legal recognition of certain same sex ways of living. Under the title 'Limited Horizons' she did not mince her words:

> [Academic analysis of German society itself] is still dominated by the conviction that 'race' is a concept which – with the exception of the years between 1933 and 1945 – is irrelevant in the German context and can thus be safely disregarded. In the case of queer identity [political praxis] is with increasing exclusiveness directed at the assimilation of white lesbians and gays to a European system whose practices of exclusion, in turn, are more and more clearly based on racist criteria.
>
> (El Tayeb 2003: 129 *et seq.*)

Probably, Fatima El Tayeb was one of the first theorists in the German speaking area to write about the role of race within a queer rights orientated strategy. In that sense she stresses that – according to the logic of a modern and liberal constitutional state – the demand for rights does not only harbour the danger of being infiltrated by heteronormative ways of thinking, but also supports a system which currently uses the concept of race as an axis of difference to justify its increasing isolation from a racialized 'outside'. By readily integrating into that system, she accordingly argues, LGBTQ[2] people take the risk of entrenching the tendency to frame whiteness or EU citizenship as norm. Consequently, race remains a category that is not reflected upon – be it as a privileging (McIntosh 2003) or as a marginalizing dimension. For LGBTQ migrants, whose experiences are essentially shaped by the marginalizing dimensions of race, there is little space left within such a strategy of rights (El Tayeb 2003: 133–136).

Meanwhile, I daresay, the category race has become an issue that at least cannot be disregarded anymore. Both in academia and in activist circles there is quite a lively and at times harsh debate about the entanglement of race and sexuality. Basically, it revolves around dimensions of cultural (Strongman 2002), respectively religious hierarchization (Dietze 2009: 42–45; Haritaworn and Petzen 2011) in relation to the (legal) recognition of same sex partnerships that, nowadays, constitutes one the most evident manifestations of LGBTQ equal rights politics. Especially the question of how these components are discursively mobilized for nation-building (Kuntsman 2008) has become a key issue. With a firm focus on the post-9/11 era the US-American theorist Jasbir Puar broke an important ground in this context by coining the term 'homonationalism'. Thereby she addresses the national inclusion of 'proper' lesbian or gay subjects contingent upon the segregation and marginalisation of racialized 'others' (Puar 2007). The hierarchy within this binary has particularly become an issue in relation to the rhetoric framing of LGBTQs as persons, who seem to be in need of protection from homophobic migrants (Haritaworn 2010). At this point it becomes apparent that LGBTQ migrants are unavoidably silenced, as soon as 'gay' and 'migrant' appear as mutually exclusive categories – a point that Fatima El Tayeb has already stressed focusing on shifts within LGBTQ communities struggling for rights. Meanwhile, this debate has in fact been taken up in broader activist circles. A well-known example was offered by Judith Butler in 2010, when she turned down the Berlin Pride Civil Courage Award. Referring to the concept of homonationalism, she accused the organisers of lacking distance from racialist politics. Refusing to be instrumentalized by such politics, she stated that she would award the price to queer of colour organisations, if she were able to (Petzen 2011; SUSPECT 2011).

With that said, I see the need to look at rights again. Precisely, I see the need to combine the insights of such a critique – that I basically describe as queer anti-racist critique – with concrete legal fields like the one on LGBTQ asylum seekers and refugees. Thereby, I aim to show how it can be made fruitful for a queer rights-orientated strategy in general and related legal reasoning in detail. In order to discuss this issue I have chosen a concrete and relevant example: the Austrian Registered Partnership Act (RPA) and the ancillary changes within the Austrian Asylum Act. The issue is all the more urgent since in fact the legal recognition of same sex partnerships is presently – after the decriminalization of consensual homosexual acts and the access to the corpus of anti-discrimination law have been achieved – considered as one of the most evident manifestations of LGBTQ equal rights politics (Valdes 2009: 95ff). Thus it offers a relevant exemplary arena to untangle legal mechanisms of segregation we implicitly serve, if we turn to a rights orientated strategy. Yet, I do not aim to simply highlight racialized segregation or ultimately condemn a queer rights-orientated strategy. Rather, I suggest questioning its 'homebase' in order to explore how legal issues present themselves, if we take the critique of normative whiteness seriously.

In other words: if we refuse to implicitly connect whiteness and queerness, what are the consequences for a rights-orientated strategy? How does the legal issue of same sex partnership change its shape, if we take the position of sexualized *and* racialized marginalization as our analytical starting point? Which legal approaches or steps become necessary, if we focus on the legal positioning of LGBTQ refugee couples?

To address these issues, I introduce the relevant legal situation in Austria first. Subsequently, I aim to sum up major implications for a queer rights-orientated strategy and link them to the debate about queer anti-racist critique. As queer approaches characteristically do not follow the logic of legal reasoning I have chosen to take up intersectionality to establish this link. By all means intersectionality is a well-discussed approach (*cf.* Davis 2008) and it has already been used to describe the existence of gay Muslims as challenge to the 'positioning of western and eastern cultures as mutually exclusive and oppositional' (Rahman 2010: 944). To enter my field I take a step further and connect intersectionality's capability to grasp the position of LGBTQ migrants with its very legal roots (Crenshaw 1989). On this basis I lastly ask for legal steps that could become necessary against the background of queer anti-racist critique. For this purpose I turn to the Convention on Human Rights (ECHR) and raise the question whether the reunification of LGBTQ refugee families under the Asylum Act may constitute a violation of Article 14 taken together with Article 8.

8.2 LGBTQ family reunification under the Asylum Act

The legal recognition of same sex partnerships in Austria has no distinguished or long history to look back on. The RPA was enacted as recently as 2010, and hardly anybody felt like celebrating. Equal rights activists were sceptical – with good reason. Joint adoption remains impossible (Paragraph 179 of the Civil Law Code) as well as joint custody, and the possibilities provided by reproductive medicine are outlawed for same sex partners (*cf.* Paragraph 2 of the Reproductive Medicine Act) – as well as, by the way, for single women. With this Act, the legislator has left no doubt about who is and is not perceived to be entitled to reproduce society – not to mention the bureaucratic discriminations same sex partners must face (*cf.* Beclin 2010: 56f). While the focus has been on arbitrary distinctions between marriage and registered partnerships, there has been little to no debate about how the RPA has affected the Austrian Asylum Act – a phenomenon that bears witness to the relatively silenced position of LGBTQ refugees.

In accordance with EU legislation – namely Articles 9–12 of the Directive 2003/86/EC (Family Reunion Directive) – persons who have been granted asylum in Austria are entitled to get their family to join them. This process of family reunification is known as 'family proceedings' (Paragraphs 2, 34 and 35 of the Asylum Act). In cases where a person belonging to the personal environment of a refugee or subsidiary protected qualifies as a 'family member' under the Asylum Act, it is enough to prove this family membership in the course of the proceedings, allowing this person the right to recognition as a refugee or as a person granted subsidiary protection as well. What makes this regulation special is that a corresponding application can be made both in Austria and in any Austrian embassy. This is the only remaining regular case where an entry permit into Austria can be obtained under Asylum law. All other refugees are forced to depend on escape agents and on illegalized migration in order to get over Europe's border fences and walls. With the enactment of the RPA, this regulation also applies to LGBTQ refugees and their registered partners. In principle, this is, of course, a positive development. However, when it comes to the question of how the family reunification in cases of LGBTQ refugees is supposed to work in practice, the legislator remained elliptical and only remarked tersely:

> Regarding the designated introduction of the institution of registered partnership for same sex couples into Austrian law effected by the passing of a federal law covering registered partnership (RPA), the Asylum Act of 2005 has to be adapted insofar as all special clauses in Asylum Act that have been standardized for spouses in the future also have to apply to registered partners. [. . .] Paragraph 2, section 1, line 22 of the current version states that the capacity of family membership for spouses is only existent if this membership, i.e. the marriage, has already existed in the country of origin. The same is henceforth of course applicable to registered partners. Thus, the registered partnership must have already existed in the country of origin.
>
> (Bundesministerium für Justiz 2009)

German text:

> Im Hinblick auf die mit der Erlassung eines Bundesgesetzes über die eingetragene Partnerschaft (EPG) vorgesehene Einführung des Instituts der eingetragenen Partnerschaft gleichgeschlechtlicher Paare in die österreichische Rechtsordnung ist das Asylgesetz 2005 insofern anzupassen, als die im Asylrecht für Ehegatten normierten Sonderbestimmungen künftig auch für eingetragene Partner gelten sollen. Dazu wird der eingetragene Partner den Familienangehörigen iSd des § 2 Abs. 1 Z 22 gleichgehalten und damit die gleichförmige Behandlung von eingetragenen Partnern und Ehegatten garantiert. [. . .] § 2 Abs. 1 Z 22 in der geltenden Fassung sieht vor, dass die Eigenschaft als Familienangehöriger bei Ehegatten nur dann vorliegt, wenn die Familieneigenschaft, also die Ehe, bereits im Herkunftsstaat bestanden hat. Gleichgelagertes soll künftig naturgemäß auch für eingetragene Partner gelten. Die eingetragene Partnerschaft muss daher bereits im Herkunftsstaat bestanden haben.

The crux of this passage lies in its very last sentence. It holds that the family member must fulfil two requirements in order to be recognized as such. The family member must be in a registered partnership for same sex couples with the person recognized as a refugee, and this partnership must have already been recognized in his or her country of origin.

As it is probably well-known that 78 countries still criminalize same sex acts between consenting adults – including five countries that punish these acts by death (Itaborahy 2012: 12 *et seq.*) – let me just illustrate the problem by quoting a decision of the Austrian Asylum Court:

> In his village in Afghanistan the appellant maintained a homosexual relationship with a man who he had lived with for about 6 months. After the relationship had been discovered, a group of men from the village attacked the appellant and his partner. In the course of this attack, the appellant was gravely injured and his partner was killed. Following this event, the appellant then left Afghanistan in the tenth or eleventh month of the year 2002.
>
> (AsylGH, 10 March 2010, Case No. C10 257854-0/2008/6E)

The Court stated these findings in March 2010 and recognized the appellant as a refugee. If his partner had survived and had made an application for family unification following the court's positive ruling, he would have needed an Afghan document proving that the partnership was registered. Such proof, however, is unknown to Afghan law. On the contrary, 'homosexual conduct' is punishable by long imprisonment; it also constitutes a Hudood crime punishable by death under Shari'a law. In the light of strong societal taboos as well as its criminalization, UNHCR considers LGBTQ people in Afghanistan 'at risk on account of their membership of a particular social group, i.e. their sexual orientation and/or gender identity, since they do not, or are perceived not to conform to prevailing legal, religious and social norms' (UNHCR 2010: 29).

In Austrian legal discourse, legal norms that are never applied are known as 'idle legislation'. In my opinion, the RPA and the subsequent amendment of the Asylum Act has created exactly such a case.[3] On the other hand, it is absolutely not unusual that – when it comes to Austrian immigration and Asylum law – referring to EU legislation is able to improve the legal position of the affected. Yet, briefly speaking, this is not the case here. Article 4 of the Family Reunion Directive defines family members basically as spouses and minor children, thereby reproducing the traditional heteronormative image of the so called 'nuclear family'. When it comes to same sex couples it is up to the Member States whether they authorise the entry of stable long-term partners or treat registered partners equally as spouses.

8.3 At the intersection of sexuality and race

Turning now to the questions which legal mechanisms of racialized exclusion are implicitly served when a rights-orientated strategy is used and how such a strategy could be influenced by queer anti-racist critique, let me refer to the work of Kimberlé Crenshaw. In her development of the concept of intersectionality, she has dealt with the marginalization of Black women in legal discourse:

> I want to suggest further that this single-axis framework erases Black women in the conceptualization, identification and remediation of race and sex discrimination by limiting inquiry to the experiences of otherwise-privileged members of the group. In other words, in race discrimination cases, discrimination tends to be viewed in terms of sex- or class-privileged Blacks; in sex discrimination cases, the focus is on race- and class-privileged women.
>
> (Crenshaw 1989: 140)

By 'single axis-framework' Crenshaw refers to the US-American anti-discrimination laws in effect at the end of the 1980s. In fact, we are confronted with a similar problem in the case of the concept of family used in the RPA and the Asylum Act nowadays. The RPA was basically written with EU-residents in mind, who are in a same sex relationship and who are so thoroughly integrated into 'bourgeois normality' that they want to institutionalize their living together. Without further ado the legislator also framed LGBTQ refugees and their partners in terms of such privileged people and treated them as if their country of origin had a legal framework similar to a Western state that offers same sex couples the possibility to institutionalize their relationship. Accordingly, the passage on family reunification in the Asylum Act was written for refugees who are privileged in their country of origin of being able to have their two-person relationships recognized – what basically applies to heterosexual people. The reality of life of LGBTQ refugee couples, however, does not fit into this logic. Their relationship is usually tied to their reasons for fleeing, and this is exactly what erases them from the opportunity of a family reunification. The Austrian legal system provides protection for refugee families and it also it recognizes same sex partnerships. But limiting this protection to the ways of living of otherwise privileged group members, the legislator has created a catch 22 for LGBTQ refugees – as soon as sexuality and origin intersect in the shape of their subject status, legal protection and recognition seems to become inaccessible. Both as LGBTQ people and as refugees, they do not conform to the privileged subject status normally used as a frame of reference by Western legal systems (i.e. heterosexual EU-citizens).

It is no coincidence that I have chosen Kimberlé Crenshaw's work on intersectionality as my current reference point. She has not only coined the term 'intersectionality', she has developed her approach out of a concrete legal problem. Even if the concept of intersectionality has been picked up and adapted variously (Davis 2008), it still rooted in legal reasoning. Some might have criticized the limitations of these roots (Grabham 2009: 183), but from the viewpoint of a well-considered rights-orientated strategy, I appreciate intersectionality as an especially fruitful approach for these very roots. It not only provides an instrument to disentangle legal mechanisms of silencing, exclusion and marginalization, but it can also be integrated into a rights-orientated strategy that aims to counter the tendency to enter legal fields from the relatively most privileged subject position (such as white, heterosexual or male). To show how such an approach towards rights and the legal discourse can actually work, let me refer to questions already prompted by Mari J. Matsuda in 1991:

> When I see something that looks racist, I ask, 'Where is the patriarchy in this?' When I see something that looks sexist, I ask, 'Where is the heterosexism in this?' When I see something that looks homophobic, I ask, 'Where are the class interests in this?'
>
> (Matsuda 1991: 1189)

Applied to the concrete example of this chapter, such an approach does not allow questions such as 'What does the RPA entail for LGBTQ people, who are refugees?' to be overlooked. We could, in that sense, not celebrate the adoption of the RPA and the ancillary changes of the Asylum Act as an unequivocal success from an anti-racist standpoint. Instead, we would have to see the RPA and the ancillary changes within the Asylum Act as a coherent, yet inconsistent legislative step that challenges a diverse rights-orientated strategy. And especially lawyers who are not willing to accept normative whiteness would be required to develop legal strategies to overcome the exclusion of same sex refugee couples. With that said, let me turn to my last point – the ECHR.

8.4 A human right to same sex family reunification?

For decades the European Court of Human Rights (ECtHR) only protected same sex relationships within the notion of 'private', but not within the notion of 'family' life in accordance with Article 8 of the ECHR. Only recently, in 2010, the ruling in the case *Schalk and Kopf v Austria* overruled the Court's case law as it stood and extended the meaning of 'family':

> In view of this evolution the Court considers it artificial to maintain the view that, in contrast to a different-sex couple, a same sex couple cannot enjoy 'family life' for the purposes of Article 8. Consequently the relationship of the applicants, a cohabiting same sex couple living in a stable *de facto* partnership, falls within the notion of 'family life', just as the relationship of a different-sex couple in the same situation would.[4]

How is this landmark decision connected to the problem at issue? Approaching this question, let me go back to the year 1985. Back then the now defunct European Commission of Human Rights rendered the judgment *Abdulaziz et al v United Kingdom*.[5] In this decision, for the first time, the applicability of Article 8 of the ECHR to requests of family reunification with non-citizens living outside the territory of a contracting State was recognized. Whereas, meanwhile, the Court has been continuously widening its understanding of family life in its case law on the application of Article 8 of the ECHR to domestic issues (*cf.* Thym 2008: 89–91), it has maintained a restrictive practice when it comes family reunion in immigration cases. Even though various applicants had referred to the principle established in the case of *Abdulaziz et al*, an affirmative judgment was not rendered until 2001 in *Sen v The Netherlands*.[6] Now that this case law on family reunion has at least apparently (see below) been made accessible by the decision in *Schalk and Kopf*, the question arises to what extent it could influence the regulation of family reunification under the Asylum Act. Thus I aim to briefly discuss the main principles that emerge from the relevant case law and relate them to the landmark judgment in the case of *Schalk and Kopf* in the following.[7]

Generally speaking, the set of principles that has emerged from the case law on family reunion corresponds to the standard reasoning in cases of expulsion and deportation (*cf.* Grabenwarter and Pabel 2012: 268–272). The peculiarity of these cases lies in the fact that the ECtHR must balance personal interests against the well-established principle that Member States have the prerogative to control immigration.[8] Hence special, partly inconsistent guideline criteria have been applied by the court (*cf.* Lambert 1999: 438–440). One of these guidelines is of particular interest for same sex refugee couples: the principal requirement of strong family ties, so that the refusal to enter a country may constitute an interference with Article 8 of the ECHR (*cf.* Lambert 1999: 435) – basically, this requirement corresponds to the reference to a stable, de facto partnership in *Schalk and Kopf*. Already in the case of *Abdulaziz et al* the Court in that sense highlighted that Article 8 'presupposes the existence of a family' (para 40). At the same time it nevertheless (and symptomatically) regards it as sufficient that '[the applicants] considered themselves to be married and that they genuinely wished to cohabit and lead a normal family life' (para 63) and states that 'not [. . .] all intended family life falls entirely outside [the] ambit [of Article 8 ECHR]' (para 62). Against this inconsistent background it is not at all certain that LGBTQ applicants would enter upon a family life that is acknowledged by the Court. Typically, they spend most of their life hiding their sexuality, a joint household or a shared household is usually not part of such ways of living. Moreover, in the decision of *Slivenko et al v Latvia* the Court has invented the term 'core family' in relation to expulsion and deportation,[9] and it is not yet clear how this idea of the core family consisting of spouses and minor children relates to decision *Schalk and Kopf*.

However, the judgment *Abdulaziz et al* is still relevant for my issue for various reasons. First, it has not yet been overruled. Second it is one of the few relevant cases that are dealing with family reunification between couples and not between spouses or parents and children. Its guidelines on the understanding of family life may therefore also be expected to be relevant for same sex couples. Third, and this is another crucial point, the applicants brought up the issue of Article 14 taken together with Article 8 of the ECHR. Returning to the intersectional view, as elaborated above, let me emphasize one more time that it is the intersection with a marginalized sexuality that basically makes family reunification inaccessible. It is not only that, as soon as they get separated, their family life is regulated through the restrictive legal procedures of family reunification. In the light of the widespread persecution of LGBTQ people, it is disproportionally more difficult for them to fulfil the legal requirement to prove the legal recognition of the partnership in the country of origin than it is for heterosexuals. Given such an intersection, the question arises whether the Court would find that Austria acts in breach of Article 14 in conjunction with Article 8 of the ECHR. In other words, it is conceivable that the undifferentiated equating of heterosexual and LGBTQ refugee couples constitutes an unjustified equal treatment of unequal circumstances.[10]

The case of *Abdulaziz et al* has, as a matter of fact, prepared the ground for such a legal reasoning.[11] Basically, the applicants in that case were three female, lawfully settled non-citizens, who were applying for their non-national spouses to enter the United Kingdom, so that they could develop their family life there. Their applications were rejected with reference to immigration rules that made it easier for a man settled in the United Kingdom to obtain entry permission for his spouse, than vice versa. The government justified this different treatment with the need to protect the labour market at times of high unemployment – men would simply be more likely to engage in paid work than women. Referring to the fact that 'the advancement of the equality of the sexes is today a major goal in the member States of the Council of Europe', the ECtHR considered the government's argumentation as insufficient to justify such a difference of treatment and concluded that the applicants had been victims of discrimination on the ground of sex, in violation of Article 14 taken together with Article 8.[12] Given the well-established case law that 'differences based on sexual orientation require particularly serious reasons by way of justification',[13] conceivably the Court passes a similar judgment in the case of family reunion under the Asylum Act. In the end it remains to be seen whether the ECtHR will maintain its view that same sex couples can enjoy family life just as different sex couples and that intended family life does not entirely fall outside the ambit of Article 8 of the ECHR or if it will finally refuse to take one step further.

8.5 Concluding remarks

Addressing LGBTQ refugees and asylum seekers, this book substantially deals with a key issue of queer anti-racist critique: it contributes to preventing and loosening the discursive link between whiteness and queerness. My aim was to make this aspect explicit and discuss homophobic and heteronormative patterns within 'the safety people seek in Europe'. Law is, in this context, certainly a focus of interest. As I was not aiming to condemn rights as such, I was basically focusing on the questions of how queer anti-racist critique can shape an approach to law and which legal steps become necessary, if we take the position of sexualized *and* racialized marginalization as our analytical starting point. First, let me conclude by stating that there is no single answer for these questions. Legal steps certainly depend on the field we approach. At the same time I consider that intersectionality has proven as a suitable analytical instrument to link the fields of anti-racist critique and law. It is not only rooted in legal reasoning, but also capable of grasping various identity shaping dimensions (such as race and sexuality) without automatically starting from a relatively privileged position. Hence it can be used to make complex structures of exclusion accessible and thereby help to dismantle the myth of 'white queerness'. In the case of the RPA an intersectional view has shown that we – even if joint adoption, etc. were not outlawed for same sex partners – could not celebrate its adoption as an unequivocal success: as soon as racialized marginalization is an issue, heteronormative structures emerge as (well-known) mechanisms of exclusion.

Basically, I consider this approach I have developed here, using the Austrian registered partnership law as an example, as a first step to be made fruitful in other legal contexts as well. Let me lastly conclude with a brief example of such a context and mention the discretion requirement (see extensively, the contributions of Weßels and Battjes to this volume) that Venice Choi so rightly describes as a catch 22:

> In this reality, refugee applicants making claims on the basis of sexual orientation and gender identity still face an unsolvable dilemma in which it is unlikely that they will pass the demeanor test: on the one hand, acting discreetly, while no longer a requirement in assessing refugee status, helps applicants avoid a threat of persecution in their home countries, yet on the other, it inhibits them from 'looking' gay as many have spent countless years 'passing' as straight.
>
> (Choi 2010: 241)

In the case of family reunification under Austrian asylum law the prohibition of discrimination (Article 14 of the ECHR) has emerged as a possible legal remedy to overcome the marginalized position of LGBTQ refugees. I consider it entirely possible that an understanding of the invisibility requirement as an intersectional issue could, for example, reshape our understanding of the right to privacy in sexualized matters as well.

8.6 Notes

* PhD Fellow, IK Gender Violence and Agency in the Era of Globalization, Faculty of Social Sciences, University of Vienna. Special thanks go to Elisabeth

Holzleithner, Isabel Lorey and Thomas Spijkerboer for their critical as well as generous comments on this text. Furthermore, I would particularly like to thank Eva Kuntschner for her translation competence that made an inevitable contribution to the development of this text. This chapter constitutes a revised and updated version of a text published in German (Sußner 2011). Thanks go to Ronald Frühwirth for his insightful comments on earlier drafts.

1 Using the term 'race' at this point, I do not necessarily refer to the way this category is usually theorized. Following the debate I aim to outline, I rather use it as an umbrella term for nationality, cultural background and racialized perception of physical appearance. As a matter of course this concept is adapted to the scope of this contribution. To further analyze this field, I consider it inevitable to use corresponding sub-categories.

2 With the term LGBTQ I refer to those who identify themselves as gay (G), lesbian (L), bisexual (B) or transgender (T). The character Q stands for queers and addresses those who cannot or do not want refer to a certain sexual status and/or gender. Additionally, it is important to mention that I mainly address transgender people (T) insofar as they are engaged in same sex partnerships. At the *fleeing homophobia* conference Søren Laursen quite rightly pointed out that transgender ways of living are often silenced within debates about LGBTQ persons. As an example he referred to a study carried out in Denmark in 2009 that has shown that even the majority of the interviewed transgender persons identified themselves as heterosexual (Laursen 2011). To avoid the perpetuation of transgender invisibility at the best possible rate, I at least stress that this chapter is basically about same sex partnership and the Austrian Asylum Act. It does not presume to further the debate on transgender refugees.

3 Certainly I do not want to conceal the fact that there can be LGBTQ refugees who have lived in a registered partnership in their country of origin. Nevertheless, I consider this possibility to be limited to such rare individual cases that I lay my focus on the other cases in this chapter, and I exclusively refer to those LGBTQ refugees who have been applying for asylum due to sexual orientation and/or gender identity.

4 ECtHR, judgment, 24 June 2010, Appl. No. 30141/04, *Schalk and Kopf v Austria*, para 94.

5 ECtHR, judgment, 28 May 1985, Appl. No. 9214/80, *Abdulaziz et al v United Kingdom*.

6 ECtHR, judgment, 21 December 2001, Appl. No. 31465/96, *Sen v The Netherlands*.

7 As a matter of course my analysis is shaped by this article's aim to incorporate the transdisciplinary critique on a racialized framing of queerness. Therefore it must be read as an attempt to reinforce the position of same sex refugee couples as racialized and sexualized 'outsiders'. Bearing in mind the restrictive practice of the Court as well as the inconsistence of the case law on family reunion (Spijkerboer 2009: 273–280), the last word definitely remains to be spoken.

8 ECtHR, judgment, 19 February 1996, Appl. No. 23218/94, *Gül v Switzerland*, para 38.

9 ECtHR, decision, 9 October 2003, Appl. No. 48321/99, *Slivenko et al v Latvia*, para 97.

10 *cf.* ECtHR, judgment, 6 April 2000, Appl. No. 34369/97, *Thlimmenos v Greece*.

11 *Abdulaziz v United Kingdom*.

12 Ibid, para 78.
13 ECtHR, judgment, 24 July 2003, Appl. No. 40016/98, *Karner v Austria*.

8.7 References

Beclin, B. (2010) 'Das Eingetragene Partnerschaft Gesetz im Lichte des Eherechts', *Zeitschrift für Ehe- und Familienrecht*, 34: 52–58.

Bundesministerium für Justiz (2009) 'Materialien zur Regierungsvorlage REGV_COO_2026_100_2_564053', available at http://www.ris.bka.gv.at/Dokumente/RegV/REGV_COO_2026_100_2_564053/COO_2026_100_2_570911.pdf (accessed 26 March 2012).

Choi, V. (2010) 'Living discreetly: a catch 22 in refugee status determinations on the basis of sexual orientation', *Brooklyn Journal of International Law*, 36: 241–258.

Crenshaw, K. (1989) 'Demarginalizing the intersection of race and sex: a black feminist critique of antidiscrimination doctrine, feminist theory and antiracist politics', *University of Chicago Legal Forum*: 139–167.

Davis, K. (2008) 'Intersectionality as buzzword: a sociology of science perspective on what makes a feminist theory successful', *Feminist Theory*, (9): 67–85.

Dietze, G. (2009) 'Okzidentalismuskritik, Möglichkeiten und Grenzen', in G. Dietze, C. Brunner and E. Wenzel (eds) *Kritik des Okzidentalismus. Transdisziplinäre Beiträge zu (Neo-) Orientalismus und Geschlecht*, Bielefeld: Transcript Verlag.

El Tayeb, F. (2003) 'Begrenzte Horizonte. Queer Identity in der Festung Europa', in H. Steyerl and E. Gutiérrez Rodriguez (eds) *Spricht die Subalterne Deutsch? Migration und postkoloniale Kritik*, Münster: UNRAST Verlag.

Grabenwarter, C. and Pabel, K. (2012) '*Europäische Menschenrechtskonvention. Ein Studienbuch*', 5th edn, München: Verlag C.H. Beck.

Grabham, E. (2009) 'Intersectionality. Traumatic impressions', in E. Graham, D. Cooper, J. Krishnadas, and D. Herman (eds) *Intersectionality and Beyond: Law, Power and the Politics of Location*, Abingdon: Routledge-Cavendish.

Haritaworn, J. (2010) 'Wounded subjects: sexual exceptionalism and the moral panic on "migrant homophobia in Germany"', in E. Gutiérrez Rodriguez, M. Boatca and S. Costa (eds) *Decolonizing European Sociology: Transdisciplinary Approaches*, Farnham and Burlington: Ashgate.

Haritaworn, J. and Petzen J. (2011) 'Integration as a sexual problem. An excavation of the German "Muslim homophobia" panic', in K. Yilmaz-Günay (ed.) *Karriere eines konstruierten Gegensatzes: zehn Jahre "Muslime versus Schwule". Sexualpolitiken seit dem 11 September 2001*, Berlin: Koray Yilmaz-Günay.

Itaborahy, L.P. (2012) 'State-sponsored homophobia. A world survey of laws criminalizing same-sex sexual acts between consenting adults', *An International Lesbian, Gay, Bisexual, Trans and Intersex Association Report*, available at http://old.ilga.org/Statehomophobia/ILGA_State_Sponsored_Homophobia_2012.pdf (accessed 18 December 2012).

Kuntsman, A. (2008) 'The soldier and the terrorist: sexy nationalism, queer violence', *Sexualities* 11: 142–170.

Lambert, H. (1999) 'The European Court of Human Rights and the right of refugees and other persons in need of protection to family reunion', *International Journal of Refugee Law*, 11(3): 428–450.

Laursen S. (2011) 'Persecution and neglect', Conference paper, *Fleeing Homophobia, Seeking Safety in Europe*, Amsterdam, September 2011.

Matsuda, M.J. (1991) 'Beside my sister, facing the enemy: legal theory out of coalition', *Stanford Law Review*, 43(6): 1183–1192.

McIntosh, P. (2003) 'White privilege and male privilege: a personal account of coming to see correspondences through work in women's studies', in N.E. Dowd and E.S. Jacobs (eds) *Feminist Legal Theory, An Anti-Essentialist Reader*, New York, NY and London: New York University Press.

Petzen, J. (2011) 'Silent echoes. The aftermath of Judith Butler's refusal on the civil courage award', in K. Yilmaz-Günay (ed.) *Karriere eines konstruierten Gegensatzes: zehn Jahre 'Muslime versus Schwule'. Sexualpolitiken seit dem 11 September 2001*, Berlin: Yilmaz-Günay, Koray.

Puar, J. (2007) *'Terrorist Assemblages. Homonationalism in Queer Times'*, Durham, NC and London: Duke University Press.

Rahman, M. (2010) 'Queer as intersectionality: theorizing gay Muslim identities', *Sociology*, 44: 944–961.

Spijkerboer, T. (2009) 'Structural instability: Strasbourg case law on children's family reunion', *European Journal of Migration and Law*, 11: 271–293.

Strongman, R. (2002) 'Syncretic religion and dissident sexualities', in A. Cruz-Malavé and M.F. Manalansan IV (eds) *Queer Globalizations. Citizenship and the Afterlife of Colonialism*, New York, NY and London: New York University Press.

SUSPECT (2011) *'Judith Butler lehnt CSD Zivilcourage-Preis ab: "Von dieser rassistischen Komplizenschaft muss ich mich distanzieren", Presseerklärung von SUSPECT zum 19. Juni 2010'*, in K. Yilmaz-Günay (ed.) *Karriere eines konstruierten Gegensatzes: zehn Jahre "Muslime versus Schwule". Sexualpolitiken seit dem 11. September 2011*, Berlin: Yilmaz-Günay, Koray.

Sußner, P. (2011) 'Totes Recht? Der asylrechtliche Familiennachzug für gleichgeschlechtliche Partnerinnen', *juridikum. zeitschrift für kritik – recht – gesellschaft*, 4: 435–444.

Thym, D. (2008) 'Respect for private and family life under Article 8 ECHR in immigration cases: a human right to regularize illegal stay?', *International and Comparative Law Quarterly*, 57: 87–112.

UN High Commissioner for Refugees (UNHCR) (2010) *UNHCR Eligibility Guidelines for Assessing the International Protection Needs of Asylum-Seekers from Afghanistan, HCR/EG/AFG/10/04*, available at http://www.unhcr.org/refworld/docid/4d0b55c92.html (accessed 27 March 2012).

Valdes, F. (2009) 'Queering sexual orientation: a call to theory as praxis', in M. Fineman, J.E. Jackson and A.P. Romero (eds) *Feminist and Queer Legal Theory: Intimate Encounters, Uncomfortable Conversations*, Burlington: Ashgate.

9 Overcoming problems with sexual minority refugee claims

Is LGBT cultural competency training the solution?

Nicole LaViolette[*]

9.1 Introduction

Problems related to sexual orientation and gender identity are often raised in relation to refugee determination proceedings. As a result, many advocates, refugee lawyers and even refugees themselves have consistently called on refugee agencies and authorities to mandate continuing professional training for personnel involved in the determination of the refugee status of lesbian, gay, bisexual and transgender (LGBT) claimants, as well as in the delivery of services to LGBT asylum seekers and refugees. While calls for training have at times outlined specific competencies required for refugee personnel and adjudicators, for the most part, proponents fail to specify the type of professional development that might foster better decision making in LGBT refugee cases.

By first considering the objectives and goals of sexual orientation and gender identity training for refugee personnel, in this chapter I argue that LGBT cultural competency training, an approach first developed in the health and social work fields, is an appropriate model for the refugee context. Use of this framework would conceptualize more clearly the professional development interventions required to improve the refugee determination process, and it would also assist in targeting the most effective training modules.

The issue of LGBT sensitivity training is examined by answering the following three queries. First, why is training seen as a solution to problems identified in LGBT refugee adjudication and service delivery? Second, if training is a useful tool, what kind of training would best address the problems? Third, towards whom should the training be targeted? Lastly, the analysis focuses on issues that suggest that training on sexual orientation and gender identity must not be seen as a panacea for the challenges facing LGBT refugee claimants. There are limitations to training and even the LGBT cultural competency training model is not a cure-all for the full range of problems facing LGBT refugees. I have been involved in professional development sessions on LGBT issues with Canadian adjudicators since 1995, and in examining these questions, I refer at times to my own experience in developing and delivering training on sexual orientation and gender identity to the Canadian Immigration and Refugee Board (IRB).

9.2 Why LGBT training?

In this section, I briefly outline the challenges confronting sexual minority refugee claimants. Furthermore, I examine the reasons for which training is often raised as a solution to the problems facing LGBT refugees when they seek protection under the international and national refugee systems.

9.2.1 Sexual minority refugees and the international refugee determination system

The international community codified the rights and status of refugees in two international instruments: the 1951 United Nations Convention Relating to the Status of Refugees (the Convention), and the 1967 UN Protocol Relating to the Status of Refugees (the Protocol). By signing the Convention and its Protocol, states have accepted the primary obligation that flows from the international instrument, which mandates that signatory states will not return any individual to a territory where his or her life or freedom would be threatened by persecution. The legal responsibility to provide protection applies only if a person meets the definition of a refugee as provided for in the Convention and Protocol. Persons seeking asylum must satisfy two main legal tests: first, they must demonstrate a well-founded fear of persecution, and, second, they must substantiate that the persecution they fear is on account of their race, religion, nationality, political opinion, or membership in a particular social group.[1]

Egregious human rights violations have compelled some LGBT individuals to seek refuge in countries that offer asylum and better human rights protection.[2] In many cases, individuals flee directly to countries where significant progress has been made on LGBT human rights and where they are able to make claims for asylum pursuant to the Convention. Indeed, several states have extended refugee protection to women and men fleeing persecution based on their sexual orientation or gender identity. For more than 30 years, decision makers in countries such as the United States, Canada, New Zealand, Australia, and several European states have granted refugee status to individuals who fear persecution based on their sexual orientation or gender identity.[3]

In other cases, as with the majority of all refugees, LGBT refugees are not able to travel to progressive countries where they can make asylum claims. According to the United Nations High Commissioner for Refugees (UNHCR), more than 80 per cent of the world's refugees remain in developing countries where most are not safe and have no possibility of integration.[4] As a result, in their search of a 'safe haven', some LGBT refugees first travel to neighbouring or transit countries, also called 'countries of first asylum'. In some cases, they will make a claim for protection as a refugee with UNHCR, and if granted, await resettlement to a country willing to offer them a permanent home. Unfortunately, LGBT refugees often face harassment, physical violence and marginalization in countries of first asylum (Kalan 2011). Indeed, when LGBT refugees flee to countries like Turkey, Kenya and Egypt, their temporary place of refuge is often as homophobic and dangerous as the country from which they fled (Helsinki Citizens' Assembly – Turkey, Refugee Advocacy and Support Program, Organization for Refuge, Asylum & Migration 2011; Human Rights First 2012; compare Cragnolini's contribution to this volume). As a result, they often need to be expeditiously resettled to safe third countries.

Whether they are in a transit country or in an asylum granting state, sexual minorities have encountered a specific set of problems in having the international refugee definition applied to their claims for asylum. According to UNHCR, as outlined in the 2008 *Guidance Note on Refugee Claims Relating to Sexual Orientation and Gender Identity* (UNHCR 2008), the growing number of asylum claims by LGBT individuals, 'has necessitated greater awareness among decision makers of the specific experiences of LGBT asylum seekers and a deeper examination of the legal questions involved'. Many scholars and advocates have stated for several years that sexual minority claimants face considerable hurdles in obtaining fair and equitable assessments of their refugee claims (LaViolette 2010a; Rehaag 2009; Kassisieh 2008; Rehaag 2008). There is, indeed, a myriad of legal, procedural, and social hurdles facing sexual minority asylum seekers. As these issues have been well canvassed in the scholarly literature and in reports issued by non-governmental organisations, this chapter only briefly enumerates the existing challenges.

The legal difficulties facing LGBT asylum seekers (LaViolette 2010a; UNHCR 2008) include: establishing whether a sexual minority claimant's fear of persecution is well-founded (LaViolette 2009; UNHCR 2008: paras 11–14, 28), assessing the persecutory impact of laws criminalizing homosexual conduct (UNHCR 2008: paras 17–22), determining whether LGBT claimants are members of a particular social group (Marouf 2008; LaViolette 1997), and establishing the sexual orientation or gender identity of a refugee claimant (McGhee 2000: 93–94; O'Leary 2008).[5] In some states, case law has focused on whether minority claimants meet the threshold of persecution rather than discrimination; on the availability of state protection in the country of origin (LaViolette 2009); or in countries of transit (Young 2010), and possible regional contrasts in the treatment of sexual minorities within a country (LaViolette 2009). Another contentious issue surfaces in the national case law of several states where a distinction has been made between discreet and non-discreet homosexuals, and some decision makers have suggested that sexual minority refugee claimants could be required to take reasonable steps to avoid persecutory harm by conducting their personal lives discreetly (Dauvergne and Millbank 2003; Kendall 2003; Johnson 2007; Millbank 2009a: 392).

Difficulties are also connected to evidentiary practices and procedures, such as assessing the credibility of a claimant's testimony (compare Middelkoop's contribution to this volume). In order to meet the requirements of the Convention definition of a refugee, a claimant must present supporting evidence, which normally consists of the testimony of the asylum seeker and general evidence of a country's human rights record. In assessing a claimant's testimony, decision makers will determine if the evidence is 'plausible, credible and frank' (Hathaway 1991: 84). For sexual minorities, sexual orientation and gender identity issues may carry with them a sense of shame, self-hating and embarrassment, given the very personal and private nature of the topic. The UNHCR Guidance Note (UNHCR 2008: para. 38) concurs and provides that a claimant 'can be reluctant to talk about such intimate matters, particularly where his or her sexual orientation would be the cause of shame or taboo in the country of origin'. The problem is also described in these terms:

> LGBTI refugees may also experience discrimination by other refugees on account of homophobic attitudes, which can lead to violence or limited access to safe shelter in settings such as detention, refugee camps and urban areas. Due to these multiple forms of discrimination, LGBTI refugees may be reluctant to reveal their sexual orientation or gender identity to national authorities or UN staff, especially if they are fleeing persecution from governments due to their sexual orientation or gender identity. Withholding of such information in asylum determination procedures can cause asylum adjudicators to question the credibility of LGBTI applicants, and has resulted in the rejection of asylum claims based on sexual orientation.
>
> (Human Rights First 2010)

Unless decision makers keep this in mind, they are likely to unfairly assess the credibility of a sexual minority's testimony.

A second evidentiary hurdle is connected to the availability of independent country of origin information. Such evidence is typically drawn from governmental, non-governmental and media reports. However, in the case of LGBT claimants, existing country documentation still fails to provide the kind of information refugees need to support their claims (LaViolette 1996a; Swink 2005–2006; de Jong 2008; O'Leary 2008: 91–92 LaViolette 2009).

Another set of problems may be encountered by LGBT asylum seekers and they are connected to the social phenomena of homophobia[6] and heterosexism.[7] When individuals apply for refugee protection in countries of first or final asylum, they will have to interact with a host of government officials, civil society agencies and community groups. This can include dealing with several of the following: visa officers, border and customs personnel, refugee and immigration adjudicators, interpreters, lawyers, immigration consultants, resettlement staff, members of ethnic diasporas, LGBT organizations, and a multitude of other personnel working in social services and government agencies. Since homosexuality and transexuality remain controversial topics around the world, there continue to be legitimate concerns that LGBT refugees encounter prejudice and hostility as they embark on the dangerous journey to a safe haven. Many frontline staff carry prevalent cultural stereotypes with them. On occasion, the problem can extend to the appointment of decision makers with clear biases against homosexuality, as was recently seen in Canada (Thompson 2009).

In the refugee process, both inland and abroad, the presence of homophobia and heterosexism may lead immigration officials and refugee adjudicators to:

- minimize the importance of sexual orientation or gender identity in a refugee claim;
- devalue a claimant's feelings and experiences;
- deny a claimant protection;
- view claimants strictly in terms of their sexual behaviour;
- assume that celibate adults and adolescents, or ones married to a person of the opposite sex, cannot identity as LGBT;
- conclude that claimants are not LGBT because they fail to meet some arbitrarily defined criterion;
- perpetuate self-hatred by some LGBT refugees; and
- result in the use of controversial interventions like phallometry or invasive medical examinations.[8]

If members of staff who interact with sexual minorities do not reflect on their own prejudices and assumptions about homosexuality and transexuality, it is unlikely they are going to be able to fairly assess asylum and resettlement claims. In essence, ignorance, fear and hostility can lead to poor decision making and substandard service and support delivery. As a result, refugee claims can be negatively impacted if any of the decision makers involved in the process are insensitive to LGBT issues or rely on stereotypes and prejudice to make their decisions. Similarly, resettlement efforts can be undermined if agency staff is homophobic or heterosexist. As stated in a report by Human Rights First (2010), '[o]n occasion negative biases among service providers, adjudicators and UNHCR staff can impinge on the ability of LGBTI asylum seekers to access services as well as fair asylum proceedings'.

9.2.2 Targeted and specialized LGBT training as a solution

In response to the specific legal and attitudinal challenges facing LGBT asylum seekers and refugees, scholars, advocates, refugee lawyers, refugees and even politicians have called on refugee adjudication and resettlement agencies to conduct professional training for decision makers and their staff. It is consistently suggested that training frontline staff and adjudicators will ensure that all parties involved are sensitized on issues relating to sexual orientation and gender identity, and that interviews with LGBT claimants will proceed in a safe and welcoming manner.

For instance, a 2011 report on LGBT asylum claims in Europe contains an explicit reference to training in its recommendations. The report recommends the following:

> Interviewers, decision makers, the judiciary and legal aid providers need to be competent and capable of taking into account the sexual orientation and gender identity aspects of asylum applications, including the process of 'coming-out' and the special needs of lesbian, gay, bisexual, trans and intersex applicants. To this end, they should be professionally trained, both in a specific basic training module and during general permanent education modules.
>
> (Jansen and Spijkerboer 2011)

The UNHCR Guidance Note (UNHCR 2008) recommends that sexual minority claimants be 'interviewed by trained officials who are well informed about the specific problems LGBT persons face'. It is further suggested that measures be adopted to ensure awareness of sexual orientation and gender identity issues, including 'targeted training sessions, mainstreaming of issues relating to sexual orientation and gender identity into the induction of new staff and training of existing staff, ensuring awareness of websites with expertise on LGBT issues, as well as the development of guidance relating to appropriate enquiries and interview techniques to use during the different stages of the asylum procedure' (UNHCR 2008). Rehaag (2008: 87) suggests that decisions will further improve if LGBT facilitators are actually included in training sessions or professional legal education courses.[9]

The call for training of UNHCR's own staff has come from non-governmental organizations and even politicians. Human Rights First, a US-based non-profit international human rights organization, has specifically called for training of UNHCR staff who deal with LGBT asylum claims (Human Rights First 2010). The Organization for Refuge Asylum & Migration (ORAM), a non-governmental organization dedicated to advocacy and research on LGBT refugees, has also called all stakeholders, including UNHCR, to 'institute trainings focused on developing an understanding of issues surrounding sexual orientation and gender identity' (Helsinki Citizens' Assembly – Turkey, Refugee Advocacy and Support Program, Organization for Refuge, Asylum & Migration 2011: 9). In a letter to Secretary of State Hillary Clinton, US Senator Kirsten Gillibrand and Congresswoman Tammy Baldwin expressed their concern for sexual minority refugees and urged the US government to support increased training of UNHCR staff on sexual orientation and gender identity issues (Gillibrand *et al.* 2010; Baldwin 2010).

The reason training is consistently called for is that it is seen to have the potential to address many of the specific problems encountered by sexual minority claimants. For instance, Kassisieh believes that:

> Sexuality training . . . can assist decision-makers in understanding the impact of actual or perceived homophobia and heterosexism in the

> experience of persecution and the refugee status determination process and could be a starting point to address the stereotypes on which many decisions are based.
>
> (Kassisieh 2008: 47)

Millbank has suggested that 'the skills and expertise of decision-makers can also be improved through ongoing training' (Millbank 2009b: 28), and more specifically, she has identified training as a tool to improve credibility assessments made by adjudicators in relation to LGBT claimants. Indeed, Millbank has called for general training on credibility assessments to be accompanied by specific training on gender and sexual orientation issues (Millbank 2009b). Millbank (2009b: 26) also points out that judicial guidance on credibility and credibility guidelines have 'not permeated the lower levels of adjudication' and cannot be a substitute for the training of decision makers.

The value of training can also extend to evidentiary challenges related to sexual minority refugee claims, as outlined by Kassisieh (2008: 48): '[s]exuality training for decision-makers could . . . also be useful in raising an awareness of the inappropriate use of country of origin information, in order to reduce inferences of fact and the weighing of evidence according to personal expectations and biases of decision-makers'. Non-governmental organizations have also suggested that skills training focused on interviewing techniques could not only avoid interactions that are offensive to sexual minority refugee claimants but also elicit the presentation of bona fide refugee claims based on sexual orientation and gender identity (Helsinki Citizens' Assembly – Turkey, Refugee Advocacy and Support Program, Organization for Refuge, Asylum & Migration 2011: 9).

It is therefore apparent that when problems related to sexual orientation and gender identity are examined or raised in the context of refugee determination systems, calls are made to mandate continuing professional education on LGBT issues for refugee personnel. Indeed, it seems a consensus has emerged that training the staff that interact with sexual minority claimants is a solution to the many legal, procedural, and social hurdles that impede access to protection under the Convention.

While the vast majority of government and civil society staff involved in refugee, migration and resettlement procedures have never received LGBT-focused training, some sensitivity and other programs have in fact been developed and implemented. One of the first LGBT training programs of refugee adjudicators was developed in Canada in 1995 after a documentary was aired on national radio during which a refugee lawyer expressed serious concern regarding the truth of some of his clients' claims to be homosexuals.[10] He asserted that a fraudulent claim to homosexuality was unlikely to be detected by adjudicators at the IRB because they were poorly prepared to question claimants' on their sexual orientation, and as a result, individuals could easily concoct false stories about being gay or lesbian. The administrative agency responded constructively by soliciting training for its decision makers in order to ensure that claims of persecution based on sexual orientation received the same professional treatment as any other claim. A training module was developed and it has since been presented to Canadian adjudicators and other IRB staff on several occasions.[11] More recently, when concerns were expressed about the negative impact of significant reforms to the Canadian asylum system on sexual minority claimants, the IRB stated it would continue specialized training in this area (McKiernan 2011).

Similar LGBT training modules have since been offered to adjudicators and frontline staff in several refugee receiving states. In Ireland, a training programme has been launched for people working with LGBT asylum seekers and refugees (RTE News Ireland 2012). Belgian interpreters and staff at asylum reception centres have received training on sexual orientation and gender identity issues (Beddeleem 2012). In the United Kingdom, the Lesbian and Gay Immigration Group provides training to LGBT and refugee organizations. In addition, a training module was developed for UK Border Agency (UKBA) staff, and the training was rolled out across the United Kingdom to all UKBA case workers and their managers in 2010 and 2011 (UK Lesbian & Gay Immigration Group 2010). The Swedish Migration Board has instituted training for its staff about sexual orientation and gender identity issues, as well as a set of guidelines, though the training is not compulsory (UNHCR 2011a). The Australian Refugee Review Tribunal has also implemented one short training session for members (Walker 2008; ABC News 2007).[12]

In the United States, Immigration Equality (n.d.), a national organization that provides legal aid and advocacy for LGBT and HIV-positive immigrants and their families, has offered training to refugee and asylum officers in several locations across the country. The United States Citizenship and Immigration Services (2011) recently prepared training materials on interviewing and adjudicating claims by sexual minority claimants. Also in the United States, a sensitivity training program geared to service providers who work with refugees, immigrants, or asylum seekers is being offered by the Heartland Alliance for Human Needs & Human Rights.[13]

At the international level, UNHCR has responded to calls for training of its own staff. In addition to including some LGBT content in its employee training, UNHCR (2011b) has turned to non-governmental organizations to provide specialized training on sexual orientation and gender identity issues. For instance, ORAM is developing a training program to be offered to frontline staff of UNHCR and non-governmental partners starting in 2012 (Grungas 2012).

9.3 What kind of training?

While calls for training have sometimes outlined particular competencies to be developed by adjudicators and other frontline staff, for the most part, few specifics are offered about the type of training that is required. Indeed, while few question the value of professional development training on sexual orientation and gender identity issues for refugee personnel, there has been little consideration regarding the type of training that will lead to stronger decision making in LGBT refugee cases.

For instance, is training to be designed to confront the homophobia and heterosexism of individual adjudicators? Is the objective to provide information about the realities of LGBT lives? Will training aim to improve adjudicators' legal interpretation of the refugee definition as it applies to LGBT cases? Is there a need to provide factual information about country conditions? Should training focus on providing adjudicators with better interviewing skills to create a safe hearing room for sexual minority refugees? Calls for training certainly seek to achieve all of these goals, and likely more; however, such diverse training objectives cannot be met in one module or one set of materials. Moreover, training with such different aims would almost certainly have to be provided by different groups of professionals or experts.

If training is not more clearly conceptualized, particularly in relation to the objectives sought, it is likely to be less effective. It is important, therefore, that calls for LGBT training become more specific and targeted. In the next section, I will present a model that could become the basis for the development of LGBT refugee training modules in order to improve the refugee determination process at both the international and national levels. The existing training construct, the 'LGBT cultural competency' model, could easily be applied to the refugee context and training on sexual orientation and gender identity issues.

9.3.1 LGBT cultural competency training

LGBT cultural competence is based on a broader concept known as cross-cultural competence, or inter-cultural competence. A person with cross-cultural competencies is defined as an individual who has an ability to understand, communicate with, and effectively interact with people originating from a variety of cultural backgrounds. The acquisition of cross-cultural competencies helps individuals to understand how behaviours, gestures and knowledge are interpreted differently across cultures. Bents-Enchill (n.d.) suggests that '[e]ffective cross-cultural communication is the ability to communicate with individuals from other cultures in a way that minimizes conflict, promotes greater understanding and maximizes [one's] ability to establish trust and rapport'. Williams (2006: 209), writing in the context of social work, defines cross-cultural competence as the 'capacity to work across multiple paradigms to find ways to engage with clients'. Williams (2006: 210) adds that '[c]ultural competence demands that we practice with skills, attitudes, and values that will make us effective and adequate in service provision to clients who originate from a variety of cultural backgrounds'.

While professions and organizations from fields as diverse as business, government, academia, and the non-profit section have all acknowledged the importance of cross-cultural competency in one way or another, historically, the fields of health care, social work and psychology led the way in developing the concept of cultural competency (Van Den Bergh and Crisp 2004: 222). In the United States, the extension of civil rights to African Americans in the 1960s and the racial and ethnic diversity that has characterized contemporary American society spurred health care providers and social justice advocates to examine their practices to determine if they were effective in delivering services to cultural and minority communities. For instance, psychologists began exploring cross-cultural counselling as far back as the 1980s (Sue *et al.* 1982; Heath, Niemeyer and Pedersen 1988; Pedersen 1988). The proliferation of academic and professional publications on cultural competencies has impacted on institutions and organizations, which have established applicable standards in their respective fields. This is the case, for instance, for doctors, nurses, psychologists, social workers, law enforcement personnel and educators (Baskir 2009). Moreover, in the United States, there are government mandated cross-cultural standards as well as state-funded programs (Baskir 2009).

There are several reasons why cross-cultural competency training is an interesting model for refugee personnel dealing with sexual minority asylum seekers and refugees. While many of the concepts and models of cultural competency training derive from the health and social work fields, the perspective adopted in this approach is useful in the broader setting of diversity work, including in the context of non-profit organizations and government agencies whose employees work with persons from different cultural/ethnic backgrounds. Cultural competency training can help conceptualize more clearly the type of LGBT sensitivity training required to overcome the challenges previously outlined in this chapter.

First, the very essence of refugee work demands that personnel possess cross-cultural competencies. Whether the refugee organization is a government department, an intergovernmental agency or a non-governmental organization, the tasks performed by frontline staff and adjudicators necessarily require them to work with individuals from different cultures. Furthermore, just as with health care providers, the consequences of poor communications between a refugee claimant and an adjudicator can have fatal consequences (Medora 2008). Cultural incompetence in the refugee business can not only have a serious psychological impact on the claimant, it can also result in poor decisions that ultimately put a claimant's life in danger if returned to a country where he or she faces persecution.

Those who work in the asylum and refugee fields have already acknowledged the importance of cross-cultural training. Agencies have developed and implemented cross-cultural training programs designed to enhance communication with refugee claimants and improve the delivery of services (Dunn and Spring Institute for International Studies 1992). As a result, frontline workers, adjudicators and resettlement staff are cognizant that they must develop the ability to work with a highly culturally diverse clientele if they are to be effective. Adding LGBT cultural competencies to existing professional development programs is therefore not an unreasonable expectation.

More important, although cultural competency initially referred to work with ethnic and racial minorities, the concept has been broadened over the years to include other culturally diverse populations (Bryant 2001: 41; Van Den Bergh and Crisp 2004: 222). Culture has been defined as 'a body of values, customs, and ways of looking at the world shared by a group of people' (Piomelli 2006: 151, citing Krieger and Neumann). Essentially, culture refers to how people understand, interpret and give meaning to their environment. Krieger and Neumann argue that cultures do not only arise out of race, ethnicity, or geography, but can be based on gender, age, religion, disability, sexual orientation, and socioeconomic status (Piomelli 2006: 151). In fact, the concept has been applied to train individuals working with LGBT clients and is referred to as 'LGBT cultural competency training'. The basic principle underlying any LGBT cultural competency training is the recognition that sexual minorities have societal characteristics and histories of social stigma and discrimination that require specific competencies to address their unique concerns.

The cultural competency model can therefore help define and implement effective training in relation to LGBT refugee adjudication and resettlement. In fact, it is already used in the refugee field, and the model has been expanded to include competencies required to work with LGBT individuals.

9.3.2 Components of an LGBT cultural competency model

It is widely held that cross-cultural competencies, including LGBT cultural competencies, can be taught and learned (Rust *et al.* 2006: 29; Elliott 2011). The scholarly and professional literature does in fact provide many examples of cultural competency training principles and tools (Reynolds 2001; Ridley, Baker and Hill 2001; Sue 2001; Alberta and Wood 2009; Sorrells 2012). It has been suggested that training and coaching are the most effective methods of improving cross-cultural communication skills and cultural competence (Bents-Enchill n.d.). It is, however, beyond the scope of this chapter to describe, in depth, the existing models of cross-cultural competency training, or to provide a critical analysis of the various approaches. Rather, the purpose here is more modest – my aim is to present how cultural competency training has been conceptualized in other disciplines and fields and to describe how the core concepts of these models are highly applicable and useful in the refugee field, especially in relation to sexual orientation and gender identity issues.

More often than not, cultural competency training is presented as a trilogy of components. Authors identify three essential cognitive components to cultural competence and cross-cultural training: (1) awareness of one's own cultural world view and attitudes toward cultural differences; (2) knowledge of different cultural practices and world views; (3) and cross-cultural skills (Sue 2006; Williams 2006; Martin and Vaughn 2012). In the following section, each of these components is explained and their relevancy to LGBT training, examined. In my view, all three components should be addressed to delineate a culturally competent approach to work with sexual minority refugees. The cross-cultural model can successfully challenge frontline staff and adjudicators to deal with homophobia and heterosexism, develop the correct cultural knowledge, and learn the right techniques to create an LGBT-positive environment (Williams 2006: 210).

9.3.2.1 Awareness and attitudes

The objective of the first cultural competency is to bring individuals' own cultural bias and beliefs into consciousness and to raise awareness of general beliefs and values about cultural differences.[14] Focussing on awareness and attitudes as a cultural competency conveys to individuals that carefully examining their own beliefs and values about cultural differences is crucial to understanding and improving their interactions with individuals from other cultures. In a training context, participants could be encouraged to focus on self-awareness of the following: one's own cultural roots, biases one might hold about those who are culturally different and one's level of comfort with a client's cultural differences (Van Den Bergh and Crisp 2004: 223). As with all of the cultural competencies, the objective of a training module focused on awareness and attitudes is to improve decision making skills and thereby enhance the ability to understand, build trust with and work with people of widely diverse backgrounds.

In the refugee context, an obvious goal of an LGBT cultural competency training program focused on 'awareness and attitudes' would be to provide frontline staff and adjudicators with a cognizance of their potential heterosexism and homophobia. It might call upon them to, for example:

- self-reflect on their own sexual orientation, in terms of its development, influences, and experiences (Van Den Bergh and Crisp 2004: 227);
- reflect upon their previous contact with LGBT individuals, both personally and professionally (Van Den Bergh and Crisp 2004: 227);
- evaluate their reactions to LGBT individuals, both in terms of positive and negative experiences (Van Den Bergh and Crisp 2004: 227);
- recognize myths, stereotypes, and prejudice about sexual minorities;
- discuss the diversity of sexual minority communities (Turner, Wilson and Shirah 2008: 67); and
- consider the importance of providing services and conducting refugee determination hearings that are inclusive and respectful of sexual minorities (Turner, Wilson and Shirah 2008: 67).

Such personal awareness will in all likelihood result in better decision making and enhanced service delivery by reducing prejudicial interactions with sexual minorities. For instance, refugee adjudicators who are able to recognize that they expect a lesbian refugee claimant to have a masculine appearance or a gay man to be effeminate have achieved a cultural awareness of their reactions to this group of refugees, and, as a result, they are more likely to be able to set aside stereotypical views of sexual minorities.

9.3.2.2 Knowledge

The knowledge component of cultural competencies generally refers to the knowledge that 'allows [a person] to successfully explain and predict the behavior of people with different cultural backgrounds within specific situations' (Rasmussen, Sieck and Osland 2010: 3). The value of gaining cross-cultural knowledge has been expressed as follows: 'The more knowledge we have about people of different cultures, the more likely we are able to avoid stepping on cross-cultural toes. Knowing how culture impacts problem solving, managing people, asking for help, etc. can keep us connected in cross-cultural interactions' (DTUI.com n.d.).

Cross-cultural knowledge includes understanding the impact of social, cultural, political and legal dynamics on the treatment of a cultural group, acquiring specific knowledge about a cultural group's values, beliefs, and norms, and being cognizant of barriers that could impede communications with a person from a different cultural group. Essentially, the objective of a training module focused on knowledge is for participants to gain a sound understanding of the situation and world view of culturally different persons; for instance, cross-cultural knowledge should enable persons to make sense of cultural behaviours that appear paradoxical (Rasmussen, Sieck and Osland 2010).

Cross-cultural knowledge is an important part of cultural competency training.[15] To be sure, 'communicating across cultures [does] not require any special knowledge of the particular culture one is dealing with' (Price-Wise n.d.). If one has attained a sufficient level of cross-cultural self-awareness, 'one can be culturally competent by asking open questions, managing one's prejudices, showing respect, and speaking in a way that does not presume that the other person shares one's own values or experiences'. However, to understand specific populations, as is required in the refugee adjudication and resettlement context, prior knowledge about the cultural group is indeed essential and required. Moreover, gaining cross-cultural knowledge helps individuals align positive cross-cultural beliefs gained through self-awareness and attitudinal training with their actual behaviours when working with people of widely diverse backgrounds. For instance, a person may believe in the equality rights of gay men and lesbians but nevertheless, in the course of a cross-cultural encounter with an LGBT person, they may, without knowing it, use an out-dated label such as 'homosexual'.[16]

Cross-cultural knowledge training focused on LGBT communities could enhance all aspects of the asylum and refugee process. For instance, the acquisition of accurate knowledge about specific LGBT populations can contribute to a better assessment of the credibility of a refugee claimant's testimony; or the learning of a culturally appropriate vocabulary can improve the communication among staff, asylum seekers and refugees. To attain LGBT cross-cultural knowledge in the refugee context, training should cover the following areas:

- key terminology and concepts used by LGBT individuals and communities (Turner, Wilson and Shirah 2008: 67);
- differentiation between sexual and gender orientation and identity (Turner, Wilson and Shirah 2008: 67);
- LGBT diversity, characteristics, history, and traditions;
- social, legal and political environment linked to LGBT experiences with discrimination and persecution (Turner, Wilson and Shirah 2008: 68);
- country conditions and persecutory practices; and
- legislative developments and legal interpretations.

It is important, however, to flag a potential pitfall of cross-cultural knowledge training: it can lead to stereotyping (Price-Wise n.d.).[17] Many factors will make individuals similar or different from their cultural group and it is unreasonable to expect uniformity of beliefs, behaviours, or experience within a cultural group (Price-Wise n.d.). It is therefore important that any LGBT cross-cultural knowledge training module underline this difficulty to participants.

9.3.2.3 Skills

The skills component is related to 'knowing how' to conduct appropriate cross-cultural interactions with individuals from diverse groups. The skills component focuses on practices that will actually make use of the beliefs and knowledge gained through the other two cultural competency components. Communication is the fundamental tool by which people interact; cross-cultural skills training aims to develop appropriate communication techniques and intervention strategies in a multicultural setting. This includes developing the ability to send and receive a wide variety of verbal and nonverbal messages and gestures, whose meanings tend to vary from culture to culture (Van Den Bergh and Crisp 2004).

In the refugee context, cross-cultural skills are essential, as frontline staff, resettlement workers and adjudicators will be engaged in daily interactions with asylum seekers and refugees from widely diverse cultural backgrounds. For instance, in a refugee status determination hearing, adjudicators must elicit a claimant's story of persecution through personal testimony. In the course of this quasi-judicial interaction, a wide variety of verbal and non-verbal queries and responses will be sent and received by all individuals involved in the hearing. In interpreting the communications and in attaching meaning to the messages, adjudicators must take into account the multicultural context of the exchanges. They will be more successful at doing this if they possess some specific skills. For instance, interviewing skills, like open-ended questions, will allow adjudicators to explore the cultural identity, beliefs, and perceptions of the refugee claimant. Adjudicators also require excellent listening skills, patience, and tolerance of silence during a claimant's testimony. They should be able to modify standardized questions to make them appropriate for use with specific cultural populations. They must be able to work with interpreters of varied linguistic and cultural backgrounds. It is also true that adjudicators must develop sensitivity to the issues of power and trust that can arise when a vulnerable refugee claimant from one country is seeking international protection from another.[18]

Skills training in relation to LGBT cultural competence would similarly seek to ensure that frontline staff and adjudicators are able to conduct appropriate interviews and hearings, and deliver suitable services to sexual minority asylum seekers and refugees. For example, skills to be developed could include:

- how to assess a claimant's perception, conceptualization and stage of gay or lesbian identity development to better situate the individual in relation to the larger cultural group;
- how to assess the ways in which sexual orientation and gender identity manifest themselves in a specific culture;
- how to recognize indications of internalized homophobia that can impact on a claimant's testimony and make it difficult for them to talk openly with refugee personnel;
- how to create a LGBT-safe milieu, for example by avoiding the use of inappropriate terms and intake forms that are replete with heterosexual assumptions, which might inhibit a claimant's honest self-disclosure;
- how to encourage discussion of LGBT experiences to allow claimants to testify openly and safely; for instance, by posing questions that allow for alternative families including two parents of the same sex.

If refugee personnel acquire such cross-cultural skills, they can create an atmosphere of openness and affirmation for LGBT asylum seekers and refugees, and, as a result, perform their duties more effectively and fairly.

9.3.2.4 Competency-appropriate training and trainers

It should be evident that an LGBT cultural competency training program that follows the model described above, with its three distinctive components, is designed to impart very different competencies to refugee personnel. As a result, it is likely that each competency will require distinct types of training and a variety of trainers with different skills and experience. For instance, in designing awareness and attitudinal training modules, the approach that is most effective may be one that is participatory and experiential, while knowledge modules could make good use of lecture and memorization-based presentations. For some participants, it may be better to frame knowledge and skills training 'in pragmatic terms relevant to their day-to-day responsibilities' and to 'incorporate more problem-based learning and role play', while an awareness and attitudinal component could focus on personal experiences that go beyond the workplace (Baskir 2009).[19] The expertise of trainers needs to match the competencies sought. For example, to address a need for country of origin information, a competency falling under the knowledge component, refugee advocates persuaded the Belgian administrative tribunal to hear from visiting LGBT human rights activists from refugee producing countries (Beddeleem 2012).

The author's experience with LGBT competency training in Canada supports the view that training modules must be clear on their objectives and offered by appropriate experts. As mentioned previously, the administrative tribunal responsible for refugee status determination in Canada, the IRB, has conducted LGBT focused training since 1995. While it is evident that members of the IRB would benefit from professional training that incorporates all three components of LGBT cultural competency, the scope has not, in fact, been this broad. As a legal expert and the person retained to develop LGBT cultural competency training, my strengths fell squarely in the knowledge component and, to some extent, in the skills fields. For instance, the training materials and modules developed for the IRB touched upon the specific legal challenges that exist in applying the refugee definition to LGBT claimants (LaViolette 2010b). In addition, materials were developed in the early sessions to assist adjudicators in questioning refugee claimants about their sexual orientation and gender identity.[20] Essentially, the training focused on imparting some knowledge and one set of interviewing skills, but did not include the awareness component and additional skills. Therefore, while having first established training of sexual orientation and gender identity issues, the IRB could improve and expand the training to touch upon all competencies.

Lastly, those advocating LGBT cultural competency training for refugee personnel should take advantage of existing models and modules. As previously mentioned, professionals in other fields such as health, social work and human resources have been developing and offering LGBT cultural competency training for many years. In addition, individuals have developed specific expertise in this field. For example, several inter-cultural experts have recently collaborated to develop and publish a training tool entitled *Cultural Detective: Lesbian, Gay, Bisexual and Transgender* (Saxena *et al.* n.d.). Designed to develop LGBT cultural competence primarily in the workplace, this resource could certainly be adapted to the refugee context. In the United States, Out & Equal Workplace Advocates, a national non-profit organization, has also developed a number of training tools and certification programs to promote LGBT cultural competency in the workplace (Out & Equal 2012). Refugee advocates therefore have at their disposal tools and modules that can serve as foundations for the development of effective and appropriate LGBT sensitivity training in the refugee context.

9.4 Training for whom?

It is also important to carefully consider to whom LGBT cultural competency training should be targeted. In many cases, the calls for training have focused on individuals making refugee status determinations. Yet when an LGBT individual makes a refugee claim, the adjudicator is often the last entity (in a long line of staff and agencies) with which the refugee has to interact. In Canada, for example, refugees can be represented by a lawyer or an immigration consultant at their hearing; the outcome for the claimant can, therefore, depend significantly on the understanding, preparation and presentation of the relevant sexual orientation or gender identity issues by the advocate. In fact, when LGBT refugee claims were first presented before the IRB, a number of claimants did not reveal their sexual orientation on the advice of their lawyers who stated that their sexual orientation would only prejudice their case.[21] Even before they deal with lawyers or adjudicators, refugees may be in contact with visa officers abroad or settlement workers in the country where they are claiming refugee status. Very little thought has been given to providing such staff with LGBT cultural competency training.

Recent reports, however, have rightly called for training for a wider range of personnel. Jansen and Spijkerboer's (2011) *Fleeing Homophobia* report mentions 'interviewers, decision makers, the judiciary and legal aid providers'. UNHCR (2008: para. 37) calls for training of officials and interpreters involved in interviews. In examining the plight of LGBT Iranians in Turkey, ORAM accurately describes the scope of training needed to improve the system as a whole:

> Significant steps need to be taken to ameliorate the plight of Turkey's LGBT asylum seekers and refugees. First and foremost, immediate steps are required to safeguard their physical security and to shield them from harassment. This will require intensive training for local police, and may include assigning LGBT asylum seekers to live in less hostile locations. Second, processing by UNHCR, the government of Turkey and resettlement countries must be accelerated to minimize LGBTs' exposure to violence. These stakeholders should also ensure that appropriate interviewing techniques are utilized in the evaluation of LGBT-based claims. Finally, ongoing trainings are needed at UNHCR, with the Turkish police, and among service providers in the health, public assistance and education sectors. Such training should extend to officers, intake workers, service providers and interpreters, increasing receptivity toward LGBT asylum seekers and refugees and creating environments where discrimination and intolerance are minimized
>
> (Helsinki Citizens' Assembly – Turkey, Refugee Advocacy and Support Program, Organization for Refuge, Asylum & Migration 2011)

LGBT cultural competency training should, therefore, be targeting a broad spectrum of staff, including the following: adjudicators and other officials involved in refugee status determinations, UNHCR staff, visa officers, refugee lawyers, immigration consultants, settlement workers, staff at refugee reception and detention centres, and interpreters. The refugee system as a whole must be sensitized to the needs of the LGBT refugee population.

9.5 Training as a panacea?

It is important to conclude on a cautionary note: LGBT cultural competency training is not a panacea. It will not be a cure-all solution for the specific problems confronting LGBT asylum seekers and refugees. Advocacy work on behalf of LGBT refugees must not only focus on the undeniable value of training, but also on many other advancements that can foster a fair and just system for all refugees, including LGBT. In my view, calls for training must be specific, targeted, and form part of a larger campaign for independent and fair refugee determination systems. I briefly canvass why LGBT cultural competency training has limitations.

9.5.1 Limited resources and time

Officials involved in the refugee determination process are often overburdened by heavy workloads and provided with little training time. In Canada, adjudicators receive what is considered a significant amount of professional development training for an administrative tribunal, which is one day a month. But this training must cover every aspect of their work, not just LGBT issues. It is unrealistic therefore to expect that, in such a context, adjudicators and other staff will get more than half or one full day of LGBT cultural competency training every few years (which is in fact what has transpired in Canada). It should be obvious that such limited training time will be insufficient if one is to adequately cover the trilogy of competencies I have outlined above. Yet building all three cultural competency components is seen as an important goal of such training:

> Attitude change alone, for example, does not lead to knowledge about different cultures. Awareness or sensitivity training does not necessarily result in acceptance of cultural differences. Teaching about cultural differences or training cross-cultural skills before understanding the individual's awareness of differences can be dangerous. There is also the problem of over-generalization. What we learn about Muslim culture, for example, may be very valuable in preparation for an assignment in Saudi Arabia, but less useful for managing a mix of first and second-generation Muslim immigrant employees in a company based in Brussels, Belgium.
>
> (Martin and Vaughn 2012)

It should be obvious that limited training time will be insufficient if one is to adequately cover the trilogy of competencies outlined above. Moreover, the effectiveness of such training is dependent on the willingness and abilities of the targeted personnel to receive the training. On this front alone, advocates must have realistic expectations of what can be achieved through LGBT cultural competency training.

9.5.2 Training can have a limited impact on an unfair refugee determination system

Training cannot overcome systemic problems in the refugee determination system. The best way to ensure positive outcomes for LGBT refugees is to advocate for independent, impartial and fair decision making for all refugees. This is an ongoing struggle because refugee-accepting countries are increasingly interested in reducing the number of refugees they accept, rather than expanding asylum protection. Refugee determination systems are, as a result, the object of reforms that impact negatively on all refugees, including measures to accelerate the decision making process,[22] create procedural obstacles,[23] eliminate appeal levels (Elliott and Payton 2012), increase the detention of refugees,[24] entrust civil servants with refugee decisions (rather than independent officials)[25] and appoint unqualified officials.[26] The impact of such reforms on LGBT refugee claimants is significant, but this is also true for all refugee claimants. Given the current restrictive climate, the fairness of refugee status determinations will be difficult to overcome by training alone.

It is, therefore, important that LGBT refugee advocates work with the larger refugee advocacy community in their efforts to improve the fairness of refugee determination systems. Many of the challenges LGBT refugees confront are the same as other refugees. Collaborating with organizations which have worked for many years on refugee protection issues and which have advocated procedural fairness and sound application of the refugee definition will only benefit LGBT refugees. By becoming part of the broader refugee advocacy communities, LGBT refugee advocates can promote LGBT specific issues, but also more generally, for an independent, impartial and fair refugee determination systems.[27]

In that context, it is important to avoid unrealistic expectations that LGBT cultural competency training will have the most significant impacts on the fairness of refugee determination systems. Broader calls and campaigns for constructive reforms may be just as important in gaining better refugee protection for LGBT asylum seekers and refugees.

9.6 Conclusion

The refugee determination process is designed to be a guardian system; it is a system that at its very core is about deciding who gets in and who does not. The best we can hope for is that staff and adjudicators will have the qualifications and resources to do the job well. LGBT refugee advocates are right to call for training to improve the LGBT competencies of decision makers. It is important, however, to take this call further and to reflect on the exact nature and content of the training that will improve international and national refugee protection systems for sexual minority refugees. This chapter has determined that models currently exist and can serve as the basis for LGBT cultural competency training for refugee personnel. At the same time, it is important to accompany calls for training with broader advocacy in support of a fair system for all refugees; this is the best way to ensure positive outcomes for LGBT refugees.

9.7 Notes

* Associate Professor, Faculty of Law, University of Ottawa. The author wishes to thank Zofia Vorontsova for her invaluable research contributions and her meticulous editing assistance. The author gratefully acknowledges the financial support of the University of Ottawa. This chapter is based on a keynote talk given at the conference 'Fleeing Homophobia' held in September 2011 at VU University Amsterdam.

1 A refugee is a person who 'owing to well-founded fear of being persecuted for reasons of race, religion, nationality, membership of a particular social group or political opinion, is outside the country of his nationality and is unable or, owing to such fear, is unwilling to avail himself of the protection of that country; or who, not having a nationality and being outside the country of his former habitual residence as a result of such events, is unable or, owing to such fear, is unwilling to return to it' (United Nations Convention Relating to the Status of Refugees, 189 UNTS 150, entered into force 22 April 1954: art. 1(2)).

2 The human rights situation of sexual minorities around the world continues to be alarming. Many countries maintain severe criminal penalties for consensual sex between persons of the same sex, including the death penalty. Sexual minorities also are frequent targets of hate crimes. In several countries, restrictions have been imposed on the freedoms of expression and association of sexual minorities, while in others, homosexuality and transexuality are perceived as Western phenomena, anti-revolutionary behaviours, crimes against religion, sexually deviant and immoral behaviours, mental disorders or unacceptable challenges to gender-specific roles. For a survey of laws prohibiting same sex sexual conduct, see Bruce-Jones and Itaborahy (2011).

3 In Canada, for instance, the first reported refugee claim based on sexual orientation dates back to 1991 (*Re R (UW)*).

4 In 2010, UNHCR estimated that over the next three to five years more than 805,000 refugees will need to be resettled in countries that are safe and provide a durable solution for displaced individuals: 'UNHCR urges more countries to establish refugee resettlement programmes' (UNHCR 2010).

5 Millbank (2009b: 392) cites an Australian decision that noted 'it is difficult for applicants to substantiate and for decision makers to evaluate [claims on sexual orientation]. By their very nature, they involve private issues of self-identity and sexual conduct, and sometimes personal issues for individuals that may be

stressful or unresolved. Social, cultural and religious attitudes to homosexuality in an applicant's society may exacerbate such problems'.

6 Crisp (2006: 115) describes this as 'a term used to refer to the broad range of negative attitudes toward gay men and lesbians'.

7 Heterosexism is a system of attitudes, biases, and discrimination that positions heterosexuality as superior and more 'natural' than homosexuality (Berkman and Zinberg 1997: 320).

8 This list is adapted from Crisp (2006).

9 Rehaag made this suggestion in the context of discussing the problems facing bisexual claimants (Rehaag 2008: 28).

10 Nick Somers made these comments in the course of an interview with Alanna Parker, a reporter with CBC Radio (Mediascan 1995).

11 The IRB has conducted professional development training focused on LGBT refugee issues on several occasions since 1995. The author of this chapter developed and presented these training seminars to RPD staff in 1995, 1999, 2003, 2004 and 2010. For an early version of the training, see LaViolette (1996b). The IRB training is also mentioned by Jiménez (2007) and by Lahey (2008). While the LGBT training is now a periodic part of the professional development programs at the IRB, a national LGBT rights organization has called for more funding to support the training and to expand the program to include other border staff (Egale Canada 2011).

12 A training session was held in 2008 by the Australian Refugee Review Tribunal in Melbourne (Star Online 2008; Walker 2008).

13 The Office of Refugee Resettlement has awarded a $250,000 grant to the Heartland Alliance of Chicago to create a training and technical assistance center to support the resettlement of lesbian, gay, bisexual, or transgender (LGBT) refugees (US Department of Health and Human Services Administration for Children and Families 2011).

14 Some authors prefer to separate the awareness and attitudinal components into separate concepts (Minami 2009; Martin and Vaughn 2012).

15 According to Williams (2006), '[t]herefore, cultural competence can be developed through the acquisition of accurate knowledge about specific cultures'.

16 Social science research indicates that values and beliefs may be inconsistent with behaviours, and individuals may be unaware of it (Devine and Monteith 1993; Devine 1996).

17 'Having specific knowledge about different cultures is essential for cultural competence but it has a pitfall: it can lead to stereotyping. Most individuals are similar to his/her racial or ethnic group in some ways and completely different from the group in other ways. Factors like a person's level of education, whether he/she grew up in a rural area or the city, his/her income level, whether he/she has traveled, and the values instilled in him/her by his/her parents will make him/her similar to or different from others in his/her racial or ethnic groups' (Price-Wise n.d.).

18 Adapted from a list of skills identified as relevant in the clinical psychology setting (Haarmans, Noh and Munger 2004: 29–30).

19 Baskir further suggests that law enforcement officers, for example, tend to prefer the pragmatic approach over more abstract, 'touchy-feely' presentations'. For a comparison of two methods of cross-cultural sensitivity training, namely an

experiential approach and a lecture-based, cognitive presentation, see Pruegger and Rodgers (1994)

20 For the first version of this training module, see LaViolette (1996b).

21 In some Canadian cases, claimants concocted false stories rather than basing their refugee claims on sexual orientation (*Re Q (BC)*, 1993; *Re J (FH)*, 1994).

22 This has been the driving force behind recent reforms to Canada's refugee determination system (Canadian Council for Refugees 2012). For problems with the UK fast-tracking provisions, see Human Rights Watch 2010).

23 For instance, the one-year filing deadline in the United States (Bowser-Soder 2010).

24 This has been the case in Australia, for instance (Refugee Council of Australia 2011). Canada has also resorted to more detention (Keung 2011). A provision in Canada's recent reforms would force asylum seekers who arrive by boat to face a year in mandatory detention (Raj 2012).

25 Canada recently decided that first instance decision makers would be civil servants, rather than Cabinet-appointees (Canadian Council for Refugees n.d.: 3).

26 Millbank has commented on the qualifications of adjudicators: 'Improving the quality of lower level decision-makers may occur through enhanced requirements for professional or educational qualifications prior to appointment, more transparent or merit-based appointment processes, greater independence of decision-making bodies from government, and the provision of initial and on-going training' (Millbank 2009b: 22, citing Crépeau and Nakache). Problems have also included appointing decision makers with clear biases against homosexuality as was recently done in Canada (Thompson 2009).

27 Some LGBT refugee advocacy groups have begun to join broad campaigns to oppose restrictive reforms. For instance, in Canada, the Rainbow Refugee Action Network of Vancouver joined other refugee advocacy groups to testify before Parliament about the unfairness of recent reforms (Rainbow Refugee Action Network n.d.).

9.8 References

ABC News (2007) 'Refugee Review Tribunal to develop sexuality training', 15 June 2007, available at http://www.abc.net.au/news/stories/2007/06/15/1952753.htm?site=news (accessed 30 October 2009).

Alberta, A.J. and Wood, A.H.A. (2009) 'Practical skills model for effectively engaging clients in multicultural settings', *The Counseling Psychologist*, 37: 564–579.

Baldwin, T. (2010) 'Baldwin, Gillibrand to Secretary Clinton: Save LGBT Refugees', 4 February 2010, available at http://tammybaldwin.house.gov/news/press-releases/2010/02/baldwin-gillibrand-to-secretary-clinton-save-lgbt-refugees.shtml (accessed 30 May 2012).

Baskir, C. (2009) 'Fostering cultural competence in justice system "gatekeepers"', *Judicature*, 92: 232–237.

Beddeleem, J. (2012) 'Proof that you are gay? Prove persecution instead', email, 20 March 2012.

Bents-Enchill, J. (n.d.) Client Communication: Measuring Your Cross-Cultural Competence, Canadian Bar Association, available at http://www.cba.org/cba/practicelink/cs/cultural.aspx (accessed 26 May 2012).

Berkman, C.S. and Zinberg, G. (1997) 'Homophobia and heterosexism in social workers', *Social Work*, 42(4): 319–332.

Bowser-Soder, B. (2010) 'Flawed U.S. filing deadline provision denies, delays protection for legitimate refugees', 30 September 2010, Human Rights First, available at http://www.humanrightsfirst.org/2010/09/30/flawed-u-s-filing-deadline-provision-denies-delays-protection-for-legitimate-refugees/ (accessed 26 May 2012).

Bruce-Jones, E. and Itaborahy, L.P. (2011) 'State-sponsored homophobia: a world survey of laws prohibiting same-sex activity between consenting adults', Belgium: International Lesbian and Gay Association, available at http://www.europarl.europa.eu/meetdocs/2009_2014/documents/droi/dv/4_04ilgareport_/4_04ilgareport_en.pdf (accessed 26 May 2012).

Bryant, S. (2001) 'The five habits: building cross-cultural competence in lawyers', *Clinical Law Review*, 8: 33–107.

Canadian Council for Refugees (2012) 'New bill further undermines refugees', 16 February 2012, available at http://ccrweb.ca/en/bulletin/12/02/16 (accessed 26 May 2012).

Canadian Council for Refugees (n.d.) 'Refugee reform: weighing the proposals', available at http://ccrweb.ca/files/c-11weighingproposal.pdf (accessed 26 May 2012).

Crisp, C. (2006) 'The gay affirmative practice scale (GAP): a new measure for assessing cultural competence with gay and lesbian clients', *Social Work*, 51(2): 115–126.

Dauvergne, C. and Millbank, J. (2003) 'Before the High Court: applicants S396/2002 and S395/2002, a gay refugee couple from Bangladesh', *Sydney Law Review*, 25: 96–124.

de Jong, A. (2008) *An Analysis of the Coverage of LGBT Issues in Country of Origin Information Reports Produced by the COI Service*, Report for the Advisory Panel on Country Information.

Devine, P.G. (1996) 'Breaking the prejudice habit,' *Psychological Science Agenda*, 9: 10–11.

Devine P.G. and Monteith, M.J. (1993) 'The role of discrepancy associated affect in prejudice reduction', in D.M. Mackie and D.L. Hamilton (eds) *Affect, Cognition, and Stereotyping: Interactive Processes in Intergroup Perception*, New York, NY: Academic Press.

DTUI.com (n.d.) 'What is cultural competence and how is it measured?', Diversityofficermagazine.com, available at http://diversityofficermagazine.com/cultural-competence-2/what-is-cultural-competence-how-is-it-measured/ (accessed 26 May 2012).

Dunn, D. and Spring Institute for International Studies (1992) *Delivering Health Care to Refugees: Cross-cultural Training to Enhance the Delivery of Quality Health Care to Culturally Diverse Persons*, Denver, CO: Spring Institute for International Studies.

Egale Canada (2010) 'Egale questionnaire – Election 2011', available at http://archive.egale.ca/home.asp?lang=&menu=1&item=1465 (accessed 26 May 2012).

Egale Canada (2011) 'Bill C-11: the Immigration and Refugee Protection Act: Summary of Recommendations', available at http://archive.egale.ca/index.asp?lang=E&menu=32&item=933 (accessed 24 December 2012).

Elliott, L. and Payton, L. (2012) 'Refugee reforms include fingerprints, no appeals for some', 15 February 2012, CBC News, available at http://www.cbc.ca/news/politics/story/2012/02/15/pol-bogus-refugees.html (accessed 26 May 2012).

Elliott, S. (2011) 'Bridging cultural divide between teachers, students: training can help bridge gap between teachers, students', *Indestar.com*, 20 November 2011, available at http://www.indystar.com/article/20111120/NEWS1003/311200003/Training-can-bridge-gap-between-students-teachers (accessed 26 May 2012).

Gilllibrand, K.E., Leahy, J.P., Akaka, D.K., Bingaman, J., Brown, S., Casey, R.P. Jr., *et al.*, (2010) 'Letter to the Honorable Hillary Rodham Clinton', available at http://tammybaldwin.house.gov/Media/PDFs/LGBT%20refugee%20letter%202.4.2010.pdf (accessed 26 May 2012).

Grungras, N. (2012) 'Re: Training', email, 30 April 2012.

Haarmans, M., Noh, S. and Munger, F. (2004) 'A review of clinical cultural competence: definitions, key components, standards and selected trainings', Ontario: Center for Addiction and Mental Health, available at http://www.problemgambling.ca/EN/Documents/AReviewClinicalCulturalCompetence.pdf (accessed 26 May 2012).

Hathaway, J. (1991) *The Law of Refugee Status*, Toronto: Butterworths.

Heath, A., Niemeyer, G.J. and Pedersen, P. (1988) 'The future of cross cultural counseling', *Journal of Counseling and Development*, 67(1): 27–31.

Helsinki Citizens' Assembly – Turkey, Refugee Advocacy and Support Program, Organization for Refuge, Asylum & Migration (2011) 'Unsafe haven: the security challenges facing lesbian, gay, bisexual and transgender asylum seekers and refugees in turkey: updated edition', available at http://www.oraminternational.org/images/stories/PDFs/oram-unsafe-haven-2011-web.pdf (accessed 26 May 2012).

Human Rights First (2010) 'Persistent needs and gaps: the protection of lesbian, gay, bisexual, transgender and intersex (LGBTI) refugees: an overview of UNHCR's response to LGBTI refugees and recommendations to enhance protection', available at http://www.humanrightsfirst.org/wp-content/uploads/pdf/Persistent-Needs_LGBTI_Refugees_FINAL.pdf (accessed 26 May 2012).

Human Rights First (2012) 'The road to safety: strengthening protection for LGBTI refugees in Uganda and Kenya', available at http://www.humanrightsfirst.org/wp-content/uploads/pdf/RPP-The_Road_to_Safety.pdf (accessed 26 May 2012).

Human Rights Watch (2010) 'UK: "fast-track" asylum fails women', 23 February 2010, available at http://www.hrw.org/news/2010/02/23/uk-fast-track-asylum-system-fails-women (accessed 26 May 2012).

Immigration Equality (n.d.) 'Lesson plan overview', available at http://www.immigrationequality.org/wp-content/uploads/2011/07/ImEq-Draft-Model-LGBT-Asylum-Guidance-2010.pdf (accessed 26 May 2012).

Jansen, S. and Spijkerboer, T. (2011) *Fleeing Homophobia, Asylum Claims Related to Sexual Orientation and Gender Identity in Europe*, COC Netherlands and VU University Amsterdam, available at http://www.rechten.vu.nl/nl/onderzoek/conferenties-en-projecten/onderzoeksproject-fleeing-homophobia/index.asp (accessed 9 December 2012).

Jiménez, M. (2007) 'Nicaraguan wins reprieve in bid to remain in Canada,' *The Globe and Mail*, 10 February 2007.

Johnson, T.A.M. (2007) 'Flamers, flaunting and permissible persecution,' *Feminist Legal Studies*, 15: 99–111.

Kalan, J. (2011) 'The gray area of gay refugees: a Ugandan couple flees to a Kenyan camp, finding little relief', *GlobalPost*, available at http://mobile.globalpost.com/dispatch/news/regions/africa/kenya/111129/gay-refugees-homosexual-rights-LGBT-uganda (accessed 26 May 2012).

Kassisieh, G. (2008) *From Lives of Fear to Lives of Freedom: A Review of Australian Refugee Decisions on the Basis of Sexual Orientation*, Sydney: Gay & Lesbian Lobby.

Kendall, C.N. (2003) 'Lesbian and gay refugees in Australia: now that "acting discreetly" is no longer an option, will equality be forthcoming?', *International Journal of Refugee Law*, 15(4): 715–749.

Keung, N. (2011) 'Refugee detention up in Canada, says UN report', *The Star*, 23 December 2011, available at http://www.thestar.com/news/investigations/immigration/article/1106661-refugee-detention-up-in-canada-says-un-report (accessed 26 May 2012).

Lahey, J. (2008) 'Sweating bullets: how Canada's gay refugees get stuck in legal limbo', *Capital Xtra*, 20 February 2008.

LaViolette, N. (1996a) 'Proving a well-founded fear: the evidentiary burden in refugee claims based on sexual orientation', in S. Levy (ed.) *Asylum Based on Sexual Orientation; A Resource Guide*, San Francisco, CA: IGLHRC.

LaViolette, N. (1996b) 'Sexual orientation and the refugee determination process: questioning a claimant about their membership in the particular social group', in S. Levy (ed.) *Asylum Based on Sexual Orientation: A Resource Guide*, San Francisco, CA: IGLHRC.

LaViolette, N. (1997) 'The immutable refugees: sexual orientation in *Canada (A.G.) v. Ward*', *University of Toronto Faculty of Law Review*, 55(1): 1–41.

LaViolette, N. (2009) 'Independent human rights documentation and sexual minorities: an ongoing challenge for the Canadian refugee determination process', *International Journal of Human Rights*, 13 (2/3): 437–476.

LaViolette, N. (2010a) 'The UNHCR's guidance note on refugee claims relating to sexual orientation and gender identity: a critical commentary', *International Journal of Refugee Law*, 22(2): 173–208.

LaViolette, N. (2010b) *Sexual orientation, gender identity and the refugee determination process*, report prepared for the Immigration and Refugee Board of Canada, Ottawa, March 2010.

Marouf, F. (2008) 'The emerging importance of "social visibility" in defining a "particular social group" and its potential impact on asylum claims related to sexual orientation and gender', *Yale Law and Policy Review*, 27: 47–106.

Martin, M. and Vaughn, B. (2012) 'Cultural competence: the nuts & bolts of diversity & inclusion', Diversityofficermagazine.com, available at http://diversity-officermagazine.com/cultural-competence-2/cultural-competence-the-nuts-bolts-of-diversity-inclusion/ (accessed 26 May 2012).

McGhee, D. (2000) 'Accessing homosexuality: truth, evidence and the legal practices for determining refugee status – the case of Ioan Vraciu', *Body & Society*, 6(1): 29–50.

McKiernan, M. (2011) 'Reforms introduce new challenges for gay refugees', available at http://www.lawtimesnews.com/201107048546/Headline-News/Reforms-introduce-new-challenges-for-gay-refugees (accessed 26 May 2012).

Mediascan (1995), *Transcript of CBC-R 'Sunday Morning'*, 29 January 1995 (on file with author).

Medora, D. (2008) 'Building a culturally competent organization', *Strategies*, 11(4): 116, available at http://www.familyresourcecenters.net/assets/library/101_summer08.pdf (accessed 26 May 2012).

Millbank, J. (2009a) 'From discretion to disbelief: recent trends in refugee determinations on the basis of sexual orientation in Australia and the United Kingdom', *The International Journal of Human Rights*, 13(2–3): 391–414.

— (2009b) '"The ring of truth": a case study of credibility assessment in particular social group refugee determinations', *International Journal of Refugee Law*, 21(1): 1–33.

Minami, M. (2009) 'Role of attitude in multicultural counselling competency', *World Cultural Psychiatry Research Review*, January: 39–46.

O'Leary, B. (2008) '"We cannot claim any particular knowledge of the ways of homosexuals, still less of Iranian homosexuals. . .": the particular problems facing those who seek asylum on the basis of their sexual identity', *Feminist Legal Studies*, 16: 87–95.

Out & Equal (2012) 'Training and education', available at http://outandequal.org/training-programs (accessed 26 May 2012).

Pedersen, P. (1988) *Handbook for Developing Multicultural Awareness*, Washington, DC: American Association for Counseling and Development.

Piomelli, A. (2006) 'Cross-cultural lawyering by the book: the latest clinical texts and a sketch of a future agenda', *Hastings Race & Poverty Law Journal*, 4: 131.

Price-Wise, G. (n.d.) 'Introduction to cultural competence in healthcare', Florida Center for Cultural Competence, available at http://www.flculturalcompetence.org/Intro_to_CC_ltrhd_3210.pdf (accessed 26 May 2012).

Pruegger, V.J and Rodgers, T.B. (1994) 'Cross-cultural sensitivity training: methods and assessment', *International Journal of Intercultural Relations*, 18(3): 369–387.

Rainbow Refugee Action Network (n.d.) 'Blog C-11 Campaign', available at http://rainbowrefugeecanada.wordpress.com/c-11-campaign-2/ (accessed 26 May 2012).

Raj, A. (2012) 'Human Rights Watch attacks mandatory one-year detention of illegal immigrants in Tory anti smuggling bill,' *Huffington Post*, 20 March 2012, available at http://www.huffingtonpost.ca/2012/03/19/human-rights-watch-canada-anti-smuggling-bill_n_1363850.html (accessed 26 May 2012).

Rasmussen, L.J., Sieck, W.R. and Osland, J. (2010) 'Using cultural models of decision making to assess and develop cultural sensemaking competence', in D. Schmorrow and D. Nicholson (eds) *Advances in Cross-Cultural Decision Making*, Boca Raton, FL: CRC Press/Taylor & Francis.

Refugee Council of Australia (2011) 'Government gets it wrong with more detention centers', 4 March 2011, available at http://www.ajustaustralia.com/releases/110304_Detention.pdf (accessed 26 May 2012).

Rehaag, S. (2008) 'Patrolling the borders of sexual orientation: bisexual refugee claims in Canada', *McGill Law Journal*, 53: 59–102.

Rehaag, S. (2009) 'Bisexuals need not apply: a comparative appraisal of refugee law and policy in Canada, the United States, and Australia', *International Journal of Human Rights*, 13(2): 415–436.

Reynolds, A. L. (2001) 'Multidimensional cultural competence: providing tools for transforming psychology', *The Counseling Psychologist*, 29: 833–841.

Ridley, C.R., Baker, D.M. and Hill, C.L. (2001) 'Critical issues concerning cultural competence', *The Counseling Psychologist*, 29(6): 822–832.

RTE News Ireland (2012) 'Training for LGBT refugee workers', 31 January 2012, available at http://www.rte.ie/news/2012/0131/lgbt.html (accessed 26 May 2012).

Rust, G., Kondwani, K., Martinez, R., Dansie, R., Wong, W., Fry-Johnson, Y., *et al.* (2006) 'A crash-course in cultural competence', *Ethnicity & Disease*, 16: s3-29–s3–36.

Saxena, V., Wuebbeler, R., O'Brien, N., Stieghorst, R., Gore, S., Pusch, R., *et al.* (n.d.) 'Cultural Detective® Lesbian, Gay, Bisexual and Transgender', available at http://www.culturaldetective.com/package.html#GAY (accessed 26 May 2012).

Sorrells, K. (2012) *Intercultural Communication: Globalization and Social Justice*, Thousand Oaks, CA: Sage.

Star Online (2008) 'Tribunal promise', 20 April 2008, available at http://www.starobserver.com.au/news/australia-news/new-south-wales-news/2008/04/20/tribunal-promise/12269 (accessed 26 May 2012).

Sue, D.W. (2001) 'Multidimensional facets of cultural competence', *The Counseling Psychologist*, 29(6): 790–821.

Sue, D.W. and Sue D. (1990) *Counselling the Culturally Different: Theory and Practice*, 2nd edn, New York, NY: John Wiley & Sons.

Sue, D.W., Bernier, J.E., Durran, A., Feinberg, L., Pedersen, P., Smith E.J., *et al.* (1982) 'Position paper: cross-cultural counseling competencies', *The Counseling Psychologist*, 10: 45–52.

Sue, S. (2006) 'Cultural competency: From philosophy to research and practice', *Journal of Community Psychology*, 34: 237–45.

Swink, A. (2005–2006) 'Queer refuge: a review of the role of country condition analysis in asylum adjudication for members of sexual minorities', *Hastings International & Comparative Law Review*, 29: 251.

Thompson, E. (2009) 'Fire anti-gay appointee', *Edmonton Sun*, 18 March 2009, available at http://www.edmontonsun.com/news/canada/2009/03/18/8791266-sun.html (accessed 26 May 2012).

Turner, K., Wilson, W. and Shirah, K. (2008) 'Lesbian, gay bisexual and transgender cultural competency for public health practitioners', in M. Shackle (ed.) *The Handbook of Lesbian, Gay, Bisexual and Transgender Public Health: a practitioner's guide*, New York, NY: Routledge.

UK Lesbian & Gay Immigration Group (2010) *Annual Report*, available at http://www.uklgig.org.uk/docs/annual_reports/Annual_Report_2010_web.pdf (accessed 26 May 2012).

UNHCR (2008) *UNHCR Guidance Note on Refugee Claims Relating to Sexual Orientation and Gender Identity*, 21 November 2008, Geneva: UNHCR, available at http://www.unhcr.org/refworld/docid/48abd5660.html (accessed 26 May 2012).

— (2010) *UNHCR Urges More Countries to Establish Refugee Resettlement Programmes*, Geneva: UNHCR, available at http://www.unhcr.org/4c31cd236.html (accessed 26 May 2012).

— (2011a) *Somewhere Over the Rainbow*, Geneva: UNHCR, available at http://www.unhcr.se/en/media/news-articles/artikel/b1bcdc68daf99579e28c57bc16f20855/somewhere-over-the-rainbow.html (accessed 28 May 2012).

— (2011b) *Working with Lesbian, Gay, Bisexual, Transgender & Intersex Persons in Forced Displacement*, Geneva: UNHCR, available at http://www.unhcr.org/refworld/docid/4e6073972.html (accessed 26 May 2012).
United Nations 'Protocol Relating to the Status of Refugees', 606 UNTS 267, entered into force 4 October 1967.
US Citizenship and Immigration Services, Refugee, Asylum, and International Operations Directorate (2011) 'Guidance for adjudication of lesbian, gay, bisexual, trangender and intersex (LBGTI) refugee and asylum claims', 28 December 2011, available at http://www.uscis.gov/USCIS/Humanitarian/Refugees%20&%20Asylum/Asylum/Asylum%20Native%20Documents%20and%20Static%20Files/RAIO-Training-March-2012.pdf (accessed 26 May 2012).
US Department of Health and Human Services Administration for Children and Families (2011) 'ACF Awards a targeted awareness training grant for LGBT Refugees', 15 June 2011, available at http://www.acf.hhs.gov/news/press/2011/training_grant_LGBT.html (accessed 26 May 2012).
Van Den Bergh, N. and Crisp, C. (2004) 'Defining culturally competent practice with sexual minorities: implications for social work education and practice', *Journal of Social Work*, 40(2): 221–238.
Walker, K. (2008) 'Re: Sexuality & Refugee Status', email, 27 March 2008.
Williams, C. (2006) 'The epistemology of cultural competence', *Families in Society*, 87(2): 209–220.
Young, J. (2010) 'The alternate refuge concept: a source of systematic disadvantage to sexual minority refugee claimants', *University of New Brunswick Law Journal*, 60: 294.

10 Sexual identity, normativity and asylum

*Thomas Spijkerboer**

In this chapter, I begin with an overview of the legal developments that followed the acceptance of sexual orientation and gender identity as a persecution ground. Quite often, important steps forward turn out to be followed by new obstacles, which can be so formidable as to undo the effects of the preceding advantages. How can we begin to understand this? In my analysis, what currently are important issues in academic writings, case law and practice are expressions of a limited number of debates about sexuality which keep re-appearing in different refugee law contexts. Having made that point, I will try to analyse how it is possible that these issues seem irresolvable and keep reappearing. This will be done by turning to the work of Foucault and Sedgwick. From Foucault, I take that sexual identity is not a cause but an effect, and from Sedgwick the inherently instability of sexual identity. The contradictions inherent in sexualities, combined with the contradictions inherent in law, create options and possibilities to do justice to lesbian, gay, bisexual and transgender (LGBT) asylum applicants, by eliminating transphobic and homophobic notions from decision making practice, as well as by formulating alternatives for pieces of legal doctrine negatively affecting LGBT claimants. But these contradictions can also be exploited by actors aiming to undo such steps forward. In this sense, I offer a more sceptical analysis than Millbank in this volume, despite the affinity between our approaches.

In this contribution, I focus on the refugee definition in the narrow sense of the word, so excluding topics such as country of origin information (Dauvergne and Millbank 2003; Swink 2006; LaViolette 2009), training (LaViolette in this volume), safe third countries (Young 2010) and reception (Cragnolini in this volume). A more comprehensive analysis than the one I undertake to make here has still to be written.

10.1 The return of the repressed

The 1951 United Nations Convention Relating to the Status of Refugees (Refugee Convention) was drafted under the spectre of totalitarianism. It protected against the risks of which the drafters were aware: persecution of political opponents as well as extermination of Jews and Kulaks in Nazi Germany and the Soviet Union. Although the refugee definition in the 1950s and 60s raised problems (as evidenced by Atle Grahl-Madsen's 1966 standard work), conceptual innovations were not necessary. Innovative efforts were aimed at deleting the temporal and geographical limitations (successful in the form of the 1966 Protocol) and at creating a subjective and enforceable right for refugees to be granted asylum (unsuccessful, see Grahl-Madsen's frustrated 1980 book).

Thinking about innovations regarding the refugee definition itself only began to develop when the so-called 'new refugees' (Goodwin-Gill 1986) entered the European scene. American and Portuguese draft evaders posed initial challenges, but their urgency disappeared with the respective finales, in 1975, of the colonial endgames in Vietnam, Angola and Mozambique. More enduring were the refugees fleeing civil strife in 'peripherous' countries: Christians and Kurds from Turkey, civilians caught up in the civil wars in Central America and Sri Lanka, civilians fleeing conflicts in Africa which are often characterised by an intractable combination of globalisation and ethnicity (Markard 2012). Now, innovations in the refugee concept did occur, and most of them stuck. Non-State agents have come to be considered as potential agents of persecution, but at the price of acceptance of the internal flight alternative and an increasingly extensive notion of agents of protection (Battjes 2012; European Court of Human Rights 28 June 2012, *A.A. and Others v Sweden*, Application 14499/09). Imputed political opinion has become a relevant persecution ground, but it is often directly or indirectly required that the intention of the agent of persecution is shown to be aimed at the purported persecution ground (persecutory intent).[1] What these innovations have in common is that they seek to apply an unchanged refugee definition to cases which did not occur in the Refugee Convention case law up until the mid-1970s.

Another wave of innovations occurred in a different context, that of equality. Feminists argued that the refugee definition was tilted, biased to the disadvantage of women. In order to do justice to the specificity of the experiences of women fleeing violence, the refugee definition had to be applied without a male bias. This gender-neutral or gender sensitive approach was sometimes thought to require amending the refugee definition (by adding a sixth persecution ground being gender), but for a mix of principled and pragmatic reasons, quite soon most agreed that membership of a particular social group would suffice. As a consequence, it became possible to base a claim to asylum on sexual violence in the context of an ethnic conflict, in a domestic setting or during interrogations. Sexual violence was reconstituted as something that was public in a normative sense, and not just tough luck. Likewise, women's activities catering for political activists or fighters, as well as activities relating to their position as women, were reframed as expressions of their political or religious opinions. At an abstract level, one might say that the feminist critique of the public/private distinction was imported in refugee law (for an overview, see Anker 2012; Crawley 2001; Spijkerboer 2000: 107–147 and 163–188). This was made feasible in part by the fact that women's issues were increasingly conceived of as human rights issues (beginning with Charlesworth, Chinkin and Wright 1991) while simultaneously the refugee definition was reconceived as being fundamentally about human rights (of which Hathaway's 1991 book is a clear expression).

It would be incorrect to say that the advocates for considering human rights violations against LGBTs as grounds for asylum merely copied feminism. The Dutch Council of State recognised sexual orientation as a species of the persecution ground social group as early as 1981,[2] and this was before second wave feminism reached refugee law. Nevertheless, the conceptual manoeuvre is similar (compare Millbank 2004 on sexual orientation, human rights and refugee law). LaViolette (2007) convincingly argues that gender, sexual orientation and gender identity are closely related as bases for asylum claims. In any case, the push for including issues of sexual orientation and gender identity in the refugee concept postdates the feminist advocacy efforts. A major point, eagerly taken up in part because it lends itself to easily formulated demands and recommendations, is recognition of sexual orientation and gender identity as a persecution ground by using particular social group.[3] It took considerable advocacy to get this accepted, but in an important way this was just the beginning. Once this hurdle was taken, four new obstacles came into view.

First, decision makers now considered the violence against LGBTs as *discrimination* not amounting to persecution. In classical refugee law doctrine, physical violence, including deprivation of liberty, was in itself considered as amounting to persecution.[4] In contrast, denial of access to the labour market, education, housing and health care were considered as only exceptionally amounting to persecution, especially when a person's life became unbearable by a combination of such measures. Surprisingly, in cases turning around sexual orientation and gender identity, physical violence was often considered as merely constituting discrimination (Spijkerboer 1998: 201–207; LaViolette 2009: 450–454; compare Saxena 2006).[5] As a consequence of the categorisation as discrimination (and not as persecution), such acts of violence were examined under the more stringent gauge of whether it made a person's life unbearable. Instead of being considered as acts of persecution, LGBT applicants must establish, for example, that such acts of violence are systematic.

A second problem that came up once sexual orientation and gender identity were recognised as a persecution ground was the idea of *discretion*. The idea behind discretion reasoning is that in many countries, even those where homosexual or transgender behaviour and/or identity are criminalised, people can live according to their identity without major risks, provided that they behave discreetly. Parks in Teheran, touristy beaches in Gambia, and the privacy of the bedroom are possibilities to which applicants are referred and where – or so decision makers claim – they can enjoy the privacy rights to which international human rights law entitles them without running excessive risk. Implicitly, the privacy rights which amount to the right to sexual autonomy are often limited to the right to have sex. These privacy rights are argued not to include the right to 'flaunting', 'conspicuous' and 'unnecessarily risky' behaviour. Applicants are, in other words, denied international protection because they are expected to protect themselves by keeping a low profile.[6] In practice, LGBT people will be expected not to share with their friends, relatives, colleagues and fellow students how they spent their weekend; they should not be seen too often with their partner; if they visit places that are marked as LGBT venues they should keep it a secret that they have gone there. They should not even think of cohabitation. And they will have to figure out an explanation for not marrying. For many people, this will mean they have to conceal, in most of their social contacts, those parts of their lives that mark them as sexual minorities. And they will have to do so for life. Relying on the rallying cry that LGBT asylum applicants should not be 'sent back to the closet', a rather successful campaign for abolishing discretion reasoning has been made (New Zealand, Australia, the Netherlands, the United Kingdom, Sweden, Finland and Norway formally abolished discretion reasoning between 2003 and 2012).[7] As with particular social group, the success of this campaign is made possible in part by the clear cutness of its demand: ban one particular ground for denying refugee status.

But discretion reasoning turns out to be a many-headed monster: once they succeeded in chopping off what brave advocates took to be its head, it turned out to have many others. For applicants who have not succeeded being discreet in their country of origin and already were in trouble there, the internal flight alternative is one such monster head. They can return to another region in the country of origin, and if they 'abide by the dominant cultural norms' (as decision makers expect they obviously will; anthropologist-style sensitivity meets refugee law restrictionism), they do not have a well-founded fear of being persecuted.[8] Another monster head rephrases discretion reasoning as *sur place* reasoning (see on this topic the contribution of Battjes in this volume). This manoeuvre is made in cases where people have succeeded in remaining closeted in the country of origin. Decision makers rule that they have only begun to be openly LGBT in the country of refuge. Once the facts of the case have been rephrased as being about *sur place*, the concomitant restrictive pieces of doctrine get on board: a purported lack of continuity between behaviour in the country of origin and the country of refuge; the unreasonableness of attracting the attention of the home country authorities before or after return; suspicions about credibility. A third monstrous head holds that some people are voluntarily discreet, and can be expected to behave as they did upon return to the country of origin (see Weßels in this volume; compare Tobin 2012: 465–466). In this line of thought, it is found to be relevant whether in the country of origin the applicant had been discreet about his or her sexuality 'voluntarily' – out of a postulated 'natural' human tendency to be discreet about sexuality, or on account of the wish not to offend relatives. In such situations, discretion is not *required* of the applicants upon return. Instead, it is held to be a reasonable *factual* prediction that, upon return, applicants will prefer to be discreet as they were before.[9] For that reason, they do not face a risk of persecution, because the potential agents of persecution will (as a matter of fact) not find out that they are LGBT. A fourth variety of discretion reasoning occurs in the definition of particular social group. Since 2006, according to some US courts a particular social group must be recognisable, i.e. socially visible. In this view, particular social groups have characteristics that are 'highly visible' and therefore 'recognizable'.[10] This may well result in denial of asylum to LGBT people who were not out in their country of origin. The social visibility approach may be used to argue that, as people who were not visibly LGBT, they were not members of the relevant particular social group which consists of people with 'highly visible' characteristics. It might be argued furthermore that upon return to their country of origin, they will most likely not be visibly LGBT (or they can be reasonably expected to be so), with the consequence that they will not be a member of the relevant particular social group.[11] Such an approach would lead to the denial of asylum to LGBT claimants on the basis of their concealment of the sexual orientation or gender identity in the past, and the expectation that they will conceal it again upon return to their country of origin. Marouf has remarked that the social visibility test may be particularly harmful for lesbians, whose social visibility tends to lower than that of gay men (Marouf 2008–2009: 87).[12] The same is true for bisexuals.

Yet another variety of the discretion requirement is at issue in one of the debates about the UK Supreme Court judgment in *HJ (Iran) and HT (Cameroon)*.[13] Discussing the question whether there is a nexus between the harm feared and the persecution ground membership of a particular social group, Hathaway and Pobjoy qualify the kind of behaviour which will count in considering whether there is a link between the harm feared and the persecution ground of membership of a particular social group. Only 'activities properly understood to be inherent' (Hathaway and Pobjoy 2012: 335) in sexual orientation (or gender identity) should be included in the 'protected interest' (Hathaway and Pobjoy 2012: 336). This excludes 'relatively trivial activity that could be avoided without significant human rights cost' (Hathaway and Pobjoy 2012: 335, 382).[14] In sum: while Hathaway and Pobjoy agree that concealment constitutes persecution (see below), the debatable notion that LGBTs can be reasonably expected to refrain from some activities expressing their sexual identity now pops up at another location in the refugee definition: whether or not the harm feared is 'on account of' the individual's sexual identity.[15]

So the second obstacle to recognition as a refugee, the discretion requirement, has been abolished in many jurisdictions but has the tendency to pop up in the context of the internal flight alternative; in rephrasing discretion cases as *sur place* cases; in the notion of 'voluntary' discretion; in the definition of the particular social group; or in the nexus between persecution and persecution ground. The issue of discretion presently is before the Court of Justice of the European Union.[16]

A third obstacle for refugee status that came into view once the issue of the persecution ground had been settled was the relevance of *criminalisation*.[17] In cases where homosexual or transgender identity or behaviour constituted a criminal offence in the country of origin, decision makers decided that this was insufficient for refugee status. Even when they admitted that, in light of the fundamental nature of sexuality, homosexual and trans people are likely to regularly engage in criminalised behaviour, they required evidence of enforcement of the criminal laws concerned. The burden of proof that enforcement (and sometimes systematic enforcement) took place remains with the applicant, and in this way the fact of criminalisation (itself already a violation of international human rights law) became irrelevant for refugee status determination. Any lack of information on enforcement became the applicant's problem. Furthermore, the fact that criminalisation makes people defenceless against extortion or violence from the side of the authorities or fellow citizens is disregarded, while human rights information on such practices is likely to be absent. Lastly, the permanent fear and anguish which results from criminalisation (the forced modification of fundamental behaviour constituting 'endogenous harm', Hathaway and Pobjoy 2012: 358 *et seq.*[18]), even if it is not formally enforced with some frequency, is held to be irrelevant for refugee status. In short, the fact that behaviour in which people are likely to engage is a criminal offence in the country of origin would seem to be an argument strongly in favour of the grant of refugee status, but it is made to evaporate. The recent judgment of the Italian Court of Cassation, ruling that criminalisation of homosexual acts constitutes persecution, goes against this trend.[19]

A final example of the obstacles to refugee status for LGBT claimants is about *credibility*. As the title (as well as the content) of Millbank's 2009 article 'From discretion to disbelief' aptly captures, when rules are adapted which favour the grant of refugee status to applicants who invoke sexual orientation or gender identity, there is a tendency among decision makers to doubt whether the people invoking such rules actually are LGBT. In doing this, they often rely on staunch stereotypes (compare Berg and Millbank 2009; Morgan 2006; O'Leary 2008). Gays may be expected to behave effeminately, know about Oscar Wilde, have gone through the stages of coming out identified in Western psychology. Lesbians may be expected to behave in a masculine way, know LGBT journals in their country of origin or LGBT symbols such as the rainbow and the pink triangle (compare Middelkoop's contribution to this volume). Remarkably, transgender asylum seekers do not frequently run into credibility problems (compare the contribution of Berg and Millbank to this volume), probably because transgender is seen as a medical condition, and not 'merely' as subjective orientation or preference.[20]

10.2 Sexual identity: a tilted concept

Advocates of granting refugee status for sexual orientation and gender identity based persecution have addressed the legal problems they encountered one by one. Initially, they tackled the issue of the persecution ground. Subsequently, they argued against improper use of the concept of discrimination, against discretion reasoning, for giving proper weight to criminalisation, and against the use of stereotypes in credibility assessment. In other words, they fought against incorrect applications of the law. However, we saw that what those advocates consider as legal improprieties keep popping up. When arguing for refugee status for persecuted LGBT people, they rely on the concept of sexual identity in one way or another. I want to point out that the improprieties seem to be merely variations of a limited number of mainstream notions about sexual orientation and gender identity. While the notion of sexual identity is crucial for formulating claims that seek to combat the exclusion and oppression of sexual minorities, that same notion at the same time is deeply influenced by such exclusion and oppression. It does not only have the potential to liberate, but also to marginalise. Asylum practice illustrates that the notion of sexual identity, while not being a poisoned gift, is a mixed blessing. I deal with three notions which play a role in the concept of sexual identity: sexual autonomy, the comprehensibility of sexual identity and sexual identity as act or identity.

A first notion is about sexual autonomy. The idea that sexual minorities must settle for less than straight people is fundamental in refugee law doctrine and practice. Even in jurisdictions where LGBT rights formally are equal to those of straight and cisgender[21] subjects, the idea that LGBT asylum seekers can be returned to situations where these rights are denied in form and substance has great plausibility for many decision makers. This can take more than one form. An extreme version holds that minority sexualities, unlike minority race, religion and political opinion, are not protected categories, and therefore cannot constitute a persecution ground. This extreme version has become rare in asylum law.[22] But there are less draconic versions of denial of sexual autonomy to sexual minorities. One of those (expressed through discretion reasoning) holds that people may be expected to repress their sexuality so as not to get in trouble – they are expected to participate in the denial of themselves. Sex (in secret) is enough, things like being open about who one's partner is are niceties which LGBT people can do without.[23] Another version presumes that physical violence, which would arguably be enough for refugee status when the applicant is, say, an Iranian democrat, is considered insufficient when it concerns violence against LGBT people. This version is implicated in the subsumption of physical violence under the concept of discrimination, and assumes that some extent of violence against LGBT people is only natural, something that one will have to put up with, and that therefore does not count. Yet another reincarnation of the denial of sexual autonomy is expressed by the notion that criminalisation of sexual orientation and gender identity is in itself insufficient for refugee status. Such criminalisation is considered a violation of the right to private life even in the absence of any enforcement (*Dudgeon*, *Norris*, *Modinos*[24]) if it occurs in Europe, but removal of a person to a country where such a violation occurs is not a violation of the same right to private life. Human rights are universal, but apparently some are more universal than others. Obviously, one may counter this idea by pointing out that while violations of Articles 2 and 3 of the European Convention on Human Rights stand in the way of removal, for the other provisions of the Convention only flagrant violations are sufficient.[25] This overlooks, however, that the intense fear and anguish which are the result of criminalisation have in other contexts been considered as a violation of Article 3 blocking removal.[26] Criminalisation is not acceptable for domestic purposes, but this is considered as a luxury item of Western lifestyle which, ultimately, one can do without if one happens not to live in the West. Therefore people can be returned to countries where their sexuality is a criminal offence.

So, even when it has been accepted that sexual orientation and gender identity are categories protected by refugee law, the debate keeps reappearing whether sexual autonomy concerns a freedom that one needs less of than political or religious freedom; and whether people in non-Western countries can do with less of it than people in the West. Yes, it is nice and desirable that LGBTs are granted equal rights. But, as we can see from asylum law, these equal rights are not fundamental, people can do without them because we can send LGBT people back to situations where equal rights are denied in significant ways. Equal rights for sexual minorities are good, but apparently not fundamental. This notion is problematic for asylum seekers, but ultimately is threatening for sexual minorities in the receiving countries as well – and not just for those seeking asylum. Apparently, LGBT rights can be undone without touching the fundaments of our constitutional systems. Minority sexualities are considered as less valid, less important, less fundamental than mainstream sexualities. Sexual minorities are, in other words, subdominant.

A second phenomenon that keeps popping up is that sexualities which deviate from the dominant norm are only comprehensible if they take a particular form. This is most easily visible in credibility assessment. It is assumed that a young Pakistani gay man has gone through the stages of denial, insecurity, guilt and potentially acceptance of his sexuality. If he has not followed this sequence, decision makers find it hard to understand how he really could be gay. Apparently, it is hard to see why an Iraqi man should be believed when he has a male partner but says he would not know whether he is gay. And how, apart from artificial insemination, can a woman claim to be lesbian *and* have a child, or be married to a man and be prepared to remain so? Non-standard sexualities are only comprehensible if they do not interfere with the stability of mainstream sexualities. LGBT people are assigned to a specific and quite narrow space where we can be LGBT – but one category at a time, preferably for life, and only to the extent they identify with one of those exact categories (Rehaag 2008; Hojem 2009: 7; Walker 2000). Another remarkable thing is that sexuality, if it is not mainstream, is to be taken quite seriously. Not only does it require (in liberal versions: passing) feelings of insecurity and guilt, but also it is presumed that one reads the journals, knows one's classics and identifies with the symbols. If one can expect a Marxist to know about Marx, why not expect a gay man to know about Oscar Wilde? And if we presume that a Christian sees the cross as an important symbol, might not a lesbian be presumed to know that the rainbow is a symbol of sexual diversity? Even if people claim to have been persecuted by their relatives or neighbours, they are supposed to have studied the law and know what the punishment for homosexuality is. Although people can have dominant sexualities without ever thinking about it, deviating from the standard is not to be taken lightly. Mainstream thinking is sure that one will not lightly accept being LGBT. Straightness is the comfortable default option; not being straight has to be a troubled and deliberate situation, because everyone who has a choice would prefer to be straight (compare Rehaag 2008: 15).

LGBT claimants are only comprehensible (and therefore credible) if they conform to the identity categories which are prevalent in receiving countries. These categories have important normative elements (such as straightness as the default option). The importance of fixed identity categories is that it allows for the construction of majority sexuality as coherent, stable and given. Being LGBT is supposed to require processes (of self-discovery, identifying the label that becomes you, coming out, dealing with shame and frustration), it consists of becoming. Straightness on the other hand simply *is*, and does not need discovery or naming. In other words, the identity of sexual minorities is assigned to a limited space, subjected to clear-cut expectations about what constitutes a real LGBT identity – it is put in a box.

A third aspect of LGBT cases is the act/identity distinction. The distinction is crucial in discretion reasoning in all its varieties: some acts (most notably, having sex with somebody else or having gender reassignment surgery) are considered as inherent in sexual identity, while other acts (varying from dressing as a member of the opposite sex, holding hands in public, or living together, to drinking the now famous multi-coloured cocktails) are considered as peripherous to sexual identity.[27] The act/identity thing also plays an important role in credibility assessment, where identity ('is this woman lesbian') is often decided on the basis of whether or not someone has performed certain acts ('but he doesn't frequent the most famous gay bar in Dublin'; compare Hanna 2005). In this case, particular acts are required to be considered as LGBT.[28] Reversely, in some situations persecution on account of same sex sexual acts is not considered persecution on account of homosexuality, because for this particular person the same sex sexual acts are not an expression of sexual identity (as when a person has sex with someone of the same sex because she or he 'had no other option' such as in separated schools, work environments or in prisons). While LaViolette in a promising way has sought to overcome the act/identity dichotomy by emphasising that LGBT people always refuse to behave in ways dictated by their biological sex and social classification (LaViolette 2007: 186; compare LaViolette 2010; Landau 2005; Neilson 2005a), in practice the ambiguity whether sexual identity is something you do or something you are is very much alive.

The strategy of LGBT advocates is based on the presumption that the problem is incorrect application of the law. This strategy has been useful. Acceptance of sexual orientation and gender identity as a persecution ground has made refugee status on those grounds possible, where that was not possible before. Abolishing discretion reasoning does lead to recognition as a refugee of people who were denied asylum before. But when the preconditions for sexuality based asylum have been met, it turns out that this is necessary but not sufficient. After refugee law doctrine has been adapted so as to be open for asylum claims by LGBTs, it became clear that even so the refugee definition can be applied in different ways so as to express different views on sexuality (compare Borg, Törner and Wolf-Watz 2010). In this way, asylum law is one of the arenas in which debates about the meaning and significance of sexual identity are waged. The successes of LGBT asylum advocates show that legal reasoning does not necessarily imply the notions on sexuality on which it was implicitly based in, say, the 1950s. The acceptance of minority sexualities in social and political discourse made it possible to articulate LGBT rights in legal discourse – asylum law, in our case. This, in turn, has reinforced the acceptance of minority sexualities in social and political discourse. But, in socio-political and in legal discourse, sexual minorities have been accepted only to a certain extent – as subdominant, boxed, and unstable categories, as I showed above. The debates about the meaning of sexuality continue, and cannot be legislated away. The mainstream notions about the subdominant, boxed and unstable nature of minority sexualities are highly mobile and adaptable. The idea that they can somehow be smoked out by doctrinal argumentation alone begins to seem futile. The debate about the legal technicalities of, say, particular social group is related to debates about sexuality.[29] As a consequence, legal technique matters. First, because the more convincing and tightly argued a position is, the more likely it is to hold; and, second, because some legal positions (such as the anti-discretion position), because of their formal status as law, can influence debates on sexuality (such as, LGBTs should be able to be just as flaunting as straights are all the time) in a way that I would find positive. But legal technique is merely one of the vocabularies in which the debate about sexuality takes place.

10.3 The tensions inherent in sexual identity

In the next two sections, I want to analyse a bit further the notions on sexuality which I found to be important in legal doctrine and practice, but without specifically focusing on either law or asylum. I do so by focusing on the work of two authors who I have found helpful in thinking about minority sexualities.

10.3.1 Foucault's subject

In this section, I want to analyse how sexual identity is an inherently problematic concept. It is not only shaped by sexual minorities themselves in the process of liberating themselves, but also (and very much so) by dominant discourse. This can help us understand how homo- and transphobic tendencies can be an integral part of the concepts of sexual orientation and gender identity.

In his 1976 book, *La volonté de savoir*, Michel Foucault dismissed what he termed the repression hypothesis, i.e. the idea that authentic and true forms of sexuality are repressed by religious, social and legal prohibitions, and can be liberated by breaking these taboos. Instead, he argued that sexuality has been made into the favourite secret of our societies. In order to be an individual, one has to discover one's secret desires, to name them, to speak about them. This requires speaking a particular language and using it to make oneself understandable to both oneself and others. Behaviour which could also have been understood as amorphous or as a number of unrelated acts is organised into a subject position through this language. Using the double meaning of the word subject, Foucault argues that one can only become a comprehensible someone (a subject) by subjecting oneself to this language and the categories it contains. The experience of authentic sexuality is an *effect* of this discursive process, and not the *source* of it.

This has important consequences for sexual minorities. If we understand the identity categories of LGBT not as expressions of authentic individual experiences, but as categories produced by dominant discourse co-opting individuals and their everyday experiences, then one thing becomes easier to understand, and another becomes less easy to understand.

If we think of sexual identities in this way, then it becomes more obvious that minority sexual identities can easily be represented as subdominant, boxed and unstable. The identities which we are seduced into assuming are not neutral but tilted. The central category is presented as unproblematic, neutral and given; this is the person who desires persons of the other sex and who identifies with the male or female gender role which has been assigned to him or her. Other categories are presented as different. Which category one belongs to is thought of as being fundamental to one's personality. The mere fact that a distinction is made between different categories implies that the difference must be delineated; whether one belongs to one category or the other makes a difference for who you are. Obviously, the border between such important categories must be delineated as sharply as possible. Therefore, the *boxed* nature of sexual identities is not coincidental, but central to the sexual subject. The identity which most people are seduced into assuming (straight and cisgender) is represented as not only that of the majority, but also as normal. If one grows up to be straight, you are not expected to have stories about how, from a very young age you felt something special, subsequently figured out what that could be about and how you came out to yourself and others. You do not need to explain yourself. In this way, the sexual identity of people who are straight and cisgender is experienced as normal, as the standard, as the fall back option when there is nothing special. Even when this difference is formulated in neutral terms, as I have tried to do just now, it is inescapable that a normative undertone slips in. The fact that minority sexualities need to explain themselves conceives them as problematic, as *subdominant*. Furthermore, the problematic 'nature' of minority sexualities indicates that it may be hard to identify oneself or others. When is the fall back option applicable? Is a person who has sex with persons of the same sex in a separated environment (a prison or a boarding school) *really* lesbian, gay or bisexual? Can a person who only has sex with one person of the other sex be lesbian, gay or bisexual? Is a person who cross-dresses but does not want gender correcting surgery transgender? Majority sexual identity is under pressure both to include many people because it is the default option, but also to exclude people who would undermine the stable and self-evident 'nature' of straight and cisgender sexual identity. This makes minority sexual identities *unstable*.

In this way, the subdominant, boxed and unstable nature of minority sexual identities are not a coincidence; they come with the notion of sexual identity as it functions in modern western societies. Whenever one speaks the language of sexual identity, the problematic aspects are lurking below the surface. And as we can see, they pop up frequently.

However, Foucault's approach to sexuality makes it harder to understand why many of us experience ourselves as LGBT – or as straight or cisgender, for that matter. Foucault refused to identify himself as gay in public. In his line of thinking, doing so would be to voluntarily assume the terms of one's own oppression.[30] On the other hand, whether or not one assumes an LGBT identity, it is imposed on people to quite some extent anyway. By not self-identifying as LGBT, you may deny something that you find important for yourself. Or having sex with people of the same sex without acknowledging you are lesbian, gay or bisexual may make you liable to blackmail. Or sexual identity may be imposed on you through violence against LGBT people. As the struggles for LGBT rights show, assuming LGBT identities may be instrumental in making the world a safer place by creating communities in which LGBT people can feel safe, by decriminalising homosexuality, introducing equal treatment legislation, and by many other effects of identity politics.

I think it is not fruitful to want to choose between either denying the categories in which sexuality is thought, or to assume sexual identity and use it as the basis of sexual politics. In actual practice, LGBT people have done one at one time, the other at other times, and a bit of both most of the time. What I want to point out here is that, if we want to advocate the right to asylum for people who fear persecution on account of their sexual or gender desires or acts, we have no other option but to use LGBT as an identity category and as a basis for human rights claims. But it should come as no surprise that, in doing so, we get on board the homo- and transphobic implications of sexual identity for free. How to deal with these implications should become a fuller and more conscious part of the LGBT rights based strategies we use in asylum law.

10.3.2 Sedgwick's closet

The argument in this sub-paragraph is that Sedgwick's focus on tensions makes it possible to see that sexual identity does have inherent homo- and transphobic tendencies (Foucault), but that by being incoherent it also creates spaces for contestation, etc.

In *Epistemology of the Closet* (1990), Eve Kosofsky Sedgwick has argued that homosexuality identity is shaped by two tensions. First, the tension between the minoritising and the universalising perspectives. The minoritising perspective relies on the notion that homosexuals are a small, distinct and relatively fixed community (Sedgwick 1990/2008: 85) – such as the idea relied on by early gay rights activists that homosexuality is inborn and therefore no fault of one's own. This minoritising perspective that homosexuals are a particular group of persons who can be identified. A consequence of this may be that special policies are formulated to protect this minority, such as anti-discrimination laws, or that a discourse on the human rights of sexual minorities is formulated. Because in this perspective people *are* homosexual, they can be LGBT regardless of their acts. On the other hand, the universalising perspective presumes that sexual desire is unpredictable even in persons with stable identities. Same sex influences and desires are crucial to heterosexual identities and vice versa (Sedgwick 1990/2008: 85). In this perspective, desire – including homosocial and homosexual desire – are everywhere. Both mainstream institutions such as the law and LGBT activists rely on both perspectives. In some settings, it made sense to represent homosexuality as innate – if people cannot help it, they should not be punished (relying on a version of the minoritising view). But in other contexts, broader coalitions could be built by emphasising sexual autonomy, regardless of sexual preference. The difference between same sex and opposite sex sexual acts is downplayed, and the commonalities are emphasised – a version of the universalising perspective. The second tension Sedgwick analyses is that between the idea that homosexuality is gender inversion, being about the borderline between the genders (a gay man has a female identity trapped in a male body, and vice versa; LGBTs are a group because they live at the borders of gender), and homosexuality as gender separatism, as being about the solidarity of women with women and of men with men (Sedgwick 1990/2008: 87–88). This tension may play out in the external signifiers of lesbian, gay and bisexual people (butch women and effeminate men versus the hyper-masculine gay clone look and lesbian separatism) as well as in politics, as became particularly clear in feminism (the tension between lesbians as part of the women's movement *versus* as part of the LGBT movement).

Sedgwick has pointed out that lesbians and gays are under a simultaneous obligation to inform their surroundings of their sexual preference and to be discreet about it. She points to US case law holding that coming out is not protected by the right to free speech because sexuality is not a matter of public concern; but at the same time, case law then still held that homosexual acts could be criminalised because they were a matter of public concern. Similarly, while a first instance court found the dismissal of a gay science teacher legitimate because he had drawn undue attention to his sexuality, the appeals court in the same case found the dismissal acceptable because he had failed to notify his employer that he had been a member of a gay students association (Sedgwick 1990/2008: 69–70). This system of double binds (be open about your sexuality at the right moment; conceal your sexuality when it is appropriate to do so), which is part of the larger system of tensions (minoritising/universalising, gender inversion/gender separatism), ensures that lesbians, gays and bisexuals are always doing *something* wrong. They mention the sexuality when they should not, and they remain silent about it while they should speak up. Their sexuality can be labelled as private when they rely on rights in the public sphere (free speech), or it can be considered as public when they rely on privacy rights.

Like Foucault, Sedgwick's analysis makes it easier to understand how sexual orientation can be such an unstable category. It makes it understandable why credibility assessment even within one country can rely on a large array of contradictory presumptions. It also enables us to rethink legal strategies. Sedgwick states that the strategy to protect LGBT rights as privacy rights is an extension of, and a testimony to the power of, the image of the closet (Sedgwick 1990/2008: 71). As a consequence, privacy is a problematic notion because it may perpetuate the closet. On the other hand (something not pointed out by Sedgwick, but in her line of thought), emphasising the public nature of sexual identity is consistent with the notion that sexual behaviour is of public concern – which makes it conceivable to criminalise it. The practice of decision makers and policy makers in asylum law, as well as the strategies used by advocates who come up against them, are full of the tensions and ambiguities that come with the notion of sexual identity. Victories are never secure – but neither is the status quo.

10.4 Contradictions: potential and risks

Contrary to the implicit assumption on which LGBT asylum advocates usually rely, proper application of the law, combined with notions of sexual identity as properly understood, will *not* lead to a stable situation in which LGBT asylum claimants with a well-founded fear of being persecuted will be granted asylum. Sexual identity is a problematic concept full of internal tensions. In addition, as Sarah van Walsum wrote, law is 'not monolithic, but fragmented and fraught with contradictions and logical flaws'. Because law serves conflicting interests, it can facilitate surprising coalitions. In this way, significant progress can be made. But such victories are not self-evident, because there is nothing inevitable or irreversible about the workings of – in our case – international asylum and refugee law (Van Walsum 2009: 311). My suggestion would be not to pretend that law (as properly applied) and sexual identity (if properly understood) will lead to a stable situation where justice will be done to LGBT asylum seekers. Instead, I propose to focus on the contradictions inherent in law and sexual identity in order to make progress, but also – once victories have been won – in order to keep the gains that have been made, to prepare for reactions, and to think about further progress.[31]

It makes sense to pursue the direction indicated by Rehaag (2008, 2009), who argues for a non-essentialist understanding of sexual identity. Looking back at the developments in the past two decades, we can go one step further than that. It is worthwhile to develop argumentations that do not choose between essentialist and constructivist notions of sexual identity, but which instead make space in refugee law discourse for the fact that people experience their sexualities in different ways. Some of us experience our identity as given, while others experience it as fluid. Likewise, it seems important to me to analyse the ways in which we rely on transphobic and homophobic notions in the very same arguments which we make in order to get LGBT people asylum. Relying on the notion of privacy may feed notions about the closet; emphasising LGBT identity may encourage decision makers to use stereotypes in credibility findings. Sexualities cannot be understood as pre-existing things out there for which we just have to find the right words. Sexualities are made and unmade by people in actions and reactions. Words, including the words of law, are among the actions and reactions that take part in shaping sexualities. Because sexualities are contradictory and contested, what we say about them can hardly be otherwise.

10.5 Notes

* I thank Sabine Jansen and Sean Rehaag for their critical comments on an earlier version of this chapter. I thank Louis Middelkoop for his research assistance, and Veeni Naganathar for her editorial assistance.

1 See on persecutory intent, Bennett 1999; Ghai 2011–2012: 540–541.

2 Afdeling rechtspraak van de Raad van State [Judicial Division of the Council of State] 13 August 1981, *Rechtspraak Vreemdelingenrecht* 1981 at 5, *Gids Vreemdelingenrecht (oud)* D12-51.

3 Arguments advocating particular social group are central to most early articles, compare Goldberg 1993; Vagelos 1993; Grider 1994; McGoldrick 1994; Park 1995; Ramanathan 1996; McGhee 2001. More generally on particular social group, see Helton 1983; Parish 1992; Fullerton 1993; Godfrey 1994–1995. See for more recent articles focusing on particular social group, Southam 2011; Sternberg 2011.

4 See for example Article 9 of EU Directive 2004/83; this provision has not been changed in Article 9 of EU Directive 2011/95.

5 This issue was included in the Fleeing Homophobia project (question 43 of the questionnaire), but was not incorporated into the final report on account of

the insufficiency of the available data. See the national reports, published at http://www.rechten.vu.nl/nl/onderzoek/conferenties-en-projecten/onderzoeksproject-fleeing-homophobia/national-questionnaire/index.asp (accessed 17 December 2012).

6 See on discretion, the contributions of Weßels and Battjes to this volume, and Choi 2010; Hanna 2005; Hinger 2010; Johnson 2007; Jansen and Spijkerboer 2011: 33–39; Millbank 2002: 171–174; LaViolette 2010. Compare on discretion in the context of political opinion, Smith 2012; Hanna 2005. For a defence of discretion reasoning, arguing that *HJ and HT* leads to refugee status for *any* infringement on the rights of LGBTs, see Buxton 2011–2012.

7 Discretion has been rejected by UNHCR, see the UNHCR *Guidance Note on Refugee Claims Relating to Sexual Orientation and Gender Identity*, 21 November 2008, paras 25–26. UNHCR *Guidelines on International Protection No. 9: Claims to Refugee Status based on Sexual Orientation and/or Gender Identity with the Context of Article 1A(2) of the 1951 Convention and/or its 1967 Protocol relating to the states of refugees*, 23 October 2012, para. 30–33. Discretion reasoning was rejected by the High Court of Australia in its judgment of 9 December 2003, *Appellant S396/2002 v Minister for Immigration and Multicultural Affairs* [2003] HCA 71, S395/2002 and 396/2202; by the New Zealand Refugee Status Appeals Authority in Refugee Appeal no. 74665/03, 7 July 2004; by a US Federal Court in United States Court of Appeal for the Ninth Circuit, 7 March 2005, *Karouni v Gonzales*, 399 F3d 1163; by the Federal Court of Canada in its judgment of 8 October 2008, *Atta Fosu v the Minister of Citizenship and Immigration*, 2008 FC 1135; in the UK Supreme Court's judgment of 7 July 2010, *HJ (Iran and HT (Cameroon) v Secretary of State for the Home Department* [2010] UKSC 21, [2011] 1 AC 596; in Finland by the Supreme Administrative Court in its judgment of 13 January 2012, KHO:2012:1; in Norway by a Supreme Court judgment of 29 March 2012, reported on http://www.unhcr.se/en/media/baltic-and-nordic-headlines/2012/april/3-4-april-2012.html (accessed 17 December 2012); in Poland by the Refuge Board's decision of 25 July 2012, *W.S. (Uganda) v Head of the Office for Foreigners*. In the Netherlands it was abolished in the Aliens Circular, Vreemdelingencirculaire 2000, C2/2.10.2; in Sweden by circular of 13 January 2011, Jansen and Spijkerboer 2011: 38. See for early literature, Millbank 1995, 2005; Walker 1996; on recent developments, Chelvan 2011; Choi 2010; Millbank 2009; Weßels in this volume.

8 See for European state practice, Jansen and Spijkerboer 2011: 43–44.

9 See Anker and Ardalan 2011–2012 on the ease with which factual prediction and requirement can trade places.

10 On the social visibility approach to particular social group and its consequences for LGBT claimants, see Marouf 2008–2009; Bresnahan 2011. Generally, Soucek 2010. A quite similar approach seems to be at work in the case law of the French Cour Nationale du Droit d'Asile, e.g. CNDA, 7 May 2008, 605398, H; see Jansen and Spijkerboer 2011: 36.

11 The social visibility test would also lead to denial of asylum to victims of domestic violence and gang related violence, Bresnahan 2011: 673–675, as well as to exclusion of family membership and human trafficking from the scope of refugee protection, Marouf 2008–2009: 91–102. One might add – although this is heavy artillery – that secular Jews in Nazi Germany would not be considered as members of a particular social group on account of the invisibility of their group membership.

12 Other authors also have pointed out that asylum claims by lesbians are particularly challenging because the threats they face emanate from family members, more so than for gay men, and similar to other women; LaViolette 2007: 188; compare Millbank 2002: 158–163.

13 UK Supreme Court, 7 July 2010, *HJ (Iran and HT (Cameroon) v Secretary of State for the Home Department* [2010] UKSC 21, [2011] 1 AC 596.

14 '(S)ome forms of behavior loosely (or stereotypically) associated with homosexuality are not presently protected at law' (Hathaway and Pobjoy 2012: 374), are not 'appropriately deemed to be included within the protected status of sexual orientation' (Hathaway and Pobjoy 2012: 374). They distinguish between a situation in which 'the activity that engenders the risk is intrinsic to one of the five forms of protected status', and a situation in which 'the activity precipitating the risk is no more than marginally connected to one of the forms of protected status' (Hathaway and Pobjoy 2012: 377–378). Hathaway and Pobjoy (2012: 379) refer to precedent holding that Pakistani Ahmadi cane be required to curb religious activity – now set aside in CJEU Case C-71/11; and to precedent holding that standing up for law and order in a corrupt system does not fall within the ambit of political opinion, which is a debatable position.

15 See for critical reactions to Hathaway and Pobjoy, Goodman 2012; Tobin 2012; Millbank 2012; Anker and Ardalan 2011–2012.

16 Cases C-199/12, C-200/12, C-201/12.

17 See Jansen and Spijkerboer 2011: 21–26.

18 Compare Anker and Ardalan 2011–2012: 534–539; Jansen and Spijkerboer 2011: 21–26. The Italian Supreme Court recently ruled that criminalisation of homosexual acts constitutes persecution, Corte Suprema di Cassazione, 29 May 2012, 15981/12.

19 Corte Suprema di Cassazione, 29 May 2012, 15981/12.

20 See on trans cases more generally, Benson 2008; Jenkins 2009–2010; Landau 2005; Mohyuddin 2001; Neilson 2005b.

21 I use the term 'cisgender' to refer to people who do identify with the gender which has been assigned to them.

22 But see Jansen and Spijkerboer 2011: 14 on Bulgaria.

23 This double standard, presuming as a factual matter that non-straight relationships are about sexual acts, has an impressive pedigree. It was relied on, for example, from the Inner London Quarter Sessions in the *Handyside* case. The British court found a passage about homosexuality in a book aimed at people between 12 and 18 years of age 'hopelessly damning' because of the 'very real danger that this passage would create in the minds of children a conclusion that that kind of relationship (i.e. a homosexual one, TS) was something permanent'. Quoted in European Court of Human Rights, 7 December 1976, *Handyside v United Kingdom*, Application 5493/72, para 34. The European Court of Human Rights found the judgment of the British court not in violation of the freedom of expression of Article 10 of the European Convention on Human Rights.

24 European Court of Human Rights, 24 February 1983, *Dudgeon v United Kingdom*, Application No. 7525/76; European Court of Human Rights, 26 October 1988, *Norris v Ireland*, Application No. 10581/83; European Court of Human Rights, 22 April 1994, *Modinos v Cyprus*, Application No. 15070/89.

25 On Article 8 of the European Convention on Human Rights in a gay asylum case, European Court of Human Rights, 22 June 2004, *F v United Kingdom*, Application

No. 17341/03; compare on Article 9, European Court of Human Rights, 28 February 2006, *Z and T v United Kingdom*, Application No. 27034/05, and on Article 6, European Court of Human Rights, 7 July 1989, *Soering v United Kingdom*, Application No. 14038/88.

26 European Court of Human Rights, 7 July 1989, *Soering v United Kingdom*, Application No. 14038/88; European Court of Human Rights, 8 November 2005, *Bader and Kandor v Sweden*, Application No. 13284/04; European Court of Human Rights, 22 June 2006, *D and others v Turkey*, Application No. 24245/02; and in other contexts than asylum, European Court of Human Rights, 18 June 1978, *Ireland v United Kingdom*, Application No. 5310/71; European Court of Human Rights, 11 January 2012, *Gorobot v Moldova*, Application No. 30951/10.

27 This distinction is central in the approach of Hathaway and Pobjoy 2012, as well as Verdirame 2012, as pointed out by Millbank 2012.

28 By the way, this raises the question as to whether someone can be lesbian, gay or bisexual without having sex with a person of the same gender. Note that this was, and in some circles still is, considered commendable behaviour for lesbian, gay or bisexual people.

29 See for an argument about decriminalization of homosexuality in the US because the US granted asylum to gay asylum seekers, Pfitsch 2006; Russ 1998.

30 This way of thinking was not unique; one can find it in the writings of Jean Genet and the films of Rainer Werner Fassbinder; see on Fassbinder's Genet film *Querelle*, Spijkerboer 1998.

31 Leitner 2004 and O'Dwyer 2008 illustrate the diversity in judicial approaches to LGBT asylum claims.

10.6 References

Anker, D. (2012) 'Gender-based particular social group claims: an overview', in *AILA Immigration and Nationality Law Handbook*, Washington, DC: American Immigration Lawyers Association.

Anker, D. and Ardalan, S. (2011–2012) 'Escalating persecution of gays and refugee protection: comment on queer cases make bad law', *New York University Journal of International Law and Politics*, 44(1): 529–558.

Battjes, H. (2012) 'Bescherming: de ontwikkeling van het begrip bescherming in het asielrecht', Amsterdam: inaugural lecture Vrije Universiteit Amsterdam.

Bennett, A.G. (1999) 'The "cure" that harms: sexual orientation-based asylum and the changing definition of persecution', *Golden Gate University Law Review*, 29(1): 279–309.

Benson, C.J. (2008) 'Crossing borders: a focus on treatment of transgender individuals in U.S. Asylum Law and society', *Whittier Law Review*, 30(1): 41–66.

Berg, L. and Millbank, J. (2009) 'Constructing the personal narratives of lesbian, gay and bisexual asylum claimants', *Journal of Refugee Studies*, 22(2): 195–223.

Birdsong, L. (2008) 'Give me your gays, your lesbians, and your victims of gender violence, yearning to breathe free of sexual persecution: the new grounds for grants of asylum', *Nova Law Review*, 32(1): 357–390.

Borg, H., Törner, E. and Wolf-Watz, O. (2010) *Norm-Critical Study of the Swedish Asylum Examination*, produced for the Swedish Migration Board by Ramböll Management Consulting.

Bresnahan, K.A. (2011) 'The Board of Immigration Appeals's new "social visibility" test for determining "membership of a particular social group" in asylum claims and its legal and policy implications', *Berkeley Journal of International law*, 29(1): 649–679.

Buxton, R. (2011–2012) 'A history from across the pond', *New York University Journal of International Law and Politics*, 44(1): 391–406.

Charlesworth, C., Chinkin, C. and Wright, S. (1991) 'Feminist approaches to international law', *American Journal of International* Law (85): 613–645.

Chelvan, S. (2011) 'Put your hands up (if you feel love)', *Immigration, Asylum and Nationality Law*, 25(1): 56–66.

Choi, V. (2010) 'Living discreetly: a catch 22 in refugee status determinations on the basis of sexual orientation', *Brooklyn Journal of International Law*, 36(1): 241–264.

Conroy, M.A. (2009) 'Real bias: how REAL ID's credibility and corroboration requirements impair sexual minority asylum applicants', *Berkeley Journal of Gender, Law and Justice*, 24(1): 1–47.

Crawley, H. (2001) *Refugees and Gender. Law and Process*, Bristol: Jordan Publishing Ltd.

Dauvergne, C. and Millbank, J. (2003) 'Burdened by proof: how the Australian Refugee Review Tribunal has failed lesbian and gay asylum seekers', *Federal Law Review*, 31(1): 299–342.

Foucault, M. (1976) *La volonté de savoir. Histoire de la sexualité 1*, Paris: Gallimard.

Frank, D.J. (2011–2012) 'Making sense of LGBT asylum claims: change and variation in institutional contexts', *New York University Journal of International Law and Politics*, 44(1): 485–496.

Fullerton, M. (1993) 'A comparative look at refugee status based on persecution due to membership in a particular social group', *Cornell International Law Journal*, 26(1): 505–564.

Gallelli, L. (2001) 'Asylum in the United States based on sexual orientation', *Journal of Legal Advocacy & Practice*, 3: 40–48.

Gehi, P. (2008–2009) 'Struggles from the margins: anti-immigrant legislation and the impact on low-income transgender people of color', *Women's Rights Law Reporter*, 30(1): 315–346.

Ghai, R. (2011–2012) 'Deciphering motive: establishing sexual orientation as the "one central reason" for persecution in asylum claims', *Columbia Human Rights Law Review*, 43(1): 521–568.

Godfrey, P.C. (1994–1995) 'Defining the social group in asylum proceedings: the expansion of the social group to include a broader class of refugees', *Journal of Law and Policy*, 3(1): 257–288.

Goldberg, S.B. (1993) 'Give me liberty or give me death: political asylum and the global persecution of lesbians and gay men', *Cornell International Law Journal*, 26(1): 605–624.

Goodman, R. (2012) 'Asylum and the concealment of sexual orientation: where not to draw the line', *New York University Journal of International Law and Politics*, 44(1): 407–446.

Goodwin-Gill, G.S. (1986) '*Non-refoulement* and the new asylum seekers', *Virginia Journal of International Law* (26): 897.

Grahl-Madsen, A. (1966) *The Status of Refugees in International Law, Vol. I*, Leiden: Sijthoff.

Grahl-Madsen, A. (1980) *Territorial Asylum*, Stockholm: Almqvist & Wiksell International.

Grider, S. (1994) 'Sexual orientation as grounds for asylum in the United States – in re Tenorio, No. A72 093 558 (EOIR Immigration Court, July 26, 1993)', *Harvard International Law Journal*, 35(1): 213–224.

Hanna, F. (2005) 'Punishing masculinity in gay asylum claims', *The Yale Law Journal*, 114(4): 913–920.

Hathaway, J.C. (1991) *The Law of Refugee Status*, Markham/Vancouver: Butterworths Canada.

Hathaway, J.C. and Pobjoy, J. (2012) 'Queer cases make bad law', *New York University Journal of International Law and Politics*, 44(1): 315–390.

Helton, A.C. (1983) 'Persecution on account of membership in a particular social group as a basis for refugee status', *Columbia Human Rights Law Review*, 15: 39.

Hinger, S. (2010) 'Finding the fundamental: shaping identity in gender and sexual orientation based asylum claims', *Columbia Journal of Gender and Law*, 19(1): 367–408.

Hojem, P. (2009) 'Fleeing for love: asylum seekers and sexual orientation in Scandinavia', New issues in refugee research, Research paper No. 181, Geneva: United Nations High Commissioner for Refugees, December 2009.

Jansen, S. and Spijkerboer T. (2011) *Fleeing Homophobia. Asylum Claims Related to Sexual Orientation and Gender Identity in Europe*, COC Netherlands and VU University Amsterdam, available at http://www.rechten.vu.nl/nl/onderzoek/conferenties-en-projecten/onderzoeksproject-fleeing-homophobia/index.asp (accessed 9 December 2012).

Jenkins, E.A. (2009–2010) 'Taking the square peg out of the round hole: addressing the misclassification of transgender asylum seekers', *Golden Gate University Law Review*, 40(1): 67–98.

Johnson, T.A.M. (2007) 'Flamers, flaunting and permissible persecution', *Feminist Legal Studies*, 15: 99–111.

Landau, J. (2005) '"Soft immutability" and "imputed gay identity": recent developments in transgender and sexual-orientation-based asylum law', *Fordham Urban Law Journal*, 32(2): 237–264.

LaViolette, N. (2007) 'Gender-related refugee claims: expanding the scope of the Canadian Guidelines', *International Journal of Refugee Law*, 19(2): 169–214.

LaViolette, N. (2009) 'Independent human rights documentation and sexual minorities: an ongoing challenge for the Canadian refugee determination process', *International Journal of Human Rights*, 13(2–3): 437–476.

LaViolette, N. (2010) 'UNHCR Guidance Note on refugee claims relating to sexual orientation and gender identity: a critical commentary', *International Journal of Refugee Law*, 22(2): 173–208.

Leitner, R.C. (2004) 'A flawed system exposed: the immigration adjudicatory system and asylum for sexual minorities', *University of Miami Law Review*, 58(2): 679–700.

Markard, N. (2012) *Kriegsflüchtlinge. Gewalt gegen Zivilpersonen in bewaffneten Konflikten als Herausforderung für das Flüchtlingsrecht und den subsidiären Schutz*, Tübingen: Mohr Siebeck.

Marouf, F.E. (2008–2009) 'The emerging importance of "social visibility" in defining a "particular social group" and its potential impact on asylum claims related to sexual orientation and gender', *Yale Law and Policy Review*, 27(1): 47–106.

McGhee, D. (2001) 'Persecution and social group status: homosexual refugees in the 1990s', *Journal of Refugee Studies*, 14(1): 20–42.

McGoldrick, B.J. (1994) 'United States immigration policy and sexual orientation: is asylum for homosexuals a possibility?', *Georgetown Immigration Law Journal*, 8(2): 201–226.

Millbank, J. (1995) 'Fear of persecution or just a queer feeling', *Alternative Law Journal*, 20(6): 261–265.

Millbank, J. (2002) 'Imagining otherness: refugee claims on the basis of sexuality in Canada and Australia', *Melbourne University Law Review*, 26(1): 144–77.

Millbank, J. (2004) 'The role of rights in asylum claims based on sexual orientation', *Human Rights Law Review*, 4(2): 193–228.

Millbank, J. (2005) 'A preoccupation with perversion: the British response to refugee claims on the basis of sexual orientation, 1989–2003', *Social Legal Studies*, 14(1): 115–138.

Millbank, J. (2009) 'From discretion to disbelief: recent trends in refugee determinations on the basis of sexual orientation in Australia and the United Kingdom', *International Journal of Human Rights*, 13(2–3): 391–414.

Millbank, J. (2012) 'The right of lesbians and gay men to live freely, openly, and on equal terms is not bad law: a reply to Hathaway and Pobjoy', *New York University Journal of International Law and Politics*, 44(1): 497–528.

Mohyuddin, F. (2001) 'United States asylum law in the context of sexual orientation and gender identity: justice for the transgendered?', *Hastings Women's Law Journal*, 12(2): 387–410.

Morgan, D.A. (2006) 'Not gay enough for the government: racial and sexual stereotypes in sexual orientation asylum cases', *Law and Sexuality*, 15: 135–162.

Neilson, V. (2005a) 'Homosexual or female? Applying gender-based asylum jurisprudence to lesbian asylum claims', *Stanford Law & Policy Review*, 16(2): 417–444.

Neilson, V. (2005b) 'Uncharted territory: choosing an effective approach in transgender-based asylum claims', *Fordham Urban Law Journal*, 32(2): 265–290.

O'Dwyer, P. (2008) 'A well-founded fear of having my sexual orientation asylum claim heard in the wrong court', *New York Law School Law Review*, 52(2): 185–214.

O'Leary, B. (2008) '"We cannot claim any particular knowledge of the ways of homosexuals, still less of Iranian homosexuals. . .": the particular problems facing those who seek asylum on the basis of their sexual identity', *Feminist Legal Studies*, 16(1): 87–95.

Parish, T.D. (1992) 'Membership in a particular social group under the Refugee Act of 1980: social identity and the legal concept of the refugee', *Columbia Law Review*, 92(4): 923–953.

Park, J.S. (1995) 'Pink asylum: political asylum eligibility of gay men and lesbians under U.S. immigration policy', *UCLA Law Review*, 42(4): 1115–1156.

Pfitsch, H.V. (2006) 'Homosexuality in asylum and constitutional law: rhetoric of acts and identity', *Law and Sexuality*, 15: 59–90.

Ramanathan, E.D. (1996) 'Queer cases: a comparative analysis of global sexual orientation-based asylum jurisprudence', *Georgetown Immigration Law Journal*, 11(1): 1–44.

Rehaag, S. (2008) 'Patrolling the borders of sexual orientation: bisexual refugee claims in Canada', *McGill Law Journal*, 53(1). 59–102.

Rehaag, S. (2009) 'Bisexuals need not apply: a comparative appraisal of refugee law and policy in Canada, the United States and Australia', *The International Journal of Human Rights*, 13(2–3): 415–436.
Russ, J.A. (1998) 'The gap between asylum ideals and domestic reality: evaluating human rights conditions for gay Americans by the United States' own progressive asylum standards', *U.C. Davis Journal of International Law and Policy*, 4(1): 29–72.
Saxena, M. (2006) 'More than mere semantics: the case for an expansive definition of persecution in sexual minority asylum claims', *Michigan Journal of Gender and Law*, 12(2): 331–358.
Sedgwick, E. Kosofsky (1990/2008) *Epistemology of the Closet,* Updated with a New Preface, Berkeley, CA: University of California Press.
Smith, P.J. (2012) 'Suffering in silence: asylum law and the concealment of political opinion as a form of persecution', *Connecticut Law Review*, 44(3): 1021–1056.
Soucek, B. (2010) 'Social group asylum claims: a second look at the new visibility requirement', *Yale Law and Policy Review*, 29: 337–345.
Southam, K. (2011) 'Who am I and what do you want me to be? Effectively defining a lesbian, gay, bisexual and transgender social group in asylum applications', *Chicago-Kent Law Review*, 86(3): 1363–1388.
Spijkerboer, T. (1998) 'Querelle asks for asylum', in P. Fitzpatrick and J.H. Bergeron (eds), *Europe's Other: European Law Between Modernity and Postmodernity*, Aldershot: Ashgate, pp. 189–217.
Spijkerboer, T. (2000) *Gender and Refugee Status*, Aldershot: Ashgate.
Sternberg, N. (2011) 'Do I need to pin a target to my back? The definition of "particular social group" in U.S. asylum law', *Fordham Urban Law Review*, 39(1): 245–298.
Swink, A. (2006) 'Queer refuge: a review of the role of country condition analysis in asylum adjudications for members of sexual minorities', *Hastings International and Comparative Law Review*, 29(2): 251–266.
Tobin, J. (2012) 'Assessing GLBTI refugee claims: using human rights law to shift the narrative of persecution within refugee law', *New York University Journal of International Law and Politics*, 44(2): 447–484.
Vagelos, E. (1993) 'The social group that dare not speak its name: should homosexuals constitute a particular social group for purposes of obtaining refugee status? Comment on Re: Inaudi', *Fordham International Law Journal*, 17(1): 229–276.
Van Walsum, S. (2009) 'Against all odds: how single and divorced migrant mothers were eventually able to claim their right to respect for family life', *European Journal of Migration and Law*, 11(3): 295–311.
Verdirame, G. (2012) 'A friendly act of socio-cultural contestation: asylum and the big cultural divide', *New York University Journal of International Law and Politics*, 44(2): 559–572.
Walker, K. (1996) 'The importance of being out: sexuality and refugee status', *The Sydney Law Review*, 18(4): 568–598.
Walker, K. (2000) 'Sexuality and refugee status in Australia', *International Journal of Refugee Law*, 12(2): 175–211.
Young, J. (2010) 'The alternate refuge concept: a source of systematic disadvantage to sexual minority refugee claimants', *University of New Brunswick Law Journal*, 60(1): 294–338.

Index